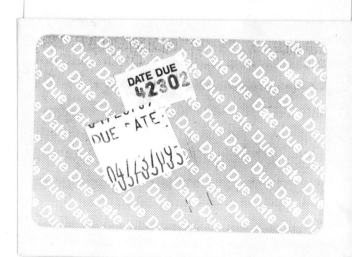

WILLIAM FAULKNER'S
GOTHIC DOMAIN

Kennikat Press
National University Publications
Literary Criticism Series

General Editor
John E. Becker

WILLIAM FAULKNER'S
GOTHIC DOMAIN

ELIZABETH M. KERR

National University Publications
KENNIKAT PRESS // 1979
Port Washington, N.Y. // London

80-973

Manufactured in the United States of America

Published by
Kennikat Press Corp.
Port Washington, N.Y. / London

Library of Congress Cataloging in Publication Data

Kerr, Elizabeth Margaret, 1905–
    William Faulkner's gothic domain.

    (Literary criticism series) (Kennikat Press national university publications)
    Bibliography: p.
    Includes index.
    1. Faulkner, William, 1897–1962–Criticism and interpretation. 2. Gothic revival (Literature)– United States. I. Title.
PS3511.A86Z8597   813'.5'2   78-27795
ISBN 0-8046-9228-9

CONTENTS

WILLIAM FAULKNER'S GOTHIC DOMAIN

I am convinced that the real world for him was Yoknapatawpha County of which he was sole lord and master.

Maurice-Edgar Coindreau

Loaded with murders, with rapes, with tortures, with castrations, with incest, with curses, with suicides, with madness, the world of Faulkner is that of the Gothic novel. . . .

Jacques Cabau

ABOUT THE AUTHOR

Elizabeth Kerr is Professor Emeritus of English at the University of Wisconsin at Milwaukee. Most of her teaching career was spent at the University of Minnesota and at the University of Wisconsin at Milwaukee. She is the author of numerous books, articles, and reviews dealing with the novel. Travel in Europe and much time spent in Faulkner's area contributed to her interest in Gothic settings.

CHAPTER ONE

FROM OTRANTO TO YOKNAPATAWPHA

FAULKNER'S GOTHIC HERITAGE

The term "Gothic" unfortunately has pejorative connotations which we must recognize before giving it the comprehensive definition necessary to an examination of the pervasive Gothic elements in William Faulkner's Yoknapatawpha novels. In current literary criticism "Gothic" either refers in the historical sense to the Gothic novel as a subgenre, from Horace Walpole through his literary successors such as Ann Radcliffe, Matthew Gregory Lewis, and Charles Maturin, or is loosely applied to various aspects of serious modern novelists such as Faulkner and Carson McCullers. The modern popular "Gothic romance," so labeled and advertised on the covers of paperback editions by a picture of an archetypal castle with a girl in flight in the foreground, is scorned by critics as sub-literary, sentimental "formula" fiction, easily recognized because, as Northrop Frye pointed out in *The Secular Scripture*, "the more undis-placed the story, the more sharply the design stands out," being undis-guised by representational realism. Like melodrama, with which it has much in common, the popular Gothic romance arouses sham terror and has a reassuring happy ending. Because such romances tend to be fab-ricated of ordinary or cheap stuff, with slick or sloppy workmanship, the critical eye may not perceive that they are often copied from such original and superior designs as those of Ann Radcliffe or the Brontës. This polluted stream of Gothicism is but a shallow branch of the deep and dark waters which, if one accepts Leslie Fiedler's thesis in *Love and Death in the American Novel*, might be called the Father of Waters of American novels, the Mississippi to which Faulkner's Yoknapatawpha River is tributary. Fully to appreciate that tributary, we must return to its deep Gothic source, for, in Harry Levin's words, "When we come to appreciate the strategic part that convention is able to play, we shall be better equipped to discern the originality of individual writers."

The origin and development of Gothic fiction played an essential part in the history of Romanticism and the Victorian novel by linking medieval romance with nineteenth-century Romanticism in such aspects as setting, time, themes, and character types. In romance, as Northrop Frye observed in *Anatomy of Criticism,* character types were often paired as moral opposites, "like black and white pieces in a chess game," a device contributing to the "general dialectic structure" of romance. The revival of interest in *The Faerie Queene* in the 1750s was, according to Maurice Lévy, one indication of the nostalgia for the marvelous and the taste for the Gothic which originated before the Gothic novel was created: "Everything 'Gothic' depends on a fantastic or grotesque imagination; every work of imagination is more or less 'Gothic.'" After the Gothic novel was established, developments analogous to Gothic fiction took place in Romantic narrative poetry, as in the works of Coleridge and Byron. Discussing the English Romantic poets, Geoffrey H. Hartman refers to "this English kind of literary mediation," bridging the otherwise too great "gap between medieval romance and the modern spirit." Prose fiction, as the Gothic novel developed, served more continuously and effectively than poetry to bridge that gap, becoming an aspect of Romanticism and sharing the qualities exhibited by the poets. Qualities of Gothicism are specified by Francis Russell Hart:

Gothic is a fiction evocative of a sublime and picturesque landscape, of an animated nature to which man is related with affective intensity. Gothic fiction is a fascination with time, with the dark persistence of the past in sublime ruin, haunted relic, and hereditary curse. The cult of ruin in Gothic, suggested Michael Sadleir, projected a symbolic bond between ruined house and nobly ruined mind. Gothic depicted a *world* in ruins, said the Divine Marquis, a world wracked by revolutionary fervor and guilt. Seen from our perspective, the Gothic signals a counter-enlightenment. . . . The Gothic novelist, still "enlightened" but imperfect in his skepticism, gave to fiction a post-Enlightenment preoccupation with the preternatural, the irrational, the primordial, the abnormal, and (tending to include the rest) the demonic.

Maurice Lévy's study of the English Gothic novel is valuable for the account of the revolution in taste which was marked by the "new category of the sublime" and which reached a climax in the Romantic passion for medieval architecture and for mountains, forests, and oceans. In choosing Yoknapatawpha as his setting, Faulkner had to forgo the ocean and the American equivalents of Alpine heights and abysses. But the obsessive images of Faulkner, like those of English Gothicism, "help to define a 'collective myth' of which one would be wrong to underestimate the importance." Lévy's comment on the Gothic novel has some pertinence to Faulkner and other modern Gothic novelists: "It is the expression of a dream suddenly released by the contemplation of prestigious vestiges of the past, a dream quite weighed down by clearly regressive symbols."

The Gothic novel can be considered also in a context more humble than that of literature and fine arts, that of current popular culture. Both the common and the sophisticated reader are attracted to the Gothic by the familiar patterns and the strategies which involve the reader by inducing him to experience vicariously the appalling plights of the characters. Gothic is one of various kinds of formula fiction seriously studied by such critics as John Cawelti because formula fiction not only confirms the Freudian and Jungian "insight that recurrent myths and stories embody a kind of collective dreaming process" but also serves a function in society by allowing individuals to act out their unconscious or repressed needs or to express latent motives not openly faced. Unlike the formula of the Western or the detective story or even the exotic spy thriller, the Gothic formula is used also in highly original ways in fiction addressed to the sophisticated reader. The constant factor in popular and literary Gothic explains its initial popularity and its survival. Elizabeth MacAndrew said the Gothic was popular because "it created, and then perpetuated, a myth necessary to its time": "The Gothic, exploring the psychology of evil in human nature, appeals to the need for mythic representation of fears and anxieties in all human beings." Observing that the romantic and the popular are closely connected "all through literature," Northrop Frye explained that popular literature "simply represents a different social development" of literature; although, in *The Secular Scripture,* he noted the merging of romance into the Gothic novel and the revival, after the 1950s, of romance in the works of Tolkien and in science fiction, he ignored the current revival of the Gothic romance.

Romanticism, like the Gothic it assimilated, is both a survival and a revival in current literature, for reasons which reflect modern culture and the human condition. In "Romanticism Re-examined" René Wellek concluded that all studies "see the implication of imagination, symbol, myth, and organic structure, and see it as part of the great endeavor to overcome the split between subject and object, the self and the world, the conscious and the unconscious." In *A Study of English Romanticism* Frye decided that Romanticism was "the first major phase in an imaginative revolution," still incomplete, and that it originated in "the revived sense of the numinous power of nature," a sense of nature "as oracular, as dropping hints of expanding mysteries into the narrowed rational consciousness." This belief, evident in Gothic novels and in Wordsworth, was accompanied by the Romantic sense of a lost Eden and was part of Faulkner's southern pastoral heritage. In a study of recent American novelists, Tony Tanner observed as a "crucial component of Romanticism . . . the desire or compulsion to project the shape of one's own unique consciousness against the imprisoning shapes of the external world."

From the Romantic period to the present, constant ingredients of the literary brew known as Gothicism have included: psychological interest and concern with the irrational and the unconscious, the dream side of the psyche; appalling situations; a Calvinistic Manichaean polarity of good and evil and/or ambivalence in the moral attitudes of characters; the abandonment of realism as a major aim; the use of setting and atmosphere to create a mood and stimulate the imagination; the reader's involvement through sharing with the characters the terror and horror which G. R. Thompson considered to be "complementary poles of a single continuum of perception and response." A comment by Joel Porte, concerning the English Gothic novel, stresses an ingredient which is essential to most southern Gothicism: "the expression of a fundamentally Protestant theological or religious disquietude."

Gothicism in nineteenth-century fiction, subsequent to the Gothic novel as such, is sporadically and insufficiently recognized because the Gothic novel, at first a recognizable tributary to the mainstream of English fiction, became mingled with and colored that stream. Among major novelists Charles Dickens is most notable as continuing the Gothic tradition, but Gothic elements are present also in the novels of Thomas Hardy and, as G. R. Thompson observed, in Conrad's *Heart of Darkness*. Such works, Thompson said, tend to be examined in a more acceptable tradition of the novel than the Gothic. The influence of Dickens and Conrad partially accounts for Gothic elements in Faulkner's novels. Dickens's use of the detective story techniques, as in *Bleak House,* helped both to create the detective story as a type of fiction and to establish its techniques among other Gothic features in mainstream novels. In relation to Dickens Archibald Coolidge analyzed the detective story pattern in Ann Radcliffe's *The Italian*. In *Anatomy of Criticism* Northrop Frye's sixth phase of comedy, "the phase of the collapse and disintegration of society," includes "ghost stories, thrillers, and Gothic romances." Dickens was no doubt a major link between the original Gothic novel and the works of such writers as Faulkner who similarly wrote Gothic novels which utilize detection techniques without being detective stories. In assessing the influence of Dickens on Faulkner, Joseph Gold noted parallel elements of Gothicism in the two novelists, including the detective story pattern, and cited specific borrowings by Faulkner. But neither Coolidge nor Gold sought what S. L. Varnado referred to as "the common denominator of a literary tradition . . . that has attracted . . . such dissimilar minds as those of Charles Dickens, Henry James, Joseph Conrad, and William Faulkner."

Between the Gothicism of Dickens, nurtured by the Romantic tradition as well as by Gothic fiction and melodrama, and the Gothicism of the present day lies the period of the Romantic decadence, the fin de siècle studied by Mario Praz in *The Romantic Agony*. Praz dealt with decadent aspects of many Gothic elements in European literature, including poetry and drama as well as fiction, with particular attention to the influence of the Marquis de Sade. Lewis J. Poteet showed the influence of *Melmoth the Wanderer* on *Dorian Gray* and observed such other Gothic themes and devices as the Faust legend. Robert Rogers defined "doubling" as "a basic literary process reflecting fundamental tendencies of the human mind." He dealt with *Dorian Gray* as representing the narcissistic double; in contrast to Dorian's "corruption and hypocrisy" and his androgynous and homoerotic nature is Basil Hallward, the painter, with his goodness and integrity. Recognition of the significance of the fin de siècle, the cultural climate of Faulkner's youth, as an influence in the Gothic tradition further illuminates what Ilse Lind, in a paper on expressionism, described as "Faulkner's allegiance to artistic ideas associated with *fin de siècle* decadence."

Thus, Gothicism in English fiction followed the course of Romanticism, through full flower to decadence; from a subgenre it became an assimilated form both in widely read novels and in those defying popular taste. The full title of Devendra Varma's study of Gothicism sums up the aspects dealt with thus far: *The Gothic Flame, Being a History of the Gothic Novel in England: Its Origins, Efflorescence, Disintegration, and Residuary Influences.* For the parallel developments in American fiction, Leslie Fiedler's *Love and Death in the American Novel* is an indispensable study of what might be called the "naturalization" of Gothicism, the process of which Faulkner's novels are thus far the most distinguished product. Fiedler's analysis of Gothic fiction provides a basis for identification in Faulkner's works of Gothic elements which show his relationship to both the European and the American tradition and which are distinctive aspects of his contribution to and influence upon American literature.

According to Leslie Fiedler, Gothic fiction in America has three dominant characteristics: the substitution of terror for love, of death for sexuality, and of dream and imagination for reason. Male protagonists flee "the confrontation of a man and woman which leads to the fall to sex, marriage, and responsibility." Moreover, Fiedler said, not only does

Thanatos stand in for Eros, but "these Gothic images" serve to project "certain obsessive concerns of our national life: the ambiguity of our relationship with the Indian and Negro, the ambiguity of our encounter with nature, the guilt of the revolutionist who feels himself a parricide—and . . . the uneasiness of the writer who cannot help believing that the very act of composing a book is Satanic revolt." This "Faustian commitment," "the diabolic bargain," was necessary for the full realization and significance of the American Gothic novel. Maurice Lévy accorded similar distinction to the Faust theme in the European Gothic novel, in Faust's descent into Hell: "The Faustian theme is the ultimate deepening of the Gothic dream."

The dream of Europe has become the nightmare of America: the age of reason was inadequate as a philosophic base for the conquest, in the New World, of the primitive in nature and in man. The revival of the Gothic in the twentieth century, the age of technology, is parallel to its birth in the eighteenth century, the age of reason. Faulkner's fellow southerner Walker Percy describes our present dilemma: "After the end of the modern age, its anthropology was still professed for a while and the denizens of the age still believed that they believed it, but they felt otherwise and they could not understand their feelings. They were like men who live by reason during the day and at night dream bad dreams." Faulkner's view of man as described by Alfred Kazin resembles the nocturnal one: "Man is a creature of passions over which his rational will has no dominion." In all his books, "The essential thing . . . was a sense of havoc and conflict, of human storm, blood madness and the irrational, of the unconscious possessing the human spirit. . . ."

Behind Gothic terror still lies the dream which men have pursued in their quest for truth, beauty, and happiness. In "white Gothic" fiction the day dream comes true in the happy ending, with virtue triumphant. Referring to this kind of fiction, Montague Summers said: "We call our dreams romance, and it was just this that the Gothic novelists gave to their readers." He agreed with Michael Sadleir that the Gothic romance "sprang from a genuine spiritual impulse," and for that reason Summers said that he called his book *The Gothic Quest* "to signify the spiritual as well as the literary and artistic seeking for beauty. . . ." The other side of the dream, the nightmare, is the black Gothic; Blanche Gelfant said, "The obverse side of a Romantic aspiration toward beauty [is] a fascination with the horrendous."

Fiedler's characterization of the American novel as lacking eroticism is confirmed not only in fact, in the comparative infrequency of eroticism in Faulkner in particular and in major American novels in general, but also in theory, by Denis de Rougement's analysis of love and passion. In *Love*

Declared he identifies three kinds of Occidental eroticism, as distinguished from sexuality (which is "instinctual and procreative"): "marriage-for-love, Tristan's mystical passion, and Don Juan's impious license," or, passion in marriage, passion beyond marriage, and license without marriage. A fourth possibility is the sublimation of sexuality through aesthetic or intellectual or spiritual endeavor such as poetry or philosophy or religion instead of through mystical passion. Passion belongs to the dark, irrational side of human nature, is born of dreams, and is the twin sister of death. As Denis de Rougemont said, "passion flings itself" on taboos "to find new pretexts for gloriously consuming itself, for defying Daylight morality in the name of Night's mysticism, and the life of rational action in the name of ecstasy and rapturous death." "Night's mysticism" and the dream side of the psyche are the essence of Gothicism, which reveals the instinctual, unconscious aspects of the psyche and abounds in literal or figurative dream-nightmare imagery and effects.

The essence of Gothicism and the source of creativity are the same. In *A Study of English Romanticism,* Northrop Frye said: "The world of sleep and dreams . . . is also the world from which the poet and the prophet draw their revelations." In *The Secular Scriptures,* Frye asserted that for the romancer, both the waking and the dreaming worlds are real. *American Dreams, American Nightmares,* the title of a collection of essays dealing with the American experience, suggests the suitability of Gothic interpretations of that experience. The aptness of the title is confirmed by the reaction of Bernard Bergonzi, a British critic of the American novel: ". . . American novels or poems are read, not so much for the literary experience they offer, as for the insights they afford into the American Myth or Dream or Nightmare."

David Madden, the editor of *American Dreams, American Nightmares,* points out that from the beginning American writers have "projected visions of dreams and nightmares" but no single dream or nightmare: "Those who say yes to the Dream have their own nightmares; those who say no have their private dreams." The "true believers," who say yes, "help make and remember heroes." The atheists, who say no, "help make and encourage victims." The agnostics say "maybe" and contemplate "the interaction between dubious heroes and their vulnerable witnesses." From the nightmare of Europe, which Gothic fiction had reflected since the mid-eighteenth century, settlers fled to the Eden of America, bringing with them their dreams, of which Robert Heilman said: "Dreams about America are an import from Europe, where they were an old habit dating from the Renaissance." In the New World dreams would play their parts; as Harry Levin said: "Both the wish-dream and the nightmare can be shared by a society, as well as introjected by an ego;

they can take on the guise of public myths as well as private fantasies." The ambivalence of the American dream is expressed by Milton Kornfeld in a study of three of the American novelists dealt with by Fiedler—Hawthorne, James, and Faulkner:

> ... belief in a deep underlying "goodness of man" has haunted American fiction in tortuous ways, for it has always been accompanied by a suspicion of the sinister, a suspicion of destructive impulses and urges which lurk beneath the benign assumptions of democracy and which have led us to distrust the very values we proclaim to be the basis of our uniqueness as a nation.

Despair over the fading of the dream and the prevalence of the nightmare gave rise, according to Madden, to contemporary antiheroes (frequent in Gothic fiction) who "assert their existence mainly as victims of the nightmare; their identity is defined mainly in terms of the false dreams they oppose."

The psychological validity of Gothic fiction is affirmed by Dr. Lawrence Kubie in "William Faulkner's *Sanctuary*." The stages in intensity in "the history of the literature of horror," from boys' tales of adventure, with "triumphs over external dangers," to "the deep and biological horrors of *Sanctuary*" are analogous to "what may occur in the psychoanalytic treatment of a patient": a series of dreams evolves to "a point at which a dream comes to the surface which can be analyzed fruitfully, throwing light retrospectively upon the mysterious shadows of all its predecessors." In less clinical terms Ihab Hassan explained that the omnipresent dreams in Capote's nocturnal style serve as "recognition of the unconscious, and all that it holds of wish and terror," and as revelation of man's "perpetual solitude . . . because his dreams must remain unsharable and his night world must rise continually against his daily actions."

"Dream," as Robert Heilman shows, has so many connotations that it requires detailed discussion, but the connotations of "nightmare" are narrower: "It may imply a gratuitous horror, a distortion of actuality, an irrational disordering where order may be expected, an unforeseen revelation of hideous truth, a truth perverted but as powerful as the real thing." The archetypal image of flight, ubiquitous on covers of paperback Gothic romances, is identified by Dr. Kubie as "one of the most characteristic nightmares of childhood, one in which the child feels helpless in the presence of danger and either runs frantically hither and thither and never escapes, or else is unable to move at all." This sense of impotence Dr. Kubie associates with "horror phantasies . . . linked to the male's constant subterranean struggle with fears of impotence." In a chapter entitled "The Gothic Novel and the Sleep of Reason," Leonard Wolf deals with nightmares in fact and fiction and shows the relationship between them.

Before the Gothic novel, there is the nightmare which, not being a literary genre, can be appreciated privately by every sleeper. The nightmare makes signals in the dark which, if they can be read and remembered in the daylight, no sane man will ignore. It is in sleep that the raw metaphors of feeling shape themselves to tell us about the motions of our day.

After citing some suitable nightmare images, Wolf continues: "In the nightmare, the claims of reason and the demands of instinct twine around each other like creepers." This general introduction to his discussion of the Gothic novel concludes: "Sleep is where the otherwise unmystical dreamer tosses in the grip of mystery and commandment. . . . The nightmare . . . is a place to encounter the primeval instincts and the unacknowledged gods without immediately having to pay the price of their recognition. For the writer, his nightmares are the sources of metaphors. . . ." Nightmare effects evoking fears and obsessions are as necessary as dreams for truly Gothic quality. Dreams and dream images, however, may be benignly romantic.

The surrealistic effect often produced by dream and nightmare images in Gothic fiction, before and after the development of surrealism in art, is frequently a clue to Gothic qualities in a work of fiction not classified as Gothic. Without identifying the pervasive Gothicism in the novels of Dickens, Joseph Gold said of them: "The intense personal dramas of their characters are combined with a descriptive clarity so vivid as to be almost surrealistic." In addition to clarity, surrealism requires exaggeration, incongruity, and irrationality. The remarkable surrealistic imagery in Ralph Ellison's *Invisible Man* puzzled critics who failed to recognize that novel as quintessentially Gothic: surrealistic effects and fantastic images are quite appropriately combined with daylight realism. The quantity and quality of Gothic devices and patterns in Ellison's tale of a quest for identity, with successive initiations, have rarely been equaled. Tony Tanner ignored the Gothic qualities but praised Ellison's achievement in *Invisible Man:* "the most profound novel about American identity written since the war."

Like Gothicism in fiction, surrealism at its source was infused "with all the obscure power of dreams, of the unconscious and of rebellion." Patrick Waldberg continued by quoting the *Manifeste du Surréalisme* (1924), defining surrealism as "pure psychic automatism . . . Thought dictated in the absence of all control exerted by reason, and outside all aesthetic or moral preoccupations." The encyclopedia definition quoted is even more pertinent to Gothicism in fiction, where psychic automatism plays no role except when it is imitated as a conscious technical device: "Surrealism is based on the belief in the superior reality of certain forms of association heretofore neglected, in the omnipotence of the dream, and in the disinterested play of thought." What Ihab Hassan said, in *The Dismemberment of Orpheus*, of the surrealist revolution applies to Gothicism: it is "ultimately grounded on a mysticism of the subconscious" and similarly opposes "the tyranny of the rational, the habitual, or the illusory world." In the works of Truman Capote, Hassan recognized the surrealist effect but not the pervasive Gothicism ("The Daydream and Nightmare of Narcissus").

There is a direct relationship between Gothicism and surrealism. Maurice Lévy gives a detailed account of André Breton's deep interest in Gothic novels and of his interpretation of them in light of his theories on art and on dialectical materialism. Breton's analysis of the ruins and ghosts of Gothicism involves revolutionary horrors and Freudian significance pertinent to Fiedler's Love and Death theme: ruins express visually the collapse of the feudal period; ghosts denote the apprehension of the return of the power of the past; subterranean passages represent the slow progress of the individual toward the day; the stormy night transposes the noise of cannons. The creatures of pure temptation embody the struggle, as Freud showed, between death and Eros, between resistance to change and acceptance of life.

Surrealism was consciously based upon a major premise implicit in Gothicism: in Paul Ray's words, "unconscious, irrational processes are instruments of investigations and exploration of the world as valid as the traditionally conscious, rational ones." The fundamental link between Romanticism and both Gothicism and surrealism is obvious. Dealing with the grotesque, which abounds in Gothicism and surrealism, Arthur Clayborough quoted William Hazlitt as saying, "Our literature is Gothic and grotesque." Herbert Gershman described surrealism as "essentially a multifaceted method for eliciting literary revelations, and as such it is indeed the prehensile tail of romanticism that Breton once termed it." In *The Surrealist Revolution in France*, Herbert Gershman regarded Surrealism as "the synthesis of Romanticism and Classicism." Such a synthesis is not essential to Gothic polarities. The primacy of the imagination, essential to Romanticism, is shared by Gothicism and surrealism, to both of which Waldberg's comments on surrealism apply: "Imagination, folly, dream, surrender to the dark forces of the unconscious and recourse to the marvellous are here opposed, and preferred, to all that arises from necessity, from a logical order, from the reasonable." Gothic fiction as created by masters like Dickens, Faulkner, Ellison, and Nathanael West achieves the aim of Breton as quoted by Waldberg: "'the future resolution of those two states, so contradictory in appearance—dream and reality—into a kind of absolute reality, of *surreality*, if one may call it so.'"

Except for the inevitable use of "surrealistic" in referring to scenes and images in Gothic fiction, such as that of the writers above, critics have generally ignored the logical and psychological relationships between Gothicism and surrealism. Carvel Collins observed parallels between *Sanctuary* and West's *The Day of the Locust*, and Bernard Bergonzi identified in West the influence of "continental surrealism" and noted affinities between West and Ellison. But neither Collins nor Bergonzi recognized the Gothic matrix of the surrealist gems in Faulkner, West, and Ellison. Harry Levin's statement of the contribution of the surrealists to the arts applies also to the serious Gothic novels of the twentieth century: ". . . the Surrealists were serious in their efforts to revive and exalt the latent imaginative strain: the visionary, the oneiric, the phantasmagorical currents that ran underground through the nineteenth century. . . . Surrealism was most meaningful in its refusal to conform with *le réalisme*." "The true meaning of the Gothic novel for surrealism," J. H. Matthews said, "lies in protest against an Age of Reason, in assertion of the fruitfulness of imaginative play, and the full development of desire outside the restrictions imposed by social and moral conventions."

In *The Romantic Rebellion* Eric Newton discussed surrealism and its predecessors in art in the chapter "The Romanticism of the Abnormal." Surrealism Newton considered to be the result of "the self-conscious pursuit of the abnormal" which marked the end of Romanticism. In the following chapter, "Conflict," Newton's explanation of the significance of unresolved tension in romantic art applies equally to the unresolved polarities in Gothic fiction: "Not conflict, . . . but the exposure of conflict, is the romantic's intention. . . . For mystery is the sign of tensions unresolved that leave behind them an unanswered question. And abnormality is a sign that the conflict is still undecided, the resolution beyond guessing at, and wonderment more potent than satisfaction."

The nightmare aspects of Gothicism—the abnormalities, the distortions, the grotesque incongruities, the horror of scene, action, and imagery, the terror aroused by danger—are heightened technically by mystery and suspense. But essentially the nightmare is created by the revelation of the blackness in the depths of human nature. In white Gothic romance, which includes most of the popular Gothic, the evil is exorcised by the triumph of goodness, confidently expected by the experienced reader. Any or all of the three kinds of Occidental eroticism identified by Denis de Rougement—"marriage-for-love . . . mystical passion, and . . . impious license"—may be involved, but the typical ending is the marriage-for-love, accomplished or imminent, of the hero and heroine. The black Gothic, however, survives in the modern *roman noir,* descended from the Marquis de Sade, and in modern Gothic novels, such as those of Faulkner and other southern writers, in which sexual perversions and aberrations and psychic horrors are not exorcised.

Relevant to sexual perversions and aberrations, which characterize both European and American black Gothic fiction, is the medieval tradition of courtly love and the related sentimental cult of chastity. In *Love and Death,* Leslie Fiedler described "the convention of sentimental love" as standing "between the codes of courtly love, on the one hand, and recent Romantic defenses of passion as the end of life, on the other." Although the Church could assimilate the courtly love cult into the cult of the Virgin, since "Mariolatry and courtly love are both aspects of the same psychic revolution, that resurgence of the female" near the end of the Middle Ages, the Church could not prevent a consequent conflict of values. "The idealized codes of love demanded the pure worship of the mistress; the flesh required sexual satisfaction; the love of God demanded the renunciation of both." This conflict resulted in a male-tempter and female-savior opposition, best exemplified by Samuel Richardson's Lovelace and Clarissa Harlowe. As Fiedler said, "A continuing tradition of prose fiction did not begin until the love affair of Lovelace and Clarissa (a demythicized Don Juan and a secularized goddess of Christian love) had been imagined."

This opposition was succeeded, after the Gretchen-Faust story, by basic character types common to both medieval romance and Gothic romance. Woman was split "into Dark Lady and Fair Maiden, savior and tempter, between whom the helpless male is eternally torn." Fiedler explained also the American development: "The symbolic vacuum left by the deposition of the Father is filled by the figure of woman, as Maiden and Mother." The triumph of the "sentimental code" over the Pauline concept of "the female as tempter," taught by Calvinistic Protestantism, was the consequence and the symptom of the decline of puritanism. Gothic fiction as "the expression of a fundamentally Protestant theological or religious disquietude," according to Joel Porte, has received "little systematic consideration." He ascribes much of the "gloomy Gothic *ambiance*" of the *genre noir,* from Godwin to Poe, to "a brooding sense of religious terror which is notably Protestant in its origin and bearing."

The sentimental code, which retained Calvinistic fear of the sins of the flesh, fostered the ideal of innocence, to be preserved mentally by taboos and physically by the rejection of sexuality, which was tantamount to the rejection of maturity and reality. Symbolic of this rejection is the evasion of initiation, defined by Fiedler in *No! in Thunder* as "a fall through knowledge into maturity." Hence the significance of initiation or the refusal of it in the Gothic novel, and the prevalence of taboo subjects such as homosexuality, perversion, and miscegenation, the knowledge of which would necessitate mature recognition of reality. In dealing with Gothicism in Carson McCullers's *The Member of the Wedding,* Robert Phillips noted as a consequence of these taboos the troubled sexuality of the characters and the violence of sexuality in thwarted characters. His observations on McCullers apply largely to Faulkner.

Rejection of adult sexuality may contribute to narcissism or incest. In *Patterns of Incest* R. E. L. Masters said: "It seems to be true that narcissism sometimes plays a part in incestuous sexual selection." In brother-sister incest, the most frequent kind in Gothic fiction, Leslie Fiedler in *Love and Death* regards the sister as "first surrogate for the mother—and the enemy is the father": "the only consummation is death." The sister is closest to the self; she is the narcissistic reflection the youth sees if he looks up from his own mirrored image. The power of sympathy could disastrously attract young people of like natures who were unaware of close blood relationship. As Montague Summers indicated, the climactic revelation of Ambrosio's villainy in Matthew Lewis's *The Monk* was that in ignorance he slew his mother and raped and killed his sister. Presumably even his villainy would have stopped short of deliberate incest. In *Love and Death* Fiedler cites Melville's *Pierre* as a notable example of brother-sister incest. Harold Bloom explained that the projection of "the ego's own self-love" onto "an outward object" can return to the ego. Object-libido and ego-libido are narrowly separated when the object is as nearly as possible like the self. Both incest and homosexuality evade mature responsibility, but homosexuality may be less self- and family-centered than incest. Enrico Garzilli regarded homosexuality as a negative interpretation of the Narcissus myth, of which the positive interpretation is "Narcissus as a creative symbol." If homosexuality occurs in the family, as it does repeatedly in Faulkner, it may, like incest, be rooted in narcissism, of which the logical extreme would be identical twins. Among numerous twins and doubles in Faulkner the Gowrie twins, Vardaman and Bilbo, in *Intruder in the Dust* represent this extreme. In *The Secular Scripture* Northrop Frye related the Narcissus theme to the romance theme of twins and confused identity.

Rejection of fertility and of life may lead to a necrophiliac cult and an obsession with the past, and may even lead to suicide. Gothic ghosts symbolize the power of the past, often a power inhibiting or destroying the individual or impelling him to self-destruction. The cult of chastity may be the source, as in Quentin Compson, of a person's choice of the dead past or even of death itself.

The cult of chastity also stimulated opposite reactions directed against it: seduction, persecution, rape. In *Love and Death* Leslie Fiedler saw in Clarissa Harlowe and Lovelace the archetypal heroine and hero of this battle of the sexes. In this conflict the masochism of the victim matches the sadism of the aggressor. The Marquis de Sade was the real father of horror-Gothic, the black Gothic strain in fiction; in theory and practice he employed all the psychological perversions characteristic of Gothic fiction. The sadistic villains of Gothic fiction are the direct descendants of the man who is immortalized in the word "sadism." Ihab Hassan described "novelists of outrage" as "the avant-garde movement in current literature, exploiting a fictional genre that may find its origins . . . in the writings . . . of Sade." Hassan dealt with the influence of Sade, including that related to Gothic fiction, in "Sade, The Prison of Consciousness" in *The Dismemberment of Orpheus.*

Prominent in, if not peculiar to, southern Gothic fiction is the significance attached to miscegenation, the sexual perversion which, in the South, is paradoxically the most prevalent and the most abhorrent. In *Love and Death* Leslie Fiedler regards miscegenation as "the secret theme" of *The Last of the Mohicans* and identifies homosexual "platonic" love between races as a theme from Cooper and Melville to the present. These themes are present in Faulkner, though less frequently than Fiedler maintains, in defiance of textual evidence.

From its beginning Gothicism had embraced medievalism, fantasy, realism, and burlesque, categories of the *roman noir* listed by Montague Summers. Burlesque, with its kinship to caricature and parody, is of special interest in a modern context. In *Love and Death* Leslie Fiedler explained the "gothic mode" as "essentially a form of parody, a way of assailing clichés by exaggerating them to the limit of grotesqueness": in *Absalom, Absalom!* Faulkner mocked "the banal harsh taunt 'Would you want a nigger to sleep with your sister!'" In "The Dream of the New" Fiedler explained further that for the American writer the only "fruitful relationship" to the past "compatible with the tradition of the New" is parody, "which simultaneously connects and rejects." Fiedler identified "conscious parody" ("one of the chief modes of our books"); "unconscious parody"; and "parody of parody"—illustrated by Mark Twain "consciously parodying Sir Walter Scott" and then being "inadvertently parodied by Ernest Hemingway." Self-parody is the fourth kind. Without reference to Gothicism, Fiedler cited Faulkner to exemplify all kinds of parody. Fiedler concluded that parody is "a kind of *necessary* final act of destroying the past, required of all who belong to the tradition of the New."

Exaggeration, one element in burlesque, is identified by Eric Bentley as a basic element in melodrama, which he defined as "the Naturalism of the dream life," akin to the exaggerated fantasies of childhood and adult dreams. Eric Newton credited "the romantic thirst for melodrama" with penetrating "so deeply into the common consciousness that excess had ceased to be ridiculous." Characteristics of melodrama given by James Smith sound much like white Gothic fiction: to provide what Michael Booth termed "'the fulfillment and satisfaction found only in dreams,'" melodrama presented stereotyped, unreal characters on a stage filled with "gigantic pictures" and "grandiose scenery," in which the hero is exposed to physical dangers. "Every act leads up to its 'tableau.'" The hero is finally rewarded by dream justice. Predictably, Smith cites among variations in melodrama the Gothic; in late Gothic the hero is sometimes "a poor man's Faust."

"Medievalism, fantasy, realism, and burlesque"—all but medievalism, in the literal sense, are found in modern American Gothic fiction. Ironic inversion, a strategy by which a kind of parody can be used seriously to convey values directly opposed to those ostensibly presented, may be used with any varieties of literary or black Gothic.

In *Love and Death* Leslie Fiedler stressed the absence in American fiction of eroticism based on adult, heterosexual love. The transformation of European Gothic themes to express the "obsessive concerns" of Americans identified by Fiedler (see p. 8 above) are all exemplified in William Faulkner's Yoknapatawpha novels, as are the general characteristics of Gothicism already dealt with. Romantic solitude sought by Old World characters was found in the New World in primeval forests or unbroken prairies, affording frontier freedom; as Fiedler said, "Scott's romantic North" became Cooper's "romantic West," and flight to escape oppressive society became flight from women and society to male companions in the wilderness. The bandits and outlaws of Europe—German freebooters and Italian banditti, according to Montague Summers—were replaced by Indians. The English gentleman-highwayman was brother under the skin to southern Civil War guerrillas. The iniquities of the Old World authoritarian church and state and corrupt social institutions were matched by New World exploitation of nature, by Negro slavery, and by frontier roughness and violence. Anti-Catholicism gave place to anti-Calvinism. The defiance of Faust, which Fiedler called "the diabolic bargain," became the center of the modern American Gothic novel, with the vast New World as the stage for the drama of superhuman ambition— a recurrent theme noted by Robert Hume in Dark Romantic writing. In a society founded by rebels, rebels and outcasts could be redeemed in the general Romantic revolt against the past and its values. Fiedler noted that the redeemed ones included Prometheus, Cain, Judas, the

Wandering Jew, and even Lucifer. The use of superstition and the supernatural, made more plausible by a medieval setting, in the New World lost its power to produce Gothic mystery, awe, and shudders. Dream experience, Howard Lovecraft said, "helped to build up the notion of an unreal or spiritual world." In fiction the supernatural could be replaced by psychological phenomena which readers could accept with at least "a willing suspension of disbelief": common experiences such as dreams; rarer phenomena such as hallucination; special power such as telepathy, prescience, and clairvoyance; psychological abnormalities, including mental deficiency and paranoia. As Leslie Fiedler observed in *Love and Death,* rejection of superstition was succeeded by the realization that such belief, "far from being the fabrication of a Machiavellian priesthood, was a projection of a profound inner insecurity and guilt, a hidden world of nightmare not abolished by manifestos or restrained by barricades. The final horrors, as modern society has come to realize, are neither gods nor demons, but intimate aspects of our own minds."

With modifications and transformations noted above, the new American literary Gothic continues the Gothic tradition, chiefly the black Gothic, in character types and psychological concerns, in settings, and in thematic ideas and narrative patterns. The character types of the Gothic novel, described by Eino Railo, largely paralleled by those in poetry and drama of the Romantic decadence, discussed by Mario Praz, flourished in both European and American fiction. Parallels also to medieval romance are obvious in such characters as the chivalric hero and the persecuted maiden, the villain and the evil woman, and in the general polarity of good and evil. Here will be listed the chief types of characters from which Faulkner, in following the Gothic tradition, could make his choice. Prominent among leading male characters are the heroes or villain-heroes descended from Elizabethan drama and from Milton's Lucifer, culminating in the Faustian or Byronic hero—handsome, melancholy, mysterious, and passionate, with exceptional capacity for both good and evil. Byron inherited this hero from Gothic romance and the poems of Sir Walter Scott. Lovecraft said that the Gothic villain and the Byronic hero are "essentially cognate types." Eric Bentley stated that villains in melodrama "stem from the archvillain Lucifer." "The dark, rebellious Byronic hero," as Byron developed the type, was described by John Ehrstine as "a composite and evolutionary figure," relentlessly pursuing in isolation "the demonic root of all evil." The Don Juan type, of which Lovelace is the prime example in the novel, is less typical of American Gothic than is the Byronic or Faustian hero. The Romantic hero is descended from the virtuous chivalric heroes but is less interesting than the knights errant. The leading female characters offer parallels to the males; the persecuted maiden, rescued from the villain by the hero, is contrasted with the evil, strong woman, often dark and sometimes a prostitute.

The relationship between the Romantic decadence and the Gothic tradition is reflected by Addison Bross's study of the influence of Aubrey Beardsley on Faulkner in *Soldiers' Pay*. Bross concluded that Beardsley contributed to "Faulkner's inherent sense of the grotesque and absurd element in man" and to the contrast between Margaret, the evil dark beauty, and the girl Cecily. In the South the Dark Lady, termed by Fiedler in *Love and Death* the "sinister embodiment of the sexuality denied the snow maiden," might be expected to have Negro blood. Faulkner did not use this contrast, not even when a woman with Negro blood was the rival to a white heroine. In *Absalom, Absalom!* Charles Bon's octoroon mistress is Judith Sutpen's rival. She is even described with explicit reference to Beardsley, as Bross and Timothy Conley noted. This passage exemplifies Conley's point that in Faulkner's mature works "his own pictorial genius" carried Beardsley's art "to its fictional heights." The octoroon is a victim, not an evil woman, and Judith provides no blonde contrast to the "magnolia-faced woman" as they stand together at the grave of Charles Bon. The octoroon suggests the Suffering Wife of the Gothic tradition, created in Horace Walpole's Hippolita and found, as Eino Railo observed, "in every later romance in which an unhappy mother and child is needed."

Development of servants as distinctive characters, whether loyal and amusing or treacherous and disgusting, was a feature of *The Castle of Otranto* in which Walpole imitated Shakespeare's servants. Only in the southern Gothic is a servant likely to be a member of the family. Clytie, half-sister in *Absalom, Absalom!* to Judith and Henry Sutpen, combines the Dark Woman with the Loyal Servant.

Most typical of Gothic fiction and least common in other kinds of narrative are the grotesque characters which, in the Gothic tradition, reflected the acceptance in eighteenth- and nineteenth-century aesthetic theory of the grotesque as an aspect of the sublime. The grotesque was one means of achieving the terror which, as Samuel Monk said, was the foundation of Edmund Burke's theory of sublimity. Ugliness could be "associated with sublimity if it is 'united with such qualities as excite strong terror.'" Maurice Lévy considered Burke's evidence valuable because "Burke formulated strictly what his epoch felt vaguely." Lévy regarded the Gothic as the product of a fantastic or grotesque imagination.

John Ruskin, however, was more influential than Burke in forming the tastes of readers and writers in nineteenth-century Romanticism. Ruskin's "Grotesque Renaissance" (chapter 3 in *The Stones of Venice*, volume 2) differentiates true or noble grotesque from false grotesque by the qualities of the spirit revealed in art. (In "The Grotesque in the Fiction of William Faulkner" Robert Ferguson applies Ruskin's categories to characters.) Howard Lovecraft referred to "the grotesque gargoyles," "the daemonic gargoyles of Notre Dame and Mont St. Michel," as gauges of "the prevalence and depth of the medieval horror-spirit in Europe, intensified by the dark despair which waves of pestilence brought." The psychological justification for the grotesque in aesthetic theory and the arts is stated by Wolfgang Kayser in "a final interpretation of the grotesque: AN ATTEMPT TO INVOKE AND SUBDUE THE DEMONIC ASPECTS OF THE WORLD." In "The Victim" Ihab Hassan noted the ancient association between "evil and the ludicrous" and cited "the grotesque magnification of evil" by Dante as a religious act. Whether "grotesque" is limited to characters or is extended to imagery and to incongruities and distortions of all kinds, the grotesque is an integral part of the total pattern of Gothic fiction and usually combines the terrible and the ludicrous in some deformation of what is regarded as natural and pleasing, some nightmarish violation of the daylight world, some ominous disruption of order and harmony.

In substantial agreement with Leslie Fiedler's basic idea in *Love and Death in the American Novel,* Irving Malin said that the "New American Gothic is in the mainstream of American fiction." Malin found the source of the grotesque in Gothic fiction to be the breakdown of order into dream effects. Agreeing with William Van O'Connor that "the grotesque is produced by disintegration," Malin observed that this disintegration, evident in narcissism and the breakdown of the family, is reflected "by the technique of new American Gothic." In "Flannery O'Connor and the Grotesque," Irving Malin grouped her "grotesquerie" with that of "Capote, Hawkes, Carson McCullers, and Purdy," all new American Gothic novelists.

Although the grotesque extends beyond characters to structure and imagery, we are concerned here only with the kinds of grotesque characters, all being deviations from the normal in appearance, capacities, and actions. Defining the grotesque as "the unresolved clash of incompatibles in work and response; the ambivalently abnormal," Philip Thomson stated that "the grotesque has a strong affinity with the *physically abnormal,*" to which our uncivilized response is "unholy glee and barbaric delight." Such grotesques include: sexual deviants who are visibly so, such as hermaphrodites, epicene persons, and transvestites; the blind, or dumb; characters whose appearance or manner shows mechanical rigidity or some other nonhuman quality; cripples; mentally deficient or insane persons. From the dwarves of medieval romance to the dwarf in Carson McCullers's *The Ballad of the Sad Café,* grotesques have been prominent in romances and novels. In modern Gothic, popular or literary, grotesque characters may even predominate, a tendency illustrated in the works of Carson McCullers, Truman Capote, and Flannery O'Connor, all southern followers of Faulkner. In *The Mortgaged Heart,* a miscellany of works by Carson McCullers, Margarita Smith, the editor and the sister of McCullers, ventured an explanation of Gothic fiction: "I wonder sometimes if what they call the 'Gothic' school of Southern writing, in which the grotesque is paralleled with the sublime, is not due largely to the cheapness of human life in the South."

A *Season of Dreams* by Alfred Appel deals with Eudora Welty. In the chapter "The Grotesque and the Gothic" Appel explains the relationship between his book and chapter titles:

The grotesque is characterized by a distortion of the external world, by the description of human beings in nonhuman terms, and by the displacement we associate with dreams. The infinite possibilities of the dream inform the grotesque at every turn, suspending the laws of proportion and symmetry: our deepest promptings are projected into the details of the scene—inscape as landscape. Because the grotesque replaces supernaturalism with hallucination, it expresses the reality of the unconscious life—the formative source which the Gothic writer, in his romantic flights, may never tap. The grotesque is a heightened realism, reminiscent of caricature, but going beyond it to create a fantastic realism or realistic fantasy that evokes pathos and terror.

Although Appel erroneously equates "grotesque" with "gothic" in his chapter title, instead of subordinating the grotesque to the encompassing Gothic configuration, his analysis sheds light on all the southern Gothic novelists.

In *Radical Innocence,* without reference to Gothicism, Ihab Hassan noted the prevalence of the grotesque in southern writers and explained the functions of grotesque characters in serious fiction.

The grotesque, as clown and scapegoat, is both comic and elegiac, revolting and pathetic. As hunchback or cripple, he is born an outsider, his very aspect an affront to appearances. His broken body testifies to the contradictions of the inner man, the impossible and infrangible dream, raging against his crooked frame and against the world in which flesh is housed.

The prominence of the grotesque in Faulkner's novels is a significant aspect of his Gothic world.

In this world "the obsessive images and recurring emblematic figures" constitute what G. R. Thompson termed "an 'iconography' of the Gothic":

the recurring character types and edifices and landscapes serve as "some sort of objective correlative" of "the themes of physical terror, moral horror, and religious mystery." The most obvious single objective correlative is derived from *The Castle of Otranto* and is suggested by the term "Gothic": the medieval castle or ancient abbey, an image of somber ruin and mystery symbolizing the past. The haunted castle, one of the three images Irving Malin deals with in *New American Gothic,* is prevalent in popular Gothic romance which clings to the splendor that "falls on castle walls" remote in time and place; in literary Gothic, with an American setting, the "castle" must be less ancient and magnificent and may be merely a ruined mansion like Faulkner's Old Frenchman's place or the Sutpen mansion. The second of Malin's images, the voyage into the forest, also has characterized Gothic fiction since Horace Walpole and Ann Radcliffe: the unaxed forest, the prairie, a mighty river, and any other scene offering solitude, danger, and mystery represent aspects of the American experience in the New World and the American dream which dominate the transformation of the Gothic novel into an American genre. Jonathan Baumbach's title *The Landscape of Nightmare* might well suggest these two images, the castle and the forest, although Baumbach selected the novels he dealt with on the basis of their treatment of a typically Gothic theme, the "spiritual passage from innocence to guilt and redemption," without regard to other Gothic features. A third kind of setting adds another nightmare image: enclosed places representing retreat and asylum or imprisonment or both. Taking the phrase from the title of Truman Capote's most Gothic novel, *Other Voices, Other Rooms,* Irving Malin in *New American Gothic* refers to the "other room" in the haunted castle which is "'the final door' through which the ghost-like forces march." The other room is the transformation in new American Gothic of the haunted castle, "the metaphor of confining narcissism, the private world." Insane asylums like the one at Jackson where Benjy Compson and Darl Bundren were sent, the jail in Jefferson, Miss Reba's brothel in Memphis, the room in Sutpen's Hundred where Henry Sutpen ended his flight and exchanged freedom for safety and care—these are only a few of the many enclosed places where people of Yoknapatawpha were trapped or hid themselves.

In front of the castle on covers of popular Gothic paperbacks forever flees the girl who represents one of a small cluster of narrative patterns of dreamlike motion. In *Love and Death* Leslie Fiedler said that the Persecuted Maiden in flight, descended from Horace Walpole's Isabella or Richardson's Clarissa, may be fleeing "through a world of ancestral and infantile fears projected in dreams"; pursued by the villain and threatened with violation, she may be fleeing from her own darker impulses as well. But according to Fiedler the flight of "the typical male protagonist of our fiction" has been from "the confrontation of a man and woman which leads to the fall to sex, marriage, and responsibility." The hero may also be in flight from guilt, pursued by conscience and justice. The ultimate issue of any flight, if escape from a fate worse than death is impossible, is suicide.

In contrast to the flight-pursuit pattern but also involving recurrent or prolonged motion is the quest, the positive journey directed toward a goal, what Northrop Frye in *The Secular Scripture* called "the epic of the creature, man's vision of his own life as a quest." In *New American Gothic* Irving Malin viewed the journey or voyage as opposed to "the other room" but equally fraught with anxiety, the movement being usually "erratic, circular, violent, or distorted." The journey in the *nouveau roman* is envisioned by Enrico Garzilli "as an anonymous quest toward self-understanding," portrayed by "the metaphor of the labyrinth." The journey in a quest for self-understanding or self-realization may follow an initiation pattern. In *The Quest* Mircea Eliade linked the initiation with the quest, noting that most "scenarios in the Arthurian cycle have an initiatory structure" and that "the pattern of initiation persists in the imaginary universes of modern man—in literature, dreams, and daydreams." Dealing in *Radical Innocence* with some of the writers that Malin discussed, Ihab Hassan saw their work as "a parody of man's quest for fulfillment," an ironic tragicomedy. A quest that resembles Hassan's parody quest was observed by Robert Phillips in the work of Carson McCullers: "the search for a sexless, dim ideal, a manifestation of the hero's avoidance and fear of reality." The quest may, however, be quite directly the equivalent of a common traditional theme, the search for identity which involves ascertaining the facts of one's parentage and finding one's father and family. In the old romances and in Gothic fiction, this search culminated in the recognition and acceptance of the hero and often in his claiming his rightful heritage. In new American Gothic the climax of the quest is more likely to be the rejection and destruction of the hero, as in *Absalom, Absalom!* The Faustian theme also usually involves a quest or purposeful journey in order to realize an ambition, such as Sutpen's design in *Absalom, Absalom!* The purpose of the quest may be evil, such as murderous revenge, or it may be a search for truth and justice involving the detective story pattern. But serious Gothic fiction is likely to have more than one pattern: the detection in *Intruder in the Dust*, for example, is subordinated to the story of Chick Mallison's successful initiation.

A third pattern of motion contrasts with both flight and quest: purposeless wandering. The stories of the Wandering Jew and of Cain have been absorbed into the Gothic tradition: wandering imposed as a doom casts a man out of human society into isolation, often literally into the wilderness. Geoffrey Hartman interprets the significance of this theme as one "which best expresses this perilous nature of consciousness":

Those solitaries are separated from life in the midst of life, yet cannot die. They are doomed to live a middle or purgatorial existence which is neither life nor death, and as their knowledge increases, so does their solitude. It is consciousness, ultimately, which alienates them from life and imposes the burden of a self which religion or death or a return to the state of nature might dissolve.

The wandering of Joe Christmas in *Light in August* combined the racial doom of alienation with a flight from both racial identities. The purgatorial life of Henry Sutpen, Faulkner's Cain, is left to our imagination until death rid him of "the burden of self."

Scenes of violence are so characteristic of Gothic themes and patterns that they are too diverse to allow specification. The effect of horror which distinguishes Gothic fiction may be secured by any and all means, realistic or fantastic, objective or psychological, but underlying all scenes of horror are the dream images and nightmare sensations in the thematic patterns noted above. Modern Gothic fiction not only makes frequent use of dreams but lends such subjective distortion to physical events that it is sometimes difficult to distinguish the inner from the outer nightmare, as in the riot scenes in West's *The Day of the Locust* and in Ellison's *Invisible Man.*

The frequency with which the landscape of nightmare in recent Gothic fiction takes on distinctly southern features is due only in part to the pervasive influence of William Faulkner upon younger southern writers. The southern background and tradition which Faulkner shared with his successors accounts in large measure for their Gothic tendencies. In explaining the prevalence of Gothic fiction in the South, Leslie Fiedler, in *The Return of the Vanishing American,* contrasted the South with "the real West," which "contains no horrors which correspond to the Southerner's deep nightmare terrors." Robert Phillips noted the frequency of violent themes in southern fiction and the shift at times to the minds of tormented souls caught in a labyrinthine life. To Jacques Cabau, the South and the North join "in nostalgia for the West, the lost prairie." Phillips observed that the southern obsession with the problem of evil sprang from a sense of guilt. Referring specifically to Flannery O'Connor, William Faulkner, Robert Penn Warren, and Eudora Welty, Carter W. Martin's view confirms that of Phillips: "The themes that arise from their use of the Gothic mode are essentially spiritual ones, for they speak

of matters of the soul and not matters of the glands or the nervous system."

Adaptation of Gothic patterns to existing social scenes has proved easier in the South than in most other regions of the United States. Indeed, some Gothic features which attract readers can be plausibly approximated in very few other American settings. Of genuine medieval ruins, of course, there is a complete lack in the United States; popular Gothic romances cherish the phony Gothic castles along the Palisades of the Hudson River. But the plantation world of antebellum days provided an analogy to feudal society and fostered chivalric ideals. The plantation aristocrat might see himself as like the lord of a manor, ruling over his serfs in a little world over which he held sovereign sway. This inclination toward medievalism accounted in part for the popularity in the South of Sir Walter Scott's novels and, in turn, strengthened by the influence of Scott, provided the foundation of the southern myth of the past, with its ideal of noblesse oblige and its devotion to a lost cause. Although, according to Fiedler, in *Love and Death,* Scott had retained Gothic devices without penetrating to the meanings of Gothic, his novels preserved and transmitted the Gothic tradition in the South. The plantation house which, in its prosperity, had stood for the orderly life of a semi-feudal society, in its ruin and decay resembled the ruined castle in Gothic novels, symbolizing the collapse of the old order. As Jacques Cabau said: "Only the South was material rich enough to express in artistic terms all the aspects—religious, social, political, psychological—of the reaction." The reaction was against liberalism and faith in human perfectibility: the most characteristic of the "artistic terms" chosen was Gothicism.

The influence of Scott strengthened also the southern white Protestant version of medieval courtly love, the cult of the White Goddess. In *Love and Death,* Fiedler cited Mark Twain's hatred of Scott as based on a conviction that Scott had "utterly corrupted the Southern imagination by dreams of chivalry and romance, which made it quite impossible for any Southern writer to face reality or describe an actual woman." In *The Mind of the South* W. J. Cash showed how southern gyneolatry developed as a consequence of cultural and literary influences and social circumstances. The sexless three decades described by Fiedler, the 1860s to the 1890s, contributed to the cult of the white virgin, which could evoke such fervid devotion only in a racially mixed society with aristocratic white leaders. Furthermore, Calvinistic repression of sex moved from New England to the South during the religious awakening of the early 1800s, with the consequent equating of sin and sex; the image of woman as temptress became the obverse of the image of woman as savior.

Fiedler in *Love and Death* sums up this duality by saying that the underside of adoration was "fear and contempt": women were goddesses or bitches. The effect of the cult of the white virgin was to inhibit healthy sexuality in upper class white women and to make them frigid physically or psychologically. Mr. Compson in *Absalom, Absalom!* well described the white gentleman's attitude toward women and his solution of his sexual problems. There were "three sharp divisions" of women: "ladies, women, females—the virgins whom gentlemen someday married, the courtesans to whom they went while on sabbaticals to the cities, the slave girls and women upon whom that first caste rested and to whom in certain cases it doubtless owed the very fact of its virginity . . ." (p. 109). Mr. Compson continued to explain how a young man on a plantation, with the first two classes inaccessible psychologically and financially, would turn to the accessible slave girls, among whom he could freely choose. Hence, the most prevalent sexual offense was miscegenation, but it was also in principle the most abhorred; miscegenation between a white woman and a Negro man was regarded as sodomy, punishable by summary death.

The remoteness and exclusiveness of the plantation contributed to other sexual aberrations than miscegenation. In the absence of eligible companions of the opposite sex, narcissism, incest, or homosexuality might result from the aristocratic self-esteem and pride that sought the image of self in the loved one. The Gothic tradition had transmitted the theme of incest which Northrop Frye, in *The Secular Scripture,* showed to be recurrent in romance and which, according to J. M. S. Tompkins, pervaded the popular eighteenth-century novel. But the plantation society after the Civil War provided a scene in which "incest was a constant," according to Andrew Lytle, not merely a literary convention which by that time had come to be regarded with horror.

This was a defeated society, cherishing the myth of the past and fostering in the southern psyche elements characteristic of romance and the Gothic tradition, with their conservative and nostalgic attitude toward the past, to which Maurice Lévy's observation that "man dreams to the right" perfectly applies. The southern myth was more aristocratic and conservative, especially in the later-settled states like Mississippi, than the past had actually been. The Gothic delight in landscape was gratified by the picturesque landscape of the South, with its moss-and-vine-draped trees and flamboyant flowers and mysterious forests and swamps. This natural setting was conducive to the paranoid "melodramatic vision" described by Eric Bentley: "We are being persecuted, and we hold that all things, living and dead, are combining to persecute us." "The landscape in *Light in August*," Francois Pitavy said, "is never immutable or dead:

motion still inhabits it and is potentially present, as in the stilled characters. Indeed, as in a dream or nightmare, the shadows tremble and bulge monstrously, and the landscape slowly alters. . . ." The landscape is "a projection or a reflection" of the characters. One is not surprised when Pitavy concludes: "The Faulknerian landscape in *Light in August* is above all the image of a state of mind." The reality, as seen by Doc Peabody, conditioned its inhabitants: rivers and land were "opaque, slow, violent; shaping and creating the life of man in its implacable and brooding image" (*As I Lay Dying*, p. 44).

The South was an agrarian society, hostile to the urban North and to evil cities, the scenes of southerners' own premeditated sins—an attitude shared with southerners by Romanticism and the Romantic decadence. London, the sum of felicity to Dr. Samuel Johnson in the age of reason, was the City of Dreadful Night to James Thomson in the next century.

Most obviously and perhaps most significantly, only the South could provide writers with an emotionally satisfying parallel for the ruined castle which was virtually the protagonist of early Gothic fiction. But the mood of tender melancholy inspired by the southern ruin had a personal, family, and community significance lacking in most haunted castles in which Gothic heroines were immured. The paintless and dilapidated mansion, vacant or inhabited, is still a familiar sight in the South, a reminder of glory and suffering only a century past, rather than a bit of stage scenery in a tale about distant times. The ghosts which haunt these southern ruins may be the living, like Faulkner's Quentin Compson, who dwell in a past more real to them than the present and who have rejected the modern world which offers them no gratifications commensurate with those of the myth of the past. The cult of the past in the South, as symbolized in its ruins, its preserved glories displayed in spring pilgrimages, its monuments and graveyards, owes less to cultural climate and imagination than to remembered history. In the South new intensity reanimates the original Gothic feeling for ruins as described by Montague Summers: "The ruin was a sacred relic, a memorial, a symbol of infinite sadness, of tenderest sensibility and regret." The southern ruin also is a symbol of a legendary Golden Age little more than a century past.

In *The Return of the Vanishing American* Leslie Fiedler's summing up of the significance of the southern plantation setting, with references to southern writers from Poe through William Faulkner to Flannery O'Connor and Truman Capote, suggests why the Gothic mode was naturalized particularly and uniquely in the South and why Yoknapatawpha was conceived in the Gothic tradition:

. . . the Southern, as opposed to the Northern, does not avoid but seeks melodrama, a series of bloody events, sexual by implication at least, played out in the blood-heat of a "long hot summer" against a background of miasmal swamps, live oak, Spanish moss, and the decaying plantation house so dear to the hearts of movie-makers. . . . The mode of the Southern is Gothic, American Gothic, and the Gothic requires a haunted house at its center. It demands also a symbolic darkness to cloak its action. . . .

Thus, the South provided William Faulkner and other southern writers with a reality which could be depicted with the strong contrasts of the Gothic genre to reveal social and psychological truths less accessible to purely objective and realistic treatment. Seldom, however, does modern southern Gothic play it straight and depict society and characters in terms of the myth and the tradition, as in the old-fashioned historical novel about the South or the modern popular Gothic romance. With a foundation of realistic displacement which conceals Gothic structure beneath the representation of modern society, all the strategies of point of view, discontinuity, ironic inversion, exaggeration, and parody are employed to give new meaning to old formulas, to "penetrate the instinctual reservoirs out of which terror arises," as Dr. Kubie said, or in Fiedler's words in *The Vanishing American*, to evoke "the nightmare terror," the "blackness of darkness."

To discern the new meaning in the old formulas, the reader must recognize what the writer could choose from in the Gothic tradition, what he did choose, and how he transformed a type of fiction originally distanced in time and space to deal with recent or present realities, often of universal urgency, the nightmares that do not vanish with the dawn. William Faulkner's Yoknapatawpha novels cover the whole range of American Gothic; his original modifications and modulations of Gothic elements are uniquely combined with non-Gothic, daylight views of the same society, within individual works or in the extended scope of the Yoknapatawpha chronicles.

CHAPTER TWO

ABSALOM, ABSALOM!

FAUST IN MISSISSIPPI, OR,
THE FALL OF THE HOUSE OF SUTPEN

Absalom, Absalom! is so obviously Gothic that critical references to it as Gothic are inevitable, but critical agreement ends with varied use of the handy label. It is as if watchers of the sky agreed on the name of a constellation but recognized only a few stars that swam into their ken and, with untrained and unaided eyes, did not identify all the stars in the configuration. Referring to *Absalom, Absalom!* as the greatest but least understood of Faulkner's novels, Cleanth Brooks in *William Faulkner* aptly described it as "more than a bottle of Gothic sauce to be used to spice up our own preconceptions about the history of American society." Analysis of the ingredients of that bottle of Gothic sauce is useful in showing how, out of traditional ingredients, Faulkner concocted a strikingly original creation, a kind of distillation of truth about American society and universal human passions. Cleanth Brooks quoted Harvey Breit's introduction to *Absalom, Absalom!* as a "terrible Gothic sequence of events" (p. ix) as a misreading because Breit did not recognize that Sutpen's innocence is the innocence of modern man, "innocence about the nature of reality." But this is also the innocence of the age of reason, as Brooks failed to perceive, against which the Gothic novel was a protest, and innocence is therefore a traditional ingredient in the Gothic sauce and an essential part of Faulkner's criticism of rationality as being inadequate for full experience and understanding of human life. In referring to *Absalom, Absalom!* as a detective story, Brooks did not recognize the detective story as an outgrowth of the Gothic tradition, a dangerous search for truth being the hero's vocation, not merely a personal quest.

To Ilse Dusoir Lind the mystery and the "macabre search" which frame the novel constitute the Gothic quality, a "melodramatic, excessive" device: "The rotting mansion is the house of the past; the death-in-life of Henry is Quentin's own." Her remark relates atmosphere to scene, character, narrative pattern, and mystery. But she omits, among other aspects of the Gothic effect, the narrative method, especially Miss Rosa as the initial narrator, who at the beginning, as Peter Swiggart said, "invests the melodramatic events of the past with a Gothic atmosphere of social sin and moral damnation." Swiggart implies, however, Victorian morality rather than the Faustian theme taken up by the last narrators from Miss Rosa's "demonizing." Concerned with the ways in which Faulkner made "technique and structure focus the meaning of the novel," Olga Vickery distinguished between "Miss Rosa's Gothic thriller" and the patterns she creates, "which some have applied to the book as a whole—the Gothic novel with its gloomy castles, dark, evil villains, and innocent victims," with its "Gothic horror and violence"—and the patterns of Mr. Compson's "deliberately rational" account. The inadequacies which she perceived in Mr. Compson's interpretation are precisely the absence of "imaginative power" and "intuitive understanding" which distinguish the Gothic version of Shreve and Quentin, an extension of Miss Rosa's demonizing.

"Darkness to Appall," Charles Gregory's title for his study of "Destructive Designs and Patterns" in some of Faulkner's characters, holds in a phrase the quintessence of Gothic effect. One is reminded that, ironically, the "Design" that appalled Robert Frost was white, not black, and one wishes that Faulkner could have alluded to Frost's design in relation to Sutpen's. Although Gregory recognized Thomas Sutpen as a hero of Gothic myth, he did not deal with Gothicism or deal with Gothic elements as such. Even an article by Max Putzel which professes to answer the question "What Is Gothic about *Absalom, Absalom!*" shows no knowledge of the essentials of the Gothic tradition or of American modifications of it as identified by Leslie Fiedler. In concluding that *Absalom, Absalom!* is not a "Gothic tale . . . intended to make us shudder deliciously at some imagined horror," Putzel limits "Gothic" to the popular, subliterary white Gothic, past or present. Mario Materassi's concept of Gothicism, based on Gothic romances, did not embrace American Gothic natural settings or recognize the rich and complex structures available in the Gothic tradition.

William Barrett used "Gothic" with perception of its deeper significance. He recognized in *Absalom, Absalom!* Faulkner's "own strange and powerful vision of the Gothic romance," in which the Civil War is "a vague nightmare in the distance." To the Protestant conscience the blacks "symbolize the qualities of spontaneity and naturalness," and the "white man's fear of the black man is his fear of what he considers the darker side of his own nature." Although Leslie Fiedler in *Love and Death in the American Novel* never applied to any of Faulkner's novels the whole Gothic pattern he well analyzed in *The Scarlet Letter, Moby-Dick,* and *Huckleberry Finn,* he regarded *Absalom, Absalom!* as "the most deeply moving of all American gothic fictions," the climax of what George Snell termed "'the demonic, macabre, apocalyptic school'" founded by Charles Brockden Brown. Fiedler cited only *Sanctuary* and *Light in August* as other Gothic novels by Faulkner.

Only when Gothic elements in setting, character types, themes, patterns of action, scenes, and episodes are considered, in novels which are predominantly or distinctly Gothic, can the significance of the Gothic tradition in Faulkner's Yoknapatawpha fiction be fully assessed. Albert J. Guerard, in *Thomas Hardy,* observed that "what both surrealism and naturalism discovered was a more than Gothic horror," revealed in *littérature noire.* He cited *Intruder in the Dust* and continued: "William Faulkner has consistently used the distortions of popular story-telling—exaggeration, grotesque horror, macabre coincidence—to achieve his darker truth; they are part of his reading of life." Faulkner's primary reason for using the Gothic mode is well stated. That "darker truth" is "darkness to appall" in *Absalom, Absalom!*

The title of a recent book on *Absalom, Absalom!* and *The Sound and the Fury* by John T. Irwin indicates that the "perspectival elements of the structure" with which he is concerned are largely Gothic, although he does not use that term: *Doubling and Incest/Repetition and Revenge.* The list of elements is expanded in the introduction: "spatial and temporal doubling, spatial and temporal incest, narcissism, the Oedipus complex, the castration complex, repetition, sameness and difference, recollection, repression, revenge, substitution, reversal, sacrifice, and mediation." Irwin's study embraces the "fruitful in-between space that exists among Faulkner's novels," specifically the two dealing with Quentin Compson. The validity of this approach is obvious, but Irwin ignores the lack of textual evidence for such assertions as: "Surely, there can be no question that Quentin reconstructs the story of Bon, Henry, and Judith in light of his own experiences with Candace and Dalton Ames. . . ." Irwin does not address himself to the question of why Faulkner seemed deliberately to avoid in *Absalom, Absalom!* precisely the interrelationships between novels that occupy the "fruitful in-between space" in most of the Yoknapatawpha cycle. The image of Quentin as the narrator, "locked in an incestuous, suicidal struggle with his dark twin, the story," Irwin extends to the novelist and "the other self of his book." Although Irwin does not recognize Gothicism as Faulkner's literary heritage or Faulkner's influence as significantly Gothic, his partial genealogy of Faulkner's ancestors includes "Poe's double stories," Mark Twain, and Henry James, and Robinson Jeffers's "Tamar."

Faulkner's use of the *paysage moralisé* in his Gothic settings (most impressive in *Absalom, Absalom!*) has been taken over, as Leslie Fiedler observed in *Love and Death,* by later southern writers, largely women: "Mississippi has taken on for the imagination of the world the symbolic values attributed in the earliest years of the gothic to Italy. Against a background of miasmic swamps and sweating black skins, the Faulknerian syndrome of disease, death, defeat, mutilation, idiocy, and lust continues to evoke in the stories of these writers a shudder once compelled only by the supernatural."

Absalom, Absalom! is the only novel by Faulkner in which the entire history of the "haunted castle" is given: in the primeval wilderness it was created by brute force directed by indomitable will; it existed in splendid isolation, the realization of Sutpen's dream, from his marriage in 1838 until the Civil War; it gradually fell into ruin during and after the war; it was destroyed by fire in 1910. Thus, the mansion is seen first as it takes shape in the wilderness, then as the center of a prosperous plantation, and finally as a "rotting shell" of a house surrounded by "fallow and rain-gutted and briar-choked old fields" (pp. 213, 214). Sutpen's original Gothic vision, "the dream of grim and castlelike magnificence" (p. 38), had been modified by the French architect.

The house as the central image, a symbol to Quentin of the South, is accompanied by such other recurrent images as closed rooms, tombstones, and the graveyard. These images and the nightmare quality they evoke are squarely in the Gothic tradition, in which, without reference to *Absalom, Absalom!*, Elizabeth MacAndrew said, "an old house or castle . . . has all the symbolic possibilities which Freud has made clear, and this dire and threatening place is representative of the villain. It is more than just his house, it is himself, . . . representation of the dark, tortured windings of ambition and cruelty, those eminently civilized vices." The creation of the house, as part of the design of Sutpen's Faustian ambition, and its destruction were effected within two generations: Henry, son of Thomas Sutpen, was destroyed with the house after a four-year living entombment in that mausoleum, as Shreve called it (p. 176). This compression in time and use of the recent past is the American modification of the Gothic traditional settings, remote in both time and place. The Sutpen "castle" is indeed haunted: by Henry, the living dead; by Quentin, to whom the past was more vivid than the present; and finally by Jim Bond, the shadowy symbol of the retribution visited upon this "House of Atreus."

The other "castle" is an ironic inversion of the tradition: in the un-painted, shabby, tomblike Coldfield house, with its "quality of grim endurance" (p. 10), the "princess" Rosa was immured, a princess whom no prince ever wooed save with an unspeakable, outrageous proposal, a princess who was born old and never grew up, a rose with a "gnarled forgotten root" (p. 144) which produced neither bud nor bloom, in the "Coldfield" of her hate. T. H. Adamowski's comparison of *Great Expectations* and *Absalom, Absalom!*, stressing melodrama rather than Gothicism, suggests a direct influence of Dickens: the Havisham and Coldfield houses are alike in their oppressive atmosphere, with no breath of fresh air or ray of sunlight, and their bizarre chatelaines, who serve "to prepare us for the extraordinary moral dramas to follow by height-ening the reader's feeling of suspense."

The claustrophobic effect is heightened by the closed rooms. Those at Coldfield's include: the room where Quentin and Miss Rosa talked, "dim hot airless" (p. 7); the attic room into which her father nailed himself and where he starved to death; the rooms outside which the child Rosa listened at closed doors and from one of which her aunt made her escape. Except for Quentin's impressions that afternoon, the experience of these closed rooms is described only by Rosa. In the Sutpen house the "other rooms" include: the one in which the fourteen-year-old Rosa, lurking from "one closed forbidden door to the next," saw the picture of Charles Bon (pp. 145, 147); the room in which, behind a closed door, Charles Bon was placed in his coffin; the darkened room to which Ellen Coldfield Sutpen retreated to live her last years; the "bare, stale room whose shutters were closed too" (p. 373) where Henry Sutpen lived his last consumptive years and where he burned to death. Without recog-nizing the closed door as a Gothic device, J. R. Raper called it "per-haps the most common Freudian symbol of repressed life force and, in females, a sign of sexual deprivation." Like the old Gothic dungeons and towers, these rooms symbolize the isolation and alienation of the characters, whose stories Quentin and Shreve recounted in a closed room at Harvard on a frigid January night. Arnold Weinstein regarded the closed door as a central thematic image: "All of the closed doors in *Absalom, Absalom!* . . . are the enclosures of blindness, the structures in which we live, walled off from life and others. They are also the doors of codes, of evidence, of fear. They are visible. Only the overpass to love can go beyond them. *Absalom, Absalom!* is about the effort to open up the closed past, closed doors, and closed minds."

Just as the castle is translated into American terms, splendid or humble, so the characters show original variations and inversions of Gothic types. At first glance, the Sutpen family somewhat resembles that of the romance, like *Clarissa Harlowe,* in which a tyrannical, patriarchal father tries to force his persecuted daughter to marry or forbids the banns, unhindered by his suffering and ineffective wife. Though Thomas and Ellen Sutpen fit the parental character types, Sutpen's interference with his daughter's marriage had rational grounds and parenthood is only one aspect of his life story. Sutpen is a Faustian obsessed villain-hero, exemplifying the "diabolic bargain" which Fiedler in *Love and Death* designated as central to the total significance of the Gothic novel. John Irwin said that Sutpen "is portrayed as a kind of Faust, whose grand design represents the rational ego's will to power in its attempt to do away with the undesigned and the irrational." From the time Sutpen as a boy was turned away from the door of a southern mansion by a liveried Negro servant, he was driven by a *"compelling dream which was insane and not his methods,"* as Miss Rosa said, who did not know the origin of the dream (p. 166). The dream begat the nightmare, and both are characteristic of the Gothic emphasis on the dream aspects of life. Both Miss Rosa and Sutpen were dreamers, whose dreams—Rosa's of the past and Sutpen's of the future—shut them off from the present reality and the lives of others. Rosa's sister Ellen as Sutpen's wife escaped from reality into a dream world and finally into death.

Quentin's situation, of repeatedly reliving a past more vivid to him than his own experience, exemplifies, as John Irwin noted, Freud's theory of the uncanny as occurring "'when infantile complexes which have been repressed are once more revived'"; Irwin continued with an explanatory comment stressing three points "that bear directly on Quentin's situation: that it is the return of the repressed that reminds us of the repetition compulsion, that the feeling of the uncanny evoked by involuntary repetition is a morbid anxiety, and that involuntary repetition recalls that sense of helplessness sometimes experienced in dreams." Quentin's repressions and the dreams of Rosa and Sutpen had similar effects in making life in the present intolerable.

In describing one kind of tragic hero in *Anatomy of Criticism,* Northrop Frye diagnosed, as it were, Sutpen as an obsessed character: "the obsession takes the form of an unconditioned will that drives its victim beyond the normal limits of humanity." Sutpen's obsession was identified by William Brown as a paranoiac dream of grandeur, involving extravagant aspiration. Sutpen's innocence, his failure to be aware of the feelings of others, is typical of paranoiacs and constitutes his tragic flaw. Sutpen's basic narcissism and inability to love others exemplifies Freud's explanation that high self-regard depends on a narcissistic libido and that love entails forfeiture of part of narcissism.

The other members of the Sutpen family show original variations of typical Gothic characters. As romantic hero and heroine Henry and Judith display a reversal of masculine and feminine characteristics: Judith was fascinated by seeing her father fight with Negroes, but Henry was nauseated. As John Ehrstine observed, the Byronic hero, "Gothic, tempestuous, and guilty," is only one of Byron's central images; the other, Cain, is exemplified in Henry Sutpen, self-exiled for fratricide for forty years before he came home to die, self-imprisoned. Judith was never the sentimental, romantic heroine; always courageous and resolute, she was forced by the Civil War to play the role of the man in the family at home, as Henry played the role in the army. Clytie, the faithful servant in the Gothic cast of characters, is never used for comic relief. The half-sister of Judith and Henry, and acknowledged to be so, Clytie was driven by her protective loyalty to Henry to destroy him and herself when she burned the house rather than let Henry be arrested, she feared, for murder. Wash Jones, another faithful but somewhat comic servant of peculiarly American nature, did not become "a criminal tool of the tyrant," like some Shakespearean and Gothic servants described by Railo, but murdered the tyrant Sutpen in a final desperate assertion of manhood.

Sutpen's other family connections multiply the typical characters. Eulalia Bon is another Suffering Wife, whether or not one accepts Shreve's interpretation of her. But her marriage to Sutpen was conventional, like Ellen's, and Sutpen did not deliberately inflict suffering on either wife. He outraged Rosa but did not persecute her; when she fled, he did not pursue. Milly, the only victim of seduction, was a willing one, easily bought by cheap gifts; Wash, her grandfather, tacitly approved of the seduction, trusting to Sutpen's honor to insure Milly's welfare. Charles Bon doubles with Henry as a romantic hero, but his sophisticated charms slightly suggest the Don Juan type. Malcolm Cowley's description of *Absalom, Absalom!* correctly identifies Charles Bon as a Byronic hero: "It seems to belong in the realm of Gothic romance, with Sutpen's Hundred taking the place of the haunted castle on the Rhine, with Colonel Sutpen as Faust and Charles Bon as Manfred." Judith being the romantic heroine, her rival, the octoroon wife of Charles, traditionally would be the evil Dark Woman, paired with a fair and delicate heroine. But Bon's octoroon wife was more delicate and romantic than Judith. At Bon's grave the "magnolia-faced woman" knelt and wept, while Judith stood "in the attitude of an indifferent guide in a museum" (pp. 193, 194).

The most obviously Gothic heroine is Miss Rosa, whose initial narrative sets the Gothic tone. Lynn Levins described Rosa as essentially a dreamer, who can comprehend reality only in a dreamer's terms, and to whom reality "assumes a nightmarish quality" when it threatens the "world of illusion." Her grotesque appearance, like "a crucified child" (p. 8),

George Lensing regarded as symbolic of the distorted roles she sought or was assigned, after "a childhood of familial fragmentation and disruption," in the Sutpen family: "mother to Henry and Judith, lover of Charles Bon, sister to Clytie, and wife to Sutpen." Rosa is a kind of parody of southern romanticism, with her poems to Confederate heroes, her dream-romance inspired by a picture of Charles Bon, her ludicrous attempts to make a trousseau for Judith. Her grotesqueness includes her becoming "all polymath love's androgynous advocate" in her dream of love (p. 146). She is one of the hermaphrodite figures traced by Joachim Seyppel in Faulkner's works. Arnold Weinstein said that Rosa was what Sutpen made her: "the wildest details of her Gothic account are relevant to an understanding of either of them. Her rage . . . becomes a medium through which the story is told." But through Rosa "Quentin and Shreve will learn her language of love": Rosa's whimpering (p. 366) "is not only a desire for touch and consummation but also a language, a mode of expression and perception." Rosa's flight, unpursued, from Sutpen, after her brief dream of being the sun in his life, was a return to the prison of her own house, to become even in her own eyes a "warped bitter orphaned country stick" (p. 168). In her progress toward becoming a ghost, Elisabeth Muhlenfeld said, Rosa was destroyed by her environment and her own romantic fantasies. But her life served one purpose: she was the catalyst who forced Sutpen's story to be considered, and her actions began and her death ended the Sutpen story for Quentin.

The actual center of the story, of course, is Quentin Compson, to whom the story is told and retold until he not only lives it more intensely than his own experience—*"If I had been there I could not have seen it this plain"* (p. 190)—but identifies himself with Henry, as Shreve identifies with Charles Bon. The theme of the double, which is suggested by the passages when "it was not two but four of them riding the two horses" (p. 334), is recurrent in Gothic fiction. In *A Psychoanalytic Study of the Double in Literature* Robert Rogers distinguished between "doubling by multiplication and doubling by division": "the division involves the splitting up of a recognizable, unified psychological entity into separate, complementary, distinguishable parts represented by seemingly autonomous characters." Doubling by multiplication is exemplified by "the appearance in a story of several characters, all of whom" represent "a single concept or attitude" toward another, such as love-hate feelings toward a father. There may be multiple father figures or a division of "the loved and hated father into two separate and seemingly unrelated persons."

Doubling frequently involves and is a clue to psychological aberrations of characters such as schizophrenia, narcissism, incest, and homosexuality.

Otto Rank defined two basic types of doubles in literature. The more modern, romantic type occurs when a narcissistic youth chooses a homosexual love object in his own image; this double is often identified with a brother, usually a twin. The doubles may be competitors for the love of a woman, sometimes the mother. If the hero is guilt-ridden, he may put on his double the responsibility for his own transgressions. Awareness of guilt "is nourished by a powerful fear of death and creates strong tendencies toward self-punishment, which also imply suicide." The slaying of a double may be "really a suicidal act." A more primitive concept is that of the double as the shadow, the embodiment of the soul; the shadow or the reflected image of the self is assurance against death. This concept "of the double as a second self and immortal soul" was explained by Freud, as Rogers noted, as springing "from the soil of man's primary narcissism," his infantile self-love.

In *Radical Innocence* Ihab Hassan explained the use of the double in the novels of Conrad and Dostoevsky as signifying "a stratagem of the ego," reverting to an early narcissistic stage which protects the child against "the foreign reality of death and corruption." The relevance of this theme to Quentin's narcissistic immaturity is evident particularly in *The Sound and the Fury*. The identification of Shreve and Quentin with Charles Bon and Henry suggests that the homosexuality ascribed by Mr. Compson to Henry, in explaining Henry's attitude toward Bon, is true also of Quentin and Shreve. Similarly, the incestuous love of Henry for Judith, in Mr. Compson's account, is paralleled in *The Sound and the Fury* by that of Quentin for Caddy, who is not mentioned or thought of in *Absalom, Absalom!* "Of the many levels of meaning in *Absalom*," John Irwin said, "the deepest level is to be found in the symbolic identification of incest and miscegenation and in the relationship of this symbolic identification both to Quentin Compson's personal history in *The Sound and the Fury* and to the story that Quentin narrates in *Absalom, Absalom!*" The reader in retrospect realizes that Quentin's imaginative identification with Charles Bon signified interracial homosexuality.

Deviations from normal sexuality are climaxed in the marriage of Charles Bon's son to a subhuman black woman; the fruit of their union is the last grotesque, the idiot Jim Bond. Rosa's dehumanizing descriptions of Sutpen and Clytie contribute materially to the impression of grotesqueness, which is augmented by such similar stylistic devices as Mr. Compson's butterfly metaphor for Ellen. But Rosa and Jim Bond are the chief grotesques, invariably making eccentricity and idiocy physically manifest.

With such American-Gothic adaptations of setting and character types, the story of Stupen as reconstructed by the narrators resembles a tragic Gothic tale of inheritance and doom. The story of Thomas Sutpen may be viewed as tragedy. Within the total scope of the novel, moreover, are encompassed all six phases of tragedy according to Northrop Frye's categories in *Anatomy of Criticism*, ending with the "undisplaced demonic vision" in which the chief symbols of the demonic vision, the prison and the madhouse, are threats removed or dispelled only by the burning of the house and the deaths of Clytie and Henry. Jim Bond is still threatened. But despite the impressive tragic qualities of *Absalom, Absalom!* provided by the addition of the other five phases to the "typical fall of the hero through hybris or hamartia," Sutpen is not truly a tragic hero in the classic sense. Robert Heilman distinguished between the tragic hero who faces "basic conflicts," "errs knowingly or involuntarily," and "comes into a larger awareness" and the hero of melodrama who is "pitted against some force outside of himself" and does not experience inner conflict. The strongly melodramatic qualities in Sutpen as a villain-hero and the shift in emphasis from the "fall of the hero" to the fates of his victims contribute to the dominance of the Gothic over the tragic, further reinforced by the other elements of Gothic characters, atmosphere, tone, and styles.

Sutpen is a Faust figure, a man on a quest to achieve his superhuman design, but without Faust's awareness of the price that may be exacted. All Sutpen's physical journeys after he left the Tidelands as a boy were in pursuit of his Grand Design: to establish an estate and a dynasty which would, as Faulkner said, "take revenge for all the redneck people against the aristocrat who told him to go around to the back door." Sutpen's insistence on a dynasty doomed him to failure because he insisted on the Tidewater pattern of inheritance through the eldest legitimate son. Sutpen's basic innocence, his attempt to live by a rational design to be achieved by will power, resulted in what Faulkner referred to as a de-humanizing "contempt for people." The humiliation which inspired Sutpen's design was suffered in turn, ironically and fatally, by Wash Jones; his murder of Sutpen is thus parallel to Sutpen's design: revenge for humiliation by an act of self-assertion in defense of honor. Wash was sane; he reacted in hot blood against the man who treated him and Milly as less than animals. Sutpen was paranoiac, taking revenge on a whole system by a mad dream; he carried out his design in cold logic, with no effect upon the source of his humiliation, the white planter and the Negro servant. A third act of revenge for humiliation, according to Lynn Levins, was Rosa's recreation of Sutpen for Quentin, a means by which she sought identity as well as the satisfaction of denouncing the dead. None of these seekers after vengeance followed the pattern of the

Elizabethan hero of revenge tragedy, that of direct action, according to plan, against the offending person who must know why he is suffering. This is what John Irwin called "the ideal situation," with the "person who initially delivered the affront . . . forced to assume the passive role . . . ; in the other situation, the revenge is inflicted on a substitute," as Sutpen inflicted "it on his own son Charles Bon." Revenge on a substitute, Irwin explained, shows the relation "between repetition and the fantasy of the reversal of generations."

Because the design required a dynasty, Sutpen's story involves the Gothic theme of inheritance: the traditional refusal of a usurper to recognize the rightful heir is inverted; Sutpen himself chose to adopt the laws of primogeniture and refused to recognize Charles Bon, his legitimate elder son and rightful heir by those laws. Like Walpole's Manfred, Sutpen turned to seduction as a last desperate means of preserving his dynasty. An interesting parallel appears between Manfred's and Sutpen's marriage plans. Manfred tried to force Isabella, who was to have been his daughter-in-law, to marry him, a marriage she regarded as incestuous. In England, the source of the cultural and legal patterns Sutpen adopted, his plan to marry Rosa, his sister-in-law, would at that time have been considered incestuous and illegal. Rosa was as willing as Isabella was unwilling. Thus, incest is suggested as a symbol of family continuity in both generations of Sutpens, father and sons.

Unlike the traditional Gothic, however, the story of Sutpen and his design, compressed into the period from 1833 to 1910 in Jefferson, epitomizes a whole society. The relationship between Sutpen and Charles, Faulkner said, "was a manifestation of a general racial system in the South," a "constant general condition." This use of the Gothic mode to present continuing social conditions in a powerfully imaginative heightening of reality is one of the achievements of the new American Gothic in which Faulkner, the originator, is still unsurpassed.

The father-son relationship is central to *Absalom, Absalom!* John Irwin noted the interchangeability of roles of Quentin and his father as narrators (pp. 261-62) and commented that "this basic interchangeability of the roles of the father and son is present in both the reversal fantasy and the incest complex" of Quentin. The story of Charles Bon, as reconstructed by the narrators, follows the quest pattern in the romance of Charles and Judith and in the theme of Charles's "desperate quest," as George Lensing called it, for identity and a father. The image of the journey in Bon's story centers in Sutpen's Hundred, which is only the final goal in Sutpen's longer quest. Charles came to Sutpen's Hundred for Christmas 1859, in the summer of 1860, and again at Christmas 1860. Sutpen's journey to New Orleans to discover the identity of Bon was followed by the crucial journey of Charles and Henry from Sutpen's Hundred to New Orleans, in December 1860. The quest was suspended during the Civil War, when Sutpen, Bon, and Henry were all in the Confederate army. Bon's return to the quest for a wife after the war, foreshadowed by his letter to Judith, a suitable Gothic "property," resulted in his meeting the fate to which his blood doomed him: Henry shot him to prevent incestuous miscegenation. According to the conjectures of Shreve and Quentin, Henry could condone simple incest.

In a kind of desperate irony Charles Etienne, son of Charles Bon, also defied the doom of blood, but by marrying a primitive, brutish Negro woman; their son was an idiot. John Hagopian's interpretation of the significance of Jim Bond and of Shreve's prophecy corrects some common misapprehensions:

> Jim Bond was conceived in hate and spite by a man who . . . wanted to outrage the bigots with his negritude. . . . Jim Bond is what will inevitably come of the white man's refusal to accept the black as both black and a man. Since Shreve believes that the South is hopelessly mired in provincial ignorance and obsessive racism, it can create only a Gothic distortion of life—rotting plantation houses and the idiot progeny of hatred and despair. Thus, far from capping the novel with a Southern racist credo, Shreve is bitterly mocking its inevitable victory with heavy irony.

That Shreve's prophecy is not Faulkner's is quite obvious in the absence in other Yoknapatawpha novels of any part-Negro idiot and the presence of a number of white ones. In *William Faulkner* Cleanth Brooks said that the pertinence of the Sutpen story "to the tragic dilemmas of the South" lies in the story of the children, "which embodied the problem of evil and of the irrational." The Gothic aspects underline these meanings.

Miss Rosa emphasized the theme of doom and retribution: without knowing Sutpen's motives or the identity of Charles Bon, she did see the design ruined and the children destroyed and was the chief witness to Sutpen's treating people like animals. The authentic Gothic note, sounded in her references to "the two accursed children" and their "devil's heritage" (p. 135), is often quoted by other narrators, referring to the destiny of the family. Observing the patterns of "jurisprudential metaphor" in Miss Rosa's narrative, Marvin K. Singleton regarded the frame of the novel as like a hearing on a bill in chancery before Quentin and Shreve. The medieval allusions and imagery, the feudal aspects of the plantation world and of Sutpen's concept of his role, and Sutpen's pompous, legalistic speech further contribute to the Dickensian impression of age-old tradition and heritage appropriate to the Gothic mode. George Lensing traced Sutpen's failure to his view of the family as "a legalistic structure devoid of human emotion." Singleton found the retelling of the Sutpen story to resemble the custom in Equity pleading that "Bills in Equity characteristically contained the same story, told three times over, though with a slightly different tonal emphasis each time. . . ." Divine and human justice doomed the house of Sutpen to destruction.

The title *Absalom, Absalom!* is a clue to the theme of inheritance; Sutpen's desire to found a dynasty was stronger than his paternal feeling. Ironically, he never uttered the lament for either of his sons that David did for Absalom; an heir was merely the necessary agent to perpetuate the Sutpen dynasty. All Sutpen needed was a male substitute for Henry. While Sutpen lived, *he* would rule. Another essential theme suggested by the title and its source is the story of brother-sister incest, involving Absalom, his sister Tamar, and Amnon, another son of David (2 Samuel 13). Absalom killed Amnon for violating Tamar; Henry, represented as desiring Judith himself and countenancing her incestuous marriage to Bon, acted in his father's stead, as Irwin believed that Absalom had done in killing Amnon, and killed Bon to prevent miscegenation. Enrico Garzilli summed up the mythic elements: "In the design of the dynasty and in the domestic crises of adultery, fratricide, incest, and blind guilt, the primitive energy of the Hebrew and Greek stories merge." Beth Haury and John Irwin both considered Robinson Jeffers's "Tamar" a major source. Thus the ancient theme of incest became the theme of miscegenation. The mystery of why Henry shot Bon is solved only at the end of the penultimate chapter, though the account of the murder is given in Miss Rosa's narrative in chapter 5; the Gothic technique of mystery and suspense serves to give maximum force to this most crucial and significant explanation, based apparently on Quentin's meeting with Henry in September.

As the story of Quentin's quest for truth and understanding, of himself and the South, *Absalom, Absalom!* takes on an added dimension. Edward Corridori viewed Quentin as the protagonist, a "questor figure" seeking meaning in a desacralized world: "Quentin's quest takes the form of a night journey into his own heritage." Quentin's one physical journey, with Miss Rosa to Sutpen's Hundred, ends in "a revelation of horror" when he encounters Henry Sutpen, "like Marlow's meeting with the dying Kurtz." Presumably Quentin learned from Henry the solution of the mystery of why he shot Bon. Quentin's role as listener and narrator, pondering over, wondering about, and reconstructing the Sutpen story, heightens the Gothic mystery and suspense. The name "Quentin," with its connotation of Quentin Durward, lends a romantic, chivalric aura to the character which, by ironic contrast, emphasizes the fact that Quentin Compson lacks the stuff of which heroes of romantic adventure are made.

The first five chapters, preceding Quentin's journey to Sutpen's Hundred in September 1909, contain Miss Rosa's information about the Coldfield-Sutpen story, the only first-hand information on the Sutpens by a narrator-character. The Gothic tone is established both by Quentin's impressions and memories, in the "dim coffin-smelling gloom" of the wistaria-scented Coldfield house, and by Miss Rosa's account of the ogre of her childhood who became the hero whom she agreed to marry. Her summary of events includes "castle," doom, hybris, heritage, violence, and mystery:

> I saw what had happened to Ellen, my sister. I saw her almost a recluse, watching those two doomed children growing up whom she was helpless to save. I saw the price which she had paid for that house and that pride; ... I saw Judith's marriage forbidden without rhyme or reason or shadow of excuse; I saw Ellen die with only me, a child, to turn to and ask to protect her remaining child; I saw Henry repudiate his home and birthright and then return and practically fling the bloody corpse of his sister's sweetheart at the hem of her wedding gown; I saw that man return—the evil's source and head which had outlasted all its victims—who had created two children not only to destroy one another and his own line, but my line as well, yet I agreed to marry him.   [P. 18]

The Gothic strategy here is not surprise but anticipation: the question is not what happened but why. The limitations of Miss Rosa's and the town's knowledge are apparent on review of the passage.

To Miss Rosa's account and the facts which were common knowledge in the town, Mr. Compson, in chapters 2 and 3, added his conjectures about some of the mysteries indicated in Miss Rosa's summary and about the characters of the Sutpens and the Coldfields, the relationships between them, and the unknown motives for their actions. In chapter 5 Miss Rosa told her own story as she and Quentin drove out to Sutpen's Hundred: her feeling toward Charles Bon, whom she never saw; the murder of Charles Bon; Sutpen's return from the war; her brief engagement to Sutpen and her outraged flight from Sutpen's Hundred. At the end, as she and Quentin approached the house, she told him: "'There's something in that house.... Something living in it. Hidden in it. It has been out there for four years, living hidden in that house" (p. 172). How she knows this, we never learn; what was hidden is disclosed only on page 373.

As Cleanth Brooks said in "The Narrative Structure of *Absalom, Absalom!*," the gradual disclosure of the truth behind the "sparse and disordered body of facts" is no "cheap mystery-mongering" but is "the most brilliant and audacious technique for fictional presentation to be found anywhere in Faulkner." Brooks identified six strata of knowledge in Quentin's process of learning about the Sutpen story: A, what he learned in boyhood up to the quail hunt in the fall of 1907 or 1908; B, what he learned during the talk in the cemetery on the quail hunt; C, what he learned from Miss Rosa, in the September afternoon in 1909; D, what he learned after C from Mr. Compson; E, what he learned after midnight of the day in September; F, what he and his father could reconstruct the day after E. In E how Quentin learned of Bon's parentage at Sutpen's Hundred remains a mystery. The Gothic tradition of mystery and suspense and the Gothic narrative techniques lent themselves to Faulkner's subtle and complex artistry.

To the end of chapter 5 the building up of mystery and suspense is the consequence of the points of view of the narrators and their limited knowledge of the facts. In the remaining chapters Quentin and Shreve are telling each other the story, which Quentin had told Shreve in part and is now completing after receiving his father's letter, dated January 10, 1910, with the news that "Miss Rosa Coldfield was buried yesterday" (p. 173). The suspense hereafter is built up by Quentin's delayed revelation of what he had known since he went out to Sutpen's Hundred: who was in the house; who and what Charles Bon was and, therefore, what Sutpen must have told Henry before Henry left home, and when he saw Henry in 1864; why Henry shot Bon; why Wash killed Sutpen. Some dust is neatly thrown in the reader's eyes when Shreve comments on how much more Quentin knows, since he had been "out there and seen Clytie" (p. 274). But Bon's parentage could not be learned by "seeing" anyone. In a previous passage, which Cleanth Brooks identified in *William Faulkner* as a late insertion in the manuscript, Quentin explained to Shreve that he told his father what he learned after the trip to Sutpen's Hundred, but he did not specify what he told. Herschel Parker's speculation about the three Sutpen faces is unconvincing. Brooks advanced the plausible theory that only through Henry could the "dark secret" be known. Thus, to maintain Gothic suspense concerning identity of characters, Faulkner was carefully manipulating his narrative to achieve maximum delay in revealing vital facts. Shreve's and Quentin's concentration on interpretation of psychological motives and reconstruction of what could never be proved, the story of Charles Bon's mother and the purely conjectural lawyer, makes Faulkner's strategy justifiable.

The central mystery is the identity of Charles Bon and the reason Henry left home, thus renouncing his heritage and thwarting Sutpen's design, and the reason that, after being Bon's comrade-in-arms throughout the war, Henry shot Bon to prevent him from marrying Judith. Three reasons were advanced. Mr. Compson's was that Bon's previous marriage to the octoroon might constitute a moral barrier, in Henry's eyes, though not in southern custom a legal barrier; this was admittedly an unsatisfactory explanation. The second reason, which introduces the theme of Bon's identity and search for a father, was that Bon was Sutpen's son and thus the marriage of Bon and Judith would be incestuous and would be part of the "current of retribution and fatality" (p. 269) started by Sutpen. But Shreve and Quentin, aided by Mr. Compson's interpretation of Henry as homosexually in love with Bon and incestuously in love with Judith, could imagine how Henry, in the arrogant pride of a scion of nobility, could justify the incest. The third reason, confirmed by Faulkner's chronology at the end of the *Absalom, Absalom!* text, is that Charles Bon's mother had Negro blood; this explanation also solves the mystery of why Sutpen put aside his first wife and child as not "conjunctive to his design." Although Quentin must have known before the beginning of chapter 6 all that his grandfather had told about Sutpen, as well as what his grandfather did not know, the reason for Sutpen's action, these facts are omitted from Quentin's and Shreve's thoughts, as they imaginatively realize the story of the other two young men, so that the disclosure will have the maximum impact. What, Shreve and Quentin wonder, could cause Henry to shoot Bon, whom he loved and with whom he had taken sides against his father, in order to prevent the marriage with Judith which Henry had initially promoted and persisted in promoting even when his father forbade it? Not the threat of bigamy. Not the threat of incest. Only the threat of miscegenation could provide an adequate motive for fratricide. Just as in unison Shreve and Quentin identified with Henry and Bon in the horsemen passages, so they seem to be imagining in unison in the dramatic reconstruction of the return of Henry and Bon to Sutpen's Hundred, when Bon says to Henry, just before Henry shoots him, *"So it's the miscegenation, not the incest, which you can't bear"* (p. 356). John Irwin regards the murder as a *Liebestod,* in which Bon, being denied his father's love, "seeks to have that love in an inverse sense . . . with that substitute for the father, the avenging brother. Henry's murder of his half-brother, the dark double, is an incestuous love-death."

The naturalization of the Gothic novel in America provided the last turn of the screw to the horror of medieval Gothic family sexual relationships. As T. H. Adamowski said: "At the heart of the baronial Mississippi family and of the elegant New Orleans bachelor is the South's terrible burden of caste. Medieval kings give such American aristocrats the latitude for committing incest, but their American heritage denies them the possibility of miscegenation."

Corollary to the themes of miscegenation and incest is the theme of Bon's search for identity and his willingness, Shreve and Quentin believed, to renounce Judith if Sutpen would give any sign of recognition of Bon as his son. Here the contrast with the traditional Gothic underlines the significance of this situation: a recognition scene would usually take place and the true heir, the elder son, would be restored to his heritage and would marry the heroine (who, of course, would not be his sister). Sutpen's failure to recognize Bon doomed Sutpen to failure in his design, as the southern system was doomed to failure through denial of blood kinship or denial of human dignity: the boy was turned away from the door from caste or class motives. To the boys at the door, Thomas Sutpen and Charles Bon, George Lensing added Quentin, as a legatee to the expanded family of the Compsons, citing the "umbilical water-cord" (p. 261) as a symbolic image for this interpretation; he observed that Quentin, as the last boy at the door, had to go in through the window. In light of this image and its Freudian implications, Quentin's suicide in *The Sound and the Fury* is the ultimate regression, a retreat to the womb and beyond, to nothingness. As John Irwin stated: "The desire to return to the womb is the desire for incest." The seriousness of the implications of the Sutpen story is increased when one remembers how Quentin ended his life on June 2, after the January scene with Shreve. Faulkner handled the Gothic pattern with such complexity in *Absalom, Absalom!* that the reader must exert great effort to understand not only the Sutpen story but the story of Quentin and his search for truth. In "Evangeline," in 1931, Faulkner had written the Sutpen story: "It began as a ghost story and ended as a tragic tale of miscegenation." The first version including Quentin, which began with Mr. Compson's letter, was dated Feb. 11, 1934, according to Joseph Blotner. Only when Faulkner fused "Evangeline" with the story of Quentin and substituted Quentin for the original narrator did the Sutpen story come alive and acquire depth and complexity which challenge the reader.

Any one of the chief techniques of Gothic fiction—the omniscient author; the first-person narrator, generally a major character and often the heroine; third person, limited point of view—would have restricted Faulkner in his strategy for establishing Gothic tone and building up Gothic suspense and would have prevented the dialectical method of conducting the "detective" search for truth. Arthur Scott explained the method of *Absalom, Absalom!* as an attempt to combine the technique "of the Cubist, the Existentialist, and the mystery writer," and noted the grotesque style and the refinement of suspense by the "carefully limited perspective" and the deliberately withheld meaning. But Scott failed to recognize that the "chaotic dream images" of surrealism also can be accommodated in the "calculated complexity of Faulkner's novels" and combined with the multiple viewpoints and the principle of simultaneity of cubism and futurism.

Miss Rosa's impassioned style and her demonizing created the Gothic tone and the character of Sutpen. As the villain-monster, Sutpen in his grotesqueness, Richard Cook said, was "both illusion and reality," evolved from her "needs and fears." Cook further explained that "the grotesque monster owes its existence as much to the personality of those who perceive it as to any of its own attributes." The creators of the character are trying to maintain their own sense of order: Rosa made an "outrageous monster" of the man who outraged her; Mr. Compson made him an unreal, tragic puppet because of his "sense of his own tragic irrelevance." The other narrators echoed Rosa's tone with variations and added their own interpretations to hers. Mr. Compson's meditative and imaginative tone could not alter the extravagant and dramatic history of Sutpen; Quentin and Shreve realized that they sounded like Mr. Compson, Shreve having heard Quentin tell it in Mr. Compson's manner (pp. 181, 207, 211, 261). The melodramatic quality that pervades the style of the narrators, despite individual variations, is justified for this southern Gothic tale couched in nineteenth-century language. As Eric Bentley said of the dialogue of melodrama: "An elevated rhetoric is a legitimate and indeed inexorable demand of melodrama. Ordinary conversation would be incongruous and anticlimactic."

Extensions of Quentin's point of view outside the dialogue, as at the beginning of the first chapter and before page 376 in the last chapter, plus a modification of that point of view by the authorial voice, as in the beginning of the second chapter, provide margins to give the necessary flexibility to the narrator technique. With this method the author's role is so inconspicuous that he need not explain Quentin's motives for withholding information from Shreve: thus, mystery and suspense are heightened, the intent and effect also of some of Faulkner's revisions in the manuscript. The Gothic tradition accommodates deviations from plausibility without rational explanations being given. The burden of imaginative reconstruction of both the story of the Sutpens and the ordeal of Quentin is thrown upon the reader, whose view of the truth is, as Faulkner said, the fourteenth way of looking at a blackbird. Quoting Faulkner, Enrico Garzilli continued: "The reader's fourteenth viewpoint is founded upon the epistemological structure which determines his own identity and persona as well as his understanding of the Sutpen story"; he is stimulated in this endeavor by the "atmosphere of creative energy" in which Miss Rosa constructed "her version of the Sutpen cosmos." Faulkner's choice of Rosa as the first narrator is essential to the Gothic effect because, as Lynn Levins said, "Gothic mystery, . . . of all genres, possesses the most affective influence upon the feelings of the reader. . . ." "Vision and Feeling" is the title of Weinstein's chapter on Faulkner and Bernanos. The reader's intellectual and emotional involvement in arriving at his own "fourteenth" perception of the truth in *Absalom, Absalom!* is an experience unique even for Gothic enthusiasts.

In comparison with the central mystery of Bon's identity and Negro blood, so carefully sustained until near the end, other minor solved or unsolved mysteries contribute to the Gothic effect: where Sutpen got his money; what deal he made with Coldfield; what he said to Rosa that enraged her; whose picture Judith held after Bon was killed; who was in the Sutpen house. These mysteries resemble those in *Great Expectations,* according to T. H. Adamowski, in constituting "an inquiry into the meaning of the relationship between an ostensibly respectable world and an ostensibly shameful world."

The answer to the last question, who was in the house, which holds the key to the other answers to the Henry-Bon-Sutpen mystery, is revealed by a memory passage when Quentin finally relived the experiences in the Sutpen house. This passage not only symbolizes the end of Sutpen's design, which involved both estate and dynasty, but is a culmination of Gothic horror exceeded only by the final holocaust. Quentin's forced entry, under cover of darkness, into the ruined mansion, haunted by all he now knows of the family tragedy; his confrontation first with Clytie, the "tiny gnomelike creature in headrag and voluminous skirts," with "a bunch of old-fashioned iron keys" in her hand (pp. 368, 369); Miss Rosa's knocking Clytie down, as no doubt she had longed to do earlier when she said, "Take your hand off me, nigger!" (p. 140); the appearance of the idiot Jim Bond, last of the Sutpen dynasty; finally the confrontation of Quentin and Henry, yellow and wasted in yellow sheets in an airless room—this memory passage induces an authentic horror which justifies the compositional maneuvering necessary to place it in this climactic position. At this point, Cleanth Brooks observed in "Narrative Structure," the ghost becomes flesh and blood in a memory scene "most cunningly delayed" for maximum intensity.

Michael Millgate refers to tableaux representing "a number of crucial moments of recognition, truth, disillusion" and cites some of them, such as Henry and his father in the library. Gothic tableaux are the fictional equivalent of tableaux of melodrama, as explained by Wylie Sypher: "The limit of the 19th Century imagination is the final expressive tableau, a stasis, a consummate act." The narrators all being products of the "19th century imagination," it is fitting that they express themselves in the Gothic mode: "Melodrama is a characteristic mode of 19th century thought and art." Their imaginations create for the reader macabre scenes, scenes of grotesque incongruity, and scenes of violence in the Gothic settings, past or narrative present. The themes involve many such Gothic scenes and episodes, in addition to the images or episodes of flights or journeys already noted. The general somberness of tone begins with the scenes of the first dialogues, in Miss Rosa's shaded room and on the Compson front gallery at dusk. Only in the last scene at Harvard are the speakers clearly visible.

Mr. Compson's letter, describing the funeral of Miss Rosa, ends the sequence of "present" events in Quentin's life and initiates the last dialogue. The letter evokes in Quentin's mind the image of the holocaust in which Clytie, mistaking for the Black Maria the ambulance brought by Miss Rosa for Henry, burned the house with herself and Henry in it. This is Northrop Frye's "point of demonic epiphany," the harvest of the dragon's teeth (*Anatomy of Criticism*). Quentin's reconstruction of the past concludes with the combination of actual past with narrative present in the death of Henry, whose life had touched Quentin's on a stifling September night; finally in the icy January night Quentin's story and his double's became one when in imagination Quentin viewed the holocaust. The major scenes in present action, as well as in the story of the past, are all Gothic. Part of the Gothic atmosphere is produced by the absence of daylight scenes in present action. Quentin said and thought "I don't hate it . . . panting in the cold air, the iron New England dark . . ." (p. 378).

Quentin's memories and related scenes emphasize death and darkness. His experiences at Sutpen's Hundred before 1909 included his flight, with other boys, from Clytie and Jim Bond and the hunting trip with his father in the rain. In the darkness under the cedars he examined the tombstones in the Sutpen family cemetery, symbols of Sutpen's megalomania. Looking at them, Quentin had a mental picture of "the ragged and starving troops without shoes" who dragged the stones from the seacoast to Mississippi (pp. 189, 190). In this cemetery Charles Bon was buried. Beside his grave had knelt his octoroon wife and delicate young son but not the stoical Judith. The murdered body of Sutpen, under the stone the troops had called "Colonel," had finally been humbled when, splendid "in his regimentals and embroidered gauntlets," it was tumbled in the ditch when the mules bolted (p. 186).

Such scenes of grotesque incongruity recur in the episodes of Gothic violence in Sutpen's story. Bernard R. Breyer's justification of violence as a literary tool in the work of Southern writers, including Faulkner, applies especially to the Gothic fiction which predominates in authors cited: "They wish simply to use it as the most dramatic manifestation of man's proud, perverse, volcanic, unregenerate . . . unreconstructed soul." No major character in modern fiction better deserves this description than does Thomas Sutpen, who died violently, in unenlightened "innocence." His design began with his first experience, when he was turned away from the front door, of such an affront to human pride and dignity as caused his violent death. Between those initial and terminal points, his life was a series of violent scenes: the slave insurrection in the West Indies, "a theater for violence and injustice and bloodshed and all the satanic lusts of human greed and cruelty," where he proved both his courage and lusts and won a wife and a fortune (p. 250); the building of Sutpen's Hundred in the wilderness, himself naked among the naked Negroes; his fighting with his own Negroes or whirling up to the church door "in a thunder and a fury of wildeyed horses and of galloping and of dust" (p. 23). The long episode in which Sutpen hunted the fugitive French architect, as if he were an animal or a slave, and in interludes told General Compson the story of his early life, is full of Gothic firelight and darkness; it is climaxed by the grotesque image of the architect in the tatters of his French elegance, surrounded by the Mississippi wilderness, the blacks, and the dogs. This tableau is premonitory of the destruction of the elegance the architect helped to create and of the purpose the elegance was intended to serve. The murder of Sutpen by the scythe in Wash's hands, cut down by man and time, equals in Gothic horror the last scenes in the ruined mansion. From Sutpen Wash derived a sense of his own dignity. Wash's ideal of manhood and his own self-esteem were destroyed at once by Sutpen's greater concern for his mare than for Milly, mother of Sutpen's daughter. Wash took his revenge for the same reason that Sutpen conceived his design. John Irwin tidily summed up the father-son and repetition patterns: Sutpen having acted the role of the son as seducer of Wash's granddaughter, Wash assumed "the role of the outraged father in relation to Sutpen. It is emblematic of the fate of the son in his battle against time that Sutpen, struggling in his old age to achieve his revenge, must again become the son and in that role be struck down by an old man with a scythe." So, too, Henry had assumed the role of the outraged father and shot Charles Bon. With a characteristic distancing of Gothic horror Faulkner had Quentin break off his account with "he put his hand on the scythe" and take up the narrative again with Wash's tender watching over Milly until he heard the men, horses, and dogs coming for him. His killing of Milly and the child with a razor-sharp knife is limited to the dialogue between Wash and Milly and the sound of the knife on the bone. This is horror restrained. Similarly restrained is the description of Wash meeting his death: "He ran with the scythe above his head, straight into the lanterns and the gunbarrels. . . " (p. 292).

The presence of traditional scenes of violence in the story of Sutpen is in contrast with the absence of the sentimental, romantic scenes associated with the Gothic heroine in the story of Judith. Judith as a woman is strong, proud, resolute, and enduring. The only romantic scene is an unrealistic, imaginary one conceived by Shreve and Quentin, of Judith and Bon in the garden. Judith brought her rival, the octoroon wife of Bon, and his child to Bon's grave; she brought the child, Charles Etienne, to live with her when his mother died and did not turn him away from the door even when he married a black. Like the scene at Bon's grave, the three scenes in which Judith gave Bon's letter to Mrs. Compson, stood in front of the closed door, holding her wedding dress, and conducted the funeral of her father were testified to by witnesses. As the tombstones, the scythe, and the regimentals are symbolic objects associated with Sutpen, the letter, the dress, and the picture of Bon's wife and child are symbols of Judith's doom. Solitary and worn out by the long ordeal of the war, Judith received her father on his return with the same cold, calm face she wore after Bon's death; she wept "instantaneous and incredible tears" only when she told Sutpen that Henry killed Bon (p. 159). If Judith had emulated her biblical namesake and committed a deed of Gothic horror, she could scarcely have been farther removed from the fragile, trembling, tearful heroine or the passionate, foolhardy one of Gothic romance.

All these scenes and images, of course, were registered in the consciousness of Quentin, in the course of his remembering, hearing, and relating the Sutpen story. From the beginning of chapter 6 Quentin's own memories with their horrifying images were breaking forth until at the end the most horrible and most forcible repressed images prevailed: those of his successive confrontations with each of the living Sutpens, Clytie, Henry, and Jim Bond. John Irwin explained that "the events of 1909 are seen as unwilled repetition of the earlier occurrences" (of the 1850s and 1860s) and that "Freud points out that the return of the repressed is a remembering that takes the form of a reliving."

The curious spiraling effect that Faulkner secured by focusing on Quentin's consciousness and adapting his own technique of withheld information to reflect Quentin's repression of thoughts and memories was heightened by his revisions of the manuscript. Gerald Langford's collation of the manuscript and the printed book revealed changes relevant to Gothic effects, of which Langford seemed unaware. His analysis of three major changes is couched in terms that are appropriate to a discussion of Gothicism and that show Faulkner's deliberate heightening of mystery and suspense to intensify his depiction of the social and psychological reality of the South. First, the mystery of Charles Bon's identity and the reason for Henry's shooting Bon depends on revisions: originally Mr. Compson knew "the truth about Bon" in chapter 2. Deletions in chapters 2 and 4, to preserve the mystery, were inconsistent with later unrevised passages; to explain discrepancies Faulkner added passages such as those cited by Cleanth Brooks (see above, p. 43). Second, the role of Quentin is upgraded, and he "becomes the one who unlocks the old mystery and who still is obsessively involved in the story of a guilt which he, as a Southerner, must share". (Quentin's thoughts and memories in chapter 6 were originally part of Shreve's narrative, recounting what Quentin had previously told him.) Thus, as Langford said, "As a result of this alteration in Quentin's role, the chronicle of the Sutpen story becomes more nearly a kind of detective story in which a missing piece of information finally makes a coherent whole out of a bewildering collection of facts." And finally, "As a result of revision at the end of the book, the heritage of man's long inhumanity to man suddenly stands before us in the blighted figure of Jim Bond": "The highly dramatic effect of the idiot Negro heir who haunts the ruins at Sutpen's Hundred was added in revision." Thus, Faulkner's most traditionally Gothic novel became even more Gothic as he relived and revised it to increase reader participation and involvement.

Absalom, Absalom! had its origin in Sutpen's daydream and ended with nightmare. The prevailing Gothic tone and atmosphere and the abundance of Gothic themes, patterns of action, and scenes are uniquely joined with a basic realism which avoids the clear moral contrasts of traditional Gothic and of the southern myth of the past, in which black and white take on racial-moral symbolism. Such elements of realism exemplify the "displacement" which Northrop Frye discussed as a means of concealing from the reader the structure of romance, "the secular scripture." The fictional structure which Irwin identified, with "the struggle between the father and the son in the incest complex . . . played out again and again in a series of spatial and temporal repetitions," has its analogue in society, where also *"nothing ever happens once and is finished"* (p. 161.) Only death without progeny can end the repetition. The social reality rests on the fact that all the descendants, legitimate or illegitimate, white or part Negro, suffer when some are denied human rights and dignity and love. This is the lightning flash of truth which breaks through the Gothic darkness if the Gothic tradition is fully recognized and its long and varied literary history is respected.

Michael Millgate was quite right when he identified both American and European influence in *Absalom, Absalom!* and concluded: "Faulkner's familiarity with English and European literature has often been ignored or underestimated by American critics, and the result has sometimes been not simply a misunderstanding of the nature and sources of many of his images and allusions but an insufficiently generous conception of the whole scale and direction of his endeavour." Millgate discussed the influence on *Absalom, Absalom!* of *Jane Eyre,* especially the parallels between Bertha Mason and Rochester, and Eulalia Bon and Sutpen. These similarities are obvious and interesting but inconsequential. Millgate failed to recognize distinctly American Gothic influences, such as the Faust theme, and he incorrectly concluded that Faulkner's use of the Gothic tradition owed as much to European sources as to American. As Leslie Fiedler demonstrated in *Love and Death in the American Novel,* such American writers as Hawthorne, Melville, Mark Twain, and Henry James had absorbed into American Gothic much of the European tradition. Faulkner continued in the American Gothic stream, with the additional influence of such favorite authors as Dickens and Conrad and of the French and British fin de siècle art and literature. In his contrast between Edgar Allan Poe and Faulkner, in a chapter entitled "William Faulkner and the Haunted South," Joseph Warren Beach arrived at a sound judgment of the distinctive achievement of Faulkner:

Faulkner is like Poe, by natural disposition, an artist in mystery and horror; but he is likewise, by disposition and training, an artist in familiar truth and fact. Of all Southern writers Faulkner is the one who has been least restrained by regard for convention or for the sensibilities of his own people. And mainly for that reason, he is the one who has done the most of all Southern writers to bring the South to life imaginatively.

He achieved that purpose in *Absalom, Absalom!* by using the resources of the Gothic tradition to explore, through the imaginations of his characters, the transmogrification of the American dream into the American nightmare. He had made less complete and less obvious use of the Gothic tradition in *The Sound and the Fury,* to tell the Compson story.

CHAPTER THREE

THE SOUND AND THE FURY

THE FREUDIAN DREAM, OR,
THE WAY TO DUSTY DEATH

Written before *Absalom, Absalom! The Sound and the Fury* deals with the Compson family; Quentin, a major figure, may be more fully understood in light of previous events presented in *Absalom, Absalom!* but not alluded to in *The Sound and the Fury*. The question arises of whether the Gothic elements inhere in the Sutpen story and, for the reader, retrospectively cast their shade on the Compsons or whether in *The Sound and the Fury* Faulkner was already experimenting with the new American Gothic in more subtle form. The latter explanation is suggested by the basic organizing pattern analyzed by William Ramsey, the two ways of perceiving the world, self-centered egoism and transcendence of family rigidity, and the psychological approach that pattern entailed.

Despite the lack of somber Gothic tones in external details, *The Sound and the Fury* is fundamentally perhaps the most Gothic of Faulkner's works in the sense that it is a dream work based on Freudian psychology. It is thus more directly opposed to a rational point of view than was Walpole's *Castle of Otranto,* which used some dream images. Ruel Foster, coauthor with Harry Modean Campbell of the first critical book on Faulkner, *William Faulkner: A Critical Appraisal* (1951), in an earlier article recognized *The Sound and the Fury* as a dream work, depending for its meaning upon Freudian insights into the manifest and latent content. James C. Cowan confirmed Foster's idea by applying the principles of Freudian analysis of dream-work to five passages in Quentin's section of *The Sound and the Fury*. Carvel Collins traced the parallels between the three Compson sons and Freud's chart of human personality, Benjy the id, Quentin the ego, and Jason the superego, all three centered in Caddy, perhaps representing the libido. Although Faulkner disclaimed direct use of Freud, he acknowledged general cultural influence. He wrote *The Sound and the Fury* at a time when Freudian psychology was being assimilated into American thought in ways discussed by Frederick Hoffman in *Freudianism and the Literary Mind* (1945).

Faulkner's denial of direct knowledge of Freud was compared by John Irwin with Freud's denial of the influence of Nietzsche. Conversations such as those in *Mosquitoes,* Irwin suggested, may be the fictional equivalent of Faulkner's sources of knowledge about Freud. To preserve his own creative energy Faulkner may have avoided more direct familiarity with Freudian psychology, of which he seemed to have an intuitive understanding.

Thus, Faulkner represents the utilization of modern psychology in work based on the unconscious, a logical development from the Gothic romance which began with the dream transmuted by Horace Walpole into *The Castle of Otranto.* Mario Materassi regarded *The Sound and the Fury* as the superposition of the psychological novel on the romance and specified the Gothic tradition and the *roman noir* among the other influences. One need not suppose that *The Sound and the Fury,* like *The Castle of Otranto,* originated in the author's dream experience. John Irwin's comparison between Quentin as narrator in *Absalom, Absalom!* and Faulkner as writer both "seeking revenge against time" is a plausible interpretation, recalling Faulkner's statement that what the writer wants is "to leave a scratch" on "the wall of oblivion"—"Kilroy was here." Even more pertinent is André Bleikasten's comment on Faulkner and Quentin in *The Sound and the Fury:* "For all the autobiographical elements that went into the character, Faulkner holds him at a distance and subjects his loveless, life-denying egocentricity to ruthless exposure.... For in exposing Quentin's blindness, Faulkner gives the full measure of his own insight and of the extraordinary self-knowledge he must have achieved by the time he wrote *The Sound and the Fury.*"

As the first booklength study of *The Sound and the Fury,* André Bleikasten's work merits special mention although it was published too late to be more fully incorporated into this chapter. Bleikasten coincidentally agrees with Irwin in some of the applications of theories of Freud and of Guy Rosolato, such as the father-son relationship and Quentin's suicide as a *Liebestod* and a return to the womb. Although Bleikasten rarely used "Gothic," as he did in describing the Compson story in Jason's soliloquy as "a burlesque Southern melodrama, a Gothic farce," he deals extensively with Gothic qualities, character types, themes, and patterns of action. The true Gothic flavor is obvious without the label.

The irrationality which is characteristic of dream psychology is clearly indicated by the title and the source passage in *Macbeth,* a title which originally was intended, Faulkner said, to refer to the first section but which finally "covered the whole family." It is easy to fit into the passage the names of the characters whose personal traits and views of life are suggested:

> Tomorrow, and tomorrow, and tomorrow,
> Creeps in this petty pace from day to day,
> To the last syllable of recorded time:
> And all our yesterdays have lighted fools
> The way to dusty death. [Mr. Compson] Out, out, brief candle!
> Life's but a walking shadow [Quentin], a poor player
> That struts [Jason] and frets [Mrs. Compson] his hour upon the stage
> And then is heard no more. It is a tale
> Told by an idiot [Benjy], full of sound and fury,
> Signifying nothing.

With his characteristic irony Faulkner told a tale that signified a great deal. The last sentence would be a suitable statement of the theme of the literature of the absurd to which the Gothic tradition contributed.

Robert Slabey identified the basic theme of *The Sound and the Fury* as related to Romanticism, which fostered the Gothic tradition: "the discrepancy between the ideal form of man's dreams and the real content of the actual world." Quentin (the strongest link between *The Sound and the Fury* and *Absalom, Absalom!*) best represents the Romantic temperament as Robert Slabey described it:

A Romantic temperament is highly subjective, strongly emotional, one that is constantly moving away from—and sometimes painfully isolated from— the actuality of everyday, present, public, rational experience. The Romantic's aspirations and idealizations are radical versions of the universal human longing for completeness and unity. It is through love that the Romantic seeks to complete his existence; he desires a perfect love, perfect both sensually and intellectually.

Charles Gregory described Quentin as a Romantic with a veneer of intellectualism, the most past-ridden of Faulkner's characters who seek in the past an escape from present reality. The name "Quentin" reinforces the Romantic suggestion: Carvel Collins observed that Quentin's human ideal, Caddy, betrayed his abstract ideal, honor, and that "Quentin" may come both from Scott's "Quentin Durward" and from Andrew Marvell's "Quaint honor turn to dust." Benjy is a Romantic figure, the "natural," the "innocent," akin to Wordsworth's "Idiot Boy," as Michael Frederickson observed. The Romantic dream and the rational experience are given a southern significance: Baxter

Hathaway perceived in the different mind-sets of Quentin and Jason the evolution of the South from "an insane transcendental dream to a low-level and frustrated rationality," or, in Faulkner's own words, "there are too many Jasons in the South who can be successful, . . . too many Quentins in the South who are too sensitive to face its reality."

Thus, the basic elements in *The Sound and the Fury* are essentially Romantic and potentially Gothic. Faulkner's account of his way of writing it, as described in *Faulkner at Nagano*, does not really fit the final product: the explanation may represent "manifest content" rather than "latent content." The difference between the story he described, which covers the grandmother's funeral, "the idiot's experience of that day" and Quentin's "version of that same day, or that same occasion," and the finished novel suggests the reconciliation of two patterns, the one he described as his initial idea and the traditional pattern of the Gothic latent in the material. It seems unlikely that Faulkner could have been unaware of the Gothic tradition when he wrote *The Sound and the Fury* and so fully aware of it when he wrote *Absalom, Absalom!* that he needed the presence of Quentin in the Sutpen story to complete it successfully.

The specific tragedy of the Compsons is in the Gothic tradition: "the tragedy of being conscious of a dying way of life and the abortive attempts of the mind to lead the individual to isolation from the world of things." This tragedy, as Robert Humphrey explained, takes place in the mind, and hence Faulkner used the stream of consciousness and the interior monologue. The method and the physical details of present action in *The Sound and the Fury* do not reinforce the Gothic elements as they do in *Absalom, Absalom!* Even Leslie Fiedler, in *No! in Thunder* acclaiming *The Sound and the Fury* as perhaps the greatest American work of fiction, did not use the term "Gothic"; his description, however, of that novel as "a vision of the meaninglessness of existence," rendering the absurdity in aesthetic form, specifies a consequent delight which is definitely Gothic: "a delight which does not deny horror but lives at its intolerable heart."

The first great contrast between *Absalom, Absalom!* and *The Sound and the Fury* in regard to major Gothic images is the treatment of the "castle," the Compson mansion and the surrounding grounds and outbuildings which are all that remain of the Compson Domain, originally consisting of a square mile. The Domain never appears in all its vicissitudes in the fiction, as the Sutpen mansion did. In the appendix the history of the Domain is given with some details from different periods; in the novel itself we first see the old Compson place in the last section, "the square, paintless house with its rotting portico" (p. 372). Like

Hawthorne's House of the Seven Gables, according to Eleanor Lang, the Compson house is the objective correlative "of the decay within."

Such limitation in objective representation is due to the subjective technique and to the restriction of both the present action and the memory of the past to the personal experiences of three young people who did not see change occur over a long period of time. The absence of a sense of the historical past is a fundamental reason that *The Sound and the Fury* lacks some of the Gothic atmosphere; Quentin, who did have a sense of the past, is here too much obsessed with his own recent past and his present to reveal the mental and emotional aspects of his nature which appear in *Absalom, Absalom!* Although the Compson Domain represents death and decay, as did Sutpen's Hundred, the process is virtually complete when the story opens, and the house, the objective symbol of that process, does not dominate the imagery but is fragmented and scattered through the action of parts 1, 3, and 4 on three spring days. The symbolic meaning of the Sutpen and the Compson mansions is similar: pride, isolation, and lack of love; the Sutpen dwelling is geographically isolated, but the Compson house is isolated in spirit from the community, and its inhabitants are alienated from each other.

The desirability of considering the whole of the Yoknapatawpha fiction when dealing with a dominant aspect or pattern in Faulkner is well illustrated by the Compson story. The end of the Compson mansion, similar to that of Sutpen's Hundred, is told in *The Mansion:* "Benjy not only burned himself up but completely destroyed the house too" (p. 322). The "sane" son, Jason, and his mother survived, but the family was ended, as was the Sutpen family when only Jim Bond still lived. The part-Negro idiot and the "sane" white son become parallel figures.

The natural settings, in themselves and as perceived by the characters, are predominantly un-Gothic: peaceful and ordinary are the Compson grounds in part 1, the remnants of the Compson Domain in which Benjy is locked in his Edenic garden for his own good, the innocent world from which Benjy cannot escape and to which Quentin cannot return; equally peaceful and ordinary are the environs of Harvard and the country along the Charles River in which Quentin rehearsed his journey to death, in 2, and the countryside around Jefferson through which Jason pursued Miss Quentin, in 3 and 4. Even more peaceful is the little Negro church on Easter morning, an ironic inversion of the ruined Gothic abbey at midnight: "A weathered church lifted its crazy steeple like a painted church, and the whole scene was as flat and without perspective as a painted cardboard set upon the ultimate edge of the flat earth, against the windy sunlight of space and April and a midmorning filled with bells" (p. 364). Edward Corridori perceived the image of the church as invested with the timelessness and spacelessness of a work of art according to Mircea Eliade's concept of sacred and profane space. The theatricality of many Gothic settings is here matched by un-Gothic theatricality.

One definitely Gothic setting appears repeatedly: the cemetery where, in turn, Damuddy, Quentin, and Mr. Compson are buried. The funeral of Mr. Compson in the rain, Benjy's "graveyard," and the routine ritual of the final Sunday drive to the cemetery are the chief visualized graveyard scenes. But the smell of death pervades the book, evoking the howls of Benjy and of successive Compson dogs.

The enclosed places are chiefly rooms in the Compson house. The rooms which represent warmth and love and a safe haven are contrasted with the "other rooms" which represent lack or loss of love, and which are traps or self-imposed prisons. Benjy's memories dwell on the living room and the kitchen and Dilsey's cabin, all offering fire and love, and on the living room after Caddy's marriage when, with the mirror gone, there was no love or firelight to be reflected. The dining room, the scene of meals which were a travesty of love and communion and to which Mr. Compson retreated to find his escape, the bottle kept in the sideboard, is the scene of action chiefly in Jason's section, 3. Mrs. Compson's room and Jason's room represent their occupants' selfish isolation: Mrs. Compson lay in the dark and complained to Dilsey; Jason kept his treasure behind a locked door and behind a locked door discovered his loss. The rooms of the two Quentins, at Harvard and in the Compson house, were anonymous, merely places to escape from; at Harvard Quentin went from his room to his death, and Miss Quentin went to her ruin from a room that had the "dead and stereotyped transience of rooms in assignation houses" (p. 352). Her desperate escape to sexuality recalls Caddy's flight, in her wedding veil in the moonlight, to an equally loveless substitute for a loveless home. For Benjy's the "other room" of the asylum is prefigured in the fence which restrains him.

The characters who occupy these rooms represent traditional types, with many ironic inversions. The Persecuted Maidens, Caddy and Miss Quentin, ironically did not defend their virginity and fled to, not from, ruin. Caddy had affairs with several boys before her marriage but was serious only about Dalton Ames. The paternity of her child is unknown; she married Herbert Head to give it a name. Any doubts one might have about Caddy's fate Faulkner resolved in the appendix, where she appeared finally, in a colored photograph, as the mistress of a Nazi general. Miss Quentin was even more the victim of a loveless home than Caddy: Miss Quentin had neither father nor brother, and her sadistic uncle, Jason, persecuted and robbed her. She went the way of her mother after similar dalliance in the swing among the cedars. The ironic contrast between Caddy and Miss Quentin and the Gothic heroines who held honor dearer than life is heightened by Quentin's ideal of virginity. By comparison with Jason's view of Caddy and Miss Quentin—"Once a bitch always a bitch"—Jason made his mistress, Lorraine, seem to represent fidelity and respectability. But he tore up her letter and burned it over the spittoon.

Quentin, as the romantic hero, had weaknesses even greater than those of Henry Sutpen, whom he somewhat resembled. Henry did protect his sister; Quentin was incapable of defending Caddy. He went through the gestures of doing so with Dalton Ames but rejected Dalton's pistol, a phallic symbol. John Irwin interpreted Quentin's virginity and his impotence as psychologically signifying his assumption of a feminine role. In Quentin's memory, Dalton plays the role of a romantic hero-villain; apparently he seduced Caddy but met with little resistance. He was a horseman, an athlete, a crack shot, and a magnanimous opponent, lying to protect Quentin and Caddy from the humiliating fact that Quentin had "passed out like a girl" (p. 201). Gerald Bland, in contrast to both Dalton and Quentin, is a parody of the romantic Don Juan southerner, with a fake British persona. When Quentin was so lost in the memory of Dalton that he confounded Dalton and Gerald and fought Gerald, Spoade provided the proper medieval term: Quentin was "the champion of dames" (p. 207). The relationship between Shreve and Quentin suggested by their identification with Charles Bon and Henry in *Absalom, Absalom!* is confirmed in *The Sound and the Fury* as homosexual: Quentin was ashamed of being a virgin and recalled that Spoade called Shreve Quentin's husband; Mrs. Bland tried twice to have Shreve moved out and a new roommate given to Quentin. The climax of Quentin's failure to play the role of the romantic hero as he conceived it was his suicide.

The two villains, in contrast with Quentin, are crass materialists and cynics. Herbert Head is an ironic villain in that he was victimized by Mrs. Compson to preserve the family's respectability and give Caddy's unborn child a father and a name. Challenged by Quentin with his past record of cheating at Harvard, Herbert referred to Quentin as a "half-baked Galahad of a brother" (p. 136). Quentin's realistic acquaintances thus recognized Quentin's self-image of the chivalric protector of feminine virtue. The other villain is Jason, who, as Quentin said, would have suited Herbert better than Quentin did. After Herbert cast out Caddy and her child and Caddy sent the baby home to be brought up by Dilsey, Jason sadistically took out on Miss Quentin his revenge on Caddy because he never got a job in Herbert's bank; he made Miss Quentin's life a hell and stole from her the money Caddy sent her. Milton Kornfeld recognized in Jason the attempt to make "experience conform to rational expectations" which was a trait of the villains of Hawthorne and Henry James. Jason's villainy being based on the profit motive, Kornfeld considered him "closer to our cultural heritage than the esoteric Faustian villain." Jason became an ironic villain, the villain-victim, when Miss Quentin stole his entire hoard, part of which was his own savings. The fact that this "trickster-tricked" pattern, frequently used in Faulkner's comic situations, serves in Jason "the function of comedy in conjunction with villainy," as Kornfeld said, is in harmony with the Gothic combination of the terrible and the ludicrous which distinguishes the grotesque.

The Compson parents are also ironic inversions of traditional Gothic types. Not only was Mr. Compson not a tyrannical father, but he was too ineffectual to protect his daughter, whom he loved so much that he drank himself to death after she left home. John Irwin interpreted Quentin as trying to force his father to play the paternal role by protecting Caddy and punishing Quentin for incest. Mrs. Compton is indeed the Suffering Wife, a role she played to the hilt. But her hypochondria inflicted suffering on the rest of the family; as a selfish, unloving mother, she was a chief cause of the misfortunes and disasters she lamented. Her empty ideal of a rigid code of conduct and her equating of virtue and virginity are parodies of Quentin's idealism: as a wife and mother she denied her own "fall" into maturity and condemned Caddy to a loveless marriage and Quentin to death.

One character in the Gothic tradition is neither ironically inverted into the opposite nor negated by inadequacy to fill the role: of all faithful servants, Gothic or otherwise, Dilsey is unexcelled. And even her occasional "impertinence," part of the tradition from *The Castle of Otranto* on, is an aspect of her humanity and compassion which constitute the one source of love and order in the household; she would not, she told Jason, blame Miss Quentin if she did break his window, "wid you naggin at her all de blessed time you in de house" (p. 347). Under her watchful eye Luster is a faithful servant, but otherwise he evades duty and is a comic prankster. The raising of Dilsey from the traditional minor, often comic, role to that of a major character, prominent in parts 1 and 3 and the center of interest in 4, is one of the most original and significant of Faulkner's modifications of the Gothic pattern. Faulkner included Dilsey with Sutpen and Joe Christmas as his three most tragic characters and said that she held the family together "not for the hope of reward but just because it was the decent and proper thing to do."

Benjy, the most obviously grotesque character, is used in a highly original way. His utter innocence is the mirror which reflects the rest of the family and reveals the warmth and tenderness of Caddy in the past and the loving care of Dilsey in the present. The Gothic effect of Benjy is modified by the fact that he is not visualized for the reader until 4: dropsical, shambling "like a trained bear," a drooling idiot, he had clear eyes, "of the pale sweet blue of cornflowers" (p. 342). Benjy was particularly grotesque with Luster, his attendant: "They looked like a tug nudging at a clumsy tanker in a narrow dock" (p. 356). William Barrett regarded as abnormal, with no reference to grotesqueness, characters who "exist at the extremity of the human situation": Benjy, the mentally deficient; Quentin, suffering from moral distortion; and Mr. Compson, the nihilist, who lived in a world without meaning. But, as Barrett said, "Sometimes one must go to the boundaries of the human condition to see what that condition implies"; the last sentence of *The Sound and the Fury* was the "last grotesque twist of Faulkner's irony."

Benjy's section was classified by James Mellard as romance, being closest to childhood and wish-fulfillment dream. Romance, however, may equally well or even better stress the dreams of youth. More pertinent to the Gothic pattern, which he does not deal with, is Mellard's comparison between Benjy and Caliban, another grotesque "natural" and, as Mellard notes, an "inverted pastoral hero." One recalls that the golf links had previously been Benjy's pasture. The most significant parallel noted by Mellard is that Benjy, like Caliban, serves to reveal the corruption and degeneracy of the world in which he lives. Prospero's words, quoted by Mellard, suggest Gothic fiction: "such stuff as dreams are made on."

The obvious parallel to Benjy in *Absalom, Absalom!* is Jim Bond, an equally extreme example of family degeneracy. Unlike Jim, however, Benjy represents degeneracy in an upper class white family, as the fruit of a fairly typical and socially respectable marriage, not of such a grotesque, untypical, unsuitable, and socially outrageous mating as produced Jim Bond. As an extrapolation of a trend in society, Shreve's prophecy that the Jim Bonds would conquer the Western Hemisphere is less sound than would be a prediction, based on Benjy, that the old "aristocracy" of the South—withdrawn, inactive, incompetent—would decline and die out. Although Benjy is not the only white idiot in Faulkner's mythical county, Jim Bond is the only mentally deficient Negro or part-Negro in Yoknapatawpha.

Whether or not Benjy was sexually molesting little girls, as Jason asserted in pressuring the family to have Benjy castrated, sexual perversions and violations of conventional behavior are numerous and significant in the Compson story. Mrs. Compson's brother, Maury Bascomb, was beaten up by a neighbor for carrying on an adulterous affair with the neighbor's wife. Maury used as his messengers his little niece Caddy and his idiot nephew, leaving a reasonable doubt as to which is more idiotic, uncle or nephew, but no doubt as to moral turpitude. Jason, the sadist and hypocrite, was Mrs. Compson's favorite child, acceptable to her, like Maury, as more a Bascomb than a Compson. Jason had a mistress but showed no other signs of attachment to others. William Brown made the plausible suggestion that, in a Freudian sense, both Benjy and Jason might unconsciously be attracted sexually to Caddy, a theory that would help to explain the violence of Jason's rational attitudes and the intensity of Benjy's instinctual reactions. Caddy and her daughter were sexually promiscuous while still in their teens, but both were doomed by the family situation in which they were victims. Doomed by that situation, his own limitations, and his idea of family honor, Quentin was narcissistic, homosexual, incestuous in feeling if not in action, and probably semi-schizoid. Irwin explained Quentin's narcissism, according to Otto Rank's theory, as "necessarily linked with his incestuous desire for his sister." Although Quentin and Henry Sutpen were similar in the above traits, Quentin showed no capacity for the masculine courage and endurance which Henry must have shown in the Civil War to survive with credit. Quentin rejected Dalton's pistol; Henry asserted his manhood with guns, in war and in murder. All three Compson brothers exhibit the narcissism identified by Irving Malin as characteristic of the "new American Gothic," as a consequence of isolation and anxiety caused by lack of communication: "New American Gothic uses grotesques who love themselves so much that they cannot enter the social world except to dominate their neighbors." Quentin loved himself in Caddy; Jason tried to dominate everyone; Benjy was totally unable to communicate and to make choices. In one respect the Compsons are unique among major upper class white families in Yoknapatawpha: they fail to exemplify the peculiarly American southern Gothic perversion, miscegenation.

There are two major sequences of action in the present: the story of Quentin's suicide on June 2, 1910 (part 2), motivated by Caddy's loss of virtue and by her wedding in May; and the story of Jason's persecution of Miss Quentin and her revenge (3 and 4), to which Benjy's section (1) provides the details of Miss Quentin and the man with the red tie, together in the swing, and of "it" climbing down the tree. In addition to the focus of 3 and 4 on the present, April 1928, Benjy's unselective memories and Quentin's more selective ones combine to develop themes and related patterns of past and present action which are predominantly Gothic, all being concerned with the search for love by Benjy, Quentin, Caddy, and Miss Quentin.

The lack of love and the disorder due to the parents' failure to fulfill their roles doomed the Compson children, as the lack of love and the father's compulsive design doomed the Sutpen children. Both "castles" represent pride and isolation from the community. Only Dilsey took an active part in the Christian community, and only Dilsey loved, with a love that recognized Benjy as the Lord's child and that triumphed over Mrs. Compson's neurotic nagging, Miss Quentin's desperate hostility, and Jason's scorn and hatred.

The lack in the Compson household of parental love and an eligible example of mature adult life affected the Compson children variously, in relation to Faulkner's theme of innocence. In *Faulkner at Nagano* Faulkner said that Benjy was fixed forever in the "self-centeredness of innocence," typified by children, and needing tenderness to shelter him. Caddy sought love where she could find it, and lost her innocence. Her love for her brother Quentin was not obsessive and exclusive, like his for her, and Faulkner stated what the fiction implies, that Quentin was not the kind of man Caddy would choose for a sweetheart. Miss Quentin, without even a brother to love, also lost her innocence and chose to be in Hell rather than where Jason was. She is one of the few Persecuted Maidens in Faulkner who literally fled, but she fled from loveless respectability and chastity, not from sexuality.

The theme of innocence is most fully and complexly developed in Quentin, whom Eleanor Lang compared with Hilda in Hawthorne's *The Marble Faun*, "the prototype of that irredeemable innocence which sees the fall of man and confesses it, but will not accept either the logical conclusions to be drawn from it or his own responsibility in it." Lawrence Bowling specified two views of innocence which are represented in *The Sound and the Fury,* the puritan concept of innocence as a virtue (the absence of wrong action rather than positive right action) and the humanist view of innocence as ignorant simplicity which must be lost to gain knowledge; each insists that the opposite of innocence is knowledge, but the puritan shuns that knowledge, whereas the humanist believes that the end of man is to know. Mrs. Compson is the puritan: "Thank God I dont know about such wickedness. I dont even want to know about it. I'm not like most people" (p. 323).

Faulkner took the humanist view: Dilsey, the only one who acted positively and unselfishly, did not remain innocent but depended on Christian faith and love as defense against sin and evil. Influenced by his mother's puritan concept and even more by the courtly love ideal of which the puritan concept is one outgrowth, Quentin tried to retain innocence and to refuse adult knowledge. Homosexual perhaps by nature, he was impelled, by his effort to remain a child, to incestuous love for Caddy, an egocentric love which evidences, according to Peter Swiggart, "a perverse response to a self-created problem." Quentin fits Denis de Rougemont's description of the quest for identity which confuses the death instinct with the necessary death of the pseudoself; Quentin narcissistically dedicated his passion to his own soul, of which Caddy would be the image. His parents' slow suicide in their flight from reality and truth became in Quentin actual suicide, a refusal to undergo the ordeal of initiation into mature knowledge and manhood, in Leslie Fiedler's phrase in *Love and Death,* a refusal "to step over the mystic barrier of twenty-one." Glenn Sandstrom applied to Quentin Compson and Joe Christmas, in *Light in August,* Erik Erikson's study of the "Problem of Ego Identity," in *Identity and Anxiety* (1960), and concluded that Faulkner showed almost "prophetic psychological ordering and vision." Quentin's suicide was the consequence of his choice of Negative Identity, the perverse opposite of acceptable roles.

Presumably, Quentin's knowledge of the Sutpen story would reinforce his incestuous desire rather than provide him with a positive example of family life and love. In discussing the eighteenth-century antibourgeois novel, in *Love and Death,* Leslie Fiedler recognized as major themes both incest, especially brother-sister incest, and suicide, a symbol of protest ennobled by the example of Werther. Without reference to Werther, William Barrett interpreted Quentin's incestuous desires as "the final overdelicate flower of inbreeding" and his romantic despair as like that of a spurned lover, "taking his own life in desperate rejection." Quentin's action, like his mental attitudes, reflects patterns and ideals from the past. In dealing with Gothic elements in *The Member of the Wedding,* Robert Phillips noted that the "rites of passage for the innocent into a violent world" is a typical Gothic theme and that "the search for a sexless, dim ideal" is "a manifestation of the hero's avoidance and fear of reality." Quentin's fear lay behind his choice of a Negative Identity and of the rites of passage of death rather than those of initiation into the world of knowledge, growth, and change. According to John Irwin's interpretation, which is in harmony with Gothic patterns, "The narcissistic origin of doubling and the scenario of madness leading to the suicidal murder of the double help to illuminate" the account of Quentin's last day. The narcissism, which is also symbolized in the death by drowning, is linked with his "incestuous desire for his sister." Quentin's rejection of the rites of initiation is emphasized by his ritualistic actions and by his choice of drowning, an ironic reversal of baptism as an initiatory rite signifying rebirth. He did not believe that Christ would raise him and the flatirons from his watery grave, only once thinking that "maybe when He says Rise the eyes will come floating up too ... to look on glory" (p. 144). Water, the dominant motif in part 2, does not symbolize regeneration. Irwin regards Quentin's death as "a suicidal *liebestod* ... in which the sexual instinct and the death instinct ... fuse in the ultimate regressive act—the suicidal return to the womb, the sexual reentry into Mother Death. ..."

The significance of "that confrontation of the 'hero' with experience which may assume the form of initiation or victimization," the central theme in Ihab Hassan's *Radical Innocence* and a major one in Fiedler's *Love and Death in the American Novel,* is confirmed by the frequency with which Faulkner used both kinds of confrontation. André Bleikasten said of Quentin and Jason: "Theirs are essentially stories of failed initiations, stories of fatal self-delusion. ..." With or without a Gothic context, the initiation pattern or an ironic inversion of it is the most frequent single pattern of action in Faulkner. The other confrontation, victimization, is by its nature eminently suitable for Gothic fiction.

The only Compson to assume an adult role is Jason, who ironically presents an image of the responsible, respectable head of a family. Actually, he is motivated by an obsessing greed and by revenge for having to assume those responsibilities without having a position in Herbert Head's bank or a Harvard education. Jason is a kind of parody of Sutpen, working toward a shabby design, a Snopesian Faust who is less clever and achieves less than the real Faust-Snopes, Flem. William Brown diagnosed Jason as paranoid, believing that "neutral actions are aimed with sinister intent" at himself, rather than, like Sutpen, having paranoiac delusions of grandeur and superhuman aspirations. The night before Miss Quentin stole Jason's nest egg, Jason stated his plans, if he should be moderately successful in playing the cotton market: "And once I've done that they can bring all Beale Street and all bedlam in here and two of them can sleep in my bed and another one can have my place at the table too" (p. 329). Jason is a shabby Faust who, having sold his soul for the four thousand dollars belonging to his niece and lost them with his own three thousand, was almost killed seeking his treasure and ended in his own Hell, "sitting quietly behind the wheel of a small car, with his invisible life ravelled out about him like a wornout sock" (p. 391).

With no reference to *The Sound and the Fury* Robert Heilman provided another insight into Faulkner's perception, whether conscious or intuitive, of both psychological and literary patterns. According to Heilman, Jason and Sutpen would be melodramatic: "The pathological extreme of the melodramatic condition is paranoia—in one phase, the sense of a hostile 'they' who will make one their victim, and, in another phase, the sense

of one's own grandeur. . . ." And Quentin approaches "the tragic condition" of which "the pathological extreme" is "schizophrenia." John
Irwin's explanation of Quentin described the specific nature of his
schizophrenia as a splitting "into a bad half and a good half," the bad
tormenting the good and the good punishing the bad. The "narrative
bipolarity" involved is "typical of both compulsion neurosis and
schizophrenia." Irwin ascribed the splitting to Quentin's inability "to
reconcile his simultaneous attraction to and repulsion by his incestuous
desire for his sister." At the end of *Absalom, Absalom!* Quentin's hysterical denial that he hated the South is a clue to the psychic disorder which
led to his suicide and thus serves as a transition to *The Sound and the
Fury;* there is no such transition between *Absalom, Absalom!* and *The
Sound and the Fury* to cover events before September 1909.

The search for identity which is a common Gothic theme takes on
special meaning in Faulkner. Frank H. Thomas, in "The Search for Identity of Faulkner's Black Characters," remarked on the new creative powers
and self-confidence of Faulkner in *The Sound and the Fury*. He examined
the Negro characters in the framework of the novel, without regard to
Gothic aspects. To Quentin, enslaved by race consciousness, Deacon,
the clever role player, represented Quentin's concept of "nigger" as
"not a person" but "a form of behavior," reflecting "the white people
he lives among" (p. 106). The problems and hazards of the Negro quest
for identity could scarcely be more succinctly stated. Dilsey sometimes
appeared in Quentin's memory but did not enter his thoughts. There is
some ambivalence in Quentin's feelings toward Negroes but none in
Jason's. Toward Job, whose self-image, Thomas noted, was uncor-
rupted by the identity he assumed on occasion, Jason took the attitude
of a redneck, not an aristocrat; toward Dilsey he was brutal, not merely
indifferent. Frank Thomas studied Dilsey in the family group, where
she was defined by the Compsons and accepted the place they assigned
her without assuming their values. Scorned by the Compsons, who could
not get along without her, the only real mother they knew, Dilsey was
respected by the black community. Sensible and perceptive, Dilsey in her
identity as mother and provider was undercut by the Compson callousness and lack of sound values. She justly took pride in the fact that her
own values sustained her; but she was denied the satisfaction of seeing
her values prevail. The lack of any vital and wholesome quest for identity
among the Compsons is contrasted with Dilsey's unflagging quest, despite
her race and the Compsons' racist attitudes, for an identity that transcends
self and race.

That contrast is represented in *The Sound and the Fury* in patterns
of motion familiar in Gothic fiction. William Barrett commented on the

peculiarity of these patterns as seen in the Compson story: "Faulkner's characters . . . often run around in frantic chase or flight, but they always turn out to be running in a circle." That circularity is seen in the activities of Benjy, Quentin, and Jason, in the first three parts. Benjy's activity is aimless wandering, within the confines of the Compson place, retracing the patterns of all his days, with past and present inextricably fused. His search for Caddy, for love and security, was recalled by the cries of "Caddy" from the golf course, his lost pasture, but he was incapable of going on a quest for her, except for his abortive escape through the gate, which Jason may have deliberately left open. Quentin spent his last day rehearsing in a round trip his solitary journey to death; at night he set out on a dead-end trip. In parts 3 and 4 Jason frantically pursued Miss Quentin and the man in the red tie, at first sadistically spying on them and then, after Miss Quentin's flight from home, trying to get back his money. His trips around town and between the hardware store and his house were in quest of profit, on the cotton market and through his trickery with the bogus checks. His journeys were circular and fruitless; as T. H. Adamowski said, "Jason, who is in search of the golden fleece, gets fleeced." In 4, in contrast to Jason's pursuit of Miss Quentin, there is a ceremonial, purposeful journey: the climax of Dilsey's routine journeys up and down stairs and around the house and outdoors, in compassionate service to those who scorned her, was her journey to church, a pilgrimage to eternity. Observing this contrast between the journey of Dilsey and those of Jason and Quentin, Edward Corridori also described Dilsey's journey as a pilgrimage, part of the contrast throughout *The Sound and the Fury* between sacred and profane space, in the terms used by Mircea Eliade. Unlike Quentin's and Miss Rosa's journeys to Sutpen's Hundred, at night, in the fall and winter, all the journeys in *The Sound and the Fury* in the present action took place in the spring or summer and, except Quentin's return trip on the trolley car, by daylight.

Equally a contrast to *Absalom, Absalom!* is the element of mystery and suspense in *The Sound and the Fury*, which depends almost wholly on the method of narration. It is the suspense of the jigsaw puzzle without a picture guide: jumbled fragments of information must be pieced together to discover what picture of the past they form. The colors of the fragments are light and dark, the sunny present being shot through with memories of night, rain, and moonlight but not predominantly somber like the Sutpen past. Much of the Sutpen story was presented in Miss Rosa's summary in the first chapter, with the sequence of events clear, however obscure some of the motives were. But the structure of *The Sound and the Fury* is dreamlike. Incongruous dovetailing of funerals and a wedding takes place in part 1. In 2 equally incongruous juxtapositions are created by shifts from present to past: the patter of Mrs. Bland, for example, is broken by Quentin's memory of telling Caddy he will confess to incest. In 1 the mystery in the present is what climbed down the tree at the end. In 2 the mystery in the present is slight, Quentin's preparations for drowning himself being obvious clues. The past mystery is chiefly what is fact and what is imagination in his memories: was he guilty of incest? and did he confess to his father?

In contrast to *Absalom, Absalom!* mystery and suspense become progressively less and coherent present action becomes greater until 3 and 4 are completely lucid, with no final revelation of deliberately withheld meaning. The lack of Gothic atmosphere and the comparative lack of mystery and suspense reduce the theatrical quality that the Gothic derives from its origins and its kinship with melodrama, strikingly evident in *Absalom, Absalom!* Substituted for melodramatic horror in *The Sound and the Fury* is psychological horror, tempered by pathos in the stories of Benjy, Quentin, and Caddy, and by satire in the characterization of Jason. In "Vision and Feeling," a chapter on Bernanos and Faulkner, Arnold Weinstein commented on the form of Faulkner's fiction as a mediation "between sight and insight": "The characteristic form of Faulkner's fiction derives from the attempt to comprehend some mysterious or extraordinary event.... This act of comprehension—be it characterized by amazement, outrage, ironic query, or passionate commitment—structures Faulkner's major fiction and brings forth an imaginative involvement from the reader." In "Faulkner's portrait of the Compson family, comprehension is defined in terms of feeling." In *The Sound and the Fury* Ralph Eberly identified components of reader interest similar to those reflected in Weinstein's analysis: "'Immediacy' is the reader's response to fictional events almost as if they were emotionally charged experiences of living persons; 'suspense' is his desire for information that the novel temporarily withholds; and 'meaning' is his awareness of the book's total comment upon the 'actual' world." Weinstein and Eberly well describe the effect sought by Gothic fiction: Gothic appeal evokes Gothic response.

The understatement of Gothic atmosphere in *The Sound and the Fury* is accompanied by an understatement of violence. There is, however, a wealth of tableaux and episodes dramatizing the themes and reinforced by symbolic images and objects such as are characteristic of Gothic fiction. The medieval influence in the Gothic tradition is often reflected in emphasis on ceremony and ritual. Rituals cover life from childhood to the grave. Faulkner's inspiration for the novel began with the image of Caddy, with her muddy drawers, up in a tree looking through the window, mistaking the ceremony she saw for a party, not a funeral. This image symbolizes dishonor, love, and death, as well as rebellious courage. As for Benjy, similarity in scene and other details between Damuddy's funeral and Caddy's wedding makes him confuse the two, suggesting that for him Caddy's wedding meant a loss like death. Quentin's preparation for death is notably ritualistic: the destruction of time by breaking the hands off his watch; the purchase and concealment of the flatirons; the writing of the suicide notes and arranging for their delivery; the "rehearsal" journey; the final ritual cleansing of himself and his clothes before the mirror. Noting Quentin's thought when removing the blood stains, "Maybe a pattern of blood he could call that the one Christ was wearing," John Irwin interpreted Quentin's suicide as part of the Christ pattern: "that self-sacrifice of the son to satisfy the father, that active willing of passivity as a self-inflicted revenge." Quentin's image of the clean flame in which he and Caddy would burn together in hell further symbolizes his refusal of initiation, of change of identity and rebirth in this world, as Dennis Murphy suggested, or of redemptive suffering in the flames of purgatory as in Dante's *Purgatorio*.

The largest group of images in Quentin's section combine the themes of time and self-punishment, a variety of Gothic masochism. Images of the shadow introduce darkness into the bright and sunny scenes. The themes and images of death in 2, a death in the North eighteen years before the Easter weekend action, are augmented by the cemetery scenes in Jefferson: Jason's memory of his father's funeral in the rain; the ritual of the carriage drive to the cemetery with which the novel ends; Benjy's confused and fragmented memories of all of the deaths—Damuddy's, Quentin's, Roskus's, Mr. Compson's; and Benjy's favorite amusement, his homemade graveyard. Most Gothic are the details of the supernatural, rare in modern literary Gothic: Benjy's smelling death, the howling of dogs when a person dies, and Luster's account of seeing his father's ghost: *"I seen him last night, waving his arms in the barn"* (p. 40).

Two meaningful rites which Dilsey conducted or participated in frame the novel: the birthday cake for Benjy's thirty-third birthday, bought with Dilsey's own money, in 1, and the Easter service to which Dilsey took Benjy, in 4. Into this novel about selfish characters obsessed with time, the expressions of Dilsey's love and the Easter sermon introduce the dimension of eternity and the power of selfless love. "De power and de glory" are contrasted with "the sound and the fury, signifying nothing." The obvious Christ symbolism—the Easter dates, allusions, and church service, and Benjy's age and his innocence—is ironic in relation to the Compsons, who certainly "never resurrected Christ" (p. 348). Benjy as the innocent one, "despised and rejected of men" but witless, and Dilsey as the potentially redemptive figure, who also was despised and whose values were ironically subverted, serve to reverse the irony of the Christ symbolism and the title, and to offer the traditional, positive significance.

Two recurrent images and associated tableaux are of particular significance in the new American Gothic. Benjy's mirror and the parallel mirror and water reflections in Quentin's section excellently exemplify the image of reflection stressed by Irving Malin. Malin's other two images have been verified: the haunted castle has become the other room, and the voyage into the forest has become movement which is "erratic, circular, violent or distorted," as has been previously indicated. The third of Malin's Gothic images Faulkner used with great originality: "the mirror in which reality is double, cracked, or wavy; only one image is constant—the beloved self." There are two actual mirrors. In one Benjy saw the fire and Caddy and Jason fighting, and Quentin saw Caddy in her wedding veil, but this mirror was gone from the wall after Caddy's wedding. Into the other mirror, at Harvard, Quentin looked to see if he had removed the stain from his vest before he went to drown himself, the final cleansing. The river, which repeatedly reflects Quentin's shadow, serves as a mirror. John Irwin explained that Quentin's drowning was "an attempt to merge the shadow and the mirror image," the mirror symbolizing Quentin's narcissism. The mirror analogues, as Lawrance Thompson indicated, also include: Benjy as the moral mirror of the Compsons, in which Caddy saw her need for cleansing; the mirroring of past action in the present—the little girl and the fight in Quentin's section reflecting Quentin's real little sister and his abortive fight with Dalton Ames; the three negative sections as reflections of the family from different angles of vision. Caddy is presented only as she is reflected in her brothers' and her mother's views. The mirror analogues do indeed serve here, in Malin's terms, as the third of the "crucial components of the new American Gothic" to "provide the scene . . . for the distortions of narcissism and the wars in the family. Without them Gothic could not exist."

The walking shadow image according to Louise Dauner occurs almost as frequently as the water image, which is often combined with the reflection image; shadows and reflections are equivalent images and the basis of similar superstitious beliefs. Quentin's shadow has both the significance derived from the title quotation from *Macbeth* and that derived from modern psychology. Fiedler's comment on Poe, in *Love and Death*, illuminates the cluster of mirror and shadow images in *The Sound and the Fury:* the incest theme signifies that the beloved is "clearly a dark projection of his psyche, as intimately related to him as his own image in the mirror. . . . She tends to become, indeed, the symbol of mortality, the figure of death itself—combining the characteristics of shadow and *anima,* as if intended to signify that the soul of a man and his death are one thing." Fiedler's comment applies to Quentin, not to Faulkner in general.

Quentin's attempt to lose or destroy his shadow is one manifestation of his death wish. Beliefs upon which taboos about shadows were based, according to Otto Rank, included the beliefs that harm to the shadow harms the owner, that the shadow symbolizes male potency, and that the shadow is a pursuing conscience. The most obvious belief, the one Quentin deliberately acted upon in anticipation of his suicide, is the belief that stepping on the shadow causes death. Louise Dauner noted the applicability of both Rank's and Jung's explanations of the symbolism of the shadow. In Rank, the shadow is the first stage in the development of the concept of the double. The shadow as the double, an evil anti-self, is suggested by Quentin's attempts to trick, trample, or destroy his shadow and finally to punish it by suicide. John Irwin applied this Freudian concept to Quentin: "the bright self, the ego controlled by the superego," was punishing "the dark self, the ego shadowed by the unconscious." Quentin's memories, Irwin observed, had emphasized "Quentin's failure as both brother avenger and brother seducer in relation to his sister Candace—failures which his drowning of himself is meant to redeem." Quentin's shadow self, the dark seducer in *Absalom, Absalom!,* was Charles Bon, whose role was linked with his Negro blood. Mary Fletcher regarded Quentin's attitude toward his shadow as evidence of his "Calvinistic sensibility" in secular manifestations.

The Jungian concept of the shadow as the negative ego, the dark side of the psyche, also explains the significance of Caddy as the anima, a false anima because she is his sister and he lacked a true anima provided by a positive relationship with a girl other than Caddy. A climactic scene in Quentin's memory of Caddy, one of the few obviously Gothic scenes of potential violence in *The Sound and the Fury,* dramatizes Quentin's failures: Quentin held a knife at Caddy's throat in what seemed to be a mutual death pact—"I can do mine then" (p. 189). This episode Irwin stressed as revealing Quentin's sense of his psychological impotence, his failure as brother seducer, as the Dalton Ames episode revealed his failure as brother avenger. The knife in the scene with Caddy and the pistol in the Ames episode are both phallic symbols, the knife also symbolizing "the threat of castration—the traditional punishment for incest." When Quentin dropped the knife and when he rejected the pistol, he shifted back from a masculine to a feminine role.

Other scenes of sexuality and sexually motivated conflict have Gothic qualities. Quentin's memory of his attempt to fight Dalton Ames fused dreamlike with his actual fight with Gerald Bland. The recurrent scene of the swing and the cedars, observed by Benjy with no sense of the time lapse between Caddy's and Miss Quentin's occupancy, was referred to by Quentin in trying to make her believe that his incestuous desires were physical fact: *"You thought it was them but it was me"* (p. 185).

This passage and many others in Quentin's memories were permeated by the sight and scent of honeysuckle as a symbol of sexuality, as the wistaria was a symbol to Miss Rosa Coldfield of romantic love and withered maidenhood. Other objective details in the Gothic tradition appear in both novels. Clytie's "bunch of enormous old-fashioned iron keys" (*Absalom, Absalom!* p. 368) and Mrs. Compson's "huge bunch of rusted keys on an iron ring like a mediaeval jailer's" (p. 351) are truly Gothic symbols of secrecy and imprisonment; neither keeper of the keys was guardian of family treasure, as were the original chatelaines; both were subjected to physical force before they gave up the keys. Judith's dress for the wedding that never took place and Caddy's dress for the wedding that never should have taken place recall the Gothic tradition of forbidden or forced or disastrous marriages. Caddy's satin slipper, a comforting fetish for Benjy, recalls one of the most Gothic figures in literature, Miss Havisham in *Great Expectations,* holding the wedding slipper that was never worn and wearing the wedding dress that, like Judith's, was never worn for a wedding. The tombstones in *Absalom, Absalom!* have their parallel in the funerals and the cemetery passages in *The Sound and the Fury.* The flight of Miss Quentin is like that of Rosa's aunt: both climbed out of a window one night, to escape from a loveless puritanic household.

Clocks are a common symbolic object in Gothic fiction: clocks and watches figure prominently in *The Sound and the Fury* to symbolize respectively Quentin's attempt to stop time, Jason's attempt to cash in on time, and the time which is out of joint in the Compson household and can be set right only by Dilsey. When the one-handed clock strikes five times, Dilsey knows that it is eight o'clock and uses her two hands to prepare breakfast. Although in Jason's section there is no subjective use of symbolism comparable with that which reflects Benjy and Quentin, there is ample use of documents, comparable to the letters in *Absalom, Absalom!* and to Quentin's suicide notes: Jason's avarice and hard-hearted revenge spawn a succession of letters, checks, and telegrams. The passes to the show Jason sadistically burned in front of the covetous Luster. Jason's "voyages" in his car, in pursuit of Miss Quentin, caused physical distress from the smell of gasoline and the mental torment of being outwitted by his niece. His second pursuit, after Miss Quentin fled with his treasure, provided one scene of physical violence: the "fatal, furious little old man" attacked Jason with a hatchet for calling him a liar, as Wash attacked Sutpen with a scythe for denying him human dignity. The ironic parallel between Jason and Sutpen is thus underlined in the contrast between Sutpen's violent end and Jason's miserable survival, to vent his frustration by striking Luster for turning the wrong way at the monument.

Each novel ends with the image of the grotesque idiot, an innocent victim: Jim Bond of loveless design, Benjy of loveless disorder. The innocent Benjy held a broken narcissus, symbol of the narcissism also of Quentin and Jason. Both families had come to an end, but Jason would continue his sterile life after his mother and Benjy were dead. Benjy's absurd quest for the lost Caddy exemplifies what James Miller, in *Quests Surd and Absurd,* termed "a descent into the vortex of time," the "basic technique" by which Faulkner explored "his major theme of absurdity." In contrasting rationality with absurdity in *The Sound and the Fury,* William Barrett used "surd," a quantity not expressed in rational numbers, to designate the heart of reality which cannot be reduced to abstraction and rational statement. The convergence of the Gothic and the literature of the absurd is thus anticipated in Faulkner's first major novel of Yoknapatawpha, in which the Gothicism is understated and the absurdity is inescapable.

The image of the idiot who represents the fate of a loveless family (like the images of the boy at the door in *Absalom, Absalom!*) illustrates the point Taylor Stoehr made about the novels of Dickens, a chief influence on Faulkner: Faulkner, like Dickens, is often "a dream novelist, who achieves his tensions between the apparent and the hidden, the dual meaning of events. . . . The essence of the dream symbol is its ability to express many things at once, to combine and condense these in a single image." The extraordinary complexity of thematic structure and richness of symbolic meaning which Faulkner achieved in *The Sound and the Fury* and *Absalom, Absalom!* are only suggested by this analysis of Gothic elements. Other approaches yield their own illuminating insights, but recognition of all the patterns of structure and symbolism and action is requisite for full appreciation of the degree to which Faulkner made original use of a multitude of traditional elements.

CHAPTER FOUR

SARTORIS

THE HAUNTED HERO, OR,
COME, SWEET DEATH

As the Gothic tradition in *The Sound and the Fury* is more clearly apparent when that novel is considered in relation to *Absalom, Absalom!* so the Gothic strain in *Sartoris* (1929) (a shortened version of *Flags in the Dust* [1973]), and *The Unvanquished* (1938) is apparent when one considers them as leading up to the last of the Sartoris sequence of novels in time of action, *Sanctuary* (1931), which is obviously and appallingly Gothic. By the time Faulkner wrote *Absalom, Absalom!* he was continuing the use of elements which he began, full scale, in *Sanctuary*.

The central story in *Sartoris* concerns young Bayard, an excellent example of the type of hero, the "rebel without cause," who is characteristic of novels by Faulkner's successors dealing with themes identified by Ihab Hassan in *Radical Innocence:* "victimization, rebellion, and alienation," implicit "in the relentless dialectic of innocence and guilt which informs the process of initiation in America." In *Flags in the Dust* the role of young Bayard as the hero is balanced by that of Horace Benbow, subjectively presented at great length; in contrast to these two heroes, Byron Snopes is fully developed as an antihero, a case history in abnormal sexual obsession and frustration. Young Bayard and Horace are Lost Generation heroes, sharing the traumatic experience of World War I in service abroad, Bayard as an aviator and Horace in the YMCA. By his social class and his lack of shared wartime experience, Byron is excluded from the Lost Generation in Yoknapatawpha. The story of young Bayard is combined with the Sartoris legend as recounted by old man Falls and remembered by old Bayard, the hero's grandfather, and as deflated by the caustic comments of Aunt Jenny on the folly of Sartoris men. Thus, the Gothic elements in both past and present Sartoris exploits are not merely understated or diminished by sunny reality in daily life, spiced with humor and touched with mild nostalgia, but are also undercut by a tone of tart commonsense and by comic minor episodes. Gothic elements in *Sartoris* involve chiefly the story of young Bayard and his wife Narcissa, and her brother Horace Benbow, both of whom reappear in *Sanctuary*. In *Flags in the Dust* the Gothic aspects of the character of Horace are more fully represented, and the Gothic abnormalities of Byron Snopes, suggested in *Sartoris*, are copiously explicit. As the dreamy, idealistic, and poetic Romantic hero, Horace is much more clearly a foil for Bayard in *Flags in the Dust* than in *Sartoris*. From his first appearance, at the end of part 1, young Bayard's recurrent nightmares and his obsessive memories of his dead twin brother mark him as a haunted Gothic hero.

The characteristic Gothic settings are described more completely and with more variety than the narrative methods of *Absalom, Absalom!* or *The Sound and the Fury* permitted: the Sartoris plantation offers an obvious parallel to Sutpen's Hundred and the Compson Domain, but when it is first depicted, as old Bayard saw it when he drove home on a spring afternoon, the house is not in ruins but resembles the stately mansions of Gothic romance. It houses no dark secret, except the inner secret of young Bayard after his return. But Sartoris is haunted by memories of past life and gaiety, symbolized by the dust-cover "shrouds" on the furniture in the little-used parlor, with its "atmosphere of solemn and macabre fustiness" (p. 60), and by the ghost of Colonel John Sartoris, with whom old Simon converses and old Bayard communes. The feeling of the ghost's presence is sufficiently pervasive to create the authentic Gothic effect, particularly as the dead colonel seems to have more vitality than his living son Bayard. Frank H. Thomas regarded "that pervasive ghostly presence, John Sartoris," as epitomizing "the old order." Charles Gregory considered Colonel John to be a vital character in *Sartoris*, a view supported by the fact that each of the five parts of *Sartoris* deals in some way with him. In parts 1, 2, and 3 he is a living legend in the memories of old Bayard, old man Falls, and Simon. In parts 4 and 5 he is represented in effigy: his monument looms over the scene of old Bayard's death in part 4, and in part 5 dominates the graves of old Bayard and young Bayard. In Aunt Jenny's mind the vital spirit of Colonel John became reduced to the cold symbol of pride (p. 374).

Sartoris is the "castle" most fully represented in Yoknapatawpha. Built to replace the house burned during the Civil War, it is seen as the center of a declining family life in different generations in "An Odor of Verbena" *(The Unvanquished)*, *Sartoris*, and *Sanctuary*. But it never became a Gothic ruin like Sutpen's Hundred, or a shabby survival like the Compson house. Old Bayard's view of Sartoris in its idyllic spring glory, Aunt Jenny's flower growing, and young Bayard's period of plantation activity and hunting provide contrast with the violence of young Bayard and the fretful passivity of old Bayard. But a pervasive melancholy that invests the house, as the dust covers shroud the furniture, is as much a part of Gothic tradition as is Gothic terror.

The countryside represents nature in its mild, bucolic aspects, and evokes a romantic feeling for the land and its people. In contrast to the quiet country setting, young Bayard's restlessness and craving for speed provided a series of violent episodes: when Bayard terrified old Simon; when he went on a drinking spree with Suratt, after riding the stallion; when he crashed his car; and when he caused his grandfather's death in a narrow escape from a wreck. A romantic interlude is added by the trip to Oxford on a moonlight night to serenade the university girls.

Most of Bayard's violence occurred in spring and summer settings which provided an ironic contrast with his mood and actions. The harvest scenes and the possum hunt, however, showed Bayard most fully in harmony with nature. Only the wintry landscape and the cold when he fled to the MacCallum farm after his grandfather's death offered a final direct parallel between Bayard's mood of bleak despair and the scene of his actions. More than either *Absalom, Absalom!* or *The Sound and the Fury*, *Sartoris* shows Gothic delight in external nature, transplanted to realistic American scenes in Faulkner's own domain and presented chiefly from an omniscient point of view. The scene with V. K. Suratt marked the beginning of Faulkner's realistic use of his native setting. Roger Davis interpreted the scene as an abortive attempt of Suratt to initiate Bayard into folk rituals which would provide an alternative to the Sartoris tradition of courting danger and death. Bayard never returned to Suratt's "small bowl of peacefulness remote from the world and time" (p. 139). Edward Corridori identified the theme of the story of young Bayard as that of man's alienation, of his lack of orientation in the cosmos through an intimate connection with sacred space. Each of Bayard's flights from the natural rhythm of the earth which might have saved him increased his alienation, until he finally fled from the earth itself. But in his despair he traversed the world of Yoknapatawpha which has the quality of sacred space.

The spaciousness of the countryside and the rhythm of the seasons throughout a single year provide contrast both with Bayard's reckless violence and with the "other rooms," the scenes of imprisonment, entrapment, or refuge. Obsessed with the memory of his twin brother John's death in a flaming plane, Bayard returned home to the room "which he and John had shared in the young masculine violence of their twinship" (p. 47). In the same room he relived in nightmares his brother's death. One such nightmare occurred when he lay imprisoned in a "damn cast-iron strait-jacket" (p. 244), after wrecking his auto. On waking he appalled and fascinated Narcissa with his brutal story of John's death. Before Bayard was free again, she had captured him. Earlier Bayard had spent a night in jail, for safe keeping until he could be sent home: for the vision of a bleak and barren world which then lay before him, he had one word—"Hell" (p. 160). After causing his grandfather's death, Bayard fled from home and took refuge with the MacCallums. At night, as he lay beside Buddy in the dark and cold, he remembered John's death again and wondered if this was Hell, if he was doomed to seek his brother forever and never find him. This is the converse of Quentin's image of Hell, burning forever with Caddy in a clean flame; both concepts reveal incestuous, narcissistic feeling to the exclusion of other emotional ties, but that of eternal separation is the more terrible, the more like a real nightmare. Both flame and ice images appear in Dante's *Inferno*. Bayard's last refuge, before the news of old Bayard's death could reach the MacCallums, was the cabin of Negroes who shared with him their meager Christmas cheer. But from his first night at home Bayard's incestuous, narcissistic love for John had cut him off from salvation by family, friends, or strangers: as he lay thinking of John, the "spirit of their violent complementing days lay like dust everywhere in the room," obliterating even the memory of his dead first wife (p. 48). The ultimate climax was "uncanny" in Freud's sense of the compulsion of doubles to repeat character traits and actions: Bayard's last flight, this time a literal one, brought him to a death much like his brother's, in a plane which was the final "other room."

As in *The Sound and the Fury, Sartoris* all but ends in the cemetery. Aunt Jenny reflected on the Sartorises and the "pagan symbols of their vainglory" (p. 376) epitomized in the effigy of Colonel John Sartoris, like the monument, the reader may reflect, to Thomas Sutpen in the Sutpen cemetery. The tone of nostalgia for a glorious past which often echoes in Gothic medievalism is heard in the well-known passage about the "glamorous fatality" in the sound of Sartoris, "like silver pennons downrushing at sunset, or a dying fall of horns along the road to Roncevaux." But Aunt Jenny's remarks just before and just after that passage should be remembered. Referring to Bayard's infant son, she said: "Do you think ... you can change one of 'em with a name?" "Do you think ... that because his name is Benbow, he'll be any less a Sartoris and a scoundrel and a fool?" (p. 380). Aunt Jenny's youthful tale of the Carolina Bayard's "hare-brained prank" which, with the tales of Colonel John's exploits and the example of young John, provided the pattern followed by young Bayard to his death, was counteracted in her old age by her scathing comments on Sartoris heroics. Thus *Sartoris* undercuts the romanticism of the Sartoris legend and the necrophiliac somberness of the Gothic, as represented by the Compson scenes in the same cemetery. Aunt Jenny not only fails to fit into the traditional Gothic character types but by her presence diminishes the Gothic effect.

But young Bayard is a perfect Gothic hero: the Romantic rebel, proud and reckless, doomed and damned. Joseph Blotner related that in 1918 "the legendary Chevalier de Bayard" was an ideal for Faulkner and quoted Malcolm Cowley as saying that "death became a romantic dream" for writers of his and Faulkner's generation. To Bayard's romantic characteristics are added another cluster even more distinctly Gothic: in his devotion to his dead twin brother, Bayard is narcissistic, homosexually incestuous, and necrophiliac. Furthermore, the twins were doubles in the most literal sense: Bayard felt incomplete without John, who had all the warmth and loving nature and cheerfulness for both. Although John and Bayard suggest what Eino Railo, discussing Doppelgängers, called "the cleavage of the ego into two separate entities," their cleavage was emotional and temperamental, not that of good-evil duality. The suggestion of homosexuality in *Sartoris* is reinforced by the male household of the MacCallums. The MacCallums, as Albert Devlin remarked, showed much "of the same perversion and frustration usually associated with the wasteland," and displayed specific psychological abnormalities. This family had no intention of introducing heterosexuality into their midst, after the mother had fulfilled her necessary function, except as "Buddy would marry and perpetuate the name" (p. 334).

John Irwin noted that the Sartoris twins, John and Bayard, succeeded the previous Bayard and John, brothers but not twins, of the Civil War period: doubles are redoubled in *Sartoris* as later in the Compson and Sutpen novels. Irwin stated the significance of the cluster of themes represented by the Sartorises (and the MacCallums): "For Faulkner, doubling and incest are both images of the self-enclosed—the inability of the ego to break out of the circle of the self and of the individual to break out of the ring of the family—and as such, both appear in his novels as symbols of the state of the South after the Civil War...." The Sartoris twins and no doubt the MacCallum twins illustrate Otto Rank's comments on doubles, twins, and narcissism: "The homosexual object was originally chosen with a narcissistic attitude toward one's own image." The double was often a brother, usually a twin. Narcissism, with its choice of a love object in its own image, usually involved abnormal sex life.

Predictably, Bayard's marriage failed to cure his psychic wound, the combination of grief and horror and guilt for whatever his responsibility might have been in John's death, or to rid him of his ambivalent feelings toward John, whom he strove to equal and perhaps had envied. In his death Bayard became Luciferian, as John and "all the dead pilots" had been: "young men like fallen angels, and of a meteoric violence like that of fallen angels, beyond heaven or hell and partaking of both: doomed immortality and immortal doom" (p. 126). Thus, in "talking of the war" Bayard was prefiguring his own death, with an image in the Byronic-Gothic tradition. Frank Thomas referred to Bayard as "the ghost of his dead brother" and to his war experiences as "the other haunting phantasms."

The Romantic hero Horace Benbow had no nightmares but dreamed of moon and starry skies and unicorns. Horace was poetic and idealistic but passive and indolent. In *Flags in the Dust* the first long description of Horace (chapter 3, p. 2) contains details of his education which do not reappear in Yoknapatawpha chronicles. As a Rhodes scholar at Oxford, "his life was a golden and purposeless dream" (p. 163). The accounts of Horace's attitude and his law practice are relevant to *Sanctuary*, where he is the leading male character. After his father's death Horace chose a life like "a topless cage": "Its direction was always upward plummeting, for a plummeting fall" (p. 162). The law practice he inherited from his father "consisted of polite interminable litigation that progressed decorously and pleasantly from conference to conference . . . without threat of consummation or of advantage or detriment to anyone involved" (p. 165). His actions and desires were like two evenly matched steeds drawing a chariot, and "the I in him" stood "above the sere and ludicrous disasters of his days" (p. 166).

Horace's relationships with women are built up in *Flags in the Dust* much more than in *Sartoris*. He flirted poetically, in pastoral mood, with the uncomprehending girl Frankie at the tennis game and was the flower-bearing courtier to Little Belle at her recital. Obviously, Horace was no prototype of Humbert Humbert in *Lolita*, but his thoughts about his sister Narcissa and Belle Mitchell, and his adolescent fear of the road ahead when he must choose between Narcissa's "still unravished quietness" and "the tiger-reek" of "Belle's rich discontent" (p. 190), introduce the elaboration of his incestuous feeling for Narcissa and his adulterous relationship with Belle, the Gothic sexual perversion and transgression which survived in abridged form in *Sartoris*. In *Flags in the Dust* Horace discussed Belle's divorce with Narcissa and said bluntly that he had exchanged Narcissa for Belle, admitting his regret: "I'm happier now than I'll ever be again" (p. 289). An episode with Belle's sister Joan, who was eliminated with Faulkner's acquiescence, by Ben Wasson, is further evidence that Horace was highly responsive to women and easily manipulated by them. Horace returned to Narcissa, after World War I, "like a swimmer into a tideless sea, into the serene constancy of her affection again" (*Sartoris*, p. 175). He yielded to the seductions of Belle, the thought of whom, "within that warm, not-yet-sleeping region where dwells the mother of dreams," enveloped him "like a rich and fatal drug, like a motionless and cloying sea in which he watched himself drown" (*Sartoris*, p. 257). Horace's account in *Sanctuary* of his married life in Kinston and his chore of fetching shrimp from the railroad station is based on a passage in *Flags in the Dust* (pp. 342–347), omitted in *Sartoris*, which prepares for his flight from Belle before the beginning of *Sanctuary*.

The excised passages in *Flags in the Dust* dealing with Horace display in style the same romantic lushness as do those retained in *Sartoris;* Faulkner's first version, therefore, exhibited even more notably than the second some of the extravagance of the nineteenth-century Gothic style and the Romantic fin de siècle decadence, in a context which does not as in *Absalom, Absalom!* evoke that tone and which is not limited to subjective characterization.

Belle, obviously the Evil Woman, has a double in *Flags in the Dust,* her sister Joan, "a lady tiger in a tea gown" (p. 292) to match Belle's "tiger-reek" (p. 190). Belle's seductive actions are simple and direct, and her victim, Horace, is a willing one. Narcissa, with her pure white clothes and serene air, seems the virtuous heroine. That she is, to the contrary, an ironic inversion of the virtuous heroine is implied in *Flags in the Dust* and *Sartoris* and demonstrated by her actions in *Sanctuary.* Horace's idealization of Narcissa, based on southern gyneolatry, encouraged her in cultivating a self-image based on the southern ideal and in playing the consequent role for Horace and the community. Her name betrays her worship of that self-image. The fuller account of Narcissa in *Flags in the Dust* adds to the version in *Sartoris* chiefly her thoughts about and reactions to men, to parallel the account of Horace and women. Her memories of John and Bayard Sartoris make explicit her "shrinking, fascinated distaste, that blending of curiosity and dread, as if a raw wind had blown into that garden wherein she dwelt" (p. 65). She remembered chiefly their violence, Bayard's "a cold, arrogant sort of leashed violence" and John's "a warmer thing, spontaneous and merry and wild" (p. 64). Narcissa's reactions to Bayard's escapades are given more fully in *Flags in the Dust.* On Horace's return from France Narcissa felt that the current of her maternalism was "undammed again" (*Flags in the Dust*, p. 160). Narcissa's dominant traits of narcissism and placidity are combined in the image of Bayard to her after Horace returned: "He was now no more than the shadow of a hawk's flight mirrored fleetingly by the windless surface of a pool, and gone; where, the pool knew and cared not, leaving no stain" (p. 160).

That Narcissa's visits to Sartoris were strategies whereby she could take the initiative when Bayard seemed unlikely to do so was presented as fact by Elnora, in "There Was a Queen," and Aunt Jenny remembered being deceived when Narcissa was engaged to Bayard all the time. Thus, in another respect Narcissa is an ironic inversion of the Romantic heroine, using dissimulation to conceal her desires and intentions. Byron Snopes's secret adoration of Narcissa may be a grotesque parallel of Narcissa's secret interest in John and then in Bayard.

The absence of autocratic elders and the lack of parents in the Sartoris family are notable. Despite her sharp tongue Aunt Jenny had no real control over either Bayard, and old Bayard had no control over his grandson. The family is less matriarchal than it was in *The Unvanquished* (1938), when Granny Millard was alive. The Sartorises lacked control even over their servants, except such as was exerted by a chunk of stove wood heaved at the impertinent Caspey. As Frank Thomas pointed out, Caspey was suffering postwar dislocation, as Bayard was; neither showed capacity for independence or inclination to engage in useful occupation. Thomas observed that the Lost Generation theme applied to both races and that Faulkner used black and white stock characters as a fictional technique because "stereotypes help produce mood and atmosphere." Bayard and Simon, for example, play "the time-honored games of the old-master-and-his-nigger," in unconscious parody of the "dying system" which they represent. Simon and Isom are not only fairly typical comic Negroes but also humorous parodies of the traditional Gothic servants.

Grotesques are present in *Sartoris* but are not especially notable. At the MacCallum farm Bayard saw a grotesque litter of pups, half hound and half fox, "monstrous and contradictory and obscene" (p. 327). One wonders whether there might be some irony in old MacCallum's amusement at the embarrassment of the sire of the pups, having "to look around on a passel of chaps like them and say . . . 'Them's my boys.' . . ." Certainly the juxtaposition of the grotesquely fat Doc Peabody and the grotesquely mechanical Dr. Alford heightens the grotesque effect. Byron Snopes, whose name better fits his romantic obsession than does his appearance, has the grotesque animal-like quality typical of the Snopes tribe. Byron's activities as a voyeur add to the sexual perversions. A recurrent grotesque spectacle in *Flags in the Dust* is provided by Byron, "wrapped in his mad unsleeping dream," pursued by his relentless blackmailing "double," Virgil Beard, who repeatedly ran Byron to earth and hounded him into flight (pp. 217, 218). Simon, the old man in love with the young Meloney and spending on her money entrusted to him by his church, is a parody of old Bayard, "putting out" money entrusted to him as a banker. From being a comic grotesque Simon became a pathetic victim of a *crime passionel.*

The themes center in the Sartoris tradition in particular and the southern myth in general: the twins reenacted the Sartoris legend of reckless violence; old Bayard retreated from reality and lived in memories of the old order. To Charles Gregory, such "pursuit of the past" to escape the present was part of the "darkness to appall." A better example than Quentin Compson of that kind of escape, old Bayard was sustained by it through a long life of inactivity. The episodes in Bayard's youth, which Faulkner later wrote as separate short stories and published finally as *The Unvanquished,* introduce scenes of Gothic violence. The most Gothic of these, lacking in *Sartoris* some of the incongruous details of the later version, is the murder of the Burdens, carpetbaggers. As told in "Skirmish at Sartoris," the shooting occurred on Colonel John Sartoris's wedding day; Drusilla, the reluctant bride, in her loathed and incongruous wedding gown and veil, after the murder acted as substitute voting commissioner at the interrupted election. The most Gothic of the tales in *The Unvanquished* Bayard did not recall in *Sartoris,* and old Falls would have no knowledge of them in their inwardness and true significance: the two stories of Bayard's initiation, his pursuit and killing of his grandmother's murderer in "Vendée" and his refusal, as a man, to avenge his father's murder in the same way, in "An Odor of Verbena." This last story marked Bayard's growth to maturity, his making his own decisions and as a man refusing to follow the tradition of blood revenge. Only Aunt Jenny approved of his moral scruples and untraditional behavior. But, as William Ramsey pointed out, Bayard was content with a personal crisis and solution in a society which needed "a new moral and ethical dispensation to replace its code of honorable murder." He never prepared himself "practically or psychologically for an active life." Ramsey's method of analysis, based on patterns of coordinate structures, provides textual evidence to support an interpretation of Bayard in *The Unvanquished,* especially in "An Odor of Verbena," which is confirmed by the account of old Bayard as the elderly banker in *Sartoris* and which thus resolves what seemed an inconsistency in characterization.

The family relics old Bayard examined are Gothic objects, some of which recall the days of his youth: the Toledo blade, the rosewood case with the dueling pistols which, in "An Odor of Verbena," he refused to use; the derringer which his father used too often; the Confederate uniform;

the family Bible. Joseph Blotner showed that the Sartoris family had earlier been traced to "Hastings and Agincourt."

The family heirlooms symbolize the Sartoris traditional code and its feudal origins. Charles Gregory recognized the tenets of the code but not its relation to the Gothic literary tradition nurtured by the influence of Sir Walter Scott. The tenets of the code included: the emphasis on tradition; the purity and superiority of southern ladies; the inferiority of Negroes; the principle of noblesse oblige in dealing with inferiors; loyalty to family; vendetta and dueling as obligations demanded by honor; truth of trial-by-combat judgments; the superiority to the law of superior men. In Yoknapatawpha, the Sartoris men most fully reflect this code and the corruption of it which produced, as Gregory said, "the amorality and moral blankness in which the Snopeses flourish." Young Bayard's mementoes reflected his devotion to John, rather than to the family; after he was injured in his car-crash, he burned a hunting coat, a bear's paw and shotgun shell, and a New Testament, along with a picture of John's Princeton club. Most frequently and with most respect Faulkner referred to Aunt Jenny's contribution to the family treasures, the colored glass she carried to Mississippi from their Carolina home, symbol of her indomitable courage and her love of beauty.

As the central character, young Bayard gave the novel its prevailing pattern of flight, in widening gyres like those of Yeats's falcon, until he escaped from his Yoknapatawpha orbit and, in literal flight, fell like Icarus. One wonders whether "The Second Coming" contributed to Faulkner's imagery in the fate of young Bayard as well as that of Quentin, whose "ceremony of innocence" was drowned. The imagery of Bayard's flights is related to the Yoknapatawpha theme of motion as symbolized by transportation. Olga Vickery listed the images: "The untamed horse, the speeding car, the untested plane: each is a propitiatory ritual performed on the altar of the two John Sartorises." Bayard's "journey into the forest" was a journey to death. Bayard rejected direct suicide. In a notable addition in *Sartoris* to *Flags in the Dust*, Bayard found a gun at the MacCallums', remembered where the shells were, and then put the gun back in the corner (p. 322). But like Quentin, he rejected the initiation which could lead to rebirth. His last flight in Yoknapatawpha was a flight from responsibility, after he caused his grandfather's death. Bayard told himself: *"You, who deliberately do things your judgment tells you may not be successful, even possible, are afraid to face the consequences of your own acts."* At this moment Bayard showed the capacity for self-observation that Freud noted as making possible a new meaning for "the old idea of a 'double'": through a division "between the critical agency and the rest of the ego," narcissism may be surmounted by censorship and self-criticism. But having made this admission, Bayard lapsed into his usual attitude: "in vindication and justification and accusation" he blamed "whom, he did not know: *You did it! You caused it all; you killed Johnny*" (p. 311). Apparently, Bayard never again faced Aunt Jenny and Narcissa. His isolation was a self-imposed exile, not expulsion from the family and the community. Aunt Jenny's telegram telling him to come home to his wife and newborn son was sent after Bayard's death. Ihab Hassan's comment on Quentin Compson applies also to Bayard, in light of the tradition of pride and courage and his twinship which, unlike Quentin's incest, was a bond with a person, not an abstract idea of honor: "The proud self retreats from the world into incest and from incest further into solipsism. Pride without courage or humility, Faulkner never tires of showing, is the brightest way to perdition."

Mystery and suspense are slight. The mystery is psychological: Why did Bayard feel such a sense of guilt over John's death? Why did John provide Bayard's only means of participating in life? The suspense is simply that of waiting to see how Bayard will finally kill himself. The Byron Snopes subplot is made clearer in *Flags in the Dust*, in which both Byron's motives and his actions are given in detail.

The other pattern of action concerns Narcissa and Horace Benbow and is relevant to *Sanctuary*. Narcissa was engaged in a kind of quest, first, to create and preserve a self-image and family image which would satisfy her ideal of southern womanhood and respectability, and second, to get the husband she needed to attain her ends. Narcissa's ambivalence, simultaneously desiring peace and being attracted to violence, is made clearer in *Flags in the Dust*. She was too self-satisfied and stupid to experience a schizophrenic split: adherence to conventionality and preservation of her self-image enabled her to sacrifice peace to violence, especially since, if she continued to live peacefully with Horace, she would have to bear the stigma of being an old maid. Bayard, the most eligible male, strangely fascinated her, as a person and as a reminder of his other and brighter self, John. Marriage to the death-seeking Bayard was almost guaranteed to bring her the status she really wanted, that of the widowed mistress of Sartoris. The reflection image implied by her name and nature was made explicit when she gazed at her reflection in a mirror (p. 248). In the Byron subplot the Gothic device of letters serves as an unusual kind of revelation, not of parentage but of character: the fact that Narcissa kept Byron's obscene letters reveals what lay beneath her surface whiteness and purity. Her worry was that "the intactness of her deep and hitherto inviolate serenity might be the sport of circumstances" (p. 301).

When this fear was realized in "There Was a Queen," she bought back the letters, case aside or lost by Byron in his flight, from the FBI agent by spending a weekend with him, preferring private shame to merely embarrassing publicity. This fact about Narcissa's shallow ideal of respectability and her lack of genuine delicacy of feeling is relevant to her actions in *Sanctuary*.

Byron Snopes, an abnormal grotesque, is a parody of the Romantic hero, the courtly lover worshiping his unattainable ideal: he is crude, vulgar, and dishonest, but he is genuinely obsessed with a hopeless passion. The most surprising difference between *Flags in the Dust* and *Sartoris* is the former's complete account of Byron's pursuit of Narcissa by means of anonymous letters, parodied by Virgil Beard's pursuit of Byron as Byron's collaborator in the letters. Details of Byron's mechanical routine at the bank and his movements around the town provide the normal pattern from which he deviated more and more frantically outside the bank, in a kind of counterpoint between control and frenzy. With an assumed air of childish innocence, Virgil confronted Byron, lost in "his mad unsleeping dream" or waking from "dreams in which her [Narcissa's] image lived and moved and thwarted and mocked him" (p. 217). In this more fully developed account of Byron, the horror grows as his frustrated passion, inflamed by jealousy, drives him to madness. The split between his methodical performance of duties and his mental turmoil is apparent in the dissociation with which he gazed "on his idle hands on the desk before him as though they were not his hands" (p. 218). That turmoil reached a climax when he learned of Narcissa's imminent marriage to Bayard, "a man whom he had hated instinctively with all his sense of inferiority" (p. 249). In *Flags in the Dust* Byron's constant drooling is more clearly than in *Sartoris* related to his obscene mental images. In *Flags in the Dust* a detailed account of Byron's theft from the bank precedes the account of his intrusion into Narcissa's room, and his retrieving of his past letters, leaving a new one. He fled to Frenchman's Bend and Minnie Sue. When she left him, "babbling a name that was not hers," "he sat where she had left him for a long time, with his half-insane face between his knees and madness and helpless rage and thwarted desire coiling within him" (p. 260). Byron's quest is the most Gothic, with passion ending in madness and flight from justice. Although Byron's name is ironic, since, unlike Gothic heroes, he was neither chivalric nor Byronic, the full-scale portrait of Byron in *Flags in the Dust* shows him to be unique among Snopeses and even in Yoknapatawpha: he was capable of an idealistic and hopeless passion for which, un-Snopeslike, he gave up the pursuit of profit and respectability. In Byron the grotesque grows less ludicrous and more terrible.

Horace is another hero in quest of an ideal, but more close to the conventional Gothic type of the sentimental romantic hero. His incestuous attachment to Narcissa and his admiration for her serenity and purity helped to form her own self-image. Horace gave up peace with Narcissa to marry Belle, as she gave up peace, for a time, to marry Bayard. The symbol of Horace's idealism is blown glass: "Macabre and inviolate; purged and purified as bronze, yet fragile as soap bubbles" (pp. 171–72). When he succeeded in blowing an "almost perfect vase of clear amber, larger, more richly and chastely serene," he called it Narcissa and apostrophized them both as "'Thou still unravished bride of quietness'" (p. 182). Horace was an easy victim for Belle Mitchell, Narcissa's antithesis. His attitude toward Narcissa is essential to motivation and action in *Sanctuary*.

The ambiguity of tone—suggested by the element of parody in the characters of Horace, Narcissa, and Byron, as well as in Bayard as a hero, neither heroic nor pathetic—obscures the Gothic elements, which are much more obvious in *Flags in the Dust* with the extended characterization of both Benbows and Byron. The combination of the story of Bayard with that of the Sartoris family, which involves humorous subplots and centers in Aunt Jenny, further diminishes the Gothic effect. The strength of the chivalric tradition among the male Sartorises and the dying out of the family are directly in the old Gothic tradition, and the problems and actions of young Bayard place him in the new American Gothic. The contrasts in the cemetery scenes at the end epitomize the combination of diverse elements: the monuments to past Sartoris glory and the simple graves of old Bayard and young Bayard; the elegiac melancholy and Aunt Jenny's recognition of the "heritage of humorless and fustian vainglory" of the men she had loved with such exasperation; the graveyard scene itself, "the black cedars from amid which the doves crooned endlessly," overarched by "the blue dappled sky" of June. The understatement of the Gothic atmosphere is a deliberate comment on the family to which that atmosphere, evocative of past glory and defeat, would appeal.

Faulkner seemed already tired of the Sartorises and their code when he undercut and inverted the Gothicism that sympathetic treatment of young Bayard's story, as that of a tragic hero, would entail. It is significant that although Bayard's role in *Sartoris* is unchanged from *Flags in the Dust*, Faulkner originally diverted attention from Bayard by the extended treatment of the two other young men. But when Ben Wasson was cutting *Flags in the Dust* to a novel of acceptable length, Faulkner was too deeply immersed in his unique Gothic variations in *The Sound and the Fury* to aid Wasson. The "Player Himself" seemed "a little wearied" of the game of Sartoris, "a game outmoded and played with pawns shaped too late and to an old dead pattern" (p. 380).

CHAPTER FIVE

SANCTUARY

THE PERSECUTED MAIDEN, OR, VICE TRIUMPHANT

Sanctuary concludes both the story of the Sartoris family as active characters in Yoknapatawpha in the twentieth century and the story of Horace Benbow. (Narcissa and Aunt Jenny reappear in "There Was a Queen.") A Gothic theme is immediately suggested by the very title, *Sanctuary*, with its meaning of a refuge and an asylum: as Faulkner said at Nagano: "some safe secure place" to which a person can flee from trouble. In *The Achievement of William Faulkner*, Michael Millgate cited passages from *Measure for Measure* and Oscar Wilde's *Salome* as clues to the meaning of "sanctuary" and "temple." The meaning of "sanctuary" as a refuge for the criminal, as revealed in the end of Temple's story, is the clue to the ironic inversion which prevails throughout the novel, lending it another dimension as a bitter satire on society and social institutions. Dr. Lawrence Kubie noted the irony in the use of this title for "a tale in which there is no right of sanctuary, where neither impotence nor potency, neither the life of the defiant rebel nor that of the acquiescent conformist, where neither the free play of instinctual expression nor the life which is dominated by a restricting conscience, provides one with any escape from an ultimate state of doom and disaster." Not only does *Sanctuary* represent the conflict between good and evil, sharply contrasted by Gothic polarity of setting and characters, but it does so in a combination of the basic seduction story with the detective story which is one of the narrative patterns derived from the Gothic novel. The irony begins with this choice of the detective story pattern, which is much more obvious in the published version than in the unpublished galleys; "the detective story," as Northrop Frye said in *The Secular Scripture*, "operates, for the most part, in a deeply conservative social area, where the emphasis is on reintegrating the existing order," rather than, as in *Sanctuary*, on exposing the iniquities of such an order.

Except for Leslie Fiedler, in *Love and Death in the American Novel*, critics have tended to recognize as Gothic only the more violent and macabre scenes in *Sanctuary*, rather than the entire pattern of inversions and the consequent force of the contrast they provide between idealism and reality. The nightmare quality in *Sanctuary*, one of the most obvious aspects of the Gothic, has been recognized and analyzed, without identifying the tradition to which the literature of nightmare belongs. Without recognizing Gothicism in general or other Gothic elements in *Sanctuary*, William Rossky stated precisely the basic nightmare effect of Gothic fiction: "Terror emanates . . . perhaps principally—from the dark vision of an irrational, nightmarish universe." Much of the reader's reaction is produced by "a technique of nightmare": "Repeatedly the narrative evokes moments of dreamlike horror typical especially of a certain kind of nightmare. The dreamer is caught in impotent terror, paralyzed, deeply frightened, trying, yet unable, to act or to scream." Rossky's description of the whole experience of *Sanctuary* is succinct and memorable: "a kind of long soundless scream." One is reminded of Edvard Munch's painting, "The Scream," which Giliane Morell cited as the visual image equivalent to Benjy's silent cries of helplessness.

Too many critics who apply "Gothic" to *Sanctuary* or any other modern American novel are unaware that Gothic has always been, as Frederick Garber explained, "an amalgam . . . which is in part a collective of other modes" and that "it is through this quality as a collective that the Gothic reaches out to fulfill its own radical form and statement." Mario Materassi saw *Sanctuary* as made up of three structures: the Gothic novel, in a modern world of delinquency and paranoia; the tall tale, in a bourgeois milieu; the tale of the antihero of the twentieth century, unable to cope with reality. The three structures are really a Gothic amalgam. Dealing with *Sanctuary* as a Gothic novel of horror, Douglas Perry analyzed it as representing the new American Gothic, defined by Irving Malin, with its "interaction of theme, image, and structure"; its themes of flight and confinement are "two sides of a coin," and narcissism is a third theme. Perry dealt also with three structural principles: *concentricity, predetermined sequence,* and *character repetition.* He explained that Faulkner, Capote, and Styron used the Gothic form "to capture the irony of our twentieth-century existence: the conviction that the search for self-awareness may not only be fatal, but fruitless, because it is equivalent to self-negation; that selfhood is an arbitrary construct of man's self-protective ignorance; that self-awareness and self-destruction are one and the same. . . ." Perry, in "Gothic as Vortex," did not relate "vortex" to "vorticism," which Donald Tritschler dealt with in "Whorls of Form in Faulkner's Fiction."

To the amalgam in *Sanctuary,* Pat Esslinger adds the influence of American comic strips and concludes: "Faulkner has indeed told an absorbing horror tale of prohibition days against the Gothic tapestry of his South, but he has also managed to embroider a magnificently grotesque thread of comic strip humor throughout his design." Joseph Blotner's account of the composition of *Sanctuary* indicates that Faulkner's character and the name "Popeye" were based on Popeye Pumphrey of Memphis and antedated the comic strip. But by the time Faulkner was writing *Sanctuary,* according to Thomas McHaney, the comic strip was new and may have influenced Faulkner's parodic development of Popeye. Esslinger points out that Horace and Popeye are doubles from the moment that their images are reflected in the pool: both are impotent, both lust after a girl to whom they bear a semipaternal relationship, and both meet their fate with resignation, defeat for Horace and death for Popeye. But unlike Faulkner's Popeye, Horace, like Popeye the Sailor Man, put a corncob to the innocent use of pipe-smoking.

More than any other novel by Faulkner *Sanctuary* structurally emphasizes the "castles" and the "other rooms"; but the novel begins with an idyllic natural setting that ironically serves to stress the polarity of characters and places. The confrontation of Horace Benbow and Popeye at the spring, in which their images are reflected, anticipates their opposition as hero and villain in the detective story plot, and differentiates natural and unnatural man, Horace at ease in this sylvan setting and Popeye terrified by a bird in flight. In picturing Popeye Faulkner carried to an extreme Charles Dickens's device of dehumanizing description which turns people into things. Traditionally, the good guy, the detective, should win, and the bad guy, the criminal, should lose in the conflict between them, and the success of the detective should represent a reassuring triumph of justice. The action of *Sanctuary* takes place in spring and summer, and the outdoor scenes in Temple's story are chiefly sunny. The most extensive and ironic use of natural setting occurs in the trip of Popeye and Temple to Memphis: the "unbelievable soft radiance of May" in that "lavender spring" (p. 133) not only is the background of the violated Temple's flight with her grotesque captor but also suggests that the action is both a modern abduction of Persephone by Pluto and an inversion of fertility rites. In both T. S. Eliot's *The Waste Land* and Sir James G. Frazer's *The Golden Bough* Thomas McHaney found parallels to scenes, plot, and characters in *Sanctuary.*

The lack of fertility is apparent in the first view of the "haunted castle": "The house was a gutted ruin rising gaunt and stark out of a grove of unpruned cedar trees" (p. 7). On the sunny afternoon when Temple and Gowan first saw it, "nowhere was any sign of husbandry—plow or tool; in no direction was a planted field in sight" (p. 40). Edward Corridori remarked on the fashion in which, in a "realistic presentation of a locale," the description may "tend toward the irrational or unreal, or, perhaps, even the surreal," terms which fit the ruined mansion and its motley crew of inmates.

In its origin the Old Frenchman place is comparable with Sutpen's Hundred or the Sartoris plantation: it was founded by Louis Grenier, who "was granted the first big land patent" and "brought the first slaves into the country" (*Requiem for a Nun*, p. 7). The house appears in Yoknapatawpha fiction only as a ruin, never in either splendor or mere shabbiness. It is not only a ruin but also the scene of evil, formerly the scene of treasure hunts by those greedy for gold and now the hangout of bootleggers and gangsters. Warren Beck referred in *Faulkner* to "the Gothic and sordid *ménage* at Frenchman's Bend," and described *Sanctuary* as one of Faulkner's "most authentically regional novels." Jean Mayoux described Frenchman's Bend as sinister and mysterious, with "an atmosphere of incoherent sorcery, of alcoholic delirium." It represents a sanctuary for lawless invaders of the county, as Sartoris, home of established aristocrats, represents a sanctuary for a homecoming native son: the two houses continue the polarity established at the spring. The technique is Dickensian, resembling the use of locales in *Bleak House,* as William Axton observed, to "discriminate between the moral qualities associated with two circles of characters," the qualities of "transience and disorder" and "permanence and order." In *Sartoris,* however, permanence and order depend on Aunt Jenny, ninety years old and confined to a wheelchair. The shift of scene to the city, Memphis, continues the polarity of setting and adds another kind of Gothic scene outside of Yoknapatawpha County. Not only did Dickens use the city as the Gothic milieu of his most evil characters and darkest deeds, but to the writers of the Romantic decadence, George Gibian reported, the city was "attractive and evil; . . . beautiful and grotesque." The completely un-Dickensian defeat of virtue in *Sanctuary* is the more impressive when the similarity to Dickensian Gothic techniques is noted.

The third mansion, Miss Reba's in Memphis, Dickens would not have dared to introduce into his novels, read aloud in the family circle, but it belongs to the Gothic tradition, brothels being not uncommon scenes. The appearance of respectability which Miss Reba maintains in her "sanctuary" is less ironic than that which Narcissa Benbow Sartoris preserved at the cost of an innocent man's life. Obviously, a brothel is a place of entrapment or imprisonment, prominent among the scenes of enclosure in *Sanctuary*. These scenes contribute, William Rossky said, to "the sense of cold paralysis, entrapment and terror which permeates *Sanctuary* and becomes a feeling about existence itself." The use of the three houses—the Old Frenchman place, Sartoris, and Miss Reba's—with Horace as the connecting character, offers a parallel to Dickens's *Great Expectations,* in which "literal landmarks," as Taylor Stoehr observed, are "landmarks of structure" as in dreams, and "place has an organizing function beyond that of mere background."

In these houses and other buildings scenes of enclosure or imprisonment are used with maximum frequency and effectiveness. In the Old Frenchman place there is a climactic succession in Temple's search for sanctuary, from the kitchen where she was safe with Ruby, to the room where she spent the night, physically unharmed, to the barn, and finally to the crib, a suitably ambiguous term. The facts that Miss Reba's is a crib in one sense and that the Grotto, the nightclub in Memphis, suggests ancient nativity scenes in a grotto establish a manger-crib association which seems further evidence of the ironic intention. Temple's room in Miss Reba's is both the scene of her imprisonment and of Popeye's voyeurism, and the scene of her confrontation with Horace, thus serving in both the seduction and the detection plots. Horace's room at Sartoris is the scene of a parallel confrontation with Narcissa which leads to her visit to the district attorney and the consequent defeat of Horace. Temple's successive refuges are paralleled, as Olga Vickery observed, by the successive scenes of literal sanctuary for Ruby—Horace's house, the hotel, the shack of the crazy woman, and the jail—but, unlike Temple, Ruby cannot save herself by flight and suffers increasing deprivation in trying to save Lee. The jail, the most obvious scene of imprisonment, ironically is a sanctuary more fully than the other refuges: Lee Goodwin was safe from Popeye when he was in jail. After the first day of the trial, Horace and Ruby shared the cell with Lee. The courtroom, the last scene of enclosure, shares with jails and prisons a long history in the Gothic novel. Devendra Varma credited Anne Radcliffe with the first use of a courtroom in a Gothic novel. In *The Secular Scripture,* Northrop Frye traced courtroom scenes to romance, in which an unjust trial was common near the end. The unjust trial in *Sanctuary* introduced the court scenes which became recurrent in Faulkner's fiction. After the trial, Lee was violently taken from the sanctuary of the jail and was lynched. Both outdoor and interior scenes in *Sanctuary* are used dramatically for contrasts between characters, for ironic contrasts between natural setting and action, and for a sense of imprisonment which may be literal with Lee and Ruby, or psychological with Temple.

Temple, a modern version of the Persecuted Maiden, most obviously represents Faulkner's inversion of characters who belong to familiar types. The strongly allegorical aspects of *Sanctuary* are suggested by some of the names. Leslie Fiedler noted in *Love and Death* that "'Temple Drake' evokes both a ruined sanctuary and the sense of an unnatural usurpation: woman become a sexual aggressor—more drake than duck." By her disobedience in going with Gowan and her refusal to leave the Old Frenchman place, Temple initiated and stimulated the events leading to her rape. The nightmare effect is so overwhelming that the reader may overlook her lack of serious effort to save herself, but her admission in *Requiem for a Nun* that she could have escaped at any time after Gowan wrecked the car confirms what the astute reader could detect through the inversion of the Gothic pattern in the character of Temple and the pattern of action. Mary D. Fletcher regarded Temple as illustrating an implicitly Calvinistic view of man as "a depraved creature who yearns not toward good but toward evil." Dr. Lawrence Kubie summed up Temple's behavior and the irony of the consequences:

It is the uttermost limits of sour irony that this impudent, tantalizing, and provocative young girl, who had played fast and loose with the men of her own world without ever giving them the gift she kept dangling in front of them, should escape the relatively honest erotic purposes of the healthy members of the band, only to taunt the impotent and tortured figure of Popeye into committing a criminal assault upon her by artificial means.

Temple is narcissistic; her compact and mirror provide repeated reflection images, most significantly when she carefully powders and preens before lying down with the expectation of being raped and before going to the Grotto with Popeye. Artificial to the point of being unnatural, with a masklike face, Temple illustrates Horace Benbow's analogy between the mirror, symbolizing Progress, and the grape-arbor, symbolizing Nature: Temple and Little Belle show the same kind of dissimulation and absorption in self. That they are doubles is revealed explicitly in Horace's nauseating vision of them merged in a surrealistic image suggesting the heroine of melodrama or early motion pictures, tied to a railroad track.

In appearance Temple is the Flapper Temptress: "arrowlike in her scant dress" she suggested a hermaphrodite figure to William Seyppel. Narcissa, a widow, was still dressed in white for her role of the Pure White Virgin. In *The Secular Scripture,* Northrop Frye cited the use in romance of "the device of the doubled heroine, sometimes represented by a dark and a fair girl, sometimes linked to a grave-and-gay contrast of temperament." Narcissa had dark hair and "a broad, stupid, serene face" (p.

25); Temple had red hair. At the trial, Temple switched roles, from the Flapper Temptress to the Persecuted Maiden, in her Violated Virgin Phase. Both Temple and Narcissa are sources of evil, overt in Temple except in the courtroom and covert in Narcissa. In *Sanctuary* Narcissa revealed how deceptive she was in appearance. She had no moral scruples, and, putting respectability above justice, she ruthlessly caused the defeat of Horace in his first serious and crucial professional case and callously sacrificed the life of Lee Goodwin. Within her own social context Miss Reba, the madam of a brothel, was motivated by the same desire as Narcissa, that of maintaining a respectable house. Grotesque as she was, Miss Reba had capacity for love and compassion and, by comparison with Narcissa's mindless serenity, was a sympathetic character instead of the traditional Evil Woman, the prostitute.

Ruby Lamar, another Evil Woman in her identity as a former prostitute and an unmarried mother, was really the Suffering Wife. Her name combines that of L. Q. C. Lamar, Oxford's most distinguished citizen before William Faulkner, with, perhaps, an allusion to the virtuous woman in Proverbs whose "price is far above rubies." Although Ruby would sacrifice her "virtue" to save Lee, Narcissa would sacrifice nothing for anyone but herself: to save her image unblemished in the public eye, Narcissa offered herself to the FBI man, in return for the mash notes of Byron Snopes, and was accepted ("There Was a Queen"). But she hounded Ruby from one refuge to another because Ruby and Lee were not married. The complete inversion in Temple and Narcissa of traditional roles is confirmed in the other works in which they appear, Temple in *Requiem for a Nun* and Narcissa in *Sartoris-Flags in the Dust* and "There Was a Queen." To some extent this inversion remains true also of Miss Reba: in *The Reivers* she reappears in her Memphis establishment but plays a completely sympathetic and highly amusing role.

Because Aunt Jenny's virtue was genuine and she scorned conventional appearances, she is never presented ironically. In "An Odor of Verbena," *Sartoris, Sanctuary,* and "There Was a Queen" she was devoid of phony gentility and sentimental romanticism. To Narcissa's wail about Horace bringing "a street walker, a murderess" into the Benbow house, Aunt Jenny retorted scornfully, "Fiddlesticks" (p. 114).

Except for Popeye as the villain, the other male characters show consistent inversion of traditional roles. Gowan Stevens is a parody of the Romantic hero; he judged a gentleman only by the way he held his liquor and, by his own standards, was no gentleman. Having chosen the role of the champion and protector of Temple, Gowan ran away and left her as soon as he was sober enough to leave the Old Frenchman place, much as Bayard Sartoris ran away when he had caused his grandfather's death. Red, Gowan's successor as Temple's champion, was much more to her taste than Gowan. Red also was cast in a hero's role and was unable to play the part. Less craven than Gowan, Red at least died as a victim instead of running away. According to tradition in either Gothic or detective fiction, Horace Benbow, the lawyer-detective, should win his case and secure the triumph of virtue over vice. But he is an idealistic hero quixotically accepting a challenge, rather than a criminal lawyer able to use the information he gathered to win the case for his innocent client. His moral courage proved ineffective when he faced collusion between the guilty ones and the other lawyers. He discovered that his society, like that described by Frye in *The Secular Scripture,* wished "to remain in a blind and gigantic darkness" in which he saw no light.

Horace's own weakness defeated him: his incestuous love for Narcissa and his adulterous and then marital love for Belle made him their victim. The romantic naiveté he showed in *Sartoris* is evident also in *Sanctuary.* (In both *Flags in the Dust* and the unpublished galleys of *Sanctuary,* Horace showed much greater self-knowledge.) In *Sanctuary* the incestuous nature of his love for Little Belle, his stepdaughter, was one of the shattering revelations he experienced in his belated initiation, at the age of forty-three, into the reality of adult life (pp. 215–16). Olga Vickery saw Popeye and Horace as polar opposites, Popeye, the villain, being "isolated by his total indifference to all moral values" and Horace, the hero, being "isolated by his dream of moral perfection." Popeye could act but not feel; Horace could feel but not act effectively. Horace is not an ironic inversion of the romantic hero; the irony lies in his inability to play the role he unselfishly chose. That he was totally unprepared for that role is clear in *Flags in the Dust* and is implied in *Sartoris.* Horace was like a man who jumped into the water to save a drowning man without being able to swim.

The only virile male character in *Sanctuary,* Lee Goodwin should be a villain: neither heroic nor respectable, he was a disreputable bootlegger engaged in no more hazardous traffic than bringing contraband liquor into Yoknapatawpha and selling it to the leading citizens. But Lee is an ironic inversion precisely as Ruby is: his name, "Lee," is that of the greatest southern hero, and "Goodwin," which means "friend of god," may also be read as Good Win, signifying the hero's triumph. As the victim, convicted of crimes of which he was innocent, and as the scapegoat who suffered a horrible death, Lee is more nearly a hero than Horace. Lee resembles the romance hero, subjected to an unjust trial, but unlike such heroes as described by Northrop Frye, Lee had "no vision of liberation." Lee tried to keep the invaders of his sanctuary from being harmed. Guilty of homicidal violence in the past, Lee was innocent of violence in *Sanctuary*. Like Marlow in *Heart of Darkness*, Lee chose his nightmare: to take sanctuary in the jail and trust that Horace could win the trial of an innocent man, rather than to inform against Popeye and be shot by him.

Popeye seems to be the only male character who does not represent an inversion of a traditional role: he is unmistakably a villain, twice a murderer in the novel. In addition, he is a sadist, a rapist, and an impotent voyeur. Leslie Fiedler in *Love and Death* described Popeye as "the most revolting avatar of the desexed seducer" and "a terrible caricature of the child witness," as he watched Red and Temple. The ugliness of this perversion is obvious, but as Olga Vickery observed, it is paralleled by "Horace's painful exclusion from the grape arbor where Little Belle casually experiments with sex." Popeye's violence is akin to Horace's "fantasy and hallucination"; "Popeye's brutal act fuses with Horace's thoughts and culminates in the nightmare vision of the rape of a composite Temple-Little Belle." Popeye's physical grotesqueness and his psychological abnormalities being caused by hereditary disease, he is not a villain in the Gothic sense of a self-willed evildoer. William Brown considered Popeye a sociopath, so closely fitting definitions of sociopathy that he was convinced that Faulkner "drew deliberately from such professional material in the creation of the characters." In other respects than as victim and violator, Temple and Popeye are doubles. In "Faulkner's Paradox in Pathology and Salvation," William Brown noted that both are "repeatedly described as 'doll-like,'" Temple "in the slang sense of a pretty but dumb girl" and Popeye "in the sense of a puppet. . . . He is a puppet physically and psychologically in that he is moved by a constitutional deformity rather than by a free mind." Jean Mayoux commented on Temple and Popeye as being grotesque in their motions, like puppets, and as showing dissociation of mind and body in a state of tension. He commented also on the effect of strangeness Faulkner created by oddity in physiognomy and on the dreamlike quality of *Sanctuary*.

The closest straight parallel to a traditional Gothic type seems to be Judge Drake, who resembles the Tyrannical Father, with a double in Ruby's father, who shot Frank. But Judge Drake's tyranny, so far as one can tell, consisted in his attempts to protect his daughter, first by laying down rules of conduct and then by making her save her reputation by perjury and the consequent miscarriage of justice. The implication of the tableau of Temple's reluctant exit from court is that Judge Drake and her four brothers used pressure to keep her from besmirching the family name by testifying truthfully. Thus, tyranny takes a new form and the judge subverts justice.

In addition to Popeye, wholly grotesque, and the grotesque aspects and un-Dickensian perversion of the characters already discussed, *Sanctuary* exhibits a larger number of minor Dickensian grotesques than any other of Faulkner's Gothic novels. Northrop Frye, in *A Study of English Romanticism,* traced back to medieval and Renaissance courts the custom, imitated in romance, of utilizing "fools, dwarfs, and cripples . . . to serve the purpose of *memento mori.*" (Horace thought that Popeye, diminutive if not a dwarf, smelled black, "like that black stuff that ran out of Bovary's mouth" [p. 7] .) With uncanny aptness in relation to *Sanctuary,* Frye referred to the grotesque in literature as "the expression . . . of the nauseated vision." Tommy, the humorous servant, was too simple and innocent to fear Popeye and was killed for trying to protect Temple, in the hope that she would keep her promise to him. The blind man at the Old Frenchman place, hands on stick, has a double at the end in Judge Drake, in the same posture, with the obvious implication of another kind of blindness. That the blind man is not merely a gratuitous horror is further made evident in the way in which, as William Rossky said, he "contributes to the sense of universal nightmare," "epitomizes . . . the horror of human decay . . . becomes man as impotent victim of the cosmic condition." He is like the blind beggar who haunted Emma Bovary. Horace's allusion to "Bovary" (p. 7) confirms Rossky's comparison. At the other end of human life is Ruby's baby, pathetically grotesque with its "putty-colored face and bluish eyelids" (p. 60).

The repulsive Clarence Snopes, the keyhole voyeur, had a putty-like, flabby face and the nose of some "weak, acquisitive creature like a squirrel or a rat" (p. 169). The physical deformity of Eustace Graham, the crippled district attorney, reflected his warped morals; his "clumsy clog-step" and finger snapping celebrated his gaining the knowledge that would serve his personal ends and cause the death of Lee Goodwin (p. 257). Miss Reba, obese, wheezy, and oddly clad, accompanied by her "white, worm-like dogs" (pp. 138–39), is an unforgettable Dickensian grotesque in appearance and speech, if not in profession. The innocence of the country bumpkins Virgil and Fonzo, who mistook Miss Reba's for a boarding house for girls and took their patronage elsewhere, serves as a contrast to the full awareness of Temple, no older than they, of the nature of the house. Dickensian burlesque with an un-Dickensian setting is also evident in the episode of Miss Reba and her decorous lady friends, mentors of the inebriated six-year-old Uncle Bud. These grotesque characters and situations visibly represent a corrupt society and its distorted values. William Rossky saw in Miss Reba's poodles a comment "on the behavior of men within the nightmare world of the novel . . . vicious, snarling and even mad in their relationship." Describing the structural principle of concentricity as like a vortex, with a series of events funneling into a final one, Douglas Perry remarked that at successive levels the main characters become more grotesque.

The two basic patterns of the action which takes place in this society, with this cast of characters, are both inverted: the seduction of Temple who refused to flee and the successful but unavailing detective search by Horace which served as a belated initiation into an adult reality too harsh for him to live in. The nightmare-dream pattern predominates in the subjective passages, which center in Temple and Horace. The alternation between these two central figures is so handled as to heighten mystery and suspense. The most traditional suspense is the delayed rape at the Old Frenchman place, a pattern which originated in Richardson's *Clarissa Harlowe*. The abrupt break after Tommy is shot is the means by which the mystery of just what did happen to Temple can be maintained until near the end of the trial. The detective story raises the usual questions: Will Horace discover the truth? Will he succeed in the trial? The obscurity of the motives of those opposed to Horace, especially the connection between Judge Drake and Popeye in concealing the truth, is due largely to the omission of details about the period between Horace's interview with Temple and the trial; Faulkner was deliberately heightening the Gothic effect.

The mysteries of Clarence Snopes's dealings with Judge Drake and the Memphis lawyer somewhat overshadow the central question: Will Temple testify to the truth? The structure, placing the court scenes very near the end, makes the revelation of the answer dramatically effective. The horrible death of Lee Goodwin diverts the reader's attention from the question which remains: Why did Temple commit perjury and cause the death of Lee Goodwin for a crime he did not commit? Dr. Kubie suggests an answer that is consistent with what happens to the virile men in the book and that might be extended from Temple and her hatred of her father and brothers to other respectable women in society: "'To be a woman is worse than death or the same as death. Therefore I will take my revenge upon all you men who are really men. . . . And finally I will be the instrument of your actual bodily destruction.'" Kubie may be right in explaining Temple's motive as revenge, a Gothic theme which Faulkner used subtly in Miss Rosa's revenge on Sutpen. Since it was Lee who suffered, Temple may have sought revenge on him because he did not respond to her coquetry, by which she invited the fate she feared.

Gothic fiction can offer few examples of the girl-in-flight pattern in which motion is so prominent in incident and imagery as in *Sanctuary*. As Leslie Fiedler said in *Love and Death*, "Faulkner's Temple figures are sheer motion, a blur of dancing legs and wind-blown hair in a speeding car. . . ." Most significant are the scenes where she is running, even running into space "right off the porch, into the weeds" (p. 63). But the flight that traditionally should save virtue is for Temple erratic and circular and is succeeded by passive captivity. The flight began when she got off the train to ride with Gowan, a flight from her father's instructions and the university rules, a flight from respectability and conventional morality. At the Old Frenchman place she refused to flee when Ruby advised her to. Temple's flights in and around the house were more provocative than elusive. As Olga Vickery explained, she never can make up her mind to take effective flight: "It is not her fear of encountering greater evils or dangers but her fascination with the idea of violence that holds her immobile." Even attempts at flight ceased when she left with Popeye. At Miss Reba's she merely played "the role of 'victim-prisoner,'" as Olga Vickery said, having abandoned "all the social values of her group without accepting the personal values which, however minimal, lend significance to the lives of Ruby and Goodwin." Faulkner confirmed this interpretation in *Requiem for a Nun,* where Temple confessed that she stayed at Miss Reba's because she was corrupt. For physical flight Temple substituted flight from reality in the fantasies she related to Horace, which add to the theme of sexuality and sexual perversion. Dr. Kubie explained that the fantasy of change of sex and her

rude awakening from this dream . . . gave rise to a secondary phantasy (one which is familiar enough to psychoanalysts in their study of illness, but rarely encountered in literature), in which there was a fusion of the ideas of rape, castration, and death. . . . From that moment Temple behaves as though she herself were dead, and the blind, dead instrument of revenge.

Temple's story led up to Horace's surrealistic and nauseating image of Temple-Little Belle. After Temple was rescued by her father and brothers, who could have rescued her much earlier if she had told Miss Reba how to reach them, she fled again, with her father, to France. Although the image of the girl in flight remains shockingly vivid, the moral significance lies in the facts that she did not actually flee to save her virtue and that she protected her violator and brought death to Lee, her protector.

As the image of Temple is flight, that of Horace is quest. But Horace began by fleeing from Belle and reality, so suddenly that he took no money with him. But when he learned of the plight of Lee Goodwin, Horace yielded to his quixotic impulses and began his purposeful journeys. Horace's physical journeys in "strenuous quest for evidence," as Warren Beck said, took him back and forth from Sartoris to Jefferson, from Jefferson to Oxford, and from Jefferson to Memphis. His journey from Sartoris to Jefferson to reside in his own house was part of his choice to struggle for justice. His short journeys in behalf of Ruby, to find lodgings for her, and to the jail, to confer with Lee, provide much of the essential action and continuity.

His quest for truth and justice is also an initiation into the nature of evil and into the reality beneath social conduct and institutions. "In nearly every one of Faulkner's novels," as Cleanth Brooks said, in "Faulkner's *Sanctuary,*" "the male's discovery of evil and reality is bound up with his discovery of the true nature of woman. Men idealize and romanticize women, but the cream of the jest is that women have a secret ·rapport with evil which men do not have, that they are able to adjust to evil without being shattered by it. . . ."

In this view of women the ironic inversion of the traditional Gothic novel is particularly obvious and significant. Brooks refers to Narcissa's shocking depravity, but he does not mention that the conventional Evil Women, Ruby and Reba, show no such depravity and do not shock Horace, except when Ruby revealed the evil in men: "'Good God,' he whispered. 'What kind of men have you known?'" (p. 268). The irony in Horace's quest and initiation is that he is a lawyer forty-three years old who has never before seriously assumed his professional and social responsibilities. Heinrich Straumann charged Horace with both his inadequacy as a counsel and his capitulation, not stoic acceptance, after losing the case. Having suffered defeat in his first defense of a legally innocent man, he fled from evil and corruption and left them to flourish without his further opposition. His lack of experience as a lawyer is even more apparent in *Flags in the Dust,* where the nature of his law practice is specified (see p. 79), than in *Sartoris,* where his chief activities were glass blowing and being seduced by Belle Mitchell.

The shock of cognition and the fall from innocence, as Frederick Garber pointed out, were characteristic of the Gothic novel and of emerging Romanticism. In *Sanctuary* the shock and the fall are experienced by a middle-aged lawyer in his native town. *Sanctuary* stops short of "the full Gothic plot," which, Garber said, "moves from an initial confrontation to a fall into self-consciousness and then . . . to a phase of coping or learning to cope." (Horace's incorrigible inability to cope may have been one reason that Faulkner permanently consigned him to Kinston and never let him reenter Yoknapatawpha.) Horace's moral enlightenment, that "there's a corruption about even looking upon evil" (p. 125), gave rise to his vision "of a world left stark and dying above the tide-edge of the fluid in which it lived and breathed," "a motionless ball in cooling space, across which a thick smell of honeysuckle writhed like cold smoke" (p. 215). Gothic fiction has few such desperate images of apocalyptic annihilation, evoked by awareness of man's sexual nature, symbolized for Horace as for Quentin Compson by the smell of honeysuckle. The moonlight scene which is the context of the quotation, preceding the surrealistic Temple–Little Belle vision, adds a new dimension to romantic moonlight as a "prop" in Gothic fiction. With no reference to the Gothic tradition Olga Vickery's explanation of Horace's reaction precisely fits the reactions which produced some of the first Gothic novels: "What reduces Horace to a state of shock is the discovery not of evil but of the shoddy foundations of his vision of a moral and rational universe, supported and sustained by the institutions of the church, the state, and the law." The degree and nature of Narcissa's betrayal of him Horace seemed not to realize; his romantic idealism and lack of self-knowledge had helped him to make Narcissa what she was. In the revisions of both *Flags in the Dust* and *Sanctuary,* Horace's similar idealization and "innocence" had concealed from him his feeling for Little Belle. His initiation involved the loss of innocence and the acceptance of guilt, personal and social. All he could do about his new maturity was to flee back to Belle and the life he had found intolerable and lock the back door, knowing that Little Belle was at a houseparty.

As the unsuccessful but sympathetically portrayed hero, the impotent Horace most fully conveys the basic theme of the impotence of modern man and his "three direct objects of fear," as dramatized, according to Dr. Kubie, in *Sanctuary:* "a fear of women, a fear of other men, and a fear of the community and of society in general." If "heterosexual" is put in place of "other," the statement is remarkably close to the thesis of Leslie Fiedler's *Love and Death in the American Novel.* Dr. Kubie noted the destruction in *Sanctuary* of the only natural, vital, and potent males, Lee Goodwin, Red, and the Negro murderer in the jail, and explained the ironic significance of Popeye: "Popeye's very figure . . . is concretely described . . . in words which make it a graphic representation of the phallus whose impotence is the root of the whole tragedy."

In addition to the flight of Temple and her father from reality and notoriety, the last chapter presents Popeye's flight from justice. Here the facts of his earlier life, with the ironic birthdate of December 25 and with details of Gothic horror, indicate that he was not responsible for the course his life had taken. By application of diagnostic criteria to the account of Popeye, in "Faulkner's Paradox" William Brown concluded that Popeye represented "pathology . . . of a specific type recognized by psychiatrists" and that in Popeye Faulkner "undoubtedly creates a constitutional abnormality." Until Popeye left Memphis, where his influence provided him with safety from the law, his flight had been more figurative than literal. After the murder of Red, Popeye started "on his way to Pensacola to visit his mother" (p. 294) and was arrested en route and charged with a murder committed at the time of Red's murder. He made no attempt to defend himself. Popeye's own trial provided what Douglas Perry called "the final gothic twist, the final concentric pattern." Thus the ultimate irony is his acceptance of the death he had avoided by destroying Lee Goodwin. Popeye's last request before execution, "Fix my hair, Jack" (p. 308), adds a grotesque detail which Joanne Creighton described as the final "macabre caricature" of concern for social appearances, forms, and rituals.

The execution which follows is covered in three words: "springing the trap." The prevalence of the grotesque in characters and scenes, and the scenes of horror and violence produce in *Sanctuary* the authentic Gothic shudder. But mere sensationalism Faulkner often avoided by distancing or understating the violence, rather than elaborating upon it.

The most Gothic sequence of action, in mood and setting and incidents, occurs at the Old Frenchman place. The ruined mansion, surrounded by desolation, and the sinister characters show the possibilities of Gothic effect from naturalistic details. The shift to subjective rendering, largely from Temple's point of view but including Tommy's and Ruby's, builds up the nightmare effect. But even here the switch to Temple's point of view omits some of the terror of the reality, as Temple's account to Horace revealed. The climax in the crib, with Temple like the cornered rat which terrifies her, stops short of the rape. The murder of Tommy is represented only by a sound "no louder than the striking of a match," the rape, only by Temple's silent scream to the old blind man, "Something is happening to me!" (pp. 98, 99).

What happened, but not how, is revealed in the account of the flight to Memphis; the beauty of the countryside is in ironic contrast to Temple's distress, which seems less than one might expect from similar experiences of the virtuous Clarissas of fiction. Temple's violation had been only physical, not moral. Despite the circumstances, speed is not stressed in Popeye's flight from the Old Frenchman place.

The room at Miss Reba's symbolizes Temple's corruption. The details of the furnishings, especially the mirrors and the one-handed china clock with its four nymphs, and the descriptions of Temple's new possessions, particularly the platinum bag with orange banknotes in it, are modernized Gothic. The most extreme example of perverted sexuality, that of Red and Temple with Popeye as voyeur, shocked even Miss Reba, "him trying to turn" her respectable house "into a peep show" (p. 248). Dr. Kubie explained Popeye's voyeurism as an acting out of "the primitive horror-ridden phantasy" of the male who "is struggling with impotence fears": "the fantasy [sic] of being helpless and bound while someone else rapes the woman he loves." More within the range of normal sexuality but with a southern "lady" as the aggressor is the scene between Temple and Red in which danger and lust are climactically mingled and Temple's eroticism is dramatically portrayed: as Fiedler said in *Love and Death*, "Not content to be violated, the woman becomes the violator," "whimpering for the consummation she had once fled in terror." (The terror, however, had been less powerful than the fascination.) The murder of Red, after this scene, is an anticlimax; it is suggested only by Popeye's "match flipped outward like a dying star in miniature" (p. 234), recalling the match that was the token of Tommy's murder.

The funeral of Red, discussed by David Frazier as an isolated Gothic scene, is most easily and convincingly explained as part of a Gothic novel, in which the macabre and grotesque details are completely appropriate. The whole ritual follows the pattern of a black mass, as William Stein demonstrated, even to the woman in red as the Whore of Babylon. The climax occurs when the corpse of Red tumbles out of the coffin and the bullet hole in its forehead is revealed. Grotesque incongruity follows: the social gathering at Miss Reba's, a parody of the decorum and respectability of the women of Jefferson, especially Narcissa, suggests that Miss Reba and her friends, grotesque as they seem, show more real feeling and sympathy than Narcissa would.

The last sequence of events, beginning with the trial, includes the quiet tension of the night Horace spent in the jail with Lee and Ruby, when he learned more about the kind of men Ruby had known and how she would have paid debts to them and about how his sheltered life looked to those who were familiar with vice and violence. On the next day of the trial, the horror of the rape is finally disclosed. The discovery and reversal occur when Temple perjures herself and Horace therefore faces defeat: he has learned the nature of reality beneath social conventions. The tableau of Temple forced out of court, surrounded by her father and four brothers, epitomizes the myth which is destroyed by the reality but preserved in appearance: the Pure Woman who has been protected by Southern Manhood with the aid of society and the legal system is in reality the cause of two murders and a lynching, as well as of her own corruption.

In addition to the scene between Temple and Red, the other scene in *Sanctuary* which receives the full Gothic treatment is what Douglas Perry called "the fiery vortex which engulfs Lee Goodwin," as witnessed by Horace who narrowly escaped Lee's fate. As William Rossky said: "The bonfire becomes the mesmerizing conflagration at the heart of everything"; "as in nightmare, the scene builds an effect of stasis in which powerlessness and enormous dread fuse." But the agonizing scene is cut short by Horace's lapse into unconsciousness.

Lee Goodwin was completely innocent of the murder of Tommy and the rape, as Temple knew. Misreading of *Sanctuary*, such as George Marion O'Donnell's, which attaches any validity to the case presented by the district attorney, deliberately framed according to the myth of the White Virgin inherited from courtly love and southern Calvinism, completely misses the whole point for which Faulkner adapted the Gothic pattern. O'Donnell described Temple as "Southern Womanhood Corrupted but Undefiled" and asserted that even when she was "hopelessly corrupted by Modern Man," she was not the cause of Lee's death. That was what O'Donnell expected to read. But by careful and virtually complete inversion of both the story of seduction and the detective story, Faulkner used the Gothic tradition much as Dickens used comparable theatrical materials, as William Axton explained, "to arouse his readers' expectations that a realistic contemporary novel will imitate an ideal mythic action and then to frustrate or disorient these expectations by departure from, inversions of, and incongruous survivals" of original motifs. The contrast between appearance and reality is sharpened by the traditional roles in which characters seem to be cast but which, when they play their parts, reveal dramatically how the forces inherent in respectable southern society have created a false image of southern womanhood and false moral views, and how justice is subverted to preserve that image and those views.

Dr. Lawrence Kubie interpreted *Sanctuary* as a dramatization of the struggle "between the forces of instinctual evil" and "the forces of an evil and savage conscience, operating through the blind vengefulness of a misdirected mob." Horace is "the weak representative of the much-battered 'Ego,' that fragment of the personality which is so often ground to pieces in the battle." The inclusion of Horace and Narcissa extends the relevance of the story beyond the story of Temple, a flapper of the twenties from Jackson. Horace and Narcissa, not having responded to the spirit of the flapper age, represent the values Temple rejected; their previous rules identify them as representing the natives of Jefferson. Thus, the attempt to secure justice and the successful action to defeat it are rooted in the community and its traditions, represented not only by the Benbows but also by the Snopeses and Eustace Graham, who were introduced in *Sartoris*. By omission of racial complications in the sexual theme, Faulkern avoided inclusion of an element so highly charged emotionally that it might obscure his inversion of characters and values.

Like *Sartoris* and *Absalom, Absalom!* the published version of *Sanctuary* differs from an earlier version and comparison of the two is pertinent to Gothic elements in the final version. In *Faulkner's Revision of "Sanctuary": A Collation of the Unrevised Galleys and the Published Book,* Gerald Langford made available the passages in the galleys which were altered or omitted in the book and showed the extensive structural changes effected through excision and rearrangement. Langford did not perceive that Gothic patterns and the detective quest-initiation are basic to the revision, in which characters, settings, and dramatic conflict are polarized.

The material from the galleys shows that Gothic elements were retained or strengthened in the following ways: retention of the violence and the horror; addition of the lynching scene and of the story of Popeye's heritage; the direct and early presentation of the story of Temple and Gowan at the Old Frenchman place; the increase of dramatic tension by the focus on Horace as the unifying "detective" protagonist, engaged in a struggle against the forces of evil.

Gothic elements which were deleted or weakened were those not essential to the dramatic present action: Horace's meditations and memories which include his consciousness of his incestuous feelings for Narcissa and greater awareness than in the novel of his feeling for Little Belle and Ruby; his dreams of his mother, Narcissa, and Ruby; the emphasis on the Benbow and the Sartoris past as reflected in the family homes and the Sartoris portraits. In the galleys Horace's consciousness of his sexual respose to all the women in his life and the four canceled passages in which he gazed at the photograph of Little Belle reduce the dramatic effect of his nausea when the images of Temple and Little Belle fused, and render the episode less convincing as a sudden traumatic revelation.

Horace's active role as the detective-protagonist who links together the diverse groups of characters and their settings is greatly strengthened by the revisions, which include the rearrangement of narrative sequences, the shift of some episodes from reminiscence to present action, and the excision of long subjective passages which develop the character of Horace beyond the requirements of his role as detective-hero and his structural function. In *Sanctuary,* the revisions, especially the addition of the lynching scene, served to make the nightmare dominate the daydream in Horace's experience.

Langford is no doubt correct in interpreting the revision of *Sanctuary* as indicating Faulkner's intention to discard Horace as a character, after trying twice, "in writing and revising *Sanctuary*," "to clarify his conception of the Horace Benbow he had created in *Sartoris.*" Of course, when Langford was making his study, *Flags in the Dust* had not been published. It seems that Ben Wasson's excisions constituted a first step in Faulkner's clarification or modification of his concept of Horace: Faulkner's deletions are in harmony with those made by Wasson. In both *Absalom, Absalom!* and *Sanctuary* Faulkner's revisions heightened the original strongly Gothic effect.

Sanctuary is Faulkner's most antibourgeois novel and in some ways his least regional. It is not, as Leslie Fiedler thought, "the least mythic," on "its more conscious levels": the mythic-Gothic pattern is ironically turned upside down. *Sanctuary* retains a basic function of Gothic novels, to induce the reader to identify with the characters in their terrifying and appalling experiences. It achieves its excruciating effectiveness by the contemporary action, the naturalistic background, and the psychological characterization. Its literary merits are those proper to Gothic fiction and require no apology for or explaining away of elements that fail to fit into other conventional patterns in the novel. As Michael Millgate concluded, Faulkner did indeed, in his own terms, make "a fair job" of revising the galleys of his shocking tale for publication. As a Gothic novel, *Sanctuary* is much better than "fair."

CHAPTER SIX

LIGHT IN AUGUST

DIANA IN DIXIE, OR, THE WAY OF THE CROSS

Light in August, an essentially Gothic and tragic story framed in a non-Gothic romance, develops Gothic themes in a study of psychological and social factors contributing to the murder with which the novel opens. The mystery and suspense lie as much in character and motivation, the roots of present action being traced to the past, as in the crime and its consequences. The action is set against Jefferson, rather than incorporated into it: none of the major characters belongs to Jefferson, as did Horace and Narcissa and Aunt Jenny in *Sanctuary.* Like *Sanctuary,* *Light in August* is based on the dream-image of flight, but to that image is added the quest, leading to disaster if devoted to the wrong dreams but having power for good if inspired by the right dreams. As Olga Vickery said, *Light in August* demonstrates that "it is man's nature to dream and dreams by their very essence are both distortions of reality and desires for a new shape to experience."

The Gothic central narrative and the comic non-Gothic romance together represent all three of Ihab Hassan's major patterns in the ironic form in *Radical Innocence,* "the closed encounter of the scapegoat, the qualified encounter of the humble hero, and the open encounter of the imposter or rogue." Hassan referred to Faulkner as one of the powerful adapters of old myths to new situations, like Joyce, Gide, Mann, and Lawrence, but he did not discuss specific novels by Faulkner. The "three types of heroes" represent *pharmakos, eiron,* and *alazon,* terms used by Northrop Frye in *Anatomy of Criticism.* The method by which Faulkner combined these types of characters to provide a morally significant contrast produced a structure somewhat like that of *Sanctuary,* in that Byron Bunch links Joe's and Lena's stories much as Horace

Benbow linked groups and places. But Joe's and Lena's stories are not dramatically merged, as the seduction and detection stories are in *Sanctuary,* nor loosely combined, as the tragedy of Bayard is fused with the amusing subplots in *Sartoris.* To the discontinuity of space in the present action of *Sanctuary* is added discontinuity of time in *Light in August:* present action, chiefly limited to Yoknapatawpha County, is interrupted or suspended by long excursions into the past histories of Joe Christmas, Gail Hightower, the Burdens, and the Hineses, none of them natives of Yoknapatawpha. The past history is presented both subjectively and by the omniscient author. The function of Byron Bunch is limited to the present action, from the discovery of the murder of Joanna Burden to the day of Joe Christmas's death, with a Byron-Lena epilogue in the last chapter. Although Byron is not a detective but only a benevolent intermediary, without his function in that role and as a moral center, *Light in August* would lack coherence and positive significance.

Despite the facts that *Light in August* involves more violence, most of it sexual or sexually motivated, than *Sanctuary,* and deals with some of the same themes as *Absalom, Absalom!* it has rarely been recognized in Faulkner criticism as essentially Gothic. The Gothic interpretation is one of four critical approaches surveyed by François Pitavy: he mentioned the violent and macabre scenes, the nightmare atmosphere, sadism, and Manichaeism, and recognized the Gothic as a persistent element in southern novels. The other three interpretations—mythologic, existentialist, and humanist—are also valid and illuminating but are less concerned than the Gothic with a specific literary tradition embracing all aspects of a novel. Although Ihab Hassan was aware of "the violent breakup of accepted literary forms" to which Faulkner contributed, he failed to note, in *Radical Innocence,* that the Gothic was one of these forms and that the "breakup" might occur within an essentially Gothic work, such as *Absalom, Absalom!* Hassan recognized the Gothic element in the novels of Carson McCullers and Truman Capote, and said that "Mrs. McCullers lacks the scope, strength, and fury of Faulkner, lacks his dark apprehension of the Southern past and his profound insight into the American wilderness, symbols both of our guilt and innocence." Hassan lists Gothic aspects but does not so label them. In *Light in August,* a novel fitting Hassan's description of "a grotesque or victim hero whose alienation defines the shape of the novel," Hassan failed to observe the "fusion of fable and fact, the ritual wedding" which he sought and which Faulkner achieved by translating Gothic elements into realistic terms and adding the mythic story of Lena. In her chapter entitled "The Shadow and the Mirror" Olga Vickery commented on "the grotesque quality" in *Light in August* and on the pattern of imagery of "the circle, the shadow, and the mirror": "the individual and the community are obverse reflections of each other." The mirror-reflection image, one of Irving Malin's three new American Gothic images, had been prominent, with the shadow, in *The Sound and the Fury.* Without identifying *Light in August* as Gothic, Dorothy Tuck described in it the typical Gothic effect and its purpose: "the immersion of the reader in the artistic creation so that he experiences the 'inwardness of the understanding,'" to arrive at "some profound and subjective apprehension of human exerience." The phrase quoted by Tuck is from Kierkegaard. She discussed *Light in August* as a psychological mystery story.

Somewhat as in *Sanctuary,* the present action in *Light in August* shifts between two chief settings in Jefferson and the vicinity, with more emphasis on interior scenes than exterior: the Burden house, like the Old Frenchman place, is outside the orbit of respectable residents of Jefferson, and Hightower's house serves like Sartoris as a setting for dialogues between major characters. But natural settings in *Light in August* more often than in *Sanctuary* are in harmony with action and feeling. The journeys of Lena across the summer landscape at the beginning and the end provide a simple pastoral setting which is augmented by the less idyllic farm scenes, in the past and the present. The season and its quality are essential to the story of Lena and thus may be in contrast with the story of Joe in present action. The title refers literally, Faulkner said, to the season: "There's a lambence, a luminous quality to the light, as though it came not from just today but from back in the old classic times, . . . a luminosity older than our Christian civilization." The world of nature, which in the Gothic romances was magnificent when not terrible, in Faulkner is simple and realistic, deeply felt but not romantically described by the omniscient author. In various wagons Lena advanced "like something moving forever and without progress across an urn," in "the hot still pinewiney silence of the August afternoon" (p. 5). The entire scene exemplifies François Pitavy's statement that "the landscape is . . . largely defined in terms of light and shade and of stillness and movement." The sentence rhythms and the evocative words invest the simple objective details with an effect of suspension of time and motion. Lena's past background was even less idyllic than the scene which lay ahead, along the monotonous red road; her home community presented a Dickensian or Conradian image of desolate, useless machinery in a worn-out land. The Armstid farm where Lena next took shelter had set upon Mrs. Armstid the mark of losing battles.

Two farms figure in Joe's story, the second also in Lena's. The McEachern farm Joe first saw in a December twilight. In a summer dusk it was starlit, bright with fireflies and musical with mockingbirds and whippoorwills. Ironically, in this musical and twinkling twilight Joe had just had a fight and was about to be thrashed. The same ambience preceded his next thrashing. The favorite Gothic moonlit landscape was the background for Joe's night escapade which ended with McEachern's pursuit and confrontation of Joe and Joe's murderous retaliation. The Burden farm, where first Joe and then Lena took shelter in carefully contrived parallel actions, was sterile, a ruined garden where Joe waited until time to murder. "This was a region of Negro cabins and gutted and outworn fields..." (p. 271). After Lena's baby was born in the cabin that had been Joe's, Hightower hoped that "luck and life" might return "to these barren and ruined acres" (p. 385). Season and time of day softened, sometimes ironically, the simple and sometimes grim rural scenes in which the action occurred.

The Burden home, reduced to a pillar of flame and smoke when the story opens, was a modest survival of the past, but somewhat comparable to survivals of more splendid mansions. When Joe first saw it, "It was a big house set in a grove of trees; obviously a place of some pretensions at one time. But now the trees needed pruning and the house had not been painted in years" (p. 213). On "a cedar knoll in the pasture a half mile from the house" (p. 235) was the family graveyard, like that at Sutpen's. In graves hidden to prevent molestation were buried the two Burdens, grandfather and grandson, who were shot by Colonel John Sartoris. Less ruinous than Sutpen's Hundred, the Burden house seemed equally somber until it, too, went up in flames.

Hightower's small dark house on a little-used street was the "castle" in which he was haunted by the cherished vision of his grandfather. ("Dark House," the title of an abortive beginning, Faulkner changed, according to Joseph Blotner, in response to a remark by Mrs. Faulkner about the special quality of "light in August.") Hightower and his "Dark House" T. H. Adamowski compared with Sir Leicester Dedlock and Chesny Wold in *Bleak House:* "The old houses and old men reek of the past," taking refuge in their houses from the present. Hightower's "brown, unpainted and unobtrusive bungalow" was almost hidden "by bushing crape myrtle and syringa and Althea" (p. 52). The window from which Hightower looked through a gap in the bushes *is* more significant than the exterior: he was usually inside, looking on reality through a glass, darkly.

Scenes of enclosure—self-imprisonment or forced imprisonment or sanctuary—are metaphors for the mental states of Hightower and other characters. For Lena, after she freed herself from her imprisoning circumstances by climbing through the window of her brother's house, rooms were refuges, accepted graciously at the Armstids' and at Mrs.

Beard's and finally in the Burden cabin. To Lucas Burch, the cabin was a trap and he, not Lena, escaped through the window. The room in which Hightower largely lived his life was the scene of numerous confrontations between him and Byron Bunch, with Hightower taking shelter behind the barrier of his desk to avoid being drawn into involvement with the human race. The same room witnessed the failure of Hightower's attempt to maintain his own immunity and to keep Byron immune: Byron and Doc and Mrs. Hines entered, to relate the terrible story of Doc's mad deeds as an instrument of divine vengeance. And ultimately, out of "the savage summer sunlight" into the "stale and cloistral dimness" of Hightower's house, Joe Christmas ran, pursued by Percy Grimm (p. 438).

Joe's story began and ended with an asylum, first the orphanage and last the unsafe sanctuary of Hightower's house. Between those points the rooms where Joe took shelter typified his loveless, alienated life. The dietitian's closet at the orphanage so sickened him with the world of women that, in his room at the McEacherns' where he suffered from beatings, he wanted no intrusion of "that soft kindness which he believed himself doomed to be forever victim of and which he hated worse than he did the hard and ruthless justice of men" (p. 158). Bobby's room, "smelling of stale scent," lighted by a single bulb, was the first of many where Joe sought love and found sex for sale (p. 183). The cabin at Miss Burden's was for a while Joe's refuge, until the traitor Burch moved in and the contest between them gave Burch cause for revenge against the "durn yellowbellied wop" (p. 260). The only rooms in Miss Burden's house to which Joe was admitted were the kitchen, as befitted his inferior caste status, and the bedroom, where in the dark all cats were gray. (Although traditionally in the South difference in caste between white men and Negro women was observed when seated but not horizontally, between white women and Negro men an insuperable barrier was supposed to exist.) The jail where Joe was imprisoned is not presented directly, as it was in *Sanctuary* when Lee Goodwin was a prisoner there. For Joe, even more than for Lee, the jail was a refuge from violence: from the time of his arrest Joe had to fear the same fate Lee suffered after his trial and conviction. From the jail to Hightower's house was for Joe a brief, frenzied, nightmare flight to a sanctuary that proved to be a death trap. Byron and Lena at the end are the only major characters who can walk out of the prisons of self and circumstance represented by the "other rooms" within the "haunted castles" in *Light in August*.

The characters not only fall into traditional types but, unlike those in *Sanctuary*, show little ironic inversion except in their humble status; none of the aristocrats have roles in *Light in August*. The male characters are numerous and varied. Of Faulkner's Gothic heroes or hero-villains, Joe Christmas is the most complex and the most representative of diverse Gothic characteristics. As a supposed mulatto, Joe represents miscegenation and the tragedy it entails. Joe resembles Charles Bon and, even more nearly, the son of Charles Bon, who could neither repudiate his heritage nor rationally accept it. Joe is explicitly referred to in Faustian terms, "exulting perhaps . . . as Faustus had," at "having put behind now at once and for all the Shalt Not, of being free at last of honor and law" (p. 194). Dorothy Tuck described Joe as Cain seeking identity and as a "parody of the innocent youth of the mythic hero, and there is a tremendous dialectical tension between the actual Joe and the archetypal echoes his actions suggest." Ishmael is a better parallel than Cain, for Joe was cast out into the wilderness, figuratively, as an infant, guiltless of any crime but being born. His hand was indeed "against every man, and every man's hand against him," and the "brethren" in whose presence he dwelt finally treated him, after they listened to "Brown's" story, as if indeed he had been the descendant of a bondwoman. Joe Christmas is referred to repeatedly in terms of crucifixion, a point discussed later. Joe's compulsive and sadistic sexuality may be, according to Richard Chase, a defense against a latent homosexuality. In light of Faulkner's detailed and uninhibited account of Joe's and Joanna's heterosexuality, there would seem no reason for less explicit treatment of homosexuality. Possibly Joe's masochistic reaction to being beaten indicates homosexuality. There is no irony in the characterization of Joe as a modern tragic hero-villain, with archetypal echoes; he transcends the literary stereotype of the tragic mulatto in American fiction.

There is, however, some irony in the pair of romantic heroes. Byron Bunch is genuinely heroic in the courage and selfless devotion with which he served Lena, his lady love, but he is so humble and self-effacing and un-Byronic that he is a comic hero, a true *eiron*. He is, in fact, so devoid of distinctive qualities as to be grotesque. As the furniture dealer said at the end, "He was the kind of fellow you wouldn't see the first glance if he was alone by himself in the bottom of a empty concrete swimming pool" (p. 469). The name "Bunch," suggesting one of the bunch, the common man, negates the "Byron," as "Snopes" made "Byron" ridiculous in *Sartoris.* "Bunch" is a common surname in Faulkner's part of Mississippi. Lucas Burch, whose name is confused with Byron's in replies to Lena's inquiries, at first glance seems more interesting than Byron, but his manner and his "alert, weakly handsome face with a small white scar beside the mouth that looked as if it had been contemplated a great deal in the mirror" (p. 32). suggest his nature, and the signs are read by Mooney and Byron: Lucas is vacuous, selfish, lazy, narcissistic, and also treacherous and mendacious, a traditional *alazon*. (The *pharmakos* in this trio of young men is, of course, Joe Christmas.) As rivals for Lena, Byron and Lucas are comic doubles. Byron chivalrously waived his claim until Lucas fled. Byron's instinctive love for Lena and the romantic idealism which invested her with unsullied purity until her baby was born reveal Byron as a humble version of the quixotic, courtly lover.

The prominence in Gothic novels of monks and nuns and other members of holy orders, usually as evil characters, suggests a traditional origin for Gail Hightower. He is evil in that he used his clerical office for ulterior purposes and abdicated his responsibility, sinking into indolent deterioration. Although Hightower was not a Calvinist like McEachern, Joanna, and Hines, he too was one of the clergy who were destroying the Church: "the professionals who control it and who have removed the bells from its steeples" (p. 461). The symbolic meaning of "Gail Hightower," "Gail" being added to a name prominent in Faulkner's Oxford, is apparent in his physical withdrawal into his house and in his own consciousness. When he entered the Church, he thought "that he could see his future, his life, intact and on all sides complete and inviolable, like a classic and serene vase, where the spirit could be born anew sheltered from the harsh *gale* of living . . ." (p. 453, italics added). He came to recognize the falseness of this concept of the seminary and the ministry.

In contrast to Byron, who came to accept life and responsibility, Gail Hightower is a kind of antihero, attempting to check Byron in his quest for self-fulfillment, self-knowledge, and love. Charles Gregory explained Hightower as the product of both his father's puritan austerity and his grandfather's Cavalier romanticism. His heritage from his father was evident in his eventual enlightenment and approach to, if not achievement of, redemption. Hightower was grotesquely fat and unkempt and unbathed. Byron implied that Hightower was thought to be a homosexual or that people would prefer to believe Hightower and Joe to be homosexuals than to believe that Joe had lived with Joanna "like a husband and then killed her" (p. 369). There is even a satanic aspect of Hightower, described objectively—"his face looked like the face of Satan in the old prints" (p. 63)—and confirmed in his thoughts: "There was within him a leaping and triumphant surge of denial behind a face which had betrayed him, believing itself safe behind the lifted hymnbook, when the photographer pressed his bulb" (p. 463). Ilse Lind considered Hightower the hero or antihero of a psychological play. He is also a scapegoat victim, a *pharmakos:* he was wounded by Joe before Joe was killed, because Hightower intervened between Grimm and the destined victim of white society.

The Tyrannical Fathers who flourished in Gothic novels and romances from the time of *The Castle of Otranto* and *Clarissa Harlowe* are, in Faulkner's works, most fully and literally represented in *Light in August*. The elder Calvin Burden threatened to "beat the loving God" into his four children, boy and girls, and took a strap to and fought his grown son (p. 230). Joanna Burden, with her repressions and her inflexible will to dominate, was one product of that family. McEachern, Joe's foster-father, was an old-fashioned Hell-and-brimstone Calvinist with a sex phobia who beat out of Joe any religion the boy might have had. Jacques Cabau well expressed the Calvinistic concepts most fully reflected in *Light in August* in McEachern: "The terror, the cruelty, the fatality are those of the Old Testament, likewise the horror of woman is that before the Virgin had atoned for the sin of Eve by giving birth to the Re-deemer." Although McEachern seemed sadistic in inflicting punishment, he was a man of deep convictions: "His clean bearded face [was] as firm as carved stone, his eyes ruthless, cold, but not unkind" (p. 141). In his granite-like inflexibility McEachern seems inhuman and therefore grotesque. Joe's grandfather, Doc Hines, was grotesque in appearance, like Pappy Yokum in "Lil' Abner." In dealing with his wife, his daughter, and Joe, Doc Hines was sadistic and mad. In him the attitudes toward sex and the will of God which were evident in McEachern were carried to the point of fanatic insanity: when he let his daughter die after childbirth, he said: "It's the Lord God's abomination, and I am the in-strument of His will" (p. 360).

Despite Faulkner's use of characters warped by Calvinistic attitudes, Mary Fletcher perceived in Faulkner "an unconscious adherence and emo-tional commitment to it [Calvinism] as a framework for his vision." But in contrast with Calvinistic unholy parents or foster parents, Faulkner presented another vision in another framework: his Holy Family—Lena, her baby, and Byron—saved by love from the Calvinism in their environ-ment.

Percy Grimm, who plays a brief but essential role, resembles McEachern and Hines as the self-appointed instrument of the Divine Will. He calls to one's mind the cruelty of Gothic inquisitors and the Nazi leaders who subsequently arose in Europe. A fanatic militant, he is the only charac-ter with a crucial role who belongs to Jefferson and who freely chooses violence. His name is as ironic a combination as Byron's; in modern society "Percy" suggests anything but the action foreshadowed by his last name. Joe Christmas was pursued by Grimm death.

The female characters are much less ironic versions of the traditional types than those in *Sanctuary*. Lena as the romantic heroine shows an ironic lack of virtue in the bourgeois sense and pursues her seducer in a parody of the usual flight-pursuit. But she is genuinely good and incorrigibly innocent and calls forth the best in others, except Lucas Burch. Although Joe and Lena never meet, they are doubles representing contrasting attitudes toward society: Joe is conditioned by the opinion of society and Lena is indifferent to it, except for her sense of decorum in manners. Joe proudly rejects what is offered to him, while Lena graciously accepts gifts and services. More than any other character, Lena breaks out of both the traditional pattern and the ironic inversion. Her femininity is too instinctive to recall that of any of the traditional heroines, aristocratic or bourgeois. The parallels with the Virgin Mary, and Mary Magdalene, and Mary sister of Martha are suggested by her blue dress and her serenity, by her name, and by her passivity in contrast with the active Martha Armstid. The parallel between Lena Grove and Diana of the Wood is less obvious but certainly is possible, especially in view of Faulkner's comment on the pre-Christian quality of "light in August," and enhances the mythic dimension of the novel.

Joe Christmas's first love, Bobbie Allen, is named to reveal her role; like Barbara Allen in the ballad, whose vengeful cruelty caused the death of her lover, she is the cruel romantic heroine. Although Dorothy Tuck correctly described Joe's love for Bobbie as "a parodic inversion of idyllic romance and first love," the inversion is implicit in the ballad; the parodic treatment is Faulkner's Gothic touch. The ironic contrast lies in the difference between Joe's naive concept of Bobbie and her actual age, character, and way of earning her living. Her grotesque hands, too large, lying on the counter "as completely immobile as if they were something she had fetched in from the kitchen" (p. 168), remind one of the unruly but also dissociated hands of Homer Simpson in *The Day of the Locust.* A Dickensian detail may have been transmitted through Faulkner to Nathanael West, in addition to the parallels Carvel Collins found between *Sanctuary* and *The Day of the Locust.* The reader sees Bobbie as the familiar prostitute of Gothic fiction long before Joe learns that she is not only a prostitute but also a sadist, like Max and his friend the stranger.

Joanna Burden is thoroughly Gothic, the Evil Woman who covers the gamut of sexuality, from complete repression "through every avatar of the woman in love" (p. 244): a kind of hermaphrodite stage in which her mannish character and training strove with her repressed femaleness; "the wild throes of nymphomania" (p. 245) which embraced "the two creatures that struggled in the one body," the duality between the "impervious and impregnable" and the "furious denial of that impregnability" through the destruction of purity (p. 246); the delusion of pregnancy; the return to a sense of sin and of mission to expiate the sin. William Brown summed up Joanna's psychological stages as sexual suppression, nymphomania, and guilt. In the depths of her degradation, her wild hair "like octopus tentacles," she is a Medusa figure, recalling the Medusan cult of beauty during the Romantic decadence, dealt with by Mario Praz in "The Beauty of the Medusa," chapter 1 of *The Romantic Agony*. Faulkner's reference to Aubrey Beardsley signifies that this cultural context was in his mind: Joanna's "formally erotic attitudes and gestures" were such "as a Beardsley of the time of Petronius might have drawn" (p. 245). In her relationship with Joe she played three roles, as Ilse Lind observed in "The Calvinistic Burden of *Light in August*": she was a white woman engaging in sexual relations with a Negro man; she was the white mistress of a household observing, for the most part, the etiquette of race relations which forbade eating together and sitting together (she did sit on his cot on one innocent occasion); she tried to be the agent of his regeneration as a Negro serving Negroes. This third role aroused Joe to murderous rage. Joanna Burden, Gail Hightower, and Joe Christmas were all victims of their family and social inheritance; by accepting the values of what Olga Vickery called their "Southern, White, and Elect" society, they became its victims and scapegoats, whereas Lena and Byron rejected those values and survived. Joanna seems to be the least culpable, in that she was warped from birth and was doomed by her puritan conscience to accept a mission which isolated her from the community and insulated her from modifying influences and experiences. Joanna and Joe are doubles in names and in upbringing and temperament, doomed to destroy each other. They are grotesque and terrible when they face each other: "the one [face] cold, dead white, fanatical, mad; the other parchment-colored, the lip lifted into the shape of a soundless and rigid snarl" (p. 262). Unlike the "good women" of *Sanctuary* who caused suffering to others and themselves escaped unscathed, Joanna, an obvious Evil Woman, brought evil on herself in terms of her own Calvinistic beliefs.

As a corollary to the abundance of Tyrannical Fathers in *Light in August*, there is an abundance of Suffering Wives. Mrs. McEachern, like her husband, is too typical to be really convincing. Her timid attempts to mother Joe met with rebuffs, and one can contemplate only with horror what her experience as a wife must have been. Hightower's mother was a Suffering Wife in the physical sense, a helpless invalid, probably as the result of malnutrition during the Civil War when her husband would not let her accept food she could not repay: "God will provide," he said" (p. 442). To their child Gail, his father was "the enemy"; what he was to his wife one can only imagine. As a Suffering Wife Mrs. Hines was the worm that turned; having let her husband in his madness kill the daughter's lover, allow the daughter to die after childbirth, and take away the infant grandchild, Mrs. Hines finally asserted herself and tried to gain at least one day in which to love her doomed grandson Joe Christmas.

Mrs. Hines is grotesque in her antiquated dress and the oddness due to isolation. But in himself, in the madness apparent in his appearance, actions, and speech, Doc Hines is the most grotesque. Hightower is grotesque in his self-neglect and obesity. François Pitavy considered Hightower too grotesque even for a Gothic interpretation, but he assumed that Hightower was intended to be "the moral center of the novel." Pitavy, however, disregarded Byron, both the moral and the structural center of the novel, who through love was both redeemed and redemptive, who not only saw his errors but was able to begin a new life and almost to persuade Hightower to give up immunity for involvement. The grotesqueness of Hightower may be one sign of his function in the Gothic context, rather than in the comic frame with its affirmative values. Richard Pearce's view of *Light in August* as presenting a grimly comic, grotesque world is a distortion due to the focus on a single aspect of Gothic and Faulknerian characteristics.

Except for such grotesque aspects of major figures as have been noted, the grotesque character is not as prominent in *Light in August* as in *Sanctuary*, with its gallery of grotesques. Grotesque incongruities in scenes and tableaux, as in the young priest aspect of Percy Grimm, and the basic grotesqueness of the multiple roles of Joe Christmas, Joanna, and Lena, are of a different order from the Dickensian caricature grotesques and the grotesquerie of purely visual Gothic effects.

Although *Light in August*, like *Sanctuary*, is in part a story of murder and detection, the murder occurred before the beginning of the story and the detection is limited to the information given by Lucas Burch, which is never investigated, much less confirmed. The pursuit of the murderer takes the place of the hunting of clues or information. But by a technique of discontinuity in time, going back to the history of Joe before the murder, Faulkner shifted the suspense from what happened and whodunit to how and why it happened. The smoke of the burning Burden house is seen by Lena, on Saturday, at the end of chapter 1; in chapter 4, after two chapters on Byron and what he knows, Byron tells Hightower about the murder and the testimony of "Brown" against Joe Christmas; chapter 5 covers Joe's actions from Thursday to the point at midnight on Friday when Joe starts toward the Burden house knowing *"Something is going to happen to me"* (p. 110). Then a long block of six chapters covers Joe's life from childhood up to the point of the second phase of Joanna's sexuality. Chapter 12 covers the third phase and the murder scene, all but the final act. After a textual hiatus, which may represent Joe's mental blackout in the act of murder, Joe gets a ride with a boy and girl and realizes, when he has got out of the car, that he flagged the car with his right hand, holding the ancient pistol Joanna had aimed at him. Chapter 13 goes back to Saturday and what was in the burning house, softening the fact that Joanna's "head had been cut pretty near off" (p. 85) to "her throat was cut" (p. 272), but adding the theory that she had been raped. In chapters 13 and 14 the story of Joe, which alternates with the story of Lena, substitutes the excitement and suspense of the chase, given both objectively and from Joe's point of view, for the mystery created by withholding facts of the murder.

Jacques Cabau compared *Light in August* with *Sanctuary* as a *roman policier* of flight and pursuit but realized that the importance of Hightower and the role of Lena are not accounted for by this classification. A significant difference between the two novels is that the chief pursuit in *Sanctuary*, Horace's pursuit of the truth, has no parallel in *Light in August*. From the entry of Doc Hines into the story when Joe is captured in Mottstown (chapter 15), the mystery of the old man and of Joe's identity, held in suspension since the orphanage sequence, predominates until the story of the Hines family, as told to Hightower, is completed in chapter 16. Another element of suspense is added by shifting from the story of Joe to the story of Lena and Byron, chapters 17 and 18, with the consequent shocking impact of the news, at the end of chapter 18, that Joe had been killed an hour previously. Again suspense is aroused by presenting the terrible fact before the antecedent circumstances, making the reader wonder how and why, rather than what. The story of Percy Grimm and his pursuit of Joe Christmas, after Joe broke away when being taken from the jail to the courthouse, is the most exciting flight and pursuit sequence in the novel, but it is told after the events, not as present action, for which Faulkner repeatedly but not consistently used the present tense in *Light in August*. Thus, in *Light in August* as published Faulkner not only used structure and narrative methods, omniscient or limited point of view, to heighten suspense and postpone the solution to the central mystery of Joe's identity but also distanced the moments of greatest horror, the two murders, by presenting them as past action and by building up the psychological study of Joe to stress motivation more than violent action. The nature of the suspense and mystery is in the oldest Gothic tradition: murder, flight and pursuit, and unknown parentage.

The mystery of Joe's identity is the basis for a cluster of themes and patterns of motion which are repeated or contrasted in the stories of other characters; alienation or withdrawal from reality offers flight-paralysis, motion-stasis contrast; quest for identity, for self-knowledge or self-fulfillment, or quest for vengeance presents journey-pursuit patterns.

The patterns of motion and stasis are reflected in the circular and linear image clusters discussed by Richard Chase. One of the most distinctive features in *Light in August* is the prominence of the theme of alienation; the major characters are ostracized or choose to remain outside the community. The basic theme in Faulkner's novels, according to Frank H. Thomas, is that "nothing worthwhile in the fabric of a small community can survive in the face of the community's unwillingness to re-examine the values it has inherited in the light of those individuals who bring different and often opposing values into it." Joanna Burden was ostracized as a northerner, of carpetbagger descent; the paths that led to her house, like the spokes of a wheel, and the volume of her correspondence show that her alienation from the white community was not that of a natural recluse. But she seemed to pursue her mission without becoming personally involved with those she served. Until the presence of Joe Christmas on the Burden place was revealed by "Brown," "there wasn't anybody" on whom to cast the eye of suspicion, to "crucify" (p. 272). Gail Hightower refused to leave the community which had tried to expel him, but he lived a life of deliberate noninvolvement and withdrawal. The ecstasy of his dream vision, a kind of self-induced hallucination for which he had sacrificed his ministry and his marriage, became the center of his life. Until Lena Grove came to Jefferson, Byron Bunch had kept aloof from others, except Hightower, in order to preserve his innocence by fleeing, not resisting, temptation: by allowing himself no leisure from work and religion, he led a blameless life. His friendship with Hightower, however, showed the alienation and withdrawal of both men to be less than complete. Byron always had to go to visit Hightower, self-imprisoned in the "castle" haunted by the vision of his grandfather. Joe, as Byron's coworker, showed an arrogant rejection of fellowship which had its source in defensive pride: "I ain't hungry. Keep your muck" (p. 31). Rejection of food, especially food offered by women, is part of a behavior pattern in Joe which acquires significance as a rejection both of women and of Christian communion. Lucas Burch is the only character whose alienation was freely chosen, along with the name "Joe Brown," whose rejection of responsibility and betrayal of trust seem to be due to some inherent weakness in character, and whose life would never be a purposeful journey but always a "flight into the forest"— facilitated by knowing how to jump a train. Burch climbed out the window and fled from Lena; Joe climbed into the window the first time he went to the Burden house and found there, for a time, a refuge and a sustained human relationship.

The quest for identity, the thematic contrast to alienation, may involve the loss of innocence and the assumption of the burden of guilt and thus combine the quest journey with flight. For the romance theme of descent, explained by Frye in *The Secular Scripture* as reflecting "a growing confusion of identity and of restrictions on action," Faulkner substituted the circle that enclosed Joe, but he inverted the ascent theme that Northrop Frye described as including "discovery of one's real identity, growing freedom, and the breaking of enchantment." Joe's identity sealed his doom, and his "growing freedom" was a brief flight to death. Lena is the one character whose motion is linear, always positive and purposeful even when she did not know her destination and had no guidance. Lena, of course, provides contrast to the Gothic characters more fully than does Byron, who moved from the Gothic orbit into Lena's romantic one. Lena's quest for the father of her child and for a refuge where she could give birth to it was undertaken with serene delight and unshaken confidence. Her acceptance of what would be shame to a respectable heroine is evidence of a kind of innocence that ignores public opinion but that, unlike Sutpen's innocence, knows the truths of the heart. Joanna Burden, whose social ostracism and Calvinistic upbringing had doomed her to sexual repression, set out on no literal journey in her quest for self-fulfillment which took her from virginity to nymphomania. But, curiously, one of the demands she imposed on Joe, during the frenzy of that phase, was a ritual flight and pursuit in which "he would have to seek her about the dark house until he found her, hidden, in closets, in empty rooms, waiting, panting, her eyes in the dark glowing like the eyes of cats," or would have to keep tryst with her "about the grounds" (p. 245). The archetypal antecedents of Gothic flight and pursuit Faulkner dredged from the depths of Joanna's unconscious.

For the three chief male characters, there is a significant change in thematic patterns of motion. Byron, in response to Lena's need and his instinctive love, accepted the quest for experience and knowledge that involved a kind of initiation, proceeding from virginity and innocence to responsibility and knowledge of good and evil and, one presumes, ultimately to normal sexuality. His quest-journeys were in behalf of Lena, in and about Jefferson. Though more limited than Horace's journeys in *Sanctuary*, Byron's journeys literally hold together the two plots. When Gail Hightower was offered a similar opportunity by Byron to assume responsibility, he fought to retain his immunity from life and to keep Byron from involvement with Lena. The reversal of Hightower's immobility, the only time when he moved farther than from his house to the store, came through Byron, who sent Hightower to aid Lena at the birth of her baby. The experience filled Hightower with such a hopeful view of the future and such a "glow of purpose and pride" (p. 383) that he returned to the cabin of his own volition. The ambivalence of his attitude is apparent, however, in his attempt to make Lena send Byron away and in his refusal later to try to save Christmas. As Olga Vickery said, "Though Hightower is willing to accept the natural world, he is not prepared to reenter the social world," to admit his responsibility for that society by interfering with its "beliefs and rituals" in behalf of Joe and thus to expose the futility of his past life, "devoted solely to the worship of a dream." Hightower returned to his "castle" and presumably died there when the world that he had shut out burst violently into his self-chosen prison: he was struck down by Joe Christmas whom he had refused to offer the figurative sanctuary of a false alibi.

The most complex quest, the one doomed to failure, was Joe's quest for identity, for self-definition. Jacques Cabau regarded that "quest for identity" as "superficially . . . the classic motive of all melodrama." To Faulkner, Joe was tragic: "His tragedy was that he didn't know what he was and would never know"; consequently "his only salvation in order to live with himself was to repudiate mankind, to live outside the human race." Doc Hines quoted a Negro as telling little Joe that Joe would never know what he was. For fifteen years, from the time he knocked down and presumably killed McEachern until he went to Jefferson, Joe fled or wandered, refusing to accept himself and his supposedly mixed blood and rejecting acceptance by others when it was offered. He could neither accept nor deny his black blood but revealed his dilemma, as Vickery said, by "his oscillation between repudiation and affirmation." Scott Greer called Joe a marginal man, living in two worlds but identifying with neither and lacking intellectual capacity to cope reflectively with his problem. Frank Thomas described Joe's road to self as full of obstacles, beginning with his victimization by those who used as weapons race and religion and who were responsible for his unsatisfactory relationships with women. Joe's life thus became, Frank Thomas said, "a constant, often agonized refusal to be what others would have him be." During the period of his involvement with Joanna, his struggle for self-definition was as a man and an individual, rather than as white or black. But such definition was impossible in the social context of Jefferson. Glenn Sandstrom explained Joe's rejection of both white and black as a choice of two kinds of negative identity. When Joanna tried to force upon him a positive Negro identity, he insisted on choosing freely a negative Negro identity, and instead of fleeing, fatally confronted her. William Brown identified Joe as a sociopath, the result of environmental influence, rather than of hereditary factors such as produced Popeye. Certainly Faulkner gave a full account of the environmental influences, but he retained the Gothic theme of blood heritage. When the mystery of Joe's identity is solved and he is revealed as the grandson of Doc Hines, his heritage becomes suspect. By giving Joe an insane religious-fanatic grandfather and exposing him to a religious-fanatic foster-father, Faulkner loaded the dice against Joe in both heredity and environment. With Joanna, of the same Calvinist breed, as mistress, the fatal consequence for Joe was inevitable as soon as Joanna's sexuality declined and religion again became an obsession, intensified by her sense of guilt and desire for expiation.

Joe's second "flight into the forest," from the Burden house, was followed with full ritual pursuit by men and dogs, as in that famous American Gothic novel, *Uncle Tom's Cabin*. Such pursuit of criminals was still a common custom in the South in Joe's time, as described by Calvin Brown and John Cullen. Cullen gives an eye-witness account of a manhunt in Oxford which somewhat parallels the pursuit of Joe. A dramatic and significant change took place in Joe during his second flight. After he had fled for several days, he emerged from a trancelike state to be aware of food given him in a Negro cabin and to regret the fear behind the gesture. He then accepted his identity as a Negro and his brotherhood with other Negroes, symbolized when he put on "the black shoes smelling of negro" (p. 313) to throw the dogs off his trail. When Joe asked what day it was, he emerged from the timeless void in which he had lived during his homeless wandering and his guilty flights and became, in Sandstrom's words, "weirdly reconciled with time." Then he desired "to see his native earth in all its phases for the first or the last time" (p. 320), and came to realize that the street he had run on for thirty years had "made a circle" and that he had "never broken out of the ring" of what he had done and could never undo (p. 321). But he played the game of capture according to the white man's rules: he made a choice and stopped running in circles. As Frank Thomas said, "He completely and finally affirmed his own individual humanity on the wagon to Mottstown," with his shoes "planted on the dashboard": "that mark on his ankles the gauge definite and ineradicable of the black tide creeping up his legs, moving from his feet upward as death moves" (p. 321).

Joe's purposeful journey back into the world of time and man, to pay for his deeds, is performed with ritualistic actions like those which had preceded his last confrontation with Joanna. He shaves himself, finally finds out the day of the week, journeys literally through the woods until he comes to a highway, gets a ride to Mottstown, on Saturday morning (more likely than "Friday") (p. 322), goes to a white barbershop and gets a shave and haircut, buys a new shirt, tie, and hat, and then walks the streets, milling with the Saturday throngs, until he is recognized, acting like neither "a nigger or a white man" (p. 331). The ritual he followed, much like that of Quentin Compson before he set out to drown himself, was intended to enable him to meet death on his own terms, with propriety and not "skulking and hiding in the woods, muddy and dirty and running" (p. 331).

After Joe's arrest Joe and the reader are kept in suspense until Doc Hines's frenzied attack on Joe and his demand that Joe be hanged forthwith are explained by the facts that Joe is Doc's grandson and that, as was apparent at the beginning of the chapter, Doc was the mysterious man at the orphanage. The traditional recognition scene, in which identity is disclosed, took place offstage: Mrs. Hines saw Joe in jail and presumably told Joe what she had told Byron and Hightower. According to Gavin Stevens, her disclosure gave Joe the patience and courage to seize the one moment when escape was possible and he could flee to sanctuary at Hightower's. The motives for this last flight are not made clear— Faulkner abdicated his omniscience. The most frantic flight and pursuit in this novel and in Faulkner's work thus took place after the revelation of identity, with the final irony that the momentous discovery which had seemed forever impossible, and which in the Gothic tradition should bring wealth and honor to the hero, precipitated his death. But Joe's "peaceful and unfathomable and unbearable eyes" may signify that his acceptance of his human condition and his one fleeting experience of kinship and love ended his alienation. Why Joe struck down Hightower remains a mystery.

This last episode also illustrates the other side of many flights, the pursuit. An unusual aspect of the flight-pursuit pattern in *Light in August* is that the motive for pursuit is repeatedly not a seducer's lust but a quest for personal or divine vengeance. Faulkner's use of clairvoyant powers in such pursuits recalls the use of the supernatural in early Gothic fiction. William Brown pointed out the relationship between the Calvinistic doctrine of predestination and the sense of prescience and clairvoyance experienced by McEachern and Percy Grimm and by Joe when fleeing after striking down McEachern. Events resulting from unconscious motivation seemed to originate outside the conscious self. Brown summed up the extreme use of this kind of "supernatural foreordained vengeful purpose": "The suspicious delusions of the insane, the religious delusions of the fanatic, and the superstitions of the fortuneteller attain here a kind of reality." Faulkner's use of such characters, representing Old Testament Protestantism, Ilse Lind cited to support her interpretation of *Light in August* as revealing "Apocalyptic Visions": "In apocalypse, revelation is conceived of as essentially a psychical phenomenon, rather than a supernatural one, expressing itself through dreams, visions, trances, and trance-like states." McEachern on the horse pursuing Joe did so with "undeviating conviction of both omnipotence and clairvoyance," as if he were being guided and "propelled by some militant Michael Himself" (p. 190). A "little mad, with frustration, outrage" (p. 309), Lucas Burch accompanied the posse on the hunt for Joe, in quest of both revenge and reward. In Doc Hines's pursuit, first of his daughter and then of Joe, Hines was less physically active than McEachern but even more implacable and relentless, as indefatigable and unshakable as the Hound of Heaven. Guided by the devil, it seemed to others, Hines thought that God "had set His will to working and had left old Doc Hines to watch it. From that very first night, when He had chose His own Son's sacred anniversary to set it a-working on, He set old Doc Hines to watch it" (p. 363). God had designated as Doc's work "that bastard": "He's a pollution and a abomination on My earth" (p. 365).

Appalling as are McEachern and Hines, one a bit mad and the other completely so, they were of an older generation, brought up like the Burdens in a stern creed. But most appalling is Percy Grimm, a young man so fanatic in his belief in the creed of white supremacy, with such "a sublime and implicit faith in physical courage and blind obedience" (p. 426), that he became self-appointed leader in the pursuit of Joe. The grotesqueness of the Grimm chase on a Western Union bicycle is authentic modern Gothic horror. Percy's "grave and reckless joy" in the pursuit, a particularly horrible touch, reached a climax when "above the blunt, cold rake of the automatic his face had that serene, unearthly luminousness of angels in church windows" (p. 437). Traditional Gothic imagery is startlingly used in a grotesquely incongruous context. With a sense of certainty like that of McEachern and Hines, Percy, "with that lean, swift, blind obedience," like a pawn moved by the Player (p. 437), ran straight to Joe in Hightower's house and completed his vengeance in the name of southern womanhood and white supremacy: "Now you'll let white women alone, even in hell" (p. 439).

With its greater scope in time and space than *Sanctuary, Light in August* includes more Gothic violence, dramatically represented. The flexibility in method and style ranges from the omniscient author, focusing on Joe or Lena to permit full subjective representation of characters who are themselves inarticulate, to the final subjective presentation of Hightower, ending with third-person stream of consciousness. Other long passages are given to a narrator, such as Joanna's story to Joe, Byron's narration of what has been going on in Jefferson, and Mrs. Hines's story of Joe's parentage. These methods permit maximum revelation of motivation, with the exception, already noted, of Joe's last flight which Faulkner chose to leave mysterious. The great range and quantity of imagery need not, with this method, be limited to what is appropriate to the point of view of the characters. Here we are concerned with imagery relevant to the Gothic tradition of dramatic tableaux and scenes of violent action.

Despite the reputation of *Sanctuary* for being Faulkner's most horrific work, *Light in August* has more scenes that are violent or macabre, especially scenes dealing with or motivated by sexuality. The initial scenes in the story of the orphan Joe, those which made him an orphan, were actions of the sex-obsessed religious fanatic Doc Hines: he shot Joe's father and left him lying dead in the rain; he kept inhuman guard over his daughter Milly to prevent aid being given her at the birth of Joe; he watched Milly die. His treatment of little Joe, in the orphanage, was sadistic in a way not perceived by that child of sin. His attack on Joe in the street in Mottstown is presented as seen by townspeople: he beat the captive Joe in maniacal frenzy until he "kind of flopped," only to recover quickly and return downtown, demanding that the "nigger" be taken from jail and hanged (p. 332). From the time that he first knew that his daughter had conceived a child in sin, Doc Hines had lived for the supreme satisfaction of this moment when God's will would be done. The prescience of Hines led him to settle in the town in which Joe's wanderings and flight would come to an end.

Joe's sexual obsessions are traced from his childhood in a series of dramatic scenes. William Brown explained the episode with the dietitian as "the central core" of Joe's "psychic makeup" in relation to "sex, guilt, and race." The "infantile amnesia" he suffered in the closet, from which he was hauled out by the furious dietitian hissing, "You little nigger bastard!" (p. 117), influenced his adult motivation by implanting seeds of sexual guilt related to Negro blood. This traumatic experience was reflected in Joe's rejection of women who tried to win him with food and kindness, especially Mrs. McEachern and Joanna Burden. The puritanic training by McEachern increased Joe's disgust with sex which was manifest in his fight with the boys who tried to initiate him into sex and in his private puberty rite with the dead sheep, by which he thought to gain immunity from his scanty and crude knowledge of sex. When Joe shot a sheep and bathed his hands "in the yet warm blood of the dying beast" (p. 174), he was, as Brown remarked, literally bathed in the blood of the lamb, but his baptism was ineffectual. His immunity ended when he fell in love with Bobbie and lost his innocence: he had a vision of "suavely shaped urns in moonlight, blanched," from each of which issued "something liquid, deathcolored, and foul" (pp. 177, 178). He overcame his revulsion and Bobbie initiated him into sexuality. His attitude toward women remained ambivalent. The urn image contrasts with the Grecian urn allusion describing Lena's progress and with Hightower's vision of his own life, "like a classic and serene vase" (p. 453). Because Joe kept

McEachern ignorant of his pathetic romance with Bobbie, only McEachern's last assault on Joe was caused by Joe's sexual transgression. When Joe raised a chair in defense, McEachern walked into it "in the furious and dreamlike exaltation of a martyr who has already been absolved," seeing Joe's face as that of Satan (pp. 191-92). The violence Joe met when he fled to Bobbie and was beaten by her friends for spoiling their racket, he met head on, "with something of the exaltation of his adopted father" (p. 204). This experience, as Olga Vickery noted, "intensifies his awareness" of the "antithesis of black and white" and initiates his provocation of racial violence from both races in "an almost joyful affirmation of the Negro-white pattern in which both Joe and his opponents are trapped." Psychologically his behavior is strikingly similar to that of Charles Etienne Bon in *Absalom, Absalom!* who first provoked fights and then accepted his Negro status by marrying a black brute. Sadism and masochism are evident in both characters, directly related to the fact or supposition of Negro blood.

The prolonged and final period of sexuality in Joe's life, the years with Joanna Burden, presents more scenes and details of various common or extraordinary and violent sexuality than can be cited. The images by which the phases in Joanna's sex life are summed up are in themselves miniature Gothic landscapes: "During the first phase it had been as though he were outside a house where snow was on the ground, trying to get into the house; during the second phase he was at the bottom of a pit in the hot wild darkness; now he was in the middle of a plain where there was no house, not even snow, not even wind" (pp. 254-55). The symbolic interpretation of Gothic landscapes in psychological terms is epitomized in these objective correlatives of sexual experience.

The final confrontation between Joe and Joanna was motivated by the decline of her sexuality and the reawakening of her sense of sin and her missionary zeal. She and Joe, in their subjection to Calvinistic teachings, Ilse Lind said, had suffered in opposite ways from analogous "cultural neuroses." When Joanna tried to bend Joe to what she conceived as the Divine Will that he should take up the black cross as a Negro among Negroes, Joe's predestined reaction was compounded of all the violence which was associated for him with sex and religion. Before going to Joanna's house, expecting something to happen, Joe observed certain rituals. These rituals included: symbolic repudiation of women in the cutting off of buttons and in the destruction of cans of whiskey, equivalents of the urns; assertion of manhood, in standing naked and shaving; and quest for racial identity, in wandering through both white and Negro sections of Jefferson. The ritual pattern itself is in keeping with the medievalism of the Gothic tradition: the repeated striking of the town clock is a specifically Gothic note.

The chapter dealing with the last confrontation of Joe and Joanna heightens the suspense by interposing Joe's recollection of the battle of wills between them, from May to August, and of her starting to pray over him two nights earlier. The striking of "the last stroke of the far clock" (p. 265) links with the clock striking twelve (p. 110). "Then it was time" (p. 266) begins the murder episode. "It wont need any light" recalls both Othello's "Put out the light, and then put out the light" and Wash Jones's "Hit wont need no light, honey" (*Absalom, Absalom!* p. 291). Joe did lay down his razor, however, and light the lamp. But the scene is utterly lacking in direct presentation of violent action. When Joanna said, "It's not I who ask it" and Joe refused to kneel in submission to the Divine Will, she pulled out an antique long revolver and Joe, unarmed, watched not the gun or her eyes, "calm and still," but the shadow of the pistol on the wall "when the cocked shadow of the hammer flicked away" (p. 267). A space on the page follows, indicating apparently a break in Joe's consciousness from that moment until he flagged down the car with the hand holding the pistol, last mentioned in Joanna's hand. The razor was not mentioned again until page 317. Joe's actions in the interval are never revealed. The young couple with whom he got the ride reported no evidence that Joe's appearance bore signs that he had committed a bloody murder, although when the body was found it was almost decapitated. The pistol, found where Joe threw it, had not been fired. Thus, not only is no murder described but the only evidence of Joe's guilt, so far as law officials and townspeople are concerned, is the word of Lucas Burch. His statement that Joe had been living with Joanna and that he had Negro blood obviated further investigation. When Joe reentered time and took up the routine of daily life, he had his razor, but there is no hint in his thoughts or in the author's comments that it was the instrument of a bloody murder. The question raised by Stephen Meats, "Who Killed Joanna Burden?" is answered only by the note on the map in *Absalom, Absalom!*: "where Christmas killed Miss Burden." This unusual twist in a Gothic novel in which violence is appropriate is not only typical of Faulkner's distancing of horror but also suggests that, so far as known facts are concerned, white society may have made Joe an innocent scapegoat, a victim of racial prejudice inflamed by the presumed sexual aspects of the murder. It is, of course, made clear to the reader that Joanna was not a victim of rape, but white society would assume that any other sexual relationship between a white woman and a Negro man was unthinkable.

Filled as the life of Joe was with scenes of sexuality and violence, episodes from the past, factually stated, add other examples. The wife of Gail Hightower was driven to infidelity by her husband's neglect and then committed suicide by jumping or falling from a hotel window.

Townsmen beat Hightower, on suspicion that he had had sexual relations with a Negro woman and a Negro man. Part of the present action is the brief fight between Byron Bunch and Lucas Burch; though Lucas fought "with the blind and desperate valor of a starved and cornered rat," Byron offered little opposition and in less than two minutes lay "bleeding and quiet" (p. 416). Not only is this fight a direct parallel of the old courtly love combats over a lady, translated into humble terms, but when Byron rises he puts into the vernacular an idea which a temporarily defeated knight-errant might express: "I'll have to get on so I can find me something else to meddle with." Faulkner's parodies of the courtly lover are one aspect of Gothic medievalism; here he named his unromantic hero to recall ironically the supremely Romantic hero. Furthermore, if Lena Grove is intended to represent "Diana of the Wood," as Beach Langston affirmed, Byron is the candidate for the priesthood who, according to Sir James G. Frazer's account in *The Golden Bough*, "could only succeed to office by slaying the priest." Faulkner's parallel ironies are likely to extend to infinity.

In addition to the scenes of sexual violence are other violent scenes, in the present or in the past which conditioned the present. The story of the shooting of the two Calvin Burdens, grandfather and grandson, by Colonel Sartoris, "over a question of Negro voting" (p. 235), significantly links *Light in August* into the Yoknapatawpha legend, where it is twice told, in *Sartoris* (1929) and *The Unvanquished* (1938); this is regional violence. The beating of the Burden children is part of the same cultural heritage as McEachern's beating of Joe Christmas: the rigors of Calvinism, mistakenly associated with Unitarianism in the Burden story, contributed to the violence displayed by Joanna and Joe. When Joe was beaten by McEachern for not learning his catechism, the uncompromising nature of man and boy was stressed. The capacity to deal out and to receive punishment was equal: "It would have been hard to say which face was the more rapt, more calm, more convinced" (p. 140). Not the influence of McEachern at this early period, but the heritage from that equally implacable but unknown grandfather is revealed in Joe. The second beating, for being late, Joe received after his fight over the Negro girl. This beating also he received unmoved: "contemplative and remote with ecstasy and selfcrucifixion" (p. 150). Twice Joe appeared as the aggressor. In the Negro church, during his flight from the Burden house, Joe assaulted the minister, knocked down an old man, and then cursed God from the pulpit: here Joe is satanic, an anti-Christ. This incident exemplifies what Ilse Lind regarded as an "innovative device," the "intercepted ritual motif": "In each instance, uncontrolled psychic energy is hurled against the very social institution which attempts to maintain moral order within the society," expressing the division in man between desire "for social integration and the destructive impulse to resist it." The episode of Joe in the church is the only example cited which involves a main character and present action. When he struck down Hightower at the end of his last flight, Joe was apparently acting in a frenzy of fear.

One whole sequence of thematic scenes in the story of Joe provides a Christ parallel, made explicit by repeated references to crucifixion, one of which is cited above. Faulkner said that "the story of Christ and the Passion" was part of his "Christian background" and that symbolism was second to the story. The regional inclination to crucify a scapegoat is mentioned and then explained in the novel: after the murder of Joanna, the townsmen, "some of them with pistols already in their pockets began to canvass about for someone to crucify" (p. 272); Doc Hines would have been crucified for holding revival services in Negro churches had he been a young man. Hightower realized that the puritanic mores produced the violence in his region: "Pleasure, ecstasy, they cannot seem to bear: their escape from it is in violence, in drinking and fighting and praying; catastrophe too, the violence identical and apparently inescapable. *And so why should not their religion drive them to crucifixion of themselves and one another?*" (p. 347). As a scapegoat, Joe Christmas fits perfectly Joel Porte's description of "the figure and fate" which have "teased, indeed tortured the Gothic and Romantic imagination endlessly": "the guilt-driven outcast, alternately a criminal and a martyr." But whereas Gothic and Romantic novels often turned to horrors of the past, Faulkner found his horrors in the living heritage from the past. And preeminent in those horrors was the one symbolized by the black cross, to which Joanna envisioned white babies nailed, the shadow which she could not escape but must raise with her: in her father's words, "'The curse of the white race is the black man who will be forever God's chosen own because He once cursed Him'" (p. 240). (The problem of "Him" was solved by Henry Pommer: autograph corrections in the manuscript show "him.")

Joe is marked as a Christ or an anti-Christ scapegoat first by his name, in which "he carried with him his own inescapable warning, like a flower its scent or a rattlesnake its rattle" (p. 29). Lucas Burch is Judas, early referred to as a disciple to Joe, the master (p. 40). Lucas betrayed Joe for the reward: "'I know who done it and when I get my reward, I'll tell'" (p. 279). Edwin Moseley identified the role of Lucas in the crucifixion of Joe Christmas: his name is "obviously derived from Luke who tells the story of Christ and from Judas who betrays the master to the deputies." Moseley did not, however, note that the assumption of the legal authorities that Joe murdered Joanna rests solely upon the word of this Judas. The account of the "crucifixion," the castration and slaying of Joe by Percy Grimm, does not establish Joe as an unequivocal Christ figure. William Brown interpreted Joe's hearing voices before the murder (pp. 97-98, 101) as a "definite sign of a psychotic schizophrenic process." He saw Joe as a Christ figure only as combining the victim-scapegoat ideas, "as the innocent and vicarious victim and expiator of the guilt of humanity."

Joe was probably guilty of murder, perhaps of both Joanna and McEachern, but not guilty of raping Joanna, the idea that aroused the most violent reaction in the community. Joe may be regarded as an anti-Christ and is so presented in the scene in the Negro church. But he is obviously a scapegoat: his guilt was not proved and he was not legally executed. As a scapegoat, made to bear the guilt of the white race toward the Negroes, he is a genuine Christ figure as described by Northrop Frye in *Anatomy of Criticism:* "All attempts to transfer guilt to a victim give that victim something of the dignity of innocence. The archetype of the incongruously ironic is Christ, the perfectly innocent victim excluded from human society." Dorothy Tuck saw in Joe also an ironic inversion of the archetypal dying god, "in whose death there are elements both of sacrifice to a higher and more fearful power" and of communion between worshipers and god and among worshipers. As Joe's story impinges on that of Lena, it expands to embrace both Christian and pagan elements to match hers. Perhaps Joe represents not Christ but a surrogate for Christ, an ironic application of the principle referring to deeds of charity: "Inasmuch as ye have done it unto the least of these my brethren, ye have done it unto me."

What concerns us here is the significance of the death of Joe as part of a Christ analogy used in a Gothic framework. The crucifixion is the ultimate horror available for use in Christian-oriented fiction. Faulkner used it in a story of alienation resulting from religious, social, and psychological influences to which a child was exposed. A suggestion of a change from alienation to an acceptance of self and of responsibility is evident in the end of Joe's flight when he goes to Mottstown and gives himself up. His last flight, unexplained, may represent a further change motivated by Joe's learning his identity; in Glenn Sandstrom's terms, Joe finally achieves "an acceptance of what he is and a belief in his own dignity and power and implacable resistance." Frank Thomas explained Joe's last flight as a way of avoiding an "execution covered with the cloak of spurious justice" and of "defining the terms of his own death." He chose the limited identity defined by T. H. Adamowski in "Joe Christmas": "the escaped-nigger-murderer-with-a-gun-in-his-hand." The mystery of why he did not fire the pistol he snatched up in a Negro cabin is not solved by Gavin Stevens's stereotyped good-white and bad-black blood theory of a moral struggle. The terror of that last Gothic flight and the horror of Joe's death Faulkner distanced and modified by relating the event after the fact and by shifting the focus to Percy Grimm. The dying god image further modifies the horror by raising it from individual suffering to regional and universal significance, well expressed by Ihab Hassan in *Radical Innocence:* ". . . Faulkner's Joe Christmas, whose name refers us back ironically to the great symbol of sacrificial redemption, is violated before our eyes, murdered and castrated, the black and white blood in his veins gushing forth to haunt our dying moments with a memory of all the outrages we have helped to perpetuate." Such a revitalization of Christian myth by means of the Gothic mode explains Faulkner's profound influence on southern writers in the burgeoning new American Gothic.

The Gothic amalgam can easily enough accommodate the tragic story of Joe Christmas as a Christ figure within the comic frame of Lena as the Virgin Mary. But although critics have perceived the thematic functions of Hightower, they have been perplexed by his structural role and his relationship to the Christ parallels. In "Apocalyptic Vision as a Key to *Light in August*" Ilse Lind offers a possible explanation of "the penultimate chapter," which she shows to be "strikingly apocalyptic." This chapter and the final one provide the other half of the initial double frame: chapter 1, the arrival of Lena, was followed by chapters 2, 3, and 4 on Byron and Hightower—what Byron and the town knew about Hightower and what Byron and Hightower knew about Joe Christmas. Chapter 5 introduces Joe directly, before the murder of Joanna Burden. Thus, the return, after the account of Joe's death, to the story of Hightower is structurally required to connect the horror of Joe's death and the happy ending of the comedy frame. The meditations of Hightower took place after he was wounded by Joe. Ilse Lind interprets Hightower as a Christ figure, "the Agony in the Garden which bodies forth Christ's spiritual ordeal." She supports her view by many impressive details, from Hightower as a man of God to the blood-sweat image. But, like Joe, Hightower is an ironic Christ figure, the man of God who betrayed his holy mission and withdrew from serving either God or man. If this fundamental inversion is kept in mind, the apocalyptic interpretation provides valuable insights into this penultimate chapter.

The setting is not in a garden: Hightower is "framed by the study window like a stage" (p. 441). The "point of epiphany" at which "the undisplaced apocalyptic world and the cyclical world of nature come into alignment" occurred on high places, according to Frye in *Anatomy of*

Criticism. Hightower's epiphany was on a low level: neither the apocalyptic world nor the world of nature had been significant in his experience, save for a brief vision of "luck and life returned to these barren acres" (p. 385) of the Burden farm, a vision unfulfilled. "Tragic enlightenment" is a better term than "epiphany" for Hightower's experience, with irony in the fact that he had been notably a man of inaction in the narrative events. But Hightower's story, from his own point of view, and the self-knowledge he attained, illuminate the whole pattern of violence which the novel presents and conclude a pattern of dream imagery and dream experience which is one of the most Gothic elements in *Light in August.* Hightower's whole life had been sacrificed to attain the hallucinatory moments of rapt vision in which he saw his grandfather, virtually apotheosized and confounded with religion, as one of Van Dorn's raiders, galloping through the darkness with sound of bugles and clash of arms. This image symbolizes the southern chivalric ideal, the same vision, in effect, of a man on a horse to which Wash Jones yielded his devotion and by which he was betrayed. The dreamlike experience of Joe on the horse, after knocking down McEachern, belongs, Lind observed, to the same cluster of images as Hightower's vision: to Joe it was "a strange dreamy effect, like a moving picture in slow motion," reaching a moment of stasis like "an equestrian statue strayed from its pedestal" (pp. 196, 197). Hightower's meditations revealed the emptiness of his life and his religion, sacrificed to a meretricious ideal. Seeing himself as if reflected in the faces of his congregations of the past, "a figure antic as a showman," he recognized his blasphemy: "a charlatan preaching worse than heresy . . . , offering instead of the crucified shape of pity and love, a swaggering and unchastened bravo killed with a shotgun in a peaceful henhouse, in a temporary hiatus of his own avocation of killing" (p. 462). By implication, this is a judgment on the ideals of the society which, without pity and love, had still crucified and which had too much cherished the memory of the Civil War, epitomized by Hightower as "a single instant of darkness in which a horse galloped and a gun crashed" (p. 465).

This whole chapter is essentially Gothic, from the family story, with the three phantoms which Hightower remembered, to his dreamlike loss of controlled thought, as the wheel of thought slowed. At this point occurs one of the two images Lind considered "strikingly apocalyptic," Hightower's vision of a "halo . . . full of faces" (p. 465), peaceful as if apotheosized, which becomes narrowed to two faces, Joe's and Percy Grimm's, which "seem to strive . . . in turn to free themselves one from the other, then fade and blend again" (p. 466). The identity of pursued and pursuer was noted by Joel Porte as a feature in Poe's doubles in

"William Wilson," which combined Gothic terror and Calvinistic theology. These doubles correspond to Northrop Frye's account, in *Anatomy of Criticism,* of the sinister parallels in apocalyptic imagery: the poles of the sinister world are: "the tyrant-leader ... who commands loyalty only if he is egocentric enough to represent the collective ego of his followers" and "the *pharmakos* or sacrificed victim, who has to be killed to strengthen the others." Hightower's final vision of the horsemen, the other "strikingly apocalyptic" passage, follows the fading of the halo: "They rush past, forwardleaning in the saddles, with brandished arms, beneath whipping ribbons from slanted and eager lances; with tumult and soundless yelling they sweep past like a tide whose crest is jagged with the wild heads of horses and the brandished arms of men like the crater of the world in explosion" (pp. 466–67). Ilse Lind explained the "apocalyptic allusions": "the horsemen as the riders of the apocalypse; the 'crater of the world in explosion' as the prognostication of the end; the haloed light as divinely inspired revelation; and the wheel—with its inherent motion and desire—as the wheel of divine purpose." This interpretation, however, neglects the characterization of Hightower throughout the novel and his admission of his own grievous errors, among which was such a vision, and ignores the fact that, as Northrop Frye demonstrated, the apocalyptic world in literature had its parallel in the sinister world, human and natural, which is represented in the novel in such fundamental aspects as the Waste Land, the demonic erotic relationships, and the demonic social relation, the mob, led and outstripped by Percy Grimm. The sinister world is "the world of the nightmare and the scapegoat, of bondage and pain and confusion. . . ."

The ambiguity of the recurrence of Hightower's vision after the enlightenment which should have exorcised it is not accounted for by Ilse Lind's interpretation, but would be consistent with the sinister world as parallel to the apocalyptic world and with the thematic implications of the novel. Olga Vickery's comment on Hightower is valid: "Hightower has the intelligence to attain this bitter self-knowledge and to realize that the responsibility rests with the individual, but he does not have the strength to live with it." Or to die with it. Hightower less resembles St. John upon Patmos than "a hollow man, dreaming of lost violent souls in death's dream kingdom."

The story of Lena and Byron concludes *Light in August,* framing the tragedy of alienation in the comedy of integration. Obviously related to the story of Joe Christmas by Lena's Virgin Mary aspect and the nativity scene, the relevance of the story of Byron to the conclusions of the stories of Joe and Hightower is not so apparent. Somewhat like Horace with Lee Goodwin, Byron had attempted to save Joe and had failed, but Byron's failure was not due to inadequacy to a professional task. Byron had saved Lena and had prepared Hightower for his enlightenment. In contrast with the nightmares of Joe and the paralyzing dreams of Hightower, Byron was motivated by a romantic dream which grew out of the realities of common experience. With no recognition of the dream elements of *Light in August* as part of the Gothic configuration, Olga Vickery stated the significance of dreams: "It is man's nature to dream and dreams by their very essence are both distortions of reality and desires for a new shape to experience." The dreams of Byron illustrate how "reason and imagination can prove an integrative force, identifying the interests of the individual with those of the community and establishing a link between the private and public worlds." In effect, this is what the original Gothic novel served in some measure to do, by restoring imagination and dreams to a culture which had too exclusively taken reason as its ideal.

Light in August, as Leslie Fiedler pointed out in *Love and Death,* is about two saviors, "Joe Christmas, in his inevitable crucifixion both Christ and anti-Christ," and Lena Grove, "an inarticulate, unvirginal Mary in search of a Joseph." Fiedler's discussion of *Light in August* in *Love and Death in the American Novel* is limited to this point. The tragic and comic aspects of *Light in August,* as Dorothy Tuck observed, "form a dialectic of irony." The last chapter not only concludes the ironic parallels to the Christ story but does so in the tradition of the Gothic romance, with a happy ending, in a most un-Gothic comic vein. As Lena and Byron and the baby ride off into Tennessee, we recall Lena's earlier journey and her serene blue figure moving across the landscape in quest of the father of her child and a place for the child to be born. As Jacques Cabau said: "From the jungle of Jefferson, from that Gothic melodrama, she, alone, departs unscathed, passing slowly from one horizon to the other. . . ." She symbolizes the paradise lost when slavery, property, and Christianity were brought to the virgin land. Lena, Byron, and the baby are Faulkner's Holy Family, fleeing to Egypt from a land where terrible things happen to children. The fact that Byron is not the child's father strengthens the Christ story suggestion—until one reflects that if Byron represents Joseph, Lucas Burch must represent the Holy Ghost. Although Faulkner's Christ parallels are never wholly consistent, one wonders whether this particular irony occurred to him. Not only is this group a Holy Family, but it is the only example in Yoknapatawpha of father, mother, and infant presented as the archetypal family group. The only parallel group, Eula, Linda, and Flem at the end of *The Hamlet,* is an Unholy Family, in view of Flem's impotence, the reasons for the marriage, and Flem's diabolic role in Ratliff's Fable of

Hell. Moreover, the birth of Lena's baby is the only birth directly presented in Yoknapatawpha. Miss Quentin and Linda Snopes were born offstage, to conceal the shame of their origins, and the birth of Benbow Sartoris is reduced to: "That day Narcissa's child was born" (*Sartoris,* p. 366). The beginning and ending of *Light in August* thus frame tragedy in comedy and extend the birth-death cycle to the rebirth, in which Lena's baby is another little Joe, as Mrs. Hines in her confused state took him to be. But Lena's child will have two parents and a reasonable hope for the future. It is doubtful that he is to be regarded as a future messiah, but at least life goes on and the last trump is not sounding. Lena and Byron on the road present an image which, Northrop Frye said in *Anatomy of Criticism,* is "inseparable from all quest literature"; the comic ending is in harmony with apocalyptic symbolism as reduced to human terms in the "analogy of innocence" which is "largely concerned with an attempt to present the desirable in human, familiar, attainable, and morally allowable terms."

The double plot structure, with Lena at both beginning and end and with carefully contrived parallel actions of Joe and Lena, was one of the most significant changes Regina Fadiman discovered in her study of Faulkner's revisions in the last handwritten manuscript of *Light in August,* in comparison with the published version. She concluded that Faulkner was an "artist in montage." Some of her specific findings in "this story of pursuit and capture" are relevant to a consideration of Gothic elements. The double plot structure, with Lucas Burch the link between the plots, involved also the opposing themes of flight and pursuit and the quest pattern. Also more fully developed in the revisions were the parallels and doubles in characters and events. The subjective characterization of Joe Christmas and Gail Hightower greatly increased the psychological study of various kinds of alienation: the long flashback of Joe's life was added after the present action had been written, and the thoughts of Hightower revealed his past life near the end. Both the Negro and the Calvinistic themes were amplified. Deliberate ambiguity was built up about Joe's racial heritage and his role in the deaths of McEachern, Joanna Burden, and Hightower. A change in Hightower's thoughts from "Maybe I am dying," in the manuscript, to "I am dying" (p. 466) supports the view that Hightower's wound was fatal. Mystery veiled Joe's motives for his last flight. Revisions played down the Christ parallels by having the birth of the baby, the death of Joe, and the epiphany of Hightower take place on the same day, a Monday. Amibguity about Joe as the grandson of Doc and Mrs. Hines was removed by revision. Gothic effects of irony, suspense, and ambiguity were heightened by the final order of events, by the distancing of violence and death, and by the enclosure of the tragic story within the comedy: the last chapter was a late addition. *Sanctuary, Light in August,* and *Absalom, Absalom!* reveal similar processes of revising and restructuring which enhance the Gothic qualities, whether or not that was Faulkner's controlling purpose.

Light in August, Faulkner's most significant use of the Gothic tradition to represent action taking place at the time of his writing, shows the forces alienating individuals and disrupting the community. Written before *Absalom, Absalom!* it anticipates the problem of miscegenation but presents it outside the context of Yoknapatawpha families. Incest is the only significant Gothic theme which Faulkner omitted in *Light in August.*

CHAPTER SEVEN

GO DOWN, MOSES

PARADISE LOST, OR, THE SECRET
OF THE LEDGERS

Although "The Bear," which is central to *Go Down, Moses* and has received more critical study than has the whole book, most fully represents the Gothic flight to the forest in Yoknapatawpha, its Gothic origins have been generally overlooked, perhaps because the tone is nostalgic rather than somber and scenes of violence are not prominent. The whole cluster of themes and patterns in *Go Down, Moses,* however, is essentially Gothic: miscegenation and incest are at the heart of the McCaslin story, and the prevailing pattern of action in the novel is flight and pursuit, chiefly of quarry and hunter. *Go Down, Moses,* the most significant Yoknapatawpha novel dealing with the theme of race relations, shows changes of intention intended to stress that theme, which became the focus of Faulkner's concern in much of his later work. The chief basic changes, those which made the Beauchamp family of Negroes the descendants, through Eunice, of Carothers McCaslin, are explained by James Early in *The Making of Go Down, Moses.*

In *Light in August* Faulkner was not dealing primarily with the leading families in Yoknapatawpha. When thereafter he wrote *Absalom, Absalom!* he made the theme of race relations central to the Sutpen story. (As Early shows, Faulkner had Negro characters named Sutpen in a typescript of "Go Down, Moses.") The theme of race relations was introduced into the Compson story when Faulkner made Quentin Compson the central consciousness, the listener-narrator, in *Absalom, Absalom!* Thus, the theme of incest of *The Sound and the Fury* is fused with the Sutpen theme of miscegenation. Because Quentin, the only sympathetic Compson character, and all the Sutpens were dead in 1910, neither Sutpens nor Compsons could be further developed in the twentieth century. Similarly, the Sartoris family had come to an end unless Faulkner wanted to develop the unpromising Benbow Sartoris. Thus, if Faulkner wanted to deal with miscegenation in its long range aspects, he had to create a new family or develop one already created which offered potentialities for growth.

The latter course Faulkner followed with the McCaslin family, which continues in the rest of the major Yoknapatawpha novels except *Snopes.* (The Snopes story had been in Faulkner's mind since the writing of *Flags in the Dust.*) Of the leading families created by the late 1930s, the McCaslins were the only ones who offered possibilities for development in the direction in which Faulkner wished to proceed. Between 1934 and the writing of *Go Down, Moses,* Faulkner had been preparing to add the McCaslins, especially Isaac, to the Yoknapatawpha cycle. In *Absalom, Absalom!* Uncle Buck (Theophilus) McCaslin was present at the burial of Charles Bon. In *The Unvanquished* (1938), an addition to "The Retreat" (1934) told of Uncle Buck's and Uncle Buddy's unconventional dealings with their slaves, and in "Vendée" (1936) Uncle Buck was a major character in a Gothic tale of pursuit and vengeance of which Bayard Sartoris, old Bayard of *Sartoris,* was the hero. Three short stories—"The Old People" (1940), "Lion" (1935), and "The Bear" (1942)—were centered in the same narrator–central intelligence, who was identified only in "Lion" as Quentin Compson. In that story Uncle Ike McCaslin was a minor figure, an old man with a grandson. In *Go Down, Moses* Faulkner made two major changes in unpublished and published works to give a prominent place to the McCaslins: he changed the narrator in "Was" from Bayard Sartoris, narrator of *The Unvanquished,* to McCaslin Edmonds, the same age as Bayard, and thus cut out the Sartorises; he put Isaac McCaslin in the role of Quentin Compson in the three short stories published independently of *Go Down, Moses,* changed the time of action to thirty years earlier, and made the necessary changes in the characters to exclude the Compsons except General Compson, whose incorrigible juvenility and pursuits were consistent with Faulkner's new plans. Thus, it is clear that Faulkner completely changed his original concept of Isaac McCaslin and radically altered the stories to fit the new concept and combined the three hunting stories about Ike McCaslin with the other four stories that make up *Go Down, Moses.* The title of the first printing, *Go Down, Moses and Other Stories,* was an error, corrected in later printings. As Malcolm Cowley and James Meriwether have indicated, Faulkner considered *Go Down, Moses* a novel.

Go Down, Moses encompasses the whole history of the McCaslins in Yoknapatawpha County, except for minor details about Isaac McCaslin as an old man in *The Mansion* and *The Reivers.* The story of Isaac McCaslin, the last to bear the McCaslin name, centers, in the hunting trilogy, in the family heritage and his repudiation of it, revealing and interpreting the larger story and accounting for the dying out of the family. The crucial part of this trilogy is the initiation of Isaac in the wilderness, Faulkner's version of the James Fenimore Cooper theme of the flight from civilization, the American Gothic flight to the forest. Leslie Fiedler's final exposition, in *The Return of the Vanishing American,* of the Gothic elements in Cooper completes his treatment of Gothicism after *Love and Death in the American Novel* and is invaluable in recognizing and interpreting this aspect of Gothicism in Faulkner, if one relies on the texts of Faulkner's works and not on Fiedler's statements about them. The story of Isaac McCaslin exemplifies the third of the four basic myths which Fiedler identifies in American life and literature; the "Good Companions in the Wilderness," the white man and the red man, are a projection in fiction of the white man's dream of joining the Indians. (Unless Roth and the Girl in "Delta Autumn" are considered to fit the first myth, the Pocahontas "Myth of Love in the Woods," Faulkner omitted that one. The second myth, of a woman abducted by the Indians, is an American modification of the basic Gothic theme used in *Sanctuary.*)

The flight into the forest and the initiation into the cult of the hunter in the McCaslin trilogy are reinforced by the repetition of the Gothic flight and pursuit or the analogous hunt patterns throughout *Go Down, Moses.* Fiedler's Rip Van Winkle "Myth of the Runaway Male," with its ritual consumption of liquor as a protest against women and domesticity, provides a second parallel to the Gothic flight pattern. The dominant theme of the Negro-white relations in the McCaslin family is also developed throughout the novel, which is as fully based on incest and miscegenation as *Absalom, Absalom!* despite the less Gothic atmosphere in *Go Down, Moses.* The sins of old Carothers McCaslin did not originally include incest: in an early genealogy of the McCaslins, conjecturally dated by Joseph Blotner in June 1941, Eunice was a Beauchamp, not a McCaslin, slave and not the mother of Tomey.

The three stories which precede the Isaac McCaslin trilogy present essential facts about the history of the McCaslin family, withholding the most significant detail, that of incest, and establish the plantation setting. "Was" combines an ironic inversion of the hunt pattern with an even more ironic inversion of the courtly lover's quest, from medieval romance, in a story which on the surface is purely comic. Walter Taylor said that "Was" illustrated Faulkner's "'walking a tightrope . . . between the bizarre and the terrible'": the themes that evoke the past are not fused but frozen "in their classical positions of sentimental defense and Gothic fright." Although Taylor's title, "Horror and Nostalgia," is practically a formula for Gothic fiction, he used "Gothic" loosely and rarely. The inversion in "Was" extends to the Gothic settings: the McCaslin "castle," the unfinished mansion begun by Carothers McCaslin, is inhabited by the plantation slaves, and their masters live in one of the Negro cabins. In the passage added to "The Retreat" in *The Unvanquished,* other Gothic details are inverted: every night the Negroes were locked in the house "with a key almost as big as a horse pistol" (p. 53), the rules of the game being that they were free to go out by the back door so long as they were in the house when it was unlocked in the morning. This comic version of the castle is a unique adaptation of the Gothic theme of captivity, with serious implications concerning the unorthodox ideas of Buck and Buddy on slavery and rules governing Negroes. The other setting is the Beauchamp plantation which Miss Sophonsiba was pleased to call Warwick, in the fond delusion that her brother was the rightful heir of Warwick. This also is a comic version of the ruined castle. Established about 1815, the "demesne" in 1859 had gateposts but no gate; the arrival of guests was heralded by a Negro boy, seated on one post, blowing a foxhorn. Unlike the other plantation mansions in Yoknapatawpha, the big houses of the McCaslins and the Beauchamps did not attain Gothic splendor before their Gothic decay.

The flight-pursuit action in "Was" is the chase of Uncle Buck and young McCaslin Edmonds after Tomey's Turl, who had fled to the Beauchamp plantation to court their slave Tennie. The terminology of the foxhunt, used throughout the chase with Turl as the fox, turns the pursuit into sport, with mythic echoes. Tomey's Turl exemplifies the dual symbolism of the foxhunt as described by Northrop Frye in *The Secular Scripture:* the fox, called by Jorrocks "'the thief of the world'" and hunted in symbolic ritual, is also "the wily and resourceful hero," the Ulysses of the animal world. Turl begins as fugitive and ends as winner in a poker game. The humorous facts that Turl is in no danger other than having his romance interrupted and that the dogs obey the quarry rather than the hunters do not conceal the serious facts that this is a comic version of the reality which survived in such incidents as the hunting down of Joe Christmas with dogs and that Uncle Buck, Turl's half-brother, treated Turl as a piece of property, with no freedom to choose a wife and marry. In "Red Leaves" the pursuit of the Negro slave who was to be offered as a sacrifice to the dead Indian chief exemplifies Faulkner's serious use of the same pattern, with Gothic setting and atmosphere.

The other part of the story concerns the romance of Miss Sophonsiba and Uncle Buck, whose sexual inclinations are suggested by his fear of marriage and his complete satisfaction in living with his twin, Uncle

Buddy, who did the cooking. One is reminded of the Sartoris twins and even more of the woman-shy MacCallum family, in the gallery of Gothic doubles. Miss Sophonsiba, despite her coy ways, is the pursuer, not the maiden in flight. The Gothic inversion is heightened by her self-image as a romantic heroine; the favor, a bit of red ribbon, which she sent Buck, the reluctant knight, he received "like it was a little water moccasin" (p. 15). None of her feminine wiles having succeeded, not even her previous trick of having her brother Hubert sneak away from the McCaslins' at midnight, leaving her there so that Buck would have to marry her to save her good name, Sophonsiba trapped Buck when he unwittingly got into bed with her—as Hubert said, crawled into the bear's den and lay down with the bear. The poker game or "tournament" between Buck and Hubert had as its stakes human destinies, those of Buck and Sophonsiba and of Turl and Tennie. Dealing in *The Secular Scripture* with themes of descent in romance, Northrop Frye explained that "cards and dice are common in descent narratives, because of their overtones of fatality and chance." If Buck won the poker game, Tomey's Turl could marry, but, with another inversion of the pattern, Buck would be saved from marriage. Buck lost, but Buddy saved him in another game, with Tomey's Turl as dealer triumphing over chance. The reality beneath the sentimental romance is concisely stated by Walter Taylor: to Buck, "the worst tragedy imaginable is marriage." The tale of how Sophonsiba finally won Buck, Faulkner never told. The comic inversion of Gothic-romance patterns in "Was" is the prelude to serious use of Gothic patterns in the rest of *Go Down, Moses.*

"The Fire and the Hearth" consists of two short stories combined, "A Point of Law" (1940) and "Gold Is Not Always" (1940), with new material linking the two plots and adding to the history of the Negro and white McCaslins. The plantation setting of "Was" is revised to represent the time of writing and action: the house, approached by a "wide carriage gate" and a drive up an "oak and cedar knoll," consisted of two log wings with a central hall and "a second storey of white clapboards" and "faced with a portico" (p. 45). This house, with the surrounding plantation, is the center of the novel. Lucas Beauchamp's cabin, central to the story of the Negro McCaslins, is much more fully described in *Intruder in the Dust* than in *Go Down, Moses.* All together, these dwellings, other Negro cabins, and the commissary and their equivalents on the Beauchamp plantation resemble the medieval manorial estate.

Two rooms are of major significance in *Go Down, Moses* and the other McCaslin stories. In Lucas's cabin ever since Lucas married Molly a fire has burned on the hearth as a symbol of a patriarchal family and of marital fidelity, ideals not only patterned after those of white society but more fully realized by Lucas than by his white kinfolk. This room is not a trap or a prison or a refuge: it is a world in itself, created by love, but threatened by the very world it reflected. The account of the fire and the moment when Lucas almost quenched it is given only in the novel version of the tale. In the other house is the room which Lucas invaded, in defiance of all racial etiquette and at risk of his life, to confront Zack Edmonds, man to man, for having kept Molly at this house as nurse for Zack's orphan son. This scene is wholly Gothic in purport and atmosphere, comparable to the confrontation of Joe Christmas and Joanna Burden before the murder but much more fully developed as a battle of wills and a physical struggle for possession of a gun. Except that there is no possible ritual to follow, the situation is essentially equivalent to a duel between two white men. Lucas discarded his razor, and the two men, foster-brothers and blood relatives, knelt on opposite sides of the bed, gripping the pistol between them. Lucas secured possession of it, and only a msifire kept him from committing murder. Emotional tension, physical struggle, and racial conflict (from the point of view of the Negro aggressor), combine to make this one of the most effective and significant Gothic episodes in Faulkner's novels. The lynching of Lee Goodwin suggests what would have happened to Lucas if he had killed Zack or if Zack had not respected Lucas as a man and a kinsman and therefore refrained from retaliation. Lucas knew, and would have paid, the price for his assertion of manhood and defense of the sanctity of marriage: instead of using the second cartridge upon himself, he *"would have waited for the rope, even the coal oil"* (p. 58).

This episode, one of the additions to the original short stories, is central to the theme of Negro-white relations in the McCaslin family and in southern society. It is also the first of the stories of initiation in *Go Down, Moses*, with a parallel in another added episode in "the Fire and the Hearth," that of Roth and Henry. Lucas asserted his manhood, at peril of his life; Roth asserted his racial superiority and ate the "bitter fruit" of his heritage (p. 114), at the cost of losing the family life beside the fire on the hearth. Henry accepted his inferior status and retained his home life but lost his companion. These truncated initiations prepare for the more extensive use of the pattern in the story of Isaac McCaslin.

The theme of the hunt in "The Fire and the Hearth" is reflected in Lucas's quest for buried treasure. "The buried treasure hoard," as Northrop Frye said in *The Secular Scripture*, "affords an obvious motive for a descent quest." The chief scenes combine Gothic darkness and suspense with grotesque incongruity: Lucas digging alone at night in the old Indian mound; Roth's pursuit of Lucas and the "borrowed" mule, ending in an incongruous tableau, seen by flashlight, of the mud-caked white salesman of the divining machine and of Lucas holding the machine "as if it were some object symbolical and sanctified for a ceremony, a ritual" (p. 87). Pride, according to Frank Thomas, was one motive which kept Lucas at his "incredible quest" for buried treasure. The salesman, seen asleep in the "wan, dew-heavy light" and later, by flashlight, digging up the salted treasure trove and seeing "the bright cascade of silver dollars glint" (p. 93), is grotesque in his corruption by greed and in his utter loss of the city-slicker sophistication by which he tried to conceal his rural origin. The final treasure-hunting scene is equally grotesque, but is pathetic, rather than comic: little Aunt Molly, trying to cure Lucas of the greed which threatened to quench the fire on the hearth, was found at noon, after being gone all night: she was "lying on her face in the mud, the once immaculate apron and the clean faded skirts stained and torn, one hand still grasping the handle of the divining-machine as she had fallen with it" (p. 125).

Faulkner had used the same theme in *The Hamlet*, where the destitute Armstid was driven mad by the cursed greed for gold. Faulkner's repetition of this theme may be explained by the facts that quest for treasure, as Northrop Frye indicates, is one of the oldest themes of romance, and that in the South legends abound of treasure buried during the Civil War. Treasure hunting with a metal-detecting machine did occur in the area in Lafayette County corresponding to Frenchman's Bend. Except the scenes with Lucas and the salesman, all the scenes referred to above were added in the revisions of the stories for *Go Down, Moses:* Faulkner introduced Gothic elements for contrast with the humorous original narrative and for the development of themes related to the whole novel.

The inclusion of "Pantaloon in Black" in *Go Down, Moses* has puzzled critics because its connection with the rest of the novel seems tenuous, consisting of the facts that Rider is one of Roth Edmonds' tenants and therefore the story has the same plantation setting as "the Fire and the Hearth," and that Rider's marriage is modeled on that of Lucas and Molly, even to the fire on the hearth. In a conversation with Malcolm Cowley, Faulkner said that Rider was a McCaslin Negro. But inclusion of "Pantaloon in Black" is justified on firmer grounds by Gothic elements in themes and patterns which serve as unifying devices in *Go Down, Moses,* notably the theme identified by John Muste as "The Failure of Love." The title of the story is grotesquely ironic, suggesting a uxorious elderly husband in a comedy, not a grief-crazed and tragic young husband, an Aristotelian tragic hero to Donald Noble. Rosemary Stephens explained the title as related to Rider's "mask and violent gestures" and regarded him as a mythic hero. A more convincing explanation of "Rider" and the title is H. R. Stoneback's. Tracing the name "Rider" to related blues songs, "Easy Rider" and "I Know You, Rider," Stoneback interprets the title as suggesting "the performer, the blues singer as 'pantaloon,' cast in a grotesquely comic role, perceived as a caricature by the detached audience of whites." Allardyce Nicoll's account of the "Pantalone" as a stock character in comedy is relevant to Faulkner's use of "Pantaloon" chiefly in the facts that the character, though elderly, was virile and vigorous and that the role was serious and dynamic but became vulgarized into "the knockabout Pantaloon and Clown." Thus, the title points to the theme of the ironic contrast between the stereotype of the Negro as a clown lacking in "the normal human feelings and sentiments of human beings" (p. 154) and Rider's inconsolable grief. Objectively viewed by the deputy sheriff, Rider's conduct after the death of Mannie confirmed the deputy's previous idea of Negro nature.

Subjectively presented in the preceding portion of the story, Rider's experiences are sheer Gothic tragedy, from the time he filled in the grave of his wife until he was lynched by hanging. The simple remembered rituals of daily life, like those in the blues song "I Know You, Rider"—"I will cut your wood baby, I will make your fire"—show that Rider's grief, after waking up like Rider in the song to find his baby gone, is inconsolable and that the rituals have lost their potency. Before he was taken out of jail to be lynched, he tore up his cell and walked off with the door because, he said, hysterically "laughing, with tears big as glass marbles running across his face . . . 'Ah just cant quit thinking'" (p. 159). His previous attempts to quit thinking involved a Gothic flight, not from animate pursuers but from grief.

Before the flight began, Rider saw the ghost of his young wife in one of the most affecting and convincing ghost scenes in modern Gothic fiction: "the insuperable barrier" of flesh and strength was raised between him and the spirit which faded from sight while he tried to entice it to return by setting a place at the table and inviting it to eat. In the ghost of Mannie, Lester Hurt said, Faulkner "creates the first successful serious ghost in western secular literature since *Hamlet*." For one short story, there is an impressive sequence of Gothic scenes: Rider's moonlight flight through woods and fields with his dog; his feats of superhuman strength at the sawmill; his flight the next night through the dark river-bottom and into the moonlight, drinking until he could not swallow; his arrival after midnight in the lumberyard "among the mute soaring of the moon-blond lumber-stacks" (p. 151); the crap game by lantern light in the tool room, ending with his whipping out his razor and cutting the throat of the white man who had been cheating the Negroes at dice for fifteen years; the jail scene and the lynching. For contrast with the

Gothic scenes there are the tender scenes with his foster-parents, who tried by love and prayer to help him, and the scene between the deputy sheriff and his indifferent wife, who cannot even imagine grief that would drive a man to frenzied activity rather than merely to take a day off, with pay, "out of pure respect no matter how he felt about his wife" (p. 156).

In the Gothic tradition of sensitivity to natural beauty, the wilderness scenes of the Isaac McCaslin trilogy of hunting stories are the most fully developed in Faulkner's fiction because Isaac McCaslin is the central intelligence and the descriptions are part of the characterization. Discussing "The Bear" in relation to Romanticism, Blanche Gelfant stressed the dreamlike quality of Ike's entrance into the wilderness and his sense of foreknowledge in finding there the confirmation of his dreams. So effective is this point of view that the wilderness theme in Faulkner leaves an impression out of proportion to his limited use of it, chiefly in this trilogy and the Indian short stories. In the first two stories, "The Old People" and "The Bear," the beauty and the mystery of the wilderness dominate. Nature in Faulkner is not idyllic and Rousseauistic but is, he said at Nagano, "a force, a blind force, that by its own standards is neither good nor bad." He denied believing that a return to nature was possible or desirable: "We mustn't go back to a condition, an idyllic condition, in which the dream [made us think] we were happy, we were free of trouble and sin. We must take the trouble and sin along with us, and we must cure that trouble and sin as we go." Nature as represented by the bear was a natural force which was "not evil, but an old obsolescence that was strong, that held to the old ways, but because it had been strong and lived within its own code of morality, it deserved to be treated with respect." Ike saw in nature more of the dream and less of the evil than Faulkner saw; the Gothic quality of evil is minimized in the natural setting because it is part of Ike's lifelong Romantic dream, the illusion, as Lewis Simpson explained, "that the ideal of pastoral permanence symbolizes the truth of existence" and that man could live outside historical reality.

The wilderness is presented in June, as well as in late fall, because the hunters went there in the green season to celebrate the birthdays of Major de Spain and General Compson, neither of whom was born in June. Thus, the solitary ordeal of young Ike took place in "the summer woods . . . green with gloom," dimmer than "in November's gray dissolution" (p. 205). The image of "a child, alien and lost in the green and soaring gloom of the markless wilderness" (p. 208), has universality equal to that of the dream image of flight. On the fall trips, more frequently represented than the June ones in Ike's education in the wilderness, there are vividly realized moments in which Ike was intensely aware of his surroundings, of the "same solitude, the same loneliness through which frail and timorous man had merely passed without altering it"; "he stood against a big gum tree beside a little bayou whose black still water crept without motion out of a cane-brake, across a small clearing and into the cane again, where, invisible, a bird, the big woodpecker called Lord-to-God by negroes, clattered at a dead trunk" (p. 202). This is American Gothic, influenced by no travel books and no Romantic landscape painters, but derived from a passion for a "postage stamp of native soil." But, like the settlers, American Gothic was directly descended from European origins. S. L. Varnado said that European Gothic used emptiness to "register a sense of the numinous," and that a constant theme was the "vacant loneliness associated with sea, desert, mountain prospects, or the night sky."

The greatest sense of mystery is conveyed by the description of the phantom buck, "moving with that winged and effortless ease with which deer move, passing within twenty feet of them, its head high and the eye not proud and not haughty, but just full and wild and unafraid" (p. 184), a phantom haunting the wilderness because, Cass explained, who himself had seen the buck that cast no shadow, life was worn out before the possibilities of living were exhausted (pp. 187, 186). From such passages and from Ike's vision of "a nirvana of pulsing life somehow free of both time and space" where he would be reunited with "the old men he had known and loved" (p. 354), Lester Hurt concluded that "of all modern writers, it was Faulkner who most dramatically and consistently argued the inevitable triumph of life over death." Ike's "nirvana" resembles the American Indians' Happy Hunting Grounds. Gloria Dussinger considered that Ike was vouchsafed "a mystical vision" in which he was taken "behind the arras-veil of phenomena to an experience in the noumenal world." Gothic supernaturalism in modern terms.

Old Ben, personified and of mythic proportions, is almost as much an apparition as was the buck: "It was just there, immobile, fixed in the green and windless noon's hot dappling, not as big as he had dreamed it but as big as he had expected, bigger, dimensionless against the dappled obscurity, looking at him" (p. 209). The last mysterious emanation of the spirit of the wilderness, though like Old Ben a creature of substance, is the snake: "the old one, the ancient and accursed about the earth, fatal and solitary and he could smell it now: the thin sick smell of rotting cucumbers and something else which had no name, evocative of all knowledge and an old weariness and of pariah-hood and of death" (p. 329). The dreamlike mystery which invests the wilderness and its creatures is essentially Gothic, despite the absence of more rugged and spectacular forms of natural scenery. But the wilderness is an imaginative recreation of an observed reality.

Nostalgia for the passing of the old wilderness fills the musing of Ike in "Delta Autumn" while he drives two hundred miles from Jefferson to find delta wilderness to hunt in. As he sees "the tall tremendous soaring of oak and gum and ash and hickory which had rung to no axe save the hunter's, had echoed to no machinery save the beat of old-time steam boats traversing it" (p. 342), he recalls "the impenetrable jungle of water-standing cane and cypress, gum and holly and oak and ash" which had given way to "cotton patches which as the years passed became fields and then plantations" (p. 340). The new hunting territory is seen chiefly in the rain at night.

Naturally, in the portions of the narrative which deal with the wilderness, images of enclosure are at a minimum, consisting chiefly of scenes in the hunting bungalow at De Spain's camp and the mere shelter of Ike's tent in "Delta Autumn." The bungalow, the "ceremonial house" of Ike's initiation, is a "sacred space," Mircea Eliade's *axis mundi,* described in *Rites and Symbols of Initiation* as "sacred with the sacrality that the earth possessed at the moment of creation." Among the dwelling motifs in the McCaslin trilogy, Edward Corridori included the hunting bungalow and the tent in "Delta Autumn," each with its fire. But Ike vainly wished to make the ceremonial dwelling places and the wilderness his true home, as it could be for none after the death of Sam Fathers. The McCaslin-Edmonds plantation is more clearly depicted in "The Fire and the Hearth" and *Intruder in the Dust* than in the hunting stories. The plantation commissary represents both the heritage and the responsibility it entailed: the supplies for the "furnish" of the tenants, to be paid for by the cotton "made and ginned and sold," and the ledgers in which the records were kept. The commissary was the scene of Ike's midnight search for what "he knew he was going to find" and did find as, "the forgotten lantern stinking anew the rank dead icy air, he leaned above the yellowed page" (p. 268). In the commissary also his later colloquy with Cass Edmonds took place.

The discovery of the dark truth in the family history as it is revealed in the ledgers is a thoroughly Gothic device presented in a thoroughly Gothic setting of a locked room at midnight: the truth was that the Negro branch of the McCaslin family were the descendants of an incestuous union between old Carothers McCaslin and his daughter Tomey, whose mother, the slave Eunice, drowned herself before Tomey's child Turl was born. Again in the Faulknerian Gothic pattern the discovery of the true heritage had no happy consequences. Ike was still the rightful heir, but he refused to take possession and relinquished the plantation to McCaslin Edmonds, his older cousin who had managed it while Ike was a minor. The confined quarters Ike chose instead of the plantation and its duties are like Hightower's house or Quentin's icy room at Harvard, a retreat from participation in life: "the little cramped icelike room in Jefferson" (p. 308); the "rented cubicle" in which his relinquishment of his inheritance cost him a son (p. 315); the house in which he lived with his "dead wife's widowed niece and her children" (p. 352). In these rooms Ike existed while waiting for November and hunting. The narrow walls of Ike's life for fifty weeks in the year represent the limitations of life and activity he chose for himself, like choosing to live in prison with a dream for fifty weeks in order to vacation in dreamland for two weeks.

The characters in *Go Down, Moses* show new and interesting variations on the Gothic types and their American adaptations, with less than the usual good-bad contrast. The male characters represent the worlds of the plantation and of the town, and of the wilderness where denizens of the other two worlds meet. Isaac McCaslin is clearly the Romantic hero. He commented on his own name, in refusing to accept his inheritance: "an Isaac born into a later life than Abraham's and repudiating immolation: fatherless and therefore safe declining the altar because maybe this time the exasperated Hand might not supply the kid—" (p. 283). The safety conferred by being fatherless has particular advantage in relation to the tyrannical "fathers" of the Gothic tradition, such as those in *Light in August* and *Absalom, Absalom!* As a boy and a young man, Ike was a gentle, heroic, and idealistic person, with no Faustian lust for wealth and power. There is no irony in his role as a Romantic hero in "The Old People" and in most of "The Bear." But in his maturity, as he is revealed in "The Fire and the Hearth" through the eyes of Lucas and in "Delta Autumn," he is much less than an ideal and becomes an ironic, unheroic elder huntsman. Leslie Fiedler's comment, in *Love and Death,* on Natty Bumppo as a "moral hermaphrodite" fits Ike: "He can only enter into an abstract and fruitless union with the wilderness itself; his true bride is . . . the forest. . . ." Gloria Dussinger regarded the quest framework as making explicit Faulkner's judgment upon Isaac McCaslin as a "Romantic hero *manqué.*" The reason for the failure of Ike's marriage was apparent before he took a wife: "He would marry someday and they too would own for their brief while that brief unsubstanced glory . . . but still the woods would be his mistress and his wife" (p. 326). Ike's wife was shut out of his dreams even as Hightower's wife was shut out of his. In light of what we know about Ike's father and mother and what little Ike's memories reveal to us, it seems likely that Ike was caught as his father was by

Sophonsiba. Buck and Buddy, however, are clearly homosexual in their chosen way of life; Ike thought that his father "should have been a woman to begin with" (p. 272), although it was Uncle Buddy who spent most of his time beside the cookstove. There is less basis for regarding Ike as homosexual.

The story of Hubert Beauchamp and his arrested development—"the boy which had existed at that stage of inviolable and immortal adolescence in his uncle for almost sixty years" (p. 303)—suggests that an implicit parallel between Ike and the other side of his inheritance may be one intention of the passage on Hubert and the legacy he left to Ike. In Ike's old age, his dream of immortal bliss was exactly the same as his daydream of earthly bliss from the time he was big enough to carry a gun: "the names, the faces of the old men he had known and loved and for a little while outlived, moving again among the shades of tall unaxed trees and sightless brakes where the wild strong immortal game ran forever before the tireless belling immortal hounds, falling and rising phoenix-like to the soundless guns" (p. 354). The part about the old men is added to the short story version of "Delta Autumn." "Phoenix-like" suggested to Lester Hurt that Faulkner saw ultimate realities in spiritual terms. Again Ike resembles Natty Bumppo, of whom Fiedler said: "The union in heaven that Natty will not grant the man and woman . . . he grants himself and his Indian friends, for they yearn to join not flesh but souls."

In his youth Ike as a Romantic hero represents the American theme of the new Adam in the new Eden, but that role cannot be sustained through a long life without becoming ironic. As Edward Corridori said, Ike tried to avoid original sin in a world already fallen, whereas man's task is both repudiation and accommodation. In Olga Vickery's words, "Having confused the wilderness with the Garden of Eden, he not only dedicates but sacrifices his life to it. Man must leave the Garden in order to discover his humanity and whatever the reason, Isaac does not do so; his knowledge stops just short of the paradox of the fortunate fall." The parallels noted by Richard Lawson between Ike McCaslin and the archetypal hero in Joseph Campbell's *The Hero with a Thousand Faces* are useful in showing a certain continuity between the ancient and the Romantic-Gothic hero types and in suggesting the significance of Ike's failure to experience an unequivocal rebirth and a return to humanity, a stage symbolized when Old Ben led Ike back to the instruments of civilization, "the tree, the bush, the compass and the watch glinting where a ray of sunlight touched them" (p. 209). In *American Dreams, American Nightmares* David Madden identified the "two major American Dream myths," the Old Testament myth of Paradise Lost and the New Testament myth of Paradise Regained, and noted that in fiction "hope for clear vision lies in the ambiguous area between Paradise Lost and Paradise Regained." He saw in "The Bear" a "classic mythic" expression "of the American dream" which suggests the possibility of redemption but distinguishes between dream and achievement. In *The Return of the Vanishing American* Leslie Fiedler contrasted the Old World and the New World versions of the Fall, in the latter of which "the Indian *is* the serpent." Fiedler regarded Ike as the "Southern alter ego of Thoreau," and cited Ike's greeting to the snake, "Chief, ... Grandfather," to support his snake-Indian thesis. The snake may also symbolize Ike's actual grandfather, a source of evil in the early settlement of the wilderness, and, as Richard Lawson observed, may signify Ike's expulsion from Eden. How far Ike was from a vision of the new Adam and Paradise Regained is apparent in his vision of heavenly bliss, which is untouched by any concepts from the New Testament despite his biblical citations in the colloquy with Cass.

A good case may be made for McCaslin Edmonds as a hero, on the basis of what we learn through Ike's consciousness without his full recognition of the significance of his knowledge. As the foster-father of a boy only sixteen years his junior, Cass performed his duties and obligations effectively, showing himself to be sympathetic and sensitive as well as practical and efficient. Ike's point of view, slanted by his preference for the wilderness world of Sam Fathers, obscures Cass's role, noted by Lawson, as a priest trying to bring Ike back into civilization. When the reader considers Cass's achievements, Ike's biased judgment becomes apparent. Cass saved the plantation after the Civil War for the benefit of Ike, the heir, and kept it "solvent and efficient and, more than that: not only still intact but enlarged, increased ... where hardly one in ten survived" (p. 298). What Cass's labors meant in terms of the welfare of all those who lived on the plantation, Ike did not consider. Despite Ike's enlightened views on Negroes, he left to Cass the task of providing employment for the Negroes on the plantation and looking after their welfare. There is no record of Ike's having done anything to help the Negroes he professed to admire, not even his own kin. If Faulkner intended Cass to be heroic, the characterization of Ike takes on additional irony.

This is the only novel before *The Reivers* in which Yoknapatawpha father figures are all benevolent: Sam, Ike's spiritual father; Theophilus (Buck), his dimly remembered physical father; Cass Edmonds, his foster-father; Major de Spain and General Compson, his initiation fathers—all encouraged Ike, gave him the benefit of their various skills and insights, and received his deepest and most lasting love. Old Sam is not only Ike's spiritual father but also the Noble Savage of both European and American Romantic and Gothic tradition. In *Go Down, Moses* Sam was the son of a quadroon and "Ikkemotubbe himself" (pp. 165, 166), not the son of a Negro woman and an Indian as in "A Justice" 1931). Sam's natural dwelling place is the wilderness because, Frank Thomas said, Sam's identity springs from his efforts to deal with his black, white, and Indian heritage, of which the Indian is most cherished. In *Go Down, Moses* Faulkner made Sam the metaphor of a central theme in Yoknapatawpha, that of the struggle of the races to live together. Sam's cage, Cass told Ike, was himself: "himself his own battleground, the scene of his own vanquishment and the mausoleum of his defeat" (p. 168). Sam's withdrawal to the wilderness may, in Cass's eyes, signify his defeat. As Frank Thomas said, Sam is "the positive moral center of *Go Down, Moses.*" He adopted the identity of caretaker of the wilderness and instructor of "those who would be a part of the holy mysteries of the wilderness." Sam's ultimate failure in that role is revealed when Ike proves unable to transmit to a younger generation what Sam taught him, a central theme in "Delta Autumn." Unlike the Romantic Noble Savage, Sam is not sentimentalized in appearance or speech but is invested with simple dignity, with a wisdom derived from the "old people" of whom he is the last descendant, and with a spiritual and mystical quality.

Grotesque humor is provided by Boon, grotesque in appearance and actions in the Dickensian fashion of dehumanized appearance and invariable behavior: he has a gargoyle-like red-walnut face, has one vice, whiskey, and one virtue, fidelity, and is totally unable to hit anything he shoots at larger than a squirrel. Boon is even more grotesque when he is seen in the incongruous setting of Memphis. Ash belongs to the southern Gothic tradition of the humorous servant. After twenty years as camp cook, Ash refused to cook unless he had a chance to go hunting; none of the shells fired until he set his gun down and forgot it.

Roth Edmonds appears in a Gothic role only in "Delta Autumn," where, as the offstage seducer of the Girl and hunter of does, he is the only real villain in *Go Down, Moses.* As noted above, the revision of "Delta Autumn" for inclusion in *Go Down, Moses* added this chapter to the McCaslin story; in the short story Uncle Ike is the only McCaslin. In "The Fire and the Hearth" Roth is overshadowed by Lucas Beauchamp, a character who fits no traditional category but who is the dominant figure among both white and Negro descendants of Carothers McCaslin. In playing the role of the Negro buffoon on occasion and in winning the battle of wits with both Roth and the divining-machine salesman, Lucas is comic. Because he can assert his manhood only at risk of his life, he is tragic, doomed like Faulkner's other Negro characters by the inexorable social laws of his time. In his invariable and antiquated costume, with the sixty-dollar beaver hat given to him by Cass Edmonds, Roth's grandfather, crowning the splendor of black clothes, white shirt, gold watch-chain, and gold toothpick, Lucas might be grotesque were it not for his imperturbable dignity. Unlike Joe Christmas, Lucas knew his ancestry and took pride in it. Refusing to be "the battleground and victim of the two strains," he was instead "a vessel, durable, ancestry-less, nonconductive, in which the toxin and its anti stalemated one another . . ." (p. 104). Roth realized that Lucas "reproduced with absolute and shocking fidelity the old ancestor's entire generation" and that he was *"both heir and prototype simultaneously of all the geography and climate and biology which sired old Carothers"* but that he had *"fathered himself, intact and complete, contemptuous . . . of all blood black white yellow or red, including his own"* (p. 118). Although Lucas inherited debasement with his Negro blood, as Frank Thomas said, he rose above his caste to take pride in and identify with his grandfather, who was a white *man*. In so doing, Lucas achieved self-assurance and a unique identity. Lucas reflected not only his grandfather's whole background but mirrored the plantation world, as Olga Vickery observed: "Lucas is the man in his house, the head of the family, the lawgiver to his wife and children," asserting in his ways that "the moral and social principles of the South are equally applicable to both Negroes and whites." Thus, although Lucas fits into no category of typical Gothic characters, he epitomizes in a positive way the Gothic search for identity and for the image of the past.

The scarcity of female characters, of whom only Molly is presented with any fullness, is a clue to the decline of the McCaslins, who failed to choose wives able to produce children and to provide a warm and loving home life; whether bachelors or widowers, the McCaslin and Edmonds men were content with a womanless home life on the plantation, where they could escape women without fleeing to the woods. The Persecuted Maiden appears in three generations, with southern Gothic modifications. A Persecuted Maiden who was a Negro and a slave could not flee, and one who was a Negro could not marry a white man. Eunice, whom old Carothers bought in New Orleans, was the mother of his daughter Tomey (see p. 140). Tomey was the mother of his son Turl, simply because Carothers could summon his property and "get a child on her" (p. 294). This combination of incest and miscegenation is the rottenness at the core of the McCaslin heritage which Isaac discovered and refused to accept, repudiating his grandfather and relinquishing his inheritance. This is the Gothic heart of *Go Down, Moses.* The third Persecuted Maiden, the Girl in "Delta Autumn," is a free agent but is nevertheless a victim, in that Roth used her love for him as Carothers had used his ownership of Eunice and Tomey, with no more intention than Carothers had of marrying the girl. The fact that the Girl is the granddaughter of James Beauchamp repeats the theme of incest, although the relationship was too remote for marriage to be forbidden. The change from Don Boyd, in the short story, to Roth Edmonds in *Go Down, Moses* involves the addition of the whole McCaslin history as background and the explicit addition of the Girl's identity and the ironic significance of Ike's rejection of her and her child. The Woman as Temptress, humorously presented in Sophonsiba in "Was," appears again in the woman Ike married. His memories give no account of the courtship; perhaps he was not fully aware of how he was captured. Faulkner confirmed what the reader infers: "She married him because she wanted to be the chatelaine of a plantation." In yielding to her for a moment and promising to take back the plantation, Ike, the wilderness Adam, yielded to the already lost Eve and her materialistic values and ambitions. But Ike had initially shut her out of his garden, which was not Eden but a male paradise. If we saw the situation from her point of view, she might seem to be a Suffering Wife, ironically so in that she ceased to be Ike's wife and denied him children.

The real Suffering Wife is not ironic. Molly Beauchamp so feared the corruption she recognized in Lucas's gold-craze and the misuse of the earth it represented that she sued for a "voce" to save herself and her daughter. Only the capitulation of Lucas saved the marriage, kept the fire burning on the hearth, and ended Molly's suffering. In romance, "the secular scripture," the theme of descent may include a quest for buried treasure and the threat of a trial, based on an unjust or mistaken charge. This trial the hero or heroine might avoid, Northrop Frye explained, "by the revelation of his or her real identity." Precisely so did Lucas avoid being sued for divorce: he admitted his errors and resumed his true identity as the responsible head of a family and a faithful husband, when he saw that his violation of the earth, aping the white man's greed, threatened to quench the sacred fire on the hearth. The ritual of reconciliation with Molly is a bit of grotesque humor: giving Molly a bag of candy, Lucas said: "Here. . . . You aint go no teeth left but you can still gum it" (p. 130).

The story of Fonsiba, as Ike remembered his one brief glimpse of her married life, adds another Suffering Wife. But she was suffering only material deprivation as the result of her free choice to marry a Negro who honorably courted and married her. She was never a Persecuted Maiden. Gloria Dussinger observed a parallel between Fonsiba's and Ike's assertions of freedom as freedom *from*, not freedom *to* moral responsibility. In youth or old age Ike saw in Fonsiba's husband only folly, not hope and pride. There is also an ironic parallel between the prosperous plantation Fonsiba left and the miserable "other room," cold and dark, in which she exercised her freedom. In that setting her husband, in unfrayed ministerial garments, reading with lensless spectacles, is grotesque.

The relatively few examples of ironic inversions and of grotesque characters in *Go Down, Moses,* seen largely through the consciousness of others, especially Ike, render it less obviously and completely Gothic than such works as *Sanctuary, Light in August,* and *Absalom, Absalom!*

Without using the term "Gothic" Mircea Eliade recognized the significance of "initiation scenarios" in such works as *Moby-Dick,* Cooper's novels, *Huckleberry Finn,* and "The Bear," which are dealt with by Fiedler in *Love and Death.* Noting that "initiatory symbols and scenarios survive, on the unconscious level, especially in dreams and imaginary universes," Eliade explained the lasting appeal of such scenarios to modern man: ". . . imaginary experiences are part of the total human being, no less important than his diurnal experiences. This means that the nostalgia for initiatory trials and scenarios, nostalgia deciphered in so many literary and plastic works, reveals modern man's longing for a total and definitive renewal, for a *renovatio* capable of radically changing his existence." After his first full-scale treatment of the initiation theme, in *Go Down, Moses,* Faulkner never abandoned that theme but finally transposed it from the Gothic to the romantic quest in *The Reivers.*

The dominant Gothic themes of initiation and inheritance in *Go Down, Moses* introduce some feeling of suspense and mystery and involve the hunt-quest pattern, which is a unifying element in the novel. The chief suspense is the prolonged contest between hunters and hunted which centers in Old Ben. To provide suspense Faulkner used a common Gothic device of anticipation: "The Bear," part 2, begins: "So he should have hated and feared Lion" (p. 209), a sentence which is repeated at the beginning of the last paragraph (p. 226), thus assuring the reader that Lion will be the means by which Ben is killed. The mystery of why Eunice committed suicide was created by the ledger entries and was solved inferentially by Ike from the clues in the dates of the death of Eunice and of the birth of Tomey's child. A slight mystery for the non-southern reader might be the reluctance of Buck and Buddy to believe that Eunice drowned herself; the southern belief that Negroes were happier than white people was indeed reinforced by the statistical fact of a low incidence of suicide among Negroes. The minor mystery of what became of James Beauchamp, whom Ike sought but could not find, was partially solved by the identity of the Girl in "Delta Autumn."

In the absence of complicated mysteries in plot, it may seem that Faulkner substituted complicated mysteries in structure and style, but only "The Bear," part 4, and reminiscent passages in "The Fire and the Hearth" present any real difficulty. It is true, however, that Ike as central intelligence creates a tone of mystery and nostalgia and that his sense of the coexistence of different periods of time introduces qualities of mind and feeling which add to the Gothic effect. Equally essential to the characterization of Ike is his impassioned colloquy with Cass, in which his mythic view of history is expressed in inflated rhetoric. The misinterpretation of Ike's views as constituting Faulkner's message to a mechanistic world was attributed by Gloria Dussinger to the self-contradictory elements in Ike's "ludicrous redaction of traditional Christian theodicy" and to the failure of critics to translate Ike's views into lucid standard diction, as she did in a footnote. She pointed out that natural man, which Ike aspired to be, "does not reason logically, seeking motives for his actions. He acts instinctively, and his deed contains its own justification." Ike's rationalization proves his "dual nature and . . . his conscious denial of the existential circumstance." Introduced into this colloquy are memories which contribute to the theme of inheritance: the legacy of Hubert Beauchamp to Ike with its mysterious changes in shape and weight proves to be an ironic transmutation of precious metals into base ones and into worthless IOUs. As Richard Lawson said, Ike's heritage from Hubert is lustful sterility and poor stewardship, to which might be added indolence. The silver cup, turned into a tin coffee pot, was transmuted from an heirloom into the grail of Ike's journeys into the forest.

The journey into the forest, the recurrent pattern of action, is both literal and figurative. It reenacts the experience of the first white settlers. Mircea Eliade's comments on the settlement of America are applicable to the Gothic tradition and to Ike's quest into the forest: ". . . the United States was the product of the Protestant Reformation seeking an Earthly Paradise. . . ." The pioneers saw life in Manichaean terms, everything reduced "to a conflict between Good and Evil." Consequently, the "vast forests, the solitude of the infinite plains, the beatitude of the rural life are set in contrast to the sins and vices of the city."

This contrast between the wilderness and the city was exemplified in one of the ordeals of Ike's initiation, his trip to Memphis as Boon's guardian. This trip, Joseph Blotner said, was based on one Faulkner made in 1918 with Buster Callicoat. Ike's reactions are not to be identified with Faulkner's; as Lewis Simpson said: "In Faulkner the search for pastoral redemption never began. His is a quest for man the historical creature."

Ike's other ordeals of initiation into the cult of the hunters follow a more obviously traditional pattern, which has a medieval parallel in initiation into knighthood. Ike was seeking not only the skills of a woodsman and his consequent acceptance into the cult of the hunters but also the moral values by which to judge himself and his heritage. His initiation fits the pattern of tribal initiation rites and secret society rites as described by Mircea Eliade: "The tribal initiation introduces the novice into the world of spiritual and cultural values and makes him a responsible member of the society" by teaching him about adult institutions and sacred traditions. Tribal and secret society initiations "correspond in every respect": "seclusion, initiatory tests and tortures, 'death' and 'resurrection,' imposition of a new name, revelation of a secret doctrine...." The chief ritual for the hunters was drinking liquor: "drinking not of the blood they spilled but some condensation of the wild immortal spirit, drinking it moderately, humbly even, not with the pagan's base and baseless hope of acquiring thereby the virtues of cunning and strength but in salute to them" (p. 192).

When the skills in which Sam had been training him from childhood enabled Ike to shoot his first deer, Sam marked Ike's face with the blood of the deer, a ritual marking, perhaps a kind of token mutilation: "He ceased to be a child and became a hunter and a man" (p. 178). (Emily Stone said that this actually happened to Phil Stone, not Faulkner.) The motif of stasis contrasts with motion: "The buck still and forever leaped, the shaking gunbarrels coming constantly and forever steady at last, crashing, and still out of his instant of immortality the buck sprang, forever immortal..." (p. 178). A sense of mystery and mysticism invests Ike's initiation; in Hyatt Waggoner's terms, "The killing of the deer has been for Ike an experience transcendent, elusive, ineffable, a religious experience." He had been washed in the blood. In the solitary ordeal whereby he earned the right to see Old Ben, Ike had to divest himself of the objects which symbolized civilization—his gun, his compass, his watch. These objects, with his tin coffee pot, his cot, and the hunting horn, are symbols not only of his initiation but of his whole life, Gothic symbols of his chosen heritage.

The climax of Ike's initiation, the death of Old Ben, is presented with Ike as a witness, not a participant. It is a ritual slaying, with Boon, the priest, killing Ben with a knife. Ike's immersion in the river previously may be significant as a ritual cleansing, a baptism, which prepared him to share in the death of Ben without being guilty of shedding his blood. Ike's innocence here foreshadows the innocence he chose by rejecting responsibility and active adult participation in the community. The yearning for immutability which inspired Ike's choice is identified by

Blanche Gelfant as "the very essence of a Romantic desire for escape from the human condition," symbolized by the Grecian urn image quoted by Cass. The introduction of this passage into *Go Down, Moses* as a memory after Ike made his choice, rather than after the fyce episode where it appeared in the short story, confirms this interpretation of Ike's motives. As Olga Vickery expressed it, "In rejecting sin, Isaac also rejects humanity." By so doing, he denied the spirit of Christ, "who did not hesitate to share in the life of man, to accept guilt, and to suffer immolation." In spirit Ike never returned from his journey into the forest. His heart remained in the forest, as Gloria Dussinger observed, and the incomplete one-way romantic journey is most apparent in "Delta Autumn."

Two other journeys follow the death of Old Ben: Ike's return to witness the passing of the wilderness when he was eighteen, "The Bear," part 5, and his trip to the delta hunting camp in "Delta Autumn." He also performed two journeys of family duty before he relinquished his inheritance when he was twenty-one: he searched for James Beauchamp in 1886 to deliver the thousand-dollar legacy, and he found Fonsiba at the end of that year and left her legacy with a banker, to insure a monthly income to keep her from starving. When he met the grand-daughter of James on his delta journey, Ike said nothing about the legacy which her grandfather had not received. Ike took no initiative in aiding his Negro kin but acted as the agent to carry out old Carothers's bequest.

The quest journey into the forest in the McCaslin trilogy began as a purposeful journey, intended as initiation leading to the road to manhood. In light of the rest of Ike's life, the journey is revealed as a flight from reality, seeking a refuge from life rather than a way of life, a relinquishment of the power to act, rather than a course of action. In a final story of hunting and initiation, Faulkner implicitly showed Ike's error. In "Race at Morning" (1955) "Uncle Ike" was a character in a story told by a boy narrator who resembles the youthful Ike. The boy was told by his foster-father that the right to hunt for two weeks was earned by farming for the rest of the year, and that the boy had to get an education because hunting and farming were no longer enough to fulfill one's human obligations: "You got to belong to the business of mankind." In commenting on "Race at Morning," Faulkner said that "this uneducated ignorant man" had learned late in life, through caring for the boy, that "no man can be an island to himself, that you have a responsibility to mankind." The foster father and his son were the "mutual salvation of one another." Faulkner also commented directly on Ike's failure. People can cope with problems in three ways: "The first says, This is rotten, I'll have no part of it, I will take death first. The second says,

This is rotten, I don't like it, I can't do anything about it, but at least I will not participate in it myself. . . . The third says, This stinks and I'm going to do something about it. McCaslin is the second. He says, This is bad, and I will withdraw from it. What we need are people who will say, This is bad and I'm going to do something about it, I'm going to change it." In *The Sound and the Fury* Faulkner used Gothic fiction to present the first type, in Quentin who substituted a death ritual for initiation; in *Go Down, Moses* he used Gothic fiction to show Ike's failure to carry into adult life what he learned in his initiation; in *Intruder in the Dust* he used Gothic fiction again to represent a successful initiation.

After Ike conducted his quest for truth in the commissary and discovered it in the ledgers, the ironic reversal began: the facts of his inheritance caused him to repudiate it; on the basis of values learned during his initiation, he rejected the participation in life for which the initiation should have prepared him. Ike's memories of his initiation never included revelation of the mysteries of human sexuality, part of both puberty and secret society rites as described by Eliade in *The Quest*. This omission may reflect the attitudes of the McCaslin-Edmonds men, represented in the initiation by McCaslin Edmonds. Because Ike married the wrong kind of woman, his repudiation resulted in his childlessness and the reduction of his active life to his hunting trips. "Delta Autumn" confirms this interpretation. The Girl, in the novel version the unwed mother of Roth's child, told Uncle Isaac that he was responsible for Roth's selfish and immature evasion of responsibility: Ike had spoiled Roth by giving the Edmonds family the property which did not belong to them. And when Ike told the Girl to forget Roth and go north and marry a Negro, she said: "Old man . . . have you lived so long and forgotten so much that you don't remember anything you ever knew or felt or even heard about love?" (p. 363). As John Muste said: "The Girl's question, and Ike's inability to answer, provide the key to the development of the stories in *Go Down, Moses*, giving it a true thematic structure," revealed in the contrast between Lucas's marriage and Ike's and between the love in the Negro branch of the McCaslin family and the absence of love among the white McCaslins. This contrast is part of the answer to the Girl's question, foreshadowed in "Was" when Tomey's Turl ran away to court Tennie and Buck ran away to escape being courted. The implication of the question in "Delta Autumn" is that Ike, in his romantic rhapsody about man and woman together being God, was still living in a romantic dream and that he had missed the realities of love other than the one sexual experience described in "The Bear," part 4. Ike had no concept of such love as was symbolized by the fire on the hearth. Despite his eloquent defense of Negroes and his repudiation of his grandfather, who bequeathed money rather than say, *"My son to a nigger"* (p. 269), Ike accepted Roth's action, which was precisely parallel to that of old Carothers except that the incest was remote and unknown to Roth; Ike paid off the Girl with Roth's money rather than acknowledge her as his kinswoman and her child as the last of the McCaslin-Edmonds family. The envelope of money symbolizes the false values of the McCaslins, now shared by Ike. The hunting horn, a gift to Ike from General Compson, which Ike gave to the child, symbolizes the tradition of the hunters which Ike failed to transmit to younger men like Roth and refused to transmit through a personal relationship to the child, to whom, in either the South or the North, the horn would be meaningless. At the end Ike realized that Roth had killed a doe, the symbol of the exploitation of the wilderness and of human beings, the wildlife symbol of the girl in flight.

The tableaux and even the scenes of violence in *Go Down, Moses* produce Gothic effects of mystery and dream rather than of horror and nightmare. The angle of vision is largely responsible for the softening of Gothic effect: Ike lived in an idyllic dream, and his consciousness controlled the narrative. The vision of the phantom buck in "The Old People" exemplifies the natural and convincing effect of supernatural phenomena in the wilderness context; as an initiate the down-to-earth Cass Edmonds had had the same vision. Such experiences, Gloria Dussinger said, constitute "a flawless, incontrovertible account of a confrontation of the noumenon." The tableau which Cass used as the occasion for his discourse on Keats's "Ode on a Crecian Urn" is the clue to Ike's desire to have life approach the stasis of art, to be like the fond lover who "could never approach any nearer and would never have to get any farther away" (p. 297). Cass's explanation of why Ike did not shoot the bear to save the fyce implies the reason that Ike stood and watched Lion and Boon kill Ben. But the virtues of the hunter—*"Courage and honor and pride and pity and love of justice and of liberty"* (p. 297)—cannot be confined to what a man does or does not do during a yearly hunting trip. Ike's dream image of stasis, the leaping buck or the looming bear, had the same effect as Hightower's dream image of action, the surge of galloping horses: neither man recognized that the reality which man must accept, or betray his human inheritance, is man in motion now, as Faulkner said at Nagano, taking along with him all the old "trouble and sin" and curing it as he goes.

In addition to the killing of the buck and the marking of Ike with the blood, narrated in "The Old People" and remembered in "Delta Autumn," Ike's most intense experience in an active role, the climax of his youthful solitary ordeal in the forest, is the mysterious apparition and vanishing of Old Ben: but as Richard Lawson pointed out, Ike failed to comprehend the significance of Old Ben's leading him back to the instruments of civilization: "By relinquishment of the material . . . one finds the spiritual, but one cannot live on spirit alone." The killing of Old Ben is the most memorable of the hunting scenes. As the climax of a long period of preparation, during which Lion was tamed to a point where he could be used, the slaying is a scene of furious action: Lion clinging to Ben's throat, Ben grasping Lion "almost loverlike" and hurling another hound five or six feet, Boon leaping on Ben's back, "and the glint of the knife as it rose and fell" (p. 241). The action is succeeded by a typical Faulknerian moment of stasis: "For an instant they almost resembled a piece of statuary: the clinging dog, the bear, the man stride its back, working and probing the buried blade." Boon pulled Ben over backward but "the bear surged erect, raising with it the man and the dog too." Then after a few steps "it fell all of a piece, as a tree falls, so that all three of them, man dog and bear, seemed to bounce once." This treelike fall marks the death of the wilderness and its creatures. The deaths of Lion and Sam follow that of Ben, but Sam's is not described. Presumably Boon shot Sam, at Sam's request, but this Gothic scene is omitted. Sam's body on the burial platform and his grave, with a can of gifts nailed to a tree for the delight of the departed spirit, lend a primitive note to the familiar Gothic graveyard scene.

Two scenes in "The Bear," part 5, introduce a note of grotesque humor into Ike's last experiences in this wilderness: the bear cub clinging to the tree, "its head ducked between its arms," terrified by the logging train, and Boon under the gum tree, frantically trying to fix his gun and claiming all the squirrels in the tree as his. Faulkner's comment on this latter scene makes clear his conscious intention to secure effects by grotesque incongruities: "To me it underlined the heroic tragedy of the bear and the dog by the last survivor being reduced to the sort of petty comedy of someone trying to patch up a gun in order to shoot a squirrel."

The last story, "Go Down, Moses," deliberately avoids direct presentation of the flight and pursuit stage of the action, the hunting down of Samuel Beauchamp by the law, and the most violent scene, his execution. Instead, the focus is on the grief of Mollie (spelled "Molly" in "The Fire and the Hearth") for her grandson and her wish for a proper burial for her "Benjamin," sold into Egypt by Roth Edmonds. Like "Pantaloon in Black" this story deals primarily with Negroes' capacity for love and grief. It does not mention Ike McCaslin but doubly reflects on him and on the consequence of his relinquishment of his inheritance. First, had Ike been running the plantation, Roth could not have sent Samuel away. Ike's failure to influence Roth, as Cass had influenced him, was apparent in "Delta Autumn." When Samuel, a teenager, was caught breaking into the commissary, Roth put him off the plantation, despite the fact that the boy was a blood relation and an orphan. Samuel's criminal career could be predicted, once he was in town and homeless. Second, Gavin Stevens and Miss Worsham, not Ike, helped Mollie. The action of Miss Worsham makes clear Ike's sins of omission by showing how Ike could have aided and comforted his Negro kin, as Miss Worsham shared the sorrow of her foster siblings "about the brick hearth on which the ancient symbol of human coherence and solidarity smoldered" (p. 380). Mollie, wife of Ike's cousin Lucas, turned for aid to Gavin Stevens and Miss Worsham, not to Ike. Faulkner could easily have put Ike in the place of Gavin, as he put Roth in the place of Don Boyd, if he had wished to revise the short story for inclusion in *Go Down, Moses*. One can only conclude that the omission of Ike was deliberate. The fatal end of this last pursuit, that of Samuel by the law, contrasts with the comic first pursuit, in "Was." "Go Down, Moses" ends with a funeral procession. Gavin said of Mollie: *"She wanted that casket and those flowers and the hearse and she wanted to ride through town behind it in a car"* (p. 383). The desire for human dignity knows no color line.

At the end of *Go Down, Moses* the Negroes are still waiting for a Moses to deliver them. Here for the first time in Yoknapatawpha fiction, Faulkner used Negroes as heroic figures, with greater capacity for love than their white kin. In his use of the Gothic tradition, Faulkner shifted emphasis away from ironic inversion in characters and away from sexual violence except as historical fact. Isaac McCaslin was more sensitively concerned with the curse of miscegenation in the past, an inherited guilt to disclaim, than with it in the present, a wrong to be mitigated or righted. Although *Go Down, Moses* not only deals with the theme of miscegenation as did *Absalom, Absalom!* but combines it with actual father-daughter incest, the Gothic horror of *Absalom, Absalom!* is lacking from *Go Down, Moses* because of the limitations in Ike's imaginative realization of the past and the absence of information beyond the ledger entries. The chief protagonist of each of these two novels is "innocent," but Ike's innocence lay in substituting dream for involvement in reality, while Thomas Sutpen's innocence lay in trying to achieve his dream in reality. Both had the wrong dreams; both "innocently" believed that they could buy freedom from guilt; both lacked capacity for mature love; both died without an heir.

CHAPTER EIGHT

INTRUDER IN THE DUST

THE PERILOUS QUEST, OR,
THE SECRET OF THE GRAVE

The continuation of the story of Lucas Beauchamp in *Intruder in the Dust* shifts from the relationship between Lucas and his white relatives to that between Lucas and the white community. But Lucas is the center of concern, not the central intelligence as he was in "The Fire and the Hearth," chapter 1. Charles Mallison is the hero of the murder-mystery-detective story and the story of initiation, in both of which the narrative content is fully Gothic. The adolescent Charles is an extraordinarily effective central intelligence because his state of tension and excitement and the dream quality which suffuses both his thoughts and his actions heighten the Gothic atmosphere.

The title of *Intruder in the Dust* is the least obvious in meaning in Yoknapatawpha fiction. It may refer to Jake Montgomery, the intruder in the dust of Vinson Gowrie's grave; it may refer to Charles as the intruder who disturbed the dust of Vinson's grave. But a sentence in Lillian Smith's *Killers of the Dream* suggests a broader meaning. To satisfy his own sense of moral obligation and to ascertain the truth, Charles defied the white community and not only disturbed the dust of a specific grave but uncovered a hidden truth. In describing the southern reaction toward such a defiance of traditional attitudes, Lillian Smith used the key word: "We alienated reason; made strangers of knowledge and facts; labeled as 'intruder' all moral responsibility for our acts."

According to Faulkner's account of the development of the story, it originated in the idea of a man in jail, "just about to be hung," who "would have to be his own detective" because "he couldn't get anybody to help him. Then the next thought was, the man for that would be a Negro." As soon as Faulkner thought of Lucas Beauchamp, "then he took charge of the story" and gave it a new shape.

The power of Lucas as a character in *Go Down, Moses* was thus the true source of *Intruder in the Dust*. The action centers in his peril, due to his behavior as an "uppity nigger," demonstrated in "The Fire and the Hearth," and in his capacity, generated by self-confidence and integrity, to stimulate a boy to daring and perilous action. The initial sequence of past action occurs on the Edmonds plantation, immediately linking *Intruder in the Dust* with *Go Down, Moses* in setting as well as character. The climax of the initiation of Isaac McCaslin, at sixteen witnessing the death of Old Ben, is paralleled by the climax of the initiation of Charles Mallison, at sixteen saving the life of Lucas. But as central intelligence Charles responded to and was involved in present action, not like Ike remembering the past as in "The Old People" and "The Bear," or contemplating the present, with echoes of the past, as in "Delta Autumn." The implications of the absence of Ike in "Go Down, Moses," already discussed, are confirmed in *Intruder in the Dust*. Roth Edmonds was in a hospital in New Orleans and thus was helpless to aid Lucas. Charles thought of Roth's "great-uncle," "Uncle Ike McCaslin . . . still alive at ninety" (p. 93), but had no idea of seeking aid or even advice from him. (Charles was realistically inaccurate; Ike would be ninety in 1957, and Roth was the great-great-grandson of Ike's Aunt Mary, sister of Buck and Buddy McCaslin.) The hold upon Faulkner's imagination of the McCaslin story and of the Gothic pattern of detection and initiation is apparent in his account of the genesis of *Intruder in the Dust*. His habitual practice of varying those patterns continues to be demonstrated.

Because *Intruder in the Dust* is a novel of detection, based on a clear moral choice of participation, rather than of withdrawal, passivity, or alienation, the Gothic aspects of the setting are markedly different from those in novels previously discussed and are more readily recognized as Gothic in the detective story context, especially the graveyard sequences. But recognition may lead to over-facile classification: Maxwell Geismar labeled this novel a Gothic romance and referred to the use of stage props and literary puppets. Since the Gothic, as has been indicated, was originally theatrical, with distinct character types, Geismar is merely naming the ingredients with which a Gothic writer begins; he fails to consider how Faulkner mixed and varied his materials. Geismar, for example, does not remark on the absence of the usual substitute for the Gothic castle. No ruined mansion figures as an essential setting because this is not a family story. The Edmonds plantation house is peripheral, and Lucas's cabin is important only in antecedent action. The Mallison house is essential but totally un-Gothic: it is a comfortable, middle class residence in Jefferson and is the center of close, harmonious, cheerful family life, not a refuge or a trap. Miss Habersham's house, carried over from "Go Down, Moses," where her name is Worsham, does fit the pattern of the decayed southern mansion. As in "Go Down, Moses," it is an ancestral mansion on the edge of town, in a "shaggy untended cedar grove," a paintless, columned colonial house with neither electricity nor water (*Intruder in the Dust,* pp. 119, 76). It reminds one of Joseph Blotner's account of Rowan Oak when the Faulkners moved into it in 1930. The Habersham house, like the Edmonds house, merely establishes the status of the family and adds a Gothic motif, rather than serving as a setting for action. Miss Habersham's indifference to conventional "respectability" and her freedom of action provide contrast with her dwelling and what it suggests.

Similarly unlike previous Gothic settings, the enclosed places do not represent self-imprisonment or withdrawal, only literal imprisonment or normal family life or practical activity. Lucas's cabin represents genuine hospitality and vital warmth for a cold and wet boy: Horace Benbow's offer of asylum to Ruby in *Sanctuary* is comparable as a generous response to need. The fifty-cent piece with which Charles tried to pay for hospitality is a major symbolic object. To Lucas, even more than to Lee Goodwin, the jail in Jefferson was not only a place of imprisonment but a sanctuary: Lee needed protection from Popeye, but Lucas needed protection from all of Beat Four and the idle youths of Jefferson. The story of the jailor's daughter adds a domestic, romantic note to the jail, which "still looked like a residence with its balustraded wooden gallery stretching across the front of the lower floor" (p. 51). The sheriff's house was another asylum for Lucas, not a prison. That house and Gavin's office represent cooperation and participation within the law but with consideration of justice and personal relationships. In fact, Gavin's office is for Charles an extension of home and family life, where he can both gain and demonstrate maturity.

Gavin's office looks out on the Square and the courthouse, and the novel begins with Chick standing across the street from the jail. Yoknapatawpha, with the courthouse in the center, exemplifies Mircea Eliade's observation in *The Quest,* that man desires to believe that he dwells at the center of the world, the *axis mundi,* and that his whole life is articulated in a system based on that belief. Faulkner's dramatization of that belief as a motivating force in Yoknapatawpha County is found in *Requiem for a Nun,* "The Courthouse" and "The Jail." The slight part the Square played in the life and thoughts of Ike McCaslin is further evidence of Ike's lack of a mature sense of community such as Chick Mallison gained through his initiation.

But if the Gothic atmosphere is notably muted in the buildings in *Intruder in the Dust,* the countryside provides background more Gothic than that in *Go Down, Moses* and comparable only to that in *Absalom, Absalom!* In the trilogy of hunting stories, the heightened sensitivity of Isaac which "registers" the wilderness is somewhat like that of Charles, but in *Intruder in the Dust* the expansion to book length of a few hours of present action allows the sensitivity of Charles to function with greater intensity and penetration, on multiple levels of consciousness. Charles's memory is as vivid as Ike's but of course covers a much briefer lapse of time. The episode at Lucas's four years before the present action is as vividly represented as the main events of the novel. Charles's memory gives a clearer picture than that in "The Fire and the Hearth" of Lucas's cabin and the fire and the hearth themselves: "the clay-daubed fieldstone chimney in which a halfburned backlog glowed and smoldered in the gray ashes" (p. 10). Edward Corridori saw in the cabin of Lucas on the hilltop a symbol of values and traditions and the center of the homogeneity Gavin praised but did not protect.

Part of the peculiarly Gothic effect of the natural settings in *Intruder in the Dust* is due to the use of light and darkness: Charles took the same trip at night and on a spring day, with conscious comparison of the visual effects. But there is no ironic contrast between setting and mood in the daylight view as there is in *Sanctuary* between the May landscape and Temple's and Popeye's flight to Memphis. The emptiness of the road at night Charles knew to be abnormal:

Yet so far he had passed nothing whatever since he left town: the road lay pale and empty before and behind him too; the lightless houses and cabins squatted or loomed beside it, the dark land stretched away into the darkness strong with the smell of plowed earth and now and then the heavy scent of flowering orchards lying across the road for him to ride through like stagnant skeins of smoke.... [P. 95]

Formulation in words of that strange emptiness "was like the struck match which doesn't dispel the dark but only exposes its terror—one weak flash and glare revealing for a second the empty road's the dark and empty land's irrevocable immitigable negation." The next day the same road was revealed in "morning's bland ineffable May": "Now he could see the white bursts of dogwood in the hedgerows marking the old section-line surveys or standing like nuns in the cloistral patches and bands of greening woods and the pink and white of peach and pear and the pink-white of the first appletrees in the orchards which last night he had only smelled ..." (p. 146). But as at night, all was "empty, vacant of any movement and any life," farmhouses and cabins alike, but "most of all, the empty fields themselves in each of which on this day at this hour on the second Monday in May there should have been fixed in monotonous repetition the land's living symbol—a formal group of ritual almost mystic significance . . ." (p. 147). Finally one such group appeared, as much an exception to Negro behavior as Charles and Gavin, who witnessed it, were to white behavior: "the man and the mule and the wooden plow which coupled them furious and solitary, fixed without progress in the earth, leaning terrifically against nothing" (p. 148).

Such tableaux of stasis in contrast with action are as characteristic of Charles's own point of view as of Faulkner's in *Light in August,* Charles being more like his creator than are most of the Yoknapatawphans and the narrative often involving furious motion in which such contrast is effective. Not only does this daylight passage present most vividly the route from Jefferson through Beat Four as seen by Charles while the exhilaration of an all-night expedition is still upon him, but it also extends the scene to the distant horizon and beyond, in a broad perspective of region and nation romantic in feeling and scope and intensely charged with love of the South in the heart of a boy "on the threshold of manhood":

—unfolding beneath him like a map in one slow soundless explosion: to the east ridge on green ridge tumbling away toward Alabama and to the west and south the checkered fields and the woods flowing on into the blue and gauzed horizon beyond which lay at last like a cloud the long wall of the levee and the great River itself . . . and beyond that stretching away east and north and west not merely to where the ultimate headlands frowned back to back upon the waste of the two oceans and the long barrier of Canada but to the uttermost rim of earth itself, the North. . . ." [Pp. 151–52]

The view Charles attained from this crest represented, according to Richard Pindell, "the consummation of a rite of passage begun at Lucas' place out of irresponsible boyhood into responsible manhood."

Against this vast panorama of the region, the nation, the earth, are enacted the specific scenes of the Gothic drama. The fact that Charles, through whose eyes and consciousness all is revealed, is in the process of becoming acutely, painfully aware of his heritage, for good and evil, and of the significance of what he has taken for granted all his life, gives such passages a function and an artistic justification lacking in the often digressive scenic effects which decorated and enhanced the original Gothic novels. The only irony in the spring scene is that created by the events themselves: inactivity due to fear keeps all Negroes in hiding and makes white farmers abandon their usual labors.

In the characters also, with one notable exception, Faulkner plays the Gothic "straight," more than ironically. Since this is a story of inner conflict, not of race conflict, and since it is subjectively presented, such polarity of characters as had been observed in *Sanctuary* or such analysis as distinguished *Light in August* had to be forgone. For the most part, Charles Mallison comes closest in Yoknapatawpha to being a genuine Romantic hero, without the Faustian or Byronic taint of evil and villainy. The nickname of Charles, "Chick," has the same symbolic significance as that of "Pip" in *Great Expectations,* as T. H. Adamowski observed: the hatching chick "pips" its way out of the shell. Chick himself provided an analogous image by which he described himself at Lucas's, "enveloped in the quilt like a cocoon." In *Rites and Symbols of Initiation* Mircea Eliade cited Buddhist imagery for spiritual birth in initiation as being "accomplished like that of the chick, . . . 'by breaking the eggshell.'" Wrappings like the quilt, according to Eliade, are used in initiations to signify gestation.

Judging Charles Mallison and Lucius Priest, narrator-hero of *The Reivers,* to be Faulkner's most admirable characters, William Brown commented on their normality and on their being products of Jefferson, rather than of country life or wilderness experience. (The initiation of Lucius follows the quest-romance, not the Gothic, pattern.) Young, idealistic, and courageous, but not foolhardy, Charles is successful, as the Romantic hero in a Gothic novel should be. But in two respects Charles is an ironic inversion—not of the Romantic hero but of the detective and of the southern hero. In *Faulkner in the University,* Faulkner commented on the fact that Lucas could not "hire a detective . . . one of those tough guys that slapped women around, took a drink every time he couldn't think of what to say next." In some essential ways Charles is untypical of southern boys, a deviation from the social tradition, if not the Gothic tradition. But Charles is less a rebel against the southern tradition than a defender of the best in his heritage.

Since this is an initiation story, there should be, and there are, benevolent father figures: the father of Charles, and his uncle Gavin Stevens. But they do not play typical roles: they are not mentors in the initiation, except after the fact. Although Aleck Sander, the companion of Charles, at first looks like the Gothic humorous servant, he too represents a deviation from the norm, but not an ironic one. He remains amusing, in his frank disinclination to be a hero and a martyr. But in his capacity to rise to what is expected of him and acquit himself well, he is admirable, and in his honest disavowal of heroic intention, he is refreshing: "I had done already told Chick I didn't aim to. Only when we got to the truck everybody seemed to just take it for granted I wasn't going to do nothing else but go and before I knowed it I wasn't" (p. 113). The example of Aleck Sander suggests a truth about human nature in general and Negro behavior in a white society in particular: people often live up, or down, to what is expected of them.

There is one thorough villain, in terms of any literary tradition: Crawford Gowrie, thief, fratricide, common murderer, who plotted to frame an innocent man for murder and who would have helped to lynch that man to conceal his own guilt. Crawford is a perfect example to support the theory of Richard Sterba, cited by Aaron Steinberg, that white hatred of Negroes is analogous to sibling hostility to a younger child: *"The hostility is repressed, but preserved in the unconscious, and then directed against the Negro as a substitute object."* Crawford, however, released his hostility and in effect murdered both his younger brother and the substitute object, Lucas, whose death by lynching was almost certain. The easily aroused hostility of the mob obscured Crawford's psychological motivations. The father of Crawford and the murdered Vinson, Nub Gowrie, is a lower class representative of the authoritarian father in Gothic romance but is not a Tyrannical Parent. His grown sons obey him, but he can grieve for Vinson and pronounce judgment on Crawford. Although Nub Gowrie is one-armed, his dignity and self-control minimize his grotesqueness. His twin sons, the ultimate extreme in identical twins as doubles, are the only genuine grotesques in the novel. Their identical appearance and their automatism make them resemble some of the mechanical characters of Dickens: "The two younger men still sat the mule identical as two clothing store dummies and as immobile," "identical as two clothes pins on a line" (pp. 162, 163). Like robots, they acted in "choreographic unison," "like a trained vauderville team" (pp. 164, 163). (The political implications of their names, Vardaman and Bilbo, Charles did not comment on, perhaps because to a southern boy at that time those names would be too familiar to excite a reaction.) Sheriff Hampton appeared grotesque when, half-dressed and tousled, he was unofficially cooking breakfast. But Constable Skipworth is essentially, not occasionally, grotesque: "a little driedup wizened stone-deaf old man not much larger than a half-grown boy with a big nickel-plated pistol loose in one coat pocket and in the other a guttapercha eartrumpet on a rawhide thong around his neck like a foxhorn" (p. 37).

Again, as in *Go Down, Moses,* Lucas Beauchamp is unique. His appearance when he is in town is still invariable: he always dressed like a white man of an older generation. His costume, particularly the beaver hat which he always kept on his head, is significant in *Intruder in the Dust* as one cause of white hostility, an unforgivable offense against racial etiquette which marked him as an "uppity nigger" and infuriated white people to the point of murderous rage. Frank Thomas pointed out the role played by the community in structuring Lucas's identity by their insistence that "niggers" observe race etiquette; the qualities Lucas developed in defying convention proved him to be superior to his detractors. The ritual reaction of conventional lower class whites toward Lucas could be triggered merely by his manner and dress, as the episode in the country store showed. In his fortitude and courage Lucas is heroic, refusing to lose his dignity even to save his life. But the circumstances exclude Lucas from most of the action in the novel. Although he is the center of concern and of reaction, as was Joe Christmas, *Intruder in the Dust* is the story of Charles, and Lucas is a kind of catalyst. As Olga Vickery said, "He is at once the 'nigger' who is to be lynched by the mob and the man who must be saved by Chick and his two companions." He is also, as Walter Brylowski remarked, "the basic symbol of the South's predicament." But as a Negro he is no more typical than he is as a character in a Gothic novel. He is sui generis.

One of the most interesting departures in *Intruder in the Dust* from the Gothic pattern in general and particularly in Faulkner, in addition to the slight use of the grotesque, is the absence of sexuality and sexual perversions. With Lucas as the man accused of a crime, a sexual offense would be much less probable than murder. Moreover, a sexual offense or even the rumor of one would be summarily dealt with, as Faulkner showed in "Dry September," in which nothing had actually happened and the lynchers had no previous ill feeling toward the man they lynched. Leslie Fiedler spied the "holy marriage of males" between almost any pair of males, especially of different colors, regardless of age, circumstances, and textual evidence. To interpret Ike McCaslin and Sam Fathers or Chick and Lucas as examples of homosexual passion as Fiedler did, in *Love and Death* and *An End to Innocence,* is unwarranted, in light of Faulkner's characterizations and of his willingness to present homosexuality without subterfuge, as in *Absalom, Absalom!* In *The Town* and *The Mansion* the devotion of Gavin Stevens to his twin sister Margaret is developed further than it is in *Intruder in the Dust,* in which the close relationship between uncle and nephew is more significant than that between brother and sister, and in which Gavin and Margaret had not yet joined the ranks of Faulkner's gallery of twin-doubles. One may well be reminded of the devotion of Gavin's predecessor Horace Benbow to his sister Narcissa, but Gavin's devotion to Margaret in "Knight's Gambit" (1949) and in *Intruder in the Dust* is that of an older brother to a sister some years younger and seems to be based on his enjoyment of the comfortable and uncomplicated life Margaret provided for him in the Mallison household, leaving Gavin free to romanticize other women before finally marrying one of them. In fact, one of the odd aspects of *Intruder in the Dust* as a Gothic novel is that it presents the most wholesome and cheerful view of family life in Yoknapatawpha County before *The Reivers.*

Margaret Mallison is neither a Suffering Wife nor a Tyrannical Parent.

Except that she is reluctant to see her son grow up and to admit that he is old enough for some independence, she has a surprising resilience and is able to give ground on one issue while making a stand on another. But she does not try to exercise undue authority over others. Aunt Molly appears again: as a "tiny old almost doll-sized woman," wearing a painted straw hat on top of her immaculate white head cloth (p. 10), she is mildly grotesque. When cause for a "voce" was past, in "The Fire and the Hearth," she ceased to be a Suffering Wife. She appeared only briefly, in Chick's memory, and had died before the present action in *Intruder in the Dust.* Grief over Molly's death rendered Lucas oblivious to the external world, and he passed Chick without seeing him. The parallel between his grief and Rider's, in "Pantaloon in Black," may be Faulkner's way of deliberately introducing again the theme of marital love among Negroes.

The uniqueness of Lucas is matched by the uniqueness of Miss Habersham. Like Lucas, she has enough innate dignity and honorable pride to escape grotesqueness despite incongruities in appearance: dressed in Sears, Roebuck print dresses, thirty-dollar shoes, and fifteen-dollar gloves, she peddled vegetables and chickens in a pickup truck. Whether she is called Worsham, as in "Go Down, Moses," or Habersham, her character is consistent: she has courage, loyalty, integrity, and compassion, and her way of supporting herself shows self-respect and independence. Anyone less in search of identity or less in flight from reality than Miss Habersham would be hard to find. But Miss Habersham as a Gothic heroine can be best appreciated by comparing her with Miss Emily Grierson, in "A Rose for Emily," who is quite similar to Miss Habersham in age, background, and circumstances. Miss Emily was self-imprisoned, the victim of a Tyrannical Father and overweening pride, and became mad and apparently necrophiliac. Gothic fiction has few more shocking "discoveries" than the body of Homer Barron, "in the attitude of an embrace," rotted and dust-covered, and next to it a second pillow, still showing "the indentation of a head" and "a long strand of iron-gray hair" (*Collected Stories,* p. 130). The bodies uncovered in *Intruder in the Dust* are commonplace by comparison. The myth of southern womanhood, of which Miss Emily was a victim, was rejected by Miss Habersham. Unique in her own society, she was also unique as a Gothic heroine, especially in a novel of initiation. Miss Habersham, not Chick's father or uncle, was his mentor. Her motivation, like Miss Worsham's in "Go Down, Moses," was love and loyalty, which sufficed to make her confident that the husband of Molly, her foster-sister, was not a murderer. She resembled Granny Millard and Aunt Jenny in *The Unvanquished,* but she played a more essential role than either in the initiation process and a less essential role than Granny in shaping the moral character of the initiate. Like the two Sartoris women, Miss Habersham represented the best in the old tradition and was able to adapt to change and to live in the present. In contrast with Gavin, the rational male, whose role as mentor she assumed when he defaulted, Miss Habersham represents the intuitive female. Her other virtues—equanimity, courage, and sturdy commonsense—are unique in nondetecting heroines in the Gothic novel but may owe something to the examples of such lady sleuths as Miss Marple, Maud Silver, and their peers.

Intruder in the Dust is not only the most Gothic of Faulkner's novels in the mystery and suspense sustained in present action, but it is also the most fully based on dream qualities and dreamlike action. Like Conrad's Marlow, in *Heart of Darkness,* Charles had a choice of nightmares and had to live through the one he chose.

The mystery and suspense are essentially similar to those prevalent in Gothic romance, and the resolution is a triumph of the "good guys," but the love interest of Gothic romance and many detective stories is totally lacking. The narrative method heightens the suspense; instead of the conventional narration after the action is complete, with "had-I-but-knowns" or other hints at the outcome, limitation to Chick's point of view, expressed in the third person and past tense, sustains the mystery and sense of danger. Both what happens and why are revealed only bit by bit, in chronological sequence; the preliminary facts concerning the murder of Vinson Gowrie and the motive of the murderer were withheld by Lucas until his innocence had been established. Chick is not a detective-participant, in the confidence of a client, but only a boy with a single task to perform, to dig up a body at night and tell the authorities what he found, what kind of gun fired the shot that killed Vinson.

Other mysteries exist at the beginning: What was the lumber deal and who was the other man involved with Vinson? What was Lucas's role? Gavin Stevens assumed that he knew the answer to the last question and Lucas did not enlighten him. The only fact that Lucas disclosed to Chick and not to Gavin is that Vinson was not shot by a .41 Colt, such as Lucas owned. In the course of the action the other mysteries arise before the initial ones are solved: Why was Jake Montgomery shot? Where is Vinson's body? Why was Montgomery's body removed, leaving an empty grave? Where was his body? What happened when a trap was set to catch Crawford? All but the last question are answered in the penultimate chapter, in the reconstruction of the whole sequence of events from before the murder of Vinson; the last question is answered parenthetically in the last chapter, in the reference to Crawford's "suicide's grave" (p. 237) which raises another question, left unanswered:

How did Crawford, in jail, get the Luger, the murder weapon, with which he then committed suicide? The gun as a Gothic object is recurrent in Faulkner, figuring notably in *The Unvanquished, Light in August,* and *Go Down, Moses.* The Luger, like an epic sword, had a history, an identity: Buddy McCallum brought it "home from France in 1919 and traded [it] that summer for a pair of fox hounds" (p. 179). This link with the McCallum episode in *Sartoris* (there spelled "MacCallum") may remind the reader of the Sartoris and McCallum twins, as parallels with the Gowrie twins as Gothic doubles.

The suspense does not depend, however, merely on the solution to the complex mystery: two themes are focused on Lucas, Chick's search for the truth which will exonerate Lucas and the community's intention to lynch Lucas as soon as the Sabbath-keeping inhabitants of Beat Four come to town on Monday. The point of view of Chick allows emphasis on both themes, on the danger to himself in his search and on the danger to Lucas, and on the urgency of time in relation to both. The discovery that it was the murderer who rode past them near the graveyard at night increases the sense of urgency and danger. The suspense concerning Lucas is lessened when Chick learns, belatedly, that Lucas is no longer in jail but has secretly been taken to the sheriff's for safety.

The chief deviations from chronological order of events as Chick participates in them or learns of them concern his previous experiences with Lucas which motivate his actions and the account of Lucas's narrow escape from violence at the country store: these are concentrated in the first chapter between Sunday noon, when Chick was waiting in the Square for Lucas to be brought to the jail, and an account of Chick's experiences from Saturday afternoon to Sunday morning. The active involvement of Chick begins with Lucas's words: "'Tell your uncle I wants to see him'" (p. 45). Charles was there where Lucas could see him because of an incident four years earlier when he fell into an icy creek near Lucas's cabin. This was the beginning of Chick's initiation which was completed four years later. The suggestion of Christian baptism is relevant. Mircea Eliade said: "Obviously, Christian baptism was from the first equivalent to an initiation." But Chick's immersion was no rite of purification or regeneration but a fall from innocence which preceded Chick's assertion of white superiority. Roth Edmonds's similar assertion had taken place in the same room, in "The Fire and the Hearth." Roth became a guest, instead of a member of the family, and was served dinner alone. Chick, a stranger, was also served dinner alone, while his wet clothes dried. Then he committed a humiliating breach of human etiquette, which transcends racial etiquette: he tried to pay for food which was offered to him as an act of hospitality to a guest. Lucas proudly refused to take or touch the money. The fifty-cent piece haunted Chick as a badge of shame which must be removed from his memory if he was to regain his dignity as a white man. T. H. Adamowski pointed out the parallel between the "two fat sweltering one-pound notes" Pip received in *Great Expectations* from his unknown benefactor and tried to repay in clean notes to Magwitch and the piece of silver which was the symbol of Chick's shame. In a kind of oneupmanship contest, Chick tried to repay Lucas with gifts, but Lucas always countered with another gift in return. Finally Lucas was in a situation where he needed what only Chick could give, a service which would humiliate neither and which it would be as blessed to receive as to give.

The first choice of nightmares which confronted Chick was to disclaim obligation and evade responsibility by saddling Highboy and riding far enough so that the lynching would be over by the time he returned: Beat Four would not break the Sabbath by lynching on Sunday and would not lynch by daylight "because then they would have to see one another's faces" (p. 114). The alternative was to accept responsibility, to choose quest rather than flight, by complying with whatever request Lucas might make. When Chick reluctantly chose quest, he engaged in a search for truth and justice which became an initiation, a nightmarish physical and mental ordeal which contributed to his maturity and sense of ethical responsibility. The daydream of flight Chick entertained recurrently until the time was past when it could become a reality. He even recalled his "first instinctive impulse" as the right one, by which he could have avoided being "responsible for having brought into the light and glare of day something shocking and shameful out of the whole white foundation of the county which he himself must partake of too since he too was bred of it, which otherwise might have flared and blazed merely out of Beat Four and then vanished back into its darkness or at least invisibility with the fading embers of Lucas's crucifixion" (pp. 137, 138). But now, not being an orphan, he could not escape, could not "even repudiate, relinquish, run" (p. 138). Faulkner's choice of words and allusions recalls other Gothic heroes: young Bayard ran; Joe Christmas was figuratively crucified; Ike McCaslin repudiated his grandfather and relinquished his inheritance. The comparison with Ike McCaslin is implicit in the diction and is most cogent. The theme of inheritance in the initiation of Chick concerns a cultural, not a family, heritage. But although the pattern of motion in Chick's reluctant initiation is that of quest, psychologically it has some of the elements of flight, flight first from the authority of the family, in his stealthy departure, and then from pursuit by the Gowries or the unknown murderer on the return from the Caledonia churchyard, "over a whole countryside already hopelessly waked and alerted" (p. 130). (This part of the journey Chick remembered in a flash after he reached home.)

This initiation was undertaken in defiance of all the traditions of the community and in opposition to his uncle's common sense. Without recognizing the initiation patterns and other Gothic characteristics, Adamowski compared *Great Expectations* and *Intruder in the Dust*. He observed that the situation in each novel "polarizes into almost Manichaean conflict of good and evil, with good in the form of error and evil in the form of apparent good," according to the standards of respectable society; in each "the social and psychological revelations" overshadow the mystery and an outcast is the principal means by which the hero achieves maturity. In Chick's unconventional initiation the ironic inversions extend to the conventional pattern, the initiate is not removed from women but owes his success in his ordeal to Miss Habersham, who furnished both the means (the pickup truck) and the moral support of her practical wisdom and ethical principles. It is a biracial initiation, participated in by Chick and Aleck Sander, as Bayard and Ringo shared the initiation ordeal of avenging Granny's murder in *The Unvanquished*. Like Ike's, the initiation journey of Chick is literally into the forest, but the skills involved are different, not woodsmanship and marksmanship but riding a horse, driving a truck, and, a new skill, digging up and filling in a grave. This ordeal not only simulates the ancient initiation ordeal of a descent into the womb of Mother Earth or into Hell in search of wisdom, described by Mircea Eliade in *Rites and Symbols,* but also exemplifies Northrop Frye's account in *The Secular Scripture* of the night world of romance and the specific theme of "a descent to a lower world of graves and caves." These ordeals took place in darkness and danger, with deprivation of food and sleep. Eliade's explanation of deprivation of sleep as an initiation ordeal is peculiarly applicable to Chick: "Not to sleep is not only to conquer physical fatigue, but is above all to show proof of will and spiritual strength; to remain awake is to be conscious, present in the world, *responsible*" (italics added). Loss of sleep adds a peculiar nightmare effect manifest in Chick's grogginess and loss of a sense of time and in sudden illusions or an effect of hypnosis, or in an inability to let go and sleep when the ordeal was over. Food and drink are stressed as part of the ritual. The coffee his mother gave him at breakfast canceled the promise that Chick was not to "ask for nor even accept a spoonful of coffee until he was eighteen years old" (p. 127). After the flight of the mob and his temporary repudiation of his people, Chick realized that "by the act of eating and maybe only by that did he actually enter the world, get himself into the world" (p. 207)—that is, be reborn, as Joe Christmas was when he accepted food with a sense of brotherhood.

Chick recognized the significance of his experience while it was going on: he was being shaped by his land into an individual, "a specific man," with "the specific passions and hopes and convictions and ways of thinking and acting of a specific kind and even race: and even more: even among a kind and race specific and unique ..." (p. 151). To achieve a full, mature sense of identity he had to achieve not only self-realization and self-acceptance but also acceptance of the community and culture to which he belonged. Revolted by the lynching mob—"not faces but a face, not a mass nor even a mosaic of them but a Face; not even ravening nor uninsatiate but just in motion, insensate, vacant of thought or even passion" (p. 182)—Charles was even more revolted when, confronted with evidence of Lucas's innocence and Crawford's guilt, they ran. This negative result of "his own one anonymous chance too to perform something passionate and brave and austere not just in but into man's enduring chronicle worthy of a place in it ..." (p. 193) caused Charles to approach repudiation like Isaac's but of a people, not just a grandfather. But Charles reaffirmed his identification with his community, "expiated his aberration from it," became "once more worthy to be received into it ... and so it must have been the eating" (p. 209). The act of communion ended his spiritual withdrawal: "He wanted no more save to stand with them unalterable and impregnable: one shame if shame must be, one expiation since expiation must surely be but above all one unalterable durable impregnable one: one people one heart one land ..." (pp. 209-10).

In his final acceptance of guilt and responsibility, Charles Mallison went beyond the point Isaac McCaslin achieved in his initiation, beyond the point achieved by any of Faulkner's other initiates: his personal morality became integrated with social morality in the recognition that the individual has a responsibility to protest against the evils he sees in his society. Gavin Stevens expressed this principle but only after Charles had acted on it when Gavin was so blinded by the stereotype of the uppity nigger that he assumed without question that Lucas "blew his top and murdered a white man" (p. 48). Thus, Gavin ironically proved his own point that "no man can cause more grief than that one clinging blindly to the vices of his ancestors" (p. 49). But after Charles repudiated those vices, Gavin encouraged him to continue his active protest: "Some things you must never stop refusing to bear. Injustice and outrage and dishonor and shame. No matter how young you are or how old you have got" (p. 206). But when Gavin said "Just dont stop," Charles had the last word: "We dont need to worry about stopping now. It seems to me what we have to worry about now is where we're going and how" (p. 210). The most unusual ironic inversion is that Charles has become mentor to Gavin. The "rational-empiric mode" which Walter Brylowski observed as an unusual experiment in Faulkner depends chiefly on the comments of Gavin after action which was based on irrational and intuitive impulses and in which he had played a belated and minor role. The triumph belongs to Charles and Miss Habersham. Gavin's rational consideration does not extend to southern society and southern tradition with enough force to move him to act upon his own precepts.

The Gothic quality of specific scenes of action or tableaux varies according to Chick's degree of awareness of what he witnessed or his relationship to events reported by others. He did not witness the scene at the country store, but he knew the place and the people, and when he heard the story he was already haunted by the half-dollar Lucas had rejected, "the dead monstrous heatless disc which hung nightly in the black abyss of rage and impotence" (p. 22). The provocativeness of Lucas's actions in the store is fully conveyed, as a prelude to the similar reaction of a similar group at the same store the day of the murder. The two murders, Crawford's murder of Vinson and of Jake Montgomery, and Crawford's suicide are distanced by being narrated after the fact or merely mentioned. Chick heard only the report of the murder of Vinson, presumably by Lucas; later he visualized Lucas standing, pistol in hand, over the body and being saved by Doyle Fraser, who had previously saved Lucas in the store. Lucas did not bother to correct Gavin's similar version of what had happened, except to deny that he had been knocked down. When the whole story of the murder of Vinson was finally told by Gavin, quoting Lucas, attention is focused on why Lucas had his pistol (it was part of his Saturday costume) and how Crawford tricked Lucas into firing his pistol at a target. The murder is notably unshocking in effect: Vinson "tripped over something and kind of bucked down onto his face" (p. 227). Psychological horror is more impressive than physical horror: Gavin's account of what Crawford's state of mind must have been during the digging up and reburying of Vinson and Montgomery is more vivid than is the crushing in of Montgomery's skull. One anticipated scene of violence never took place: the expected attack by Crawford on the sheriff and Lucas as they crossed Whiteleaf bottom in low gear. The murders in *Intruder in the Dust* are as unsanguinary as those in *Sanctuary* and are similarly distanced.

The suspense centers chiefly in danger and potential violence. After the murder of Vinson the sequence of events is a ritual as Olga Vickery said, as predictable as was the dispatching of a posse of men with dogs to track down Joe Christmas: "There is no confusion, no haste, because the performers know their roles as well as the inexorably increasing tempo that will culminate in the violence of the Negro's death." All the forms of justice are followed, as they were in *Light in August;* the local officials are all conscientious but without sympathy for the prisoner. Previous Gothic novels by Faulkner serve to explain the tension by illustrating what is likely to happen to Lucas: Lucas had dared the "coal-oil and the rope" when he confronted Zack in "The Fire and the Hearth"; mobs took Rider and Lee Goodwin from the jail and lynched them, Rider by hanging and Goodwin by burning; Joe Christmas was castrated and killed without a trial. The scene of the arrival of Lucas at the jail, as seen by Chick from across the street, is impressively Gothic: the sudden appearance of the crowd of men, the nucleus of a mob; the arrival of the sheriff's car; Lucas's slow descent, knocking off the hat which symbolized his defiance of racial etiquette; the threats of the crowd; and, finally, just as Chick was ready to go and saddle Highboy, Lucas's request. This is the first scene in the ritual of race relations.

The second scene adds the Gothic details of the jail, with the incongruous barred window in its galleried brick front. Will Legate as armed guard is mild and matter-of-fact, but the massive door and padlock at the top of the stairs, the bullpen, and Lucas's bare cell are in marked contrast with Lucas's imperturbability. His two confrontations, first with Gavin and Chick and then with Chick, dramatize the desperation of a man who must put his faith in such frail agents for rescue. His look of mute urgency made Chick return alone for the second confrontation. Chick asked the right question, upon which the life of Lucas and his own rebirth depended: "What do you want me to do?" (p. 68). Lucas's insistence that he wanted to engage legal services signified his rejection of white patronage. Chick recognized his own responsibility to perform an impossible task in insufficient time in order to prevent "the death by shameful violence of a man who would die not because he was a murderer but because his skin was black" (p. 72). The imperturbability of Lucas, in contrast with traditional Gothic melodrama, is nowhere more telling than when he said to Chick, with invasion by a lynch mob imminent, "I'll try to wait" (p. 73).

That part of the ritual which involves the mob is most fully represented in two antithetical movements, noted by Olga Vickery: "Just as the murder of a Gowrie by a Negro served to unite the mob, so the killing of a Gowrie by a Gowrie serves to disperse it. . . ." The same unnatural absence of normal activity which Chick observed in the country, night and morning, is ominously evident in Jefferson—until he sees the Square: "a moil and mass of movement, one dense pulse and hum filling the Square as when the crowd overflows the carnival midway or the football field"; the mob might be triggered into action by the most trivial incident, "perhaps even a child running toward the jail" (pp. 135, 137). As an allegorical tableau, Margaret Mallison and Miss Habersham sitting with their mending in front of the jail is comparable with Judge Drake and his sons taking Temple from the courtroom: Southern Manhood protecting Southern Womanhood by suppressing the truth has given place to Southern Womanhood preventing violence by Southern Manhood until the truth can defuse passions. The stasis that represents potential violence is followed by the motion that represents renunciation of violence. The flight of the cars from the Square, in all directions, seemed to Chick like a stage battle scene in which "the marching or charging troops as soon as they reached the wings break into a frantic stumbling run swapping coats and caps and fake bandages as they doubled back behind the rippling cheesecloth painted with battle and courage and death to fall in on their own rear and at heroic attention cross the footlights again" (p. 185). Still groggy from loss of sleep, Chick daydreamed of the steady stream of fleeing vehicles causing Miss Habersham to travel for miles around Jefferson to reach her home, until he broke into hysterical laughter at his own fantasy and his disillusionment: "They ran" (p. 192).

The shift from the threat of violence to the effect upon Chick of the flight of the mob is perfectly appropriate to this Gothic novel of initiation: to mob violence Chick would have been only a witness. The true Gothic climaxes are the paired scenes in the churchyard, where Chick was first a major participant and then the instigator of the actions of others. The lonely ride out to the churchhard in the dark is followed by a succession of tense moments for Chick, Miss Habersham, and Aleck Sander: Highboy smelled quicksand; a mule and rider, with a mysterious burden, came down the hill and passed the three intruders in the dust; in frantic haste the trio found the grave, moved the flowers, uncovered the coffin, opened it—and found the corpse was Jake Montgomery, not Vinson. The reversal of the process, still in frantic haste, Chick remembered later. The darkness, with only a flashlight for light, the need for silence, and such incongruous details as Miss Habersham, "the round hat on the exact top of her head such as few people had seen in fifty years and probably no one at any time looking up out of a halfway rifled grave" (p. 103)— this whole episode is completely Gothic in imagery and feeling. The significance as an initiation is brought out in Chick's thoughts; as he rode through the empty darkness, he recognized that in one day from being "a swaddled unwitting infant in the long tradition of his native land . . . a witless foetus . . . blind and insentient" he had come to a realization that the economy of the land was founded upon the dark people who had turned their backs "in one irremediable invincible inflexible repudiation, upon not a racial outrage but a human shame" (pp. 96-97).

The consciousness of Charles Mallison as represented by Faulkner seems to reflect what Mircea Eliade called "the perennial significance of the traditional patterns of initiation," as if "initiation and its patterns were indissolubly linked with the very structure of spiritual life; as if initiation were an indispensable process in every attempt at total regeneration. . . ." A communion motif associated with the food and drink ritual is introduced by the winey fragrance of the pines and Chick's thought that communion wine did not count as wine: "the deathless blood of our Lord not to be tasted, moving not downward to the stomach but upward and outward into the Allknowledge between good and evil and the choice and the repudiation and the acceptance forever" (p. 100). The combination of levels of awareness, ranging from absorption in urgent action to meditation on personal and universal truths, characterizes the consciousness of Charles Mallison and brings to the Gothic suspense and atmosphere an original modification.

If this narrative sequence is the most mysterious, because of the limited visibility, the parallel daylight incident is the most macabre. The group of characters at first includes the sheriff, with his convict laborers, and Gavin Stevens and Chick. Now we can *see* the scene: the church a "plank steepleless box" which said "Burn"; the graveyard "a fenced square of earth" smaller than many garden plots, overgrown with weeds, the graves marked by canted "shingle-thin slabs of cheap gray granite"; the raw grave with the flowers, which Chick and Aleck Sander had put back in place, now tossed to one side (pp. 157–59). Again the succession of tense moments leads up to a surprise finish: the arrival of the Gowries, a grotesque trio; the digging up of the grave by the twins, "kneedeep then waistdeep, working with a grim and sullen speed, robotlike and in absolute unison" (p. 165); the opening of the coffin, to find it empty. This time a second succession of even tenser moments follows: the amazed group around the coffin; the reconstruction of what must have happened; the resultant search in the sand of the branch-bed, following the mule tracks of the previous night; the discovery of the second burial place, scarcely covered, which held, not Vinson, but Jake Montgomery. The climax is the height of the macabre and grotesque: old Gowrie leaped into the quicksand and stood there "as if his legs had been cut off at the loins by one swing of a scythe, leaving his trunk sitting upright on the bland depthless milklike sand. 'All right, boys!' old Gowrie cried, brisk and carrying: 'Here he is. I'm standing on him'" (p. 177).

Extrication of the body of Vinson is equally grotesque and macabre: "the body coming out now feet first, gallowsed up and out of the inscrutable suck to the heave of the crude tackle then free of the sand with a faint smacking plop like the sound of lips perhaps in sleep and in the bland surface nothing . . ." (p. 177). Old Gowrie looked at the body, "his face wrenched and his upper lip wrenched upward from the lifeless porcelain glare and the pink bloodless gums of his false teeth" (p. 178).

Charles's memories of the previous night and his imaginative reconstruction of what the man on the mule had done, "the anguish, the desperation, the urgency in the black dark," again adds to the exciting narrative another dimension, which is a distinctive feature of his consciousness. The tempo of his mental processes, compounded of perception, reminiscence, reverie, imagination, anticipation, and meditation, accelerates or decelerates. His reactions become exacerbated or blunted as fatigue, hunger, and sleeplessness affect him. Content, imagery, and style reflect this complexity to produce effects eminently suitable in a modern version of Gothic subjectivism and nightmare psychology.

In *Intruder in the Dust* Faulkner presented his most direct fictional treatment of basic issues of southern justice and ethics, as perceived by a sensitive young man aware of both the strengths and the weaknesses of the old tradition. The reiterated statement of those issues as human, not racial, echoes other presentations of the same themes in other Gothic novels: the right of the individual to recognition and to dignity, whether he is a young Thomas Sutpen or a Milly Jones or a Joe Christmas or a Lucas Beauchamp. The most severely criticized aspect of *Intruder in the Dust* is the propagandist harangues of Gavin Stevens. The thoughts of Charles Mallison can and do accommodate reflections on the same themes; Charles also remembers what he has previously learned from Gavin, such as the account of the feeling of southern boys for the past which most aptly concludes: "You escape nothing, you flee nothing; the pursuer is what is doing the running and tomorrow night is nothing but one long sleepless wrestle with yesterday's omissions and regrets . . ." (p. 195). What Gavin had taught Charles is, as it were, admissible evidence in the process of initiation. But when Gavin reacted in a thoroughly traditional fashion to Lucas, assuming that Lucas was guilty because he had apparently behaved as a nigger was expected to, Gavin was no better than Mr. Lilly, his social and intellectual inferior whose mental processes Gavin was explaining. Thus, Gavin forfeited his right to be Chick's initiation mentor, and Chick gave up the attempt to make Gavin take seriously what Lucas had told Chick to do. Miss Habersham therefore became his mentor.

Gavin's view on the race question should be suspect since, like Isaac McCaslin, he never demonstrated his sincerity as a defender of Negroes, though as a lawyer he was even better trained to aid Negroes than Isaac was. The artistic validity of the inclusion of large chunks of Gavin's views in a Gothic novel with a limited point of view, a strong and exciting plot, and a single center of interest has been questioned. But perhaps Gavin's function and significance have been too narrowly interpreted; perhaps his inactivity was deliberately paralleled by his loquacity. For Gavin to confirm the principles behind the actions of Chick and Miss Habersham and Aleck Sander, who "have defied and so transcended and revivified the social norm," is eminently suitable, as Olga Vickery said; Chick did have to learn to accept his society, as well as criticize it; he had to fuse the action of the mob and the actions of himself and his companions "into a single emotional acceptance of his land." When Gavin deals with general principles of moral conduct, he stays within a dramatically suitable role, urging Charles to continue to act with the courage of his convictions.

Gavin's long disquisitions on the race question, however, represent a departure from his dramatic role. In these passages, as William Steinberg said, the "syntax is garbled, his speeches bloated, irrational and without logic." Steinberg explained the style much as Gloria Dussinger explained Ike's inflated rhetoric in "the Bear," part 4: rationalization of irrational feelings is betrayed by inflated rhetoric. Through Gavin, Steinberg believed, Faulkner was presenting "the conscious Southern attitude toward Negroes, an attitude motivated by the unconscious forces that Chick has uncovered" in digging up the grave, against Gavin's wishes. In light of Faulkner's contrast between Chick and Gavin, all to the credit of Chick, and Faulkner's own nonfiction statements on racism, it may well be that when Gavin seems to step out of his dramatic role, he speaks for some southerners but not for Faulkner, and that he is confirming his unworthiness to serve as Chick's mentor and is not to be regarded as a source of what Wayne Booth, in *The Rhetoric of Fiction*, calls "Reliable Commentary." Gavin's initial attitude toward Lucas, which was proved fallacious, was consistent with and evoked self-justifying rationalization. Gavin's use of "Sambo," as both Steinberg and Frank Thomas observed, is sufficient to warn the reader that Gavin's attitude toward the Negro is "belittling and hostile," based on racial stereotypes which he disclaims.

The humorous note at the end of *Intruder in the Dust* is somewhat like the incident of Boon under the gum tree at the end of "The Bear": the humor provides an ironic contrast to the preceding potentially tragic situation and is related to a major theme. Lucas's insistence on paying for Gavin's services, since he cannot pay Charles, is part of his insistence on being treated like an adult, instead of being denied mature dignity by accepting white patronage. The fifty pennies Lucas counted out reduced the fifty-cent piece which had haunted Chick to the triviality

of small change. The difference between a social and a professional relationship, between hospitality and a financial transaction, was underlined
by Lucas's previous invitation to Chick to come out to the plantation
again: "'You'll be welcome without waiting for a freeze'" (p. 241). The
last words of Lucas conclude the book and return the situation to a
professional relationship. Asked by Gavin what he was waiting for, Lucas
answered, "My receipt." Only on the surface is this a comic ending.
As Frank Thomas said, it signifies that "the only footing on which the
white and the black man can and must equitably face each other is on payment in kind." Chick and Lucas understand that; perhaps now Gavin does
too.

The contrast between the initiation of Charles Mallison and that of
Isaac McCaslin is significant. Charles chose to play an active and dangerous
part in opposing a human shame for which he had no responsibility
and no guilt; Isaac chose inaction and evasion of responsibility for his
own heritage and his own kinsmen. His repudiation, unlike Charles's,
was never followed by acceptance of his family and society. The merits
of Charles shine the more brightly in contrast with the deficiencies of
Isaac: Isaac was the second type, who says, "This is bad and I will withdraw from it." Although Faulkner did not name Charles in that context, Charles does exemplify the third type, who says, "This is bad and
I'm going to do something about it, I'm going to change it." The fact
that all three types, exemplified by Quentin, Isaac, and Charles, are dealt
with in Gothic novels, with initiation a major pattern in the stories of
Isaac and Charles and providing an ironic parallel to Quentin's rites of
passage, shows Faulkner's continuing interest in the initiation theme in
particular and in the use of the Gothic tradition in general to convey his
most serious reflections on man and society. Faulkner's final use of the
initiation theme, as I indicated in my article on *The Reivers,* followed
the quest-romance pattern.

At Nagano, when one of Faulkner's questioners in a colloquy commented on the similarity between a selection from Faulkner's *The
American Dream* and *Intruder in the Dust,* Faulkner replied: "...
Intruder in the Dust was an effort to show in action what this speaks
of in theory. . . . And somebody somewhere must do something to rectify,
cure injustice, rather than just philosophize about it." Faulkner's definition of the American Dream in his essay "On Privacy" is relevant to
Intruder in the Dust, to his use of Gothic elements, and to the whole
naturalization of Gothic fiction in American literature: "This was the
American Dream: a sanctuary on the earth for individual man," where
he could be free of hierarchies of power and of the mass into which
"church and state had compressed and held him individually thralled

and individually impotent." The founders of the New World said "as with one simultaneous voice: 'We will establish a new land where men can assume that every individual man . . . has inalienable right to individual freedom within a fabric of individual courage and honorable work and mutual responsibility." Behind the revival of Gothic fiction by serious writers lies the anguished realization that the American Dream has been transmogrified into the American Nightmare.

The merits of *Intruder in the Dust* have unfortunately been obscured, partly by misinterpretation of Gavin's role and the assumption that he spoke for Faulkner and partly by failure of readers and critics to realize that Faulkner's use of Gothicism and other strategies of popular fiction was concomitant with great seriousness of purpose. William Steinberg summed up Faulkner's achievement as "Psychologist of the Southern Psyche": "In *Intruder in the Dust* . . . Faulkner delineates the Southern psyche on a two-fold level. He dramatizes an unconscious reason for race hatred (what Chick discovers in the grave). He shows the Southerner consciously reacting to this unconscious reason (the arguments of Stevens). In its totality, Faulkner's analysis of the Southern malady in *Intruder in the Dust* parallels what Sterba has discovered through his psychoanalytic investigations."

CHAPTER NINE

SNOPES

"FROM RAGS TO RICHES"
"THE KNIGHT OF THE RUEFUL COUNTENANCE"
"THE REVENGER'S TRAGEDY"

Following *Intruder in the Dust* Faulkner continued the stories of Gavin Stevens and Charles Mallison in *The Town* and *the Mansion*, in a non-Gothic thematic pattern. But between *Intruder in the Dust* (1948) and *The Town* (1957) *Knight's Gambit* (1949) provided a link which continued the Gothic pattern but prepared for the new theme in *The Town*. *Knight's Gambit* is a collection of detective stories with Gavin Stevens as the hero. His nephew, Charles Mallison, is the narrator in "Monk," "An Error in Chemistry," and "Tomorrow," a study of character more than of detection. In the novella "Knight's Gambit" Charles, the third-person central intelligence, became eighteen in December 1941; in *Intruder in the Dust* he was sixteen after the death of Molly Beauchamp, who was still living in 1941 in "Go Down, Moses." Only "Knight's Gambit" requires consideration in relation to Faulkner's longer Gothic narratives.

The role of Charles as central intelligence in "Knight's Gambit," written in a shorter version, according to Joseph Blotner, late in 1941, anticipates his role in *Intruder in the Dust*. More an observer-catalyst than a main actor, he provides a clue which enables Gavin to prevent a murder. After some strongly Gothic scenes, such as the moonlight scenes which lead to a climax with a vicious horse, the Gothic tale of detection shifts to the romance of Gavin Stevens. Several clues and motifs in "Knight's Gambit" prepare for Gavin's role in *The Town*, which ends in 1929, and *The Mansion*, in which the first ten of the seventeen chapters precede December 1941, the time of action in "Knight's Gambit." The title "Knight's Gambit" is explained by an analogy referring to Gavin, Captain Gualdres, whose life Gavin saved, and Melisandre Harriss: "A knight comes suddenly out of nowhere—out of the west, if you like—and checks the queen and the castle all in that same one move. What do you do?" (p. 218). Charles knew the answer: "You save the queen and let the castle go." After the queen was safe, however, Gavin let the knight, Captain Gualdres, go, with Melisandre's daughter, and kept the queen, Melisandre, and the castle for himself.

The clue to the theme represented by the chessmen is provided by Leslie Fiedler in *Love and Death:* "Mariolatry and courtly love are both aspects of the same psychic revolution, that resurgence of the Female which, toward the close of the Middle Ages, left its impress everywhere, even on the chessboard, where the queen appears for the first time as the all-powerful piece." Associating chess with themes of ascent in *The Secular Scripture*, Northrop Frye said: "Chess and other board games, despite *The Waste Land*, appear more frequently in romance and in Eros contexts, as *The Tempest* . . . reminds us." Melisandre as the queen and her ancestral estate (remodeled Hollywood-fashion by her bootlegger husband) as the castle are more in the tradition of romance than in the Gothic modification of romance. Since neither Gavin's romance nor his marriage plays a prominent part in Yoknapatawpha fiction, "Knight's Gambit" needs no further consideration here. The image of the chessmen is part of a recurrent pattern of chivalric images, noted by Warren Beck, which point to Gavin as "Faulkner's Roland," standing "first and unique among several protagonists by virtue of his chivalry." Beck did not regard Gavin as conceived in irony. As the unsuccessful and Quixotic courtly lover, Gavin is the center of the theme of romantic, idealistic love in *The Town* and *The Mansion*. His marriage to Melisandre, after almost twenty years of devotion to Eula and her daughter Linda, is an anti-climax. Charles referred flippantly to calling on "the squire and his dame among his new ancestral white fences and electric-lit stables" (*The Mansion*, p. 256). The squire of dames has ironically become the country squire. But since the pattern of romance is more pertinent to the story of Gavin than is the Gothic pattern to which romance contributed, Gavin will be dealt with in *Snopes* chiefly as he is involved in the definitely Gothic theme of revenge.

Faulkner had used the quest-romance pattern in an early novel, *As I Lay Dying*, and returned to it in his last novel, *The Reivers*, where he made the initiation theme central to the quest-romance, rather than sub-ordinate, as in *As I Lay Dying*. Although *As I Lay Dying* has some Gothic elements and creates a macabre atmosphere which is lacking in *The Reivers*, both works belong essentially to the romance tradition; I have analyzed them elsewhere in relation to that tradition. The relation-ship between *The Reivers* and such dissimilar Gothic works as *Sanctuary* and "The Bear" is established by the reappearance in *The Reivers* of Miss Reba and Boon Hogganbeck and Ike McCaslin. Thus, Faulkner at the end of his writing shifted his emphasis from Gothic to romantic elements, a modulation in tone which was facilitated by the many characteristics of theme, setting, character, and patterns of action shared by the two kinds of narrative. Ironic inversion is used in *The Reivers* somewhat as it was in *Sanctuary*, except that Miss Reba and Everbe become heroines by their own actions, not by contrast with "good women" like Narcissa and Temple, and their virtues are rewarded in the happy ending.

The combination of Gothic with non-Gothic elements has been noted in earlier works such as *Light in August*. The counterpointing in *Snopes*, however, is more complicated than the double themes of Lena and Joe. *The Hamlet* develops three themes, centered respectively in Eula Varner, Flem Snopes, and Mink Snopes: love and sexuality; money and social status; outrage and revenge. Only the third, revenge, is developed consistently with atmosphere, characters, and incidents which are distinctly Gothic. In *The Town* the theme of love and sexuality becomes chiefly the theme of courtly love and offstage adulterous passion: the theme of money and social status continues, modified into money and respectability. Observing the shift from myth to romance in *The Town*, Walter Brylowski described Gavin as quixotic, with Ratliff as Sancho Panza in their unsuccessful alliance against Snopesism. (In *Faulkner in the University*, Faulkner said that he reread *Don Quixote* every year.) In *The Mansion* the revenge tragedy is the major action, the courtly love continues and finally merges with the revenge tragedy, and the money-respectability theme, having reached its limit in the career of Flem Snopes, is echoed in the story of Orestes Snopes. In *Snopes*, *The Town* is least essential in relation to the Gothic theme but is necessary to the romance theme, linking *The Hamlet* with *The Mansion;* Mink Snopes, villain-hero of the revenge plot, is in prison during the present action in *The Town*. Revenge, however, is a motive in some episodes in *The Town*. Even the more preposterous events in *The Town* appear in the light of reason as narrated by Gavin Stevens, Charles Mallison, and V. K. Ratliff, spokesmen for the people of Jefferson and proponents of decency, self-restraint, and order. William Brown considered these three narrators as normal individuals in Faulkner's terms, representing the humanistic virtues of truth, love, honor, and sacrifice and striving to maintain "a tenuous balance ... during which chaos is staved off." Because of the narrative method all of *The Town* is on the conscious level and in the oral tradition.

In *The Hamlet*, however, the treatment of love and money involves either Gothic elements or inversion of Gothic types and patterns. The pastoral tone in *The Hamlet,* as Olga Vickery observed, contrasts with the revenge theme: "Ike's pasture is replaced by Mink's dark and terrifying forest and by the barren land despoiled by the insane Armstid. As the comedy grows darker, the idyllic is overshadowed by the grotesque, the macabre, and the demonic, producing the complex tonal quality of *The Hamlet.*" The grotesque is not limited to the revenge theme but contributes to a larger configuration of motifs and images and scenes which complements the Gothic narrative.

The theme of courtly love is parodied in the story of Eula, grotesquely mammalian and inert, and Labove, whom Eula aptly described as an Ichabod Crane. Eula's failure to flee from Labove's attack—"she had not even moved to avoid him"—and her escape from the ensuing wrestling match by "a full-armed blow," which left her virtue intact and herself in effect "unexercised and unbreathed," is even more amusing when recognized as the inversion of the familiar maiden in flight: "She stood over him, breathing deep but not panting and not even dishevelled. 'Stop pawing me,' she said. 'You old headless horseman Ichabod Crane,'" (p. 122).

Leslie Fiedler's misreading, in *Love and Death in the American Novel,* is testimony to the suggestive force of traditional patterns. His error should be an object lesson showing the necessity of observing closely how an author uses such patterns: "The scene in which the schoolmaster Labove, helpless with the desire that an eleven-year-old girl has stirred up in him and will not satisfy, chases her mindless quivering flesh round and round the classroom comes closer than anything in American literature to the horrific vision of *Death in Venice....*" Although Fiedler described *The Hamlet* as "more comic than Gothic," he described a Gothic scene that existed only in his imagination: Faulkner's whole point is that Eula did not flee. Her lack of fear, her easy mastery of Labove, and her ignoring the incident as not worth mentioning to her brother constitute the unbearable humiliation by which she took her revenge on Labove. When Jody assumed that Labove had come to complain about a window sash, Labove was denied "that last vindication, the ratification of success which he had come to buy with his life" (p. 126). In his grotesqueness and his frustrated obsession, Labove belongs to the Gothic counterpoint on the romantic theme. Labove's "gangrened lust" and his fantasies of being both the sadistic seducer and the masochistic maiden, as noted by Myron Weybright, contributed to the comic tensions created by the contrast between Labove and Eula's teenage suitors, and thus to the tension between humor and horror.

In addition to the younger suitors who clustered around Eula, displaced by Flem Snopes after he married Eula, a considerable group of other characters, mostly grotesque to some degree, are related to the themes of love and marriage, or trade and barter, or revenge, associated respectively with Eula, Flem Snopes, and Mink Snopes. All the Snopeses exemplify the success of Flem's strategy in providing places in Frenchman's Bend for his kinfolk. Ab and his first wife, in Ratliff's horse-swapping tale, introduce the chief male-female symbols, the horse and the cow, and initiate the literal or figurative horse-trading episodes, with the frequent "trickster tricked" twist. Of the non-Snopes minor characters, Henry and Mrs. Armstid are miserable grotesques representing female subjugation to the male and male greed and self-assertion that ends in madness. The other extreme is seen in the Tulls, Vernon being dominated by his wife and daughters. Both Henry and Vernon suffered grotesque accidents during the moonlight stampede of the spotted horses. Jody Varner, Eula's older brother and self-appointed guardian of her virginity, "emanated a quality of invincible and inviolable bachlordom" (p. 6) and was fairly ridiculous both in his appearance and in the futility of his endeavors. Only V. K. Ratliff, a bachelor on affable terms with both sexes, and Mrs. Littlejohn, a self-supporting widow, represent the male-female contrast without notable grotesqueness.

The most extreme example of grotesqueness in the love theme, of course, is Ike Snopes and his love for the cow. In his lack of greed and his capacity for love and devotion, Ike is the polar opposite of Flem, as William Ramsey noted. Ike belongs to the same group of Gothic grotesques as Benjy Compson, Jim Bond, and Popeye's henchman Tommy. The idyll of Ike's faithful service, through fire and water, to his beloved creature is told in a heightened style which is the comic variety of romantic-Gothic rhetoric. Joseph Blotner related how, in a self-parody, Faulkner had told the fire episode in "Afternoon of a Cow," by "Ernest V. Trueblood," with Mr. Faulkner in the role of hero; the parodic element is still present in the version in *The Hamlet,* which raises the "barnyard comedy" to mythic dimensions. The prototypes of Ike and the cow are Zeus and Io. Walter Brylowski noted that Ike, in rescuing the cow from a ring of fire, suggests the Wagnerian Siegfried saving Brunhilde. Eula is later described as Brunhilde, standing at a window in the moonlight: "To those below what Brunhilde, what Rhinemaiden on what spurious river-rock of papier-mâché, what Helen returned to what topless and shoddy Argos, waiting for no one" (p. 306). The combination in *The Hamlet* of Gothic grotesque and mythic echoes and parody of chivalric romance contributes to the Gothic imagery and provides contrast with the Gothic tone and atmosphere. The story of Ike and the cow is sustained parody in context and style that transcends the grotesque subject, nowhere more amazingly than in the transmutation of the Narcissus image into the reflection of Ike's image in the eyes of the cow and of Ike's and the cow's images in the water from which they drink (pp. 182, 183, 186). Myron Weybright commented on these images as suggesting the unique qualities of experience. In *The Secular Scripture* Frye commented on the Narcissus image on lower levels as reflected in a sinister Doppelgänger and on demonic sexual parody as represented in the combination of male animal and female human being. These images of Ike and the cow exemplify the originality with which Faulkner used traditional patterns, here changing the sinister version of the Narcissus image and the demonic sexual parody to innocent idiocy, which is nevertheless a source of corruption in society.

The image of Eula in the moonlight is the climax of a change from the parodic characterization of her as a mammalian fertility goddess to a poetic representation of her as a mythic heroine, like Helen of Troy in attracting suitors. Even at the age of five or six, Eula was grotesque in size and inertia; carried by her mother's Negro servant, she was an "already indisputably female burden like a bizarre and chaperoned Sabine rape" (p. 96). The youthful suitors, eventually driving their own chariots in their pursuit of Eula, are a kind of chorus for the rejected villain and the accepted hero of Eula's romance, Labove and Hoake McCarron. The ironic inversion in this mythic romance lies in Hoake's desertion of the girl he ruined and the flight of his envious rivals, leaving Eula to be sold to the detestable and impotent Flem. Eula, the earth goddess and queen of hearts, bore one child, Linda, fathered by McCarron.

The whole sequence of characters and episodes representing the theme of love and fertility reveals similar ironies and grotesqueries. The romantic-Gothic moon shone on Eula and on the bed of Houston, placed "to catch the moon's full of April through the window," a fact that the widowed and childless Houston remembered just before Mink shot him (pp. 215, 216). Brylowski saw Houston as a courtly lover, responding to a mysterious, irresistible attraction to a woman; but his murder belonged to the Gothic, not the romantic vein, and to the theme of revenge, not of love. The same moon shone on the stampeding spotted horses; Ratliff's equine adversary emerged on Mrs. Littlejohn's veranda "and took the railing and soared outward, hobgoblin and floating, in the moon" (p. 303). The excitement of the men and the violence and destruction wrought by the horses, male symbols, are contrasted with the beauty of Eula and of the pear tree in the moonlight, the female and the symbols of fertility. The moon and the references to Eula as the Helen of Frenchman's Bend link Eula with Ike and the cow in their sylvan Arcadia, where dawn is suspired "from the earth itself," "the blind dark of time's silt and rich refuse ... Troy's Helen and the nymphs and the snoring mitred bishops . . ." (p. 181). Faulkner's use of the courtly love tradition in counterpoint with the Gothic tradition serves as a reminder that the Gothic is derived in part from chivalric romance and retains elements in common with it.

The Hamlet thus prepares for the theme of courtly love in *The Town*, with Gavin Stevens as the hero, chivalrously loving Eula Snopes and serving her with no hope of requital of his love. This thematic sequence, recalling Ike as the courtly lover in *The Hamlet*, suggests that Gavin is not to be taken with complete seriousness and that there is a bit of parody also in *The Town*. Faulkner confirmed the interpretation of Gavin as in flight from reality, a theme suited to a Gothic context: Gavin postponed marriage, in part by his safe devotion to Eula and Linda, because "he might get too involved with the human race if he married one of them." Faulkner suggested that in *Intruder in the Dust*, which occurs after *The Town*, Gavin had probably learned something from experience. There is a touch of satire in the portrayal of Gavin, revealed through his own words or through Ratliff and Charles as narrators: Gavin is a bit of a Prufrock, a middle-aged man who is still incorrigibly adolescent. Gavin's role as a courtly lover in *The Town* and *The Mansion* seems to be a kind of extension of his role in "Knight's Gambit," in which he married Melisandre Backus Harriss, the sweetheart of his youth. Melisandre appeared in the 1941 version of "Knight's Gambit"; by 1943 she was provided with ancestors in a Bayard Sartoris story, "My Grandmother Millard." In continuing Gavin's role in *Snopes* from that in "Knight's Gambit," Faulkner seems to have found difficulty in keeping Gavin a bachelor until time for his marriage to Melisandre in *The Mansion*. In *The Town*, Melisandre had preceded Linda as a girl with a mind to be formed by Gavin, but no reader unfamiliar with "Knight's Gambit" is prepared for Melisandre's reappearance in *The Mansion*, after her marriage to Gavin while Linda was still in Pascagoula "riveting ships to save Democracy" (p. 356). Gavin, the courtly lover, violated the ideal by marrying one of the objects of his devotion, but he waited to do so until he might become an instant grandfather as well as a husband. In Horace Benbow in *Sanctuary* and in Gavin Stevens in *The Town* we see the Romantic hero in a Gothic and in a non-Gothic context. Gavin replaced Horace in the roster of characters in Yoknapatawpha. In *The Town* and *The Mansion* Gavin was never enmeshed in evil as fully as Horace was, never suffered such an appalling revelation of dark reality, never moved in such places of lawlessness and iniquity. Not until Gavin became involved in Mink's pardon and release from prison was he shown to be fully engaged in matters of life and death of others and to be acting to change the course of events. Thus, his role as the quixotic lover in

The Town and *The Mansion* changed when he briefly and finally was caught up in the revenge tragedy of Mink and Linda. In *The Mansion,* despite his success in winning Melisandre as his wife, Gavin was conquered by his delusions and was a failure as a lawyer, accessory before the fact of murder and agent in paying blood money to the murderer.

Gavin's quixotic tilting at windmills was stimulated by Flem Snopes. Flem also fails to be a Gothic figure but bears an ironic resemblance to Sutpen as hero, or antihero, in a success story. T. H. Adamowski described Flem as "on a quest for success," with experiences ironically parallel to those in Northrop Frye's account of quest romance. The crowning irony is that Flem does win the beautiful bride but is interested only in her dowry. Charles Gregory compared Flem and Sutpen, noting that they share the Faust theme and that they seem to experience no inner conflict. He failed to stress the vital difference, that Sutpen's design included a dynasty, an impossible ambition for the impotent Flem. Flem was a kind of Horatio Alger version of Faust, lacking the imagination required for a genuine Faustian rise and fall. Milton Kornfeld contrasted Flem's "grotesquely comic rise" to wealth and respectability with "the darker and more tragic fable" of Sutpen. In Ratliff's fable of Flem in Hell, Flem is raised to what Kornfeld called "the comic apotheosis of Faustian myth"; he diminishes progressively in *The Town* and *The Mansion.* Flem and the lesser Snopeses were compared by Lewis Lawson to "a devil surrounded by his imps." Walter Brylowski observed that the satanic qualities of Ab Snopes in "Barn Burning" are continued in motifs in *The Hamlet* such as the fire images and Jody Varner's exclamation, "Hell fire." Ab's satanic qualities are analyzed by William Bysshe Stein in "Faulkner's Devil." Although there is opposition of good and evil in *Snopes,* the evil does not involve such violence and corruption as that in *Sanctuary* but is more like the "innocence" of Sutpen: both Sutpen and Flem treated human beings in accordance with the prevailing business practices but with a ruthless system of values based on personal aggrandizement and on imitation of their social and economic superiors. The conflict between the materialistic values of Flem and the more humane ones of Gavin and Ratliff is chiefly anecdotal and comic except in *The Hamlet,* where the rise of Flem is attended by darker episodes of Gothic quality and where only V. K. Ratliff can tangle with Flem in the game of "horse-trading" without catastrophic loss of money and self-esteem.

Flem's story in *The Town* impinges on Gavin's because of Gavin's platonic love for Eula and then for Linda, her daughter, and his attempt to remove Linda from Flem's influence. A similar connection is established in *The Mansion* with Linda's return to Jefferson and to Flem's house, but Flem was less active in the community than before, and the conflict subsided. In *The Hamlet* Flem's story contrasts with Mink's, Flem rising socially and financially while Mink barely subsists. Mink's initial grievance against Flem, for which he sought revenge, began in *The Hamlet.* Although Mink gained another and stronger motive during the period covered by *The Town,* that motive is revealed only in *The Mansion,* which overlaps with and supplements Mink's story as given in *The Hamlet. The Mansion,* as the Gothic story of Mink's revenge, involves Flem as antagonist-victim.

Except for grotesque appearance, Flem is not treated as a Gothic figure and is unsuited for such treatment, unless in ironic inversion as an unvillainous villain. He somewhat resembles Popeye in *Sanctuary* in that he is a flat character, presented objectively. Observing that Flem was sexually and emotionally impotent like Popeye, Milton Kornfeld disregarded Flem's lack of Popeye's voyeuristic interest in sex. Applying Annie Reich's "The Structure of the Grotesque-Comic Sublimination," Lewis Lawson described Flem as "a villain *manqué* . . . a grotesque-comic figure" which, as a special type, is "'characterized by a special form of disguise, that is by particular disfigurement and deformation'": the particular disfigurement by which Flem is rendered contemptible is dehumanizing disparagement, which diminishes the dignity of the object. Unlike Popeye, Flem is "pseudo-normal," according to William Brown, exhibiting no evidence of psychic disturbance or moral impulse but showing rather the "vacancy of mind, anonymity of purpose and conformity to type" of mass society. Flem is the essence of a rudimentary rationalism: utterly lacking in imagination and capacity to dream fine dreams, he can only copy others, within the narrow limits of observation afforded by Jefferson. Sutpen's design was creative; Flem's plan was merely imitative. Flem began with nothing and ended with emptiness, symbolized by his chewing on air. On the rare occasions when Flem stopped chewing, he thus manifested, according to Lawson, a negative response to setbacks or defeats, which suggests that chewing "seems to symbolize . . . aggression." When Flem resumed chewing before Mink shot him, he made "what amounts to a heroic gesture with which to end his life."

Both within and outside the Gothic narrative patterns and themes, there is in *Snopes* considerable use of grotesqueness. As Warren Beck observed, in *Man in Motion,* "That Faulkner's work abounds in the grotesque brooded upon until it deepens into a kind of Gothic darkness is undeniable." In noting the prevalence of grotesqueness in the behavior of both the wrongdoers and the admirable characters, Beck explained that it is not mere melodrama but "the shadowing forth of a realistic world-view" to which extravagance is essential. This worldview, of course, impelled Faulkner to use repeatedly all the resources of the Gothic tradition. Beck recognized the similarities between the fiction of Faulkner and that of such authors as the Brontës and Dickens and Conrad, but he did not realize that in Gothicism they shared a well-defined common tradition. This, without distinguishing between the Gothic and the non-Gothic narrative lines in *Snopes,* Beck dealt with the fantastic as an aid to imaginative expression and with grotesqueness in imagery as expressing either the characters or the author. As he pointed out, the protagonists and especially the narrators in *The Town* and *The Mansion* "share the power of grotesque imaging and imagining," and grotesque characters and episodes abound in the comic action. "Terror thus continuously shades into laughter," as Alan Howard said. The literary conventions of Ratliff's frontier tales have been superseded by "violence, inhumanity, and chaos" as "human realities which force Ratliff to acknowledge both the darkness of the human soul and its extraordinary vulnerability to the destructive forces ranged against it." Howard failed to see that the "two radically different, perhaps irreconcilable literary modes, the comic mode of frontier humor and the grotesquerie of psychological or metaphysical terror," can in fact be reconciled in the new American Gothic novel.

Although Warren Beck realized that "seen in context, the darkly shaded grotesquerie in Faulkner's work . . . is for thematic emphasis, by those main bold lines which as in caricature bound the concept at its limits and thereby starkly contain basic implication," he did not see that the context most frequently is Gothic. He observed that "as grotesqueness enters into a resistance of the exaggerated forms which evil takes, the crusades of Faulkner's champions become a series of sallies afoot," which, he said, is realism: "Where find the complete and proper champion, this side of romantic melodrama?" The answer is simple: in Gothic fiction, which lies between romance and melodrama on the one hand and realistic prose fiction on the other. Or, to use Ihab Hassan's terms, in "The Daydream and Nightmare of Narcissus," for Truman Capote's fiction, the daylight style of humor and the nocturnal style of the supernatural bring together, especially in *The Hamlet* and *The Mansion,* "dread and humor, dream and reality, in-sight and ex-perience." Beck's excellent discussion of grotesque elements in style brings out a point which explains such combination of the Gothic, with its distinctive grotesqueness, and the comic as has already been noted in *Sanctuary* and *Light in August:* "The grotesque, under the control of irony, may become the medium of the tragicomic. . . ."

Lewis Lawson's observation on Faulkner's depiction of the Snopeses "as grotesque monsters" reinforces the continuity of the Gothic tradition from the Middle Ages to the present. Faulkner's "medieval cast of mind," Lawson said, is apparent in his making Flem a gargoyle and in his references suggesting "that he knew of the Temptation of Saint Anthony motif that runs through grotesque painting from the Middle Ages to Salvador Dali." The demonstration of a straight line of descent in the grotesque in art from the Middle Ages to the present, parallel to that in literature represented by Gothicism, is offered by *Fantastic Art* (edited by David Larkin) and includes reproductions of four of the paintings referred to by Lawson, by artists from the fifteenth to the seventeenth century: Hieronymus Bosch, Matthias Grünewald, Jean Mandyn, Salvatore Rosa. Rosa was a favorite with the first generation of Gothic novelists. The "fantastic art" represented extends from Bosch to the post-surrealists and includes surrealists Max Ernst, Paul Delveaux, Richard Oelze, and Salvador Dali. In literature as well as in art the fantastic persists because it is, Thomas Hafner said (plate 36), "a deeply felt and personal way of expressing a view of the world."

In view of Warren Beck's ample treatment of the grotesque in *Snopes,* discussion here will be limited to grotesque characters and to grotesque aspects of the Gothic tragedy of revenge, with Mink as villain-hero and Flem as villain-victim.

Flem and Mink had little in common except the name "Snopes," but that name bound them together as long as they both lived and was to Mink a cause for murder: Flem, the Snopes who had made good, ignored the ties of kinship and neither aided nor even visited Mink when he was on trial for the murder of Houston. The parallels and contrasts between Flem and Mink are symbolized by their dwellings, by their prisons, literal or figurative, and by their relationship to the land. In *The Hamlet* they began on the same level, as poverty-stricken tenant farmers. The cabin Mink lived in until he left it for the state penitentiary was the antithesis of the Gothic mansion, however ruinous:

the paintless two-room cabin with an open hallway between and a lean-to kitchen, which was not his, on which he paid rent but not taxes, paying almost as much in rent in one year as the house had cost to build; not old, yet the roof of which leaked and the weather-stripping had already begun to rot away from the wall planks and which was just like the one he had been born in which had not belonged to his father either, and just like the one he would die in if he died indoors. . . ." [P. 219]

This cabin, Mink was convinced, was owned by Flem.

A few years earlier Flem had lived in one like it: "the sagging broken-backed cabin set in its inevitable treeless and grassless plot and weathered to the color of an old beehive . . ." (p. 18). From the time Flem began to work for the Varners, he steadily ascended the scale of dwellings. By the end of "Flem," he had moved into the Varners' house, which he left temporarily when he took Eula to Texas and left permanently when they moved to Jefferson. He had displaced Will and Jody Varner in the store and at the gin, and finally took Will's place in the barrel chair at the Old Frenchman's place, the usurper on the throne instead of the rightful heir. Flem's career began to look like a kind of revenge for past humiliations and deprivations. After he owned the Old Frenchman's place, his reward for marrying Eula, he tricked Ratliff into trading in for the old ruin Ratliff's share of a restaurant in Jefferson. Flem and Eula and the baby lived in a tent behind the restaurant until Flem rented a house on a back street and after a time bought the house. He finally achieved his ambition, ownership of the mansion which represented success in southern terms and reprisal in personal terms. When his wife Eula committed suicide and Manfred de Spain, her lover for eighteen years, had to leave town, Flem got not only Manfred's position as president of the bank but also the De Spain family mansion, originally "jest a house, two storey with a gallery" (*The Mansion*, p. 153).

This "mansion," after Flem had it renovated, is unusual, if not actually unique, among southern Gothic "castles" in not being decayed at the time of the narrative. According to Ratliff's description, it was a bit more than life-size, with "colyums across the front now": "I mean the extry big ones so even a feller that never seen colyums before wouldn't have no doubt a-tall what they was, like in the photographs where the Confedrit sweetheart in a hoop skirt and a magnolia is saying good-bye to her Confedrit beau jest before he rides off to finish tending to General Grant . . ." (*The Town*, p. 352). The mansion is Hollywood-romantic, rather than Gothic. As the climax to Flem's steady rise in prosperity and respectability, the mansion is a direct contrast to Mink's cabin which, when Flem was living in the mansion, had collapsed into the orifice of its foundation. As the crowning achievement of an impotent man who had cut loose from family ties and could enjoy nothing in the house except "sitting in a swivel chair like in a bank or an office, with his feet propped against the chimney and his hat on" (*The Mansion*, p. 412), the mansion is an ironic Gothic "castle."

In fact, *The Mansion* was ironically parallel to Mink's habitation during the years when Flem lived behind the "colyums": Flem had condemned himself to what amounted to solitary confinement, and Mink in the penitentiary was at least not in solitary. Images of enclosure predominate in the life of Mink, who spent thirty-eight years in prison. The jail in Jefferson, the most Gothic structure in town and the most frequently used as a setting in Faulkner's Gothic novels, housed Mink during long weeks when "he would stand at the little window of his cell, his grimed hands gripped among the bars and his face craned and pressed against them, to watch a slice of the street before the jail . . . which his cousin would have to cross to come to the jail and abolish the dream, free him, get him out" (*The Mansion*, p. 40).

But although Flem did not visit Mink in jail, let alone get him out, Flem did visit Montgomery Ward Snopes in that same jail, sat there in a chair toted up from the jailer's kitchen, with Montgomery Ward on the cot with the bedbugs, and blackmailed Montgomery Ward into conning Mink to attempt an escape from Parchman. Thus, Flem bought as many years of life as would be added to Mink's sentence in the penitentiary as punishment for his attempt to escape. This episode, told by Montgomery Ward in *The Mansion* (chapter 4), is totally new information concerning the episode in *The Town* in which he was sent to Parchman, on rigged evidence, for the locally acceptable offense of possessing bootleg liquor, instead of to the federal prison for purveying pornography. In *The Town* Flem was apparently wreaking revenge on Montgomery Ward for jeopardizing Flem's respectability.

To these Gothic scenes in jail the story of Montgomery Ward allows Faulkner to add another familiar Gothic setting, Miss Reba's house in Memphis, the year after Fonzo and Virgil (and, the reader of *Sanctuary* adds, Temple and Popeye) stayed there. Miss Reba's house had not changed since it had returned to its normal unabashed activities after Virgil and Fonzo left. The fact that Faulkner used Miss Reba and her house again in *The Reivers* increases the significance of this setting as part of the pattern of room images related to the theme of literal or psychological imprisonment.

The ultimate in the images of enclosure, after Mink and Flem had ended their terms in the Big House and the mansion, respectively, is seen in the final parallel between them: Flem is in his grave and Mink is in the cellar where Gavin and Ratliff had found him: "On a crude platform he had heaped together, the man they sought half-squatted half-knelt blinking up at them like a child interrupted at its bedside prayers . . . kneeling in the new overalls which were stained and foul now, his hands lying half-curled on the front of his lap . . ." (p. 432). This image of a man sixty-three years old, never much given to prayer, who had shot his cousin in cold blood after serving thirty-eight years in prison for another cold-blooded murder, would be the height of ironic grotesqueness but for the fact that Mink had a kind of childlike simplicity and ignorance and even innocence. Mink had not returned to his birthplace but to the old cellar of the last in a succession of miserable hovels that punctuated a landless tenant farmer's life. Mink remained there when Ratliff and Gavin left, yielding to the pull of earth against which he had guarded himself while he still had a purpose in life.

Flem never had to guard against any such attraction to Mother Earth. In their attitudes toward nature Flem and Mink were as opposite as were Popeye and Horace in *Sanctuary,* except that Flem did not fear nature—he exploited it. We do not see nature or anything else from Flem's point of view. When he lived at Frenchman's Bend, Flem rode around the countryside with Varner, examining fields in which they had a financial interest. But to Mink, the land was more than the soil he cultivated; he felt that nature was a source of mystic power that threatened man's freedom, an imaginative concept born perhaps of the harsh reality that he was a slave to the land. But even his endless labor on the land did not blind Mink to its beauty:

He walked through the bright sweet young summer morning between the burgeoning woodlands where the dogwood and redbud and wild plum had long since bloomed and gone, beside the planted fields standing strongly with corn and cotton, some of it almost as good as his own small patches . . . treading peacefully the rife and vernal earth boiling with life—the frantic flash and glint and crying of birds, a rabbit bursting almost beneath his feet, so young and thin as to have but two dimensions, unless the third one could be speed. . . . [*The Mansion,* p. 26]

In a long passage in *The Mansion,* when Mink reflected on the difference between the not uncongenial labor of working on the prison farm and farming elsewhere, he recognized his enslavement: "It was the land itself which owned them," no matter what worthless land they occupied: "the land, the earth itself passing their doomed indigence and poverty from holding to holding of its thralldom as a family or clan does a hopelessly bankrupt tenth cousin" (p. 91). In the ironic contrast between what the land meant to Mink and what it meant to Horace Benbow or Charles Mallison, may be seen the range of Faulkner's use of natural setting in Gothic fiction, from the naturalistic passages which cover with excruciating realism the pitiful rituals of the poorest tenant farmer to the still realistic but beautiful spring scenes which Charles saw on the way to Caledonia church. But when Mink left prison in October, seeing in the delta country only the "cotton stalks and cypress needles" he had seen thirty-eight years before, he remembered the fall "back home in the hills": "all the land would be gold and crimson with hickory and gum and oak and maple, and the old fields warm with sage and splattered with scarlet sumac . . ." (p. 104). He remembered a squirrel-hunting episode from his incredibly deprived childhood, when he had to steal a gun and try with one shell to get a squirrel for food for his sick aunt, and recalled the autumn woods, "unaxed in memory and unaxeable, inviolable and immune, golden and splendid with October" (p. 106). The style of such passages transcends the language of Mink's thoughts and is typical of that representing Mink's moments of intense consciousness; such style is more suitable to the heightened rhetoric of the Gothic tradition than to photographic and tape-recorded naturalism.

Mink's autumn memories illustrate the elegiac tone which Olga Vickery identified as the third tonal variation in *Snopes,* succeeding the pastoral tone of *The Hamlet* and the ironic tone of *The Town:* "The tone is one of diffused melancholy, weariness, and sense of loss that permeates both the human and the natural worlds." The new and bewildering world which, after thirty-eight years in prison, confronted this little Rip Van Winkle as he approached Memphis at night is one of speed and light: "as if all the earth was hurrying, plunging, being sucked, decked with diamond and ruby lights, into the low glare on the sky as into some monstrous, frightening, unimaginable joy or pleasure" (p. 283). But the world of tenant farmers, on the road to Jefferson, Mink found unchanged, the dirt road with "wisps of cotton lint snared into the roadside weeds and brambles from the passing gin-bound wagons" and the Negro cabin, "a weathered paintless dog-trot cabin enclosed and backed by a ramshackle of also-paintless and weathered fences and outhouses" (pp. 398, 399). The seasonal details of fall contrast with the spring details in *The Hamlet,* but both concern the labors of poor farmers. Only the squirrel-hunting memory reflects pure joy in nature on a rare escape from toil. The Gothic delight in landscape is translated into the relation between man and nature in a struggle for mere subsistence. But Mink retained a closeness to the soil which Flem lost when he chose the world of money.

The two chief characters in the revenge plot, Mink and Flem, represent a similar scaling down from the spectacular and the heroic to the subnormal and the less than human. The technique of disfigurement by diminution is modified in the treatment of Flem after *The Hamlet,* and is lessened by the subjective presentation of Mink in both *The Hamlet* and *The Mansion,* a technique that conveys both his limitations, his physical and mental subnormality, and his human pride and dignity. As the villain-hero, Mink is a grotesque version of the revenge villain. Hyatt Waggoner aptly described Mink as a "fierce little Ahab." Since, like Sutpen, Mink experienced no inner conflict but was inflexibly resolute in purpose, he was, in Robert Heilman's terms, a melodramatic rather than a tragic villain-hero. Like all the genuine Snopeses, excluding Eck and his sons as pseudo-Snopeses, Mink is referred to in animal terms, such as "that durn little half-starved wildcat" (*The Mansion,* p. 374). To develop the themes of *The Hamlet,* the avenger must also be a lover:

therefore Faulkner changed the murderer in "The Hound," a bachelor, Ernest Cotton, to Mink Snopes in revising the story for inclusion in *The Hamlet,* much as he had revised stories for *Go Down, Moses* to concentrate on the McCaslins. As Olga Vickery noted, Houston, Mink, and Labove are similar in that "the lover neither chooses his role nor the object of his love," but is "driven by his own nature to enact the ritual of sexual pursuit," even at the cost of "his cherished masculine freedom." These three men and Ike Snopes, the idiot, "all share the same identity as lover and all become part of the natural and timeless world of love." The combination of love and revenge would seem to be in the Elizabethan-Gothic tradition. But there is no relation between the two themes in *The Hamlet.* Mink murders not out of rivalry or jealousy but to avenge an intolerable affront to his dignity and manhood: what he would have said to Houston, had there been time "between the roar of the gun and the impact of the shot," was: "'I killed you because of that-ere extry one-dollar pound fee'" (*The Mansion,* p. 39). This scheme of values, as Olga Vickery said, is a "grotesque absurdity," but it is part of the grotesqueness of the Gothic. What is perhaps unprecedented in Gothic fiction is Faulkner's achievement in raising to semiheroic stature this grotesque, subnormal, childlike, but terrifying little man with his distorted sense of values. By sympathetic, subjective, but unsentimental portrayal, in which Gothic scenes and actions are represented in heightened style to convey intensity of feeling beyond Mink's powers of expression or conceptualization, Faulkner conveys the integrity of Mink's motive, to assert his identity and thus to count for something in life and to wipe out the insult of being denied human dignity by contending, as Edward Corridori observed, with the forces of earth, law, and society. This motive, similar to that of Wash Jones, belongs not only to the romantic-Gothic tradition but also to the tradition of modern tragedy as represented by Arthur Miller: "The fatal wound from which the inevitable events spiral is the wound of indignity, and its dominant force is indignation." In "essence," Miller said, "the tragic hero is intent upon claiming his whole due as a personality, and if this struggle must be total and without reservation, then it automatically demonstrates the indestructible will of man to achieve his humanity."

Houston, Mink's first victim—to Mink the personification of arrogant pride—is Byronic: a proud, passionate, and lonely figure. In *The Hamlet* the omniscient author's account of Houston makes him a more sympathetic character than he appeared to be to Mink. After Jack, the schoolboy, ate the apples with which Lucy tempted him and "they had looked upon the olden Snake" (p. 208), Houston fled, "not from his past, but to escape his future" (p. 211). Lucy did not pursue him; she waited. The stallion which symbolized Houston's manhood killed Lucy when the moon of April had shone on their bed. Mink's grievance began when Houston on his stallion almost ran down Mink, who astutely observed that Houston had bought this stallion after killing the one which caused the death of Lucy. In *The Hamlet* Houston, lying solitary in the moonlight of fertility, "rigid, indomitable, and panting" (p. 216), resembles the grieving Rider in "Pantaloon in Black," whose grief was literally intolerable.

Flem, Mink's second victim, is so completely un-Gothic as to be an ironic inversion as either the villain-hero of the Faust plot or the villain-victim in the revenge plot. Flem is presented so objectively and seems so entirely lacking in imagination and ability to dream that he personifies the rational man, a type which the Gothic novel was a reaction against. Thus, in a Gothic context Flem, like Jason Compson in *The Sound and the Fury*, is a natural villain. The parallels between Flem's quest for mere money and respectability and Sutpen's quest for magnificence and a dynasty are largely ironic; their poor-white origins are similar. Flem is grotesque in appearance: he had "a broad still face containing a tight seam of mouth stained slightly at the corners with tobacco, and eyes the color of stagnant water, and projecting from among the other features in startling and sudden paradox, a tiny predatory nose like the beak of a small hawk" (*The Hamlet*, p. 51). The slight variations in Flem's otherwise invariable dress and gestures are part of his grotesque and inhuman rigidity: the changes in headgear from a cloth cap to a black felt planter's hat; the changes in footgear from farmer's brogans to tennis shoes to polished city shoes; the invariable little bow tie; the constant chewing, first tobacco, then gum, then air. Although Flem's "innocence," revealed in his imitation of his superiors, seems like Sutpen's, Flem's lack of creative imagination and activity, symbolized in his sexual impotence, contrasts with Sutpen's sexual potency and his creation of plantation and mansion in what had been wilderness. Similarly, Flem's sedentary habits in *The Mansion* contrast with Sutpen's constant physical activity and his striving for what was beyond his grasp. Flem's impotence, unlike Popeye's, did not impel him to seek abnormal sexual gratification. As Lewis Lawson observed, Flem's impotence serves as a device to introduce "a thematic point that extends throughout the trilogy: the evil that Flem represents is sterile and self-consuming." The chief example of Gothic sexual perversion is the pornographic atelier of Montgomery Ward Snopes and its clients. As proprietor, he seemed more interested in his profits than in his stock in trade, and he apparently lacked the sexual prowess of Virgil Snopes in *Sanctuary*.

In *The Town* and *The Mansion* Gavin Stevens as the courtly lover and

V. K. Ratliff as his confidant and companion represent romance rather than Gothic types. In romance or in traditional Gothic fiction, they should be victorious heroes, as champions of virtue. But Gavin could only serve without reward, first Eula and then Linda; he was no more capable than was Horace Benbow of accepting reward, when it was offered, for services to women. In their brief activity as detectives, also, Gavin and Ratliff were not successful: they did not intercept Mink and prevent the murder of Flem.

Outside the major Gothic revenge story there are other grotesque characters which affect the contextual tone and atmosphere of the revenge story and sometimes echo the revenge motive. *The Hamlet* includes: the barn-burning Ab Snopes and his bovine daughters; the insane Armstid, whose life, like Mink's, had been one of harsh poverty; the idiot Ike Snopes; the candy-consuming robot Saint Elmo Snopes; I. O. Snopes, the bigamous, talkative weasel, fount of garbled proverbs. *The Town* includes: the "centawyer," comprised of Tom Tom and Turl on their comic Gothic flight in the moonlight; Old Het and Mrs. Hait, involved in the flight of the maiden, the cow (and the attendant hens), pursued by the villain, the mule, "in automatic compact of female with female against the world of mules and men"—to be specific, I. O. Snopes (p. 238); the savage, half-Indian children of Byron Snopes, dog-eaters and man-burners *manqué*. Saved from being burned at the stake, Clarence Snopes ended in *The Mansion* the political career in which he was engaged in *Sanctuary*. Lewis Lawson pointed out that Clarence's defeat exemplifies the medieval tradition of the devil as clown, repelled by "animal discharge"; Lawson cited instances also in *The Hamlet* of what might be called excremental repetition as a device for rendering Snopeses grotesque and contemptible. In *The Mansion* the last of the grotesque Snopeses, Orestes, engaged in a comic but potentially deadly feud with the last and most grotesque of the Tyrannical Fathers, Meadowfill, "a retired wheel-chair old gentleman" (p. 331). His daughter, made bold by love, defeated the old man. Revenge or reprisal is involved in Ab's barn burning, Tom Tom's and Turl's alliance after Flem tried his "divide and conquer" tactics, Mrs. Hait's animosity toward I. O. Snopes, and the Orestes-Meadowfill feud.

Mrs. Meadowfill was a "gray drudge of a wife" like Mrs. Henry Armstid in *The Hamlet*. Within the revenge story Mink's wife was a Suffering Wife like Ruby in *Sanctuary* and used the same means as Ruby did to get money to help her husband. Mink's wife was not only a prostitute like Ruby but was a nymphomaniac, whose sexual prowess amounted to "that perfect marriage of will and ability with a single undiffused object" which made her like "the confident lord of a harem" (p. 237). By introducing Montogomery Ward Snopes into the story of Flem and Mink, Faulkner could logically include Miss Reba Rivers and her brothel, repeating the stories of Miss Reba and Mr. Binford and of Virgil and Fonzo from *Sanctuary*.

The central woman character in the Flem-Mink story and in the courtly love story is Linda Snopes Kohl, the first female hero in Jefferson. A kind of grotesque Diana, a deaf beauty with a quacking voice, Linda is presented only as seen by the three narrators. As Warren Beck said, "The resultant picture of her, a genuine grotesque, is a faceted, almost fractured representation, like a Picasso multiple-profile face." Beck's defense of the grotesque in the character of Linda applies also to much of Faulkner's use of the grotesque in other Gothic fiction, but Beck does not recognize the relationship between the device and the subgenre: "That the grotesque, intensified by severally overlaid views of it, is made to enhance the essence of an authentic and representative subject of realistic fiction is a particular aesthetic triumph." Beck used Linda in *Faulkner* to exemplify his statement that the "grotesqueness in Faulkner's fiction" is not "mere expedient melodrama" but rather "the shadowing forth of a realistic world-view, with a conviction integrated against prevalent vulgarities, indifference, inequities, and aggression": "With her quacking voice and the tablet for Gavin to write on, living with Flem her not-father in his ill-gotten mansion, in a suspension of her womanly life that makes her seem a lady bewitched in an ogre's castle, where she herself turns avenger, she is certainly a figure shadowed and weird." Here Beck almost perceived the Gothic pattern. As the heroine of a tragedy of revenge, Linda is a kind of inversion of the traditional roles: she neither motivated nor committed the deed. She secured Mink's release from prison with the expectation that he would kill Flem and thus avenge Eula's suicide and Linda's other grievances. No Clytemnestra, Linda postponed action and did not wield the weapon herself. The somewhat masculine quality in Linda, heightened by her work in a shipyard during World War II and by her fondness for wearing masculine coveralls and a stained burberry, suggests that if Eula was a Helen, Linda was a Diana—especially when she protected Mink, in name and nature like a small animal.

Neither Gavin's sister, Margaret Mallison, nor his wife, Melisandre, played any part in the revenge tragedy in which Linda deceptively involved Gavin. In *The Town* both Margaret and Melisandre represent upper-class southern women who genuinely possess the virtues which Narcissa Benbow imitated and Temple Drake used as a shield. These potential heroines in *Snopes* function chiefly as subordinate figures related to the theme of courtly love. In *The Town* Margaret is Gavin's twin sister, not his younger sister as in previous narratives. With unfailing sisterly devotion and an intuitive understanding of Gavin based on twinship, Margaret aided Gavin in his idealistic pursuit of Eula and then of Linda. In *The Town* Melisandre is only a few years younger than Gavin and Margaret, nearer Gavin's age than in "Knight's Gambit." Gavin had had a youthful romance with Melisandre which mysteriously failed to culminate in marriage, and she married Mr. Harriss, a wealthy bootlegger. Gavin's marriage to Melisandre in *The Mansion,* prepared for in "Knight's Gambit," occurred after he refused to marry the deaf and widowed Linda, of whom there is no hint in "Knight's Gambit." Gavin's refusal to marry Linda and his subsequent marriage to Melisandre are facts to be reckoned with in the involvement of Linda with Mink.

The role of Mink as both a murderer fleeing from justice and a revenge villain-hero involves him in two alternating ritualistic movements, flight and quest. In both quests for revenge, against Houston and against Flem, Mink was seeking revenge for denial of recognition, first as a man struggling for human dignity and second as a Snopes, kinsman to Flem. In the second motive there is a variation in the Gothic theme of identity: Mink did not need to prove who he was but merely needed to have Flem recognize the claims of kinship. With the sensitivity to indignity of a man whose whole life had left him naked to scorn, Mink responded in the same way to Houston's arrogance and to Flem's callousness. In *The Hamlet* and *The Mansion* there are numerous discrepancies in the accounts of events leading up to the murder of Houston. *The Mansion,* the more detailed concerning motives and preparation for the murder, in the early summer, was written much later than *The Hamlet,* which gives the more complete account of the flight after the murder, in September. Since only the Gothic aspects of the story are relevant here, the more complete accounts will be considered, with little regard to alterations between earlier and later versions.

In *The Mansion* Mink's life before the murder was a series of journeys "into the forest" and out again. One sequence of circular journeys took him back and forth between Houston's prosperous farm and his own poor one: first, to get the cow which had wintered in Houston's pasture and which Mink falsely claimed to have sold and which Houston would not release without pay for feed and for servicing by his bull. Then, when Houston's claims were supported by Will Varner, justice of the peace, Mink journeyed the two miles to Houston's after sundown for thirty-seven days to dig postholes and stretch wire, in payment for his cow; he worked around the clock to do his own plowing and work at Houston's, going to sleep in the furrow at sunset. After the journey to get his cow, when he had worked out his debt only to find that he owed an additional dollar pound fee, he walked four miles to Varner's store, "through the bright sweet young summer morning," and waited, without food, until Varner returned in midafternoon and confirmed that Mink owed "two more days for the pound fee" (p. 28). The next morning he walked to Houston's and returned at sundown, went home and slept, and at midnight walked back for the last stint. At noon he finally drove his cow home. Rarely have so many weary journeys and so much labor provided a motive for murder, a privilege earned, according to Mink's code of ethics, by completely discharging his obligation to Houston before killing him. At least Mink's last journey before the murder was less monotonous than the earlier ones: he rode to Jefferson and back with the mail carrier, being robbed of five dollars and beaten up by the carrier when he protested. When Ike McCaslin refused to sell Mink two buckshot shells because there was no game at Frenchman's Bend requiring buckshot, Mink spent the night enjoying what free excitement nocturnal Jefferson provided, especially the passing trains. After his return with the mail carrier to Varner's store, Mink still had five miles to walk home. He returned to the bridge between Houston's and Varner's store uncounted days before Houston rode into his ambush.

The effect of this oppressive first chapter is to arouse amazement at Mink's endurance and his inflexible purpose, first to fulfill his obligations without accepting any favors and then to take vengeance for that final dollar, which Varner would gladly have given him. The alternation of day and night scenes, with Mink's sense of time often blurred by weariness, provides Gothic contrasts. But in general Mink remained alert and cunning and intensely conscious of his surroundings when he was not working around the clock.

In *The Hamlet* after the murder of Houston, Mink began his nightmare flights and journeys, literally into the forest, simultaneously fleeing from the law and seeking to silence the hound and dispose of the body. Since most of this action takes place at night, with the focus on Mink's state of mind, these are the most Gothic scenes, in both content and tone, in Mink's story, the most nightmarish in repeated and circular journeys in the darkness, in the frantic haste and the disordered sense of time, and in the suspension of normal life and human contacts.

Oddly enough, after the murder Mink's actions were dominated more by purpose than by panic, and his journeys into the forest rarely became flight. Mink's dominant characteristic was "the incorrigible singleness of his will" which made his mind the master of his body: "His mind, his will, stood like an unresting invincible ungrazing horse while the puny body which rode it renewed its strength" (*The Hamlet*, pp. 227, 228). Consequently, Mink knew "no blind, instinctive, and furious desire for flight which he had to combat and curb" (p. 218), but for three days he acted deliberately, in the belief that he had an "alternative between planned and intelligent escape and mere blind desperate harried fleeing . . ." (p. 242). Then his cousin Lump's greed for the money in Houston's pockets interfered with Mink's actions and made him realize that he had "lost that privilege of choice" and that "all which remained to him of freedom lay in the shortening space" between the light where he could keep straight on to the railroad and escape or turn off to his cabin (p. 242). Even his incorrigible will did not keep him from realizing his initial mistake: "I thought that when you killed a man, that finished it. . . . But it dont. It just starts then" (p. 243). This tragic enlightenment did not, however, prevent him from committing a second murder of revenge.

Thus, Mink's will and the practical requirements of the situation, as long as he hoped for a planned escape, necessitated a series of journeys between his cabin and the "forest," the wooded area where he killed Houston: going home to wash his shoes and gun and to eat and sleep, alone after his wife took the children and left; at the howling of Houston's hound summoning strength and will for "the phase of harried and furious endeavor which his life was about to enter" (p. 223); hiding the body in a hollow tree; following a mechanical, half-conscious routine of hiding at home by day and going into the forest at night; finally shooting the persistent hound. Then "the tremendous silence . . . roared down about him," even more terrifying than the howls: for the first time his will failed him and "he was running, blindly in the pitch darkness" (p. 230). Sound and eventually smell guided him in the blackness, which intensified the nightmarish effect. By the time he got home, after throwing his gun in a stream, three days had passed since the murder.

Mink's first journey out of the forest and away from his cabin was to Varner's store. There Lump's blackmailing threat to reverse the lies he had told to protect Mink, unless Mink shared with him what money Houston had carried, ended the possibility of Mink's successfully carrying out his plan to dispose of the body again before the buzzards revealed its location. Now Mink's involuntary flight began. After knocking out Lump, Mink looked frantically for the tree where he had left the axe when Lump was trailing him. Then "in the roar not of silence now but of time's friction," the "too loud" sound of time, he ran to a Negro cabin and seized an axe (p. 249). Then, after controlling his impulse to run from the barking dog, and to run when he was lost, he finally ran and fell into the sunken road he was seeking, dropped the axe, and circled back home. Here he found his own axe, knocked Lump out a second time, and returned to the hollow tree which held the body. Ironically, even the final direct journey to the tree became circular: Mink discovered that the body had an arm missing and had to go back to retrieve it. These repeated circular journeys, which turned into flights under pressure of the macabre incidents and such complications as the howling of the hound and the intrusion of Lump, ended in his capture. On his last journeys, to the jail in Jefferson and to the state prison in Parchman, Mink finally rode.

At Parchman, tricked by Montgomery Ward at Flem's orders, Mink was transformed into the most grotesque maiden in flight in Gothic fiction. Even then he had enough self-control to follow Montgomery Ward's advice and walk, not run, to the nearest exit: "the damn little thing looking like a little girl playing mama in the calico dress and sunbonnet . . . as forlorn and lonely and fragile and alien in that empty penitentiary compound as a paper doll blowing across a rolling mill; still walking even after he had passed the point where he couldn't come back and knew it; even still walking on past the moment when he knew that he had been sold . . ." (*The Mansion*, p. 85). Even Montgomery Ward was human enough to have sympathy for Mink. The revenge that seemed excessive for Flem's failure to aid Mink when Mink's guilt was unquestioned no longer seems excessive for this indignity into which Flem tricked him and which cost him a twenty-year extension of his sentence.

Mink's thirty-eight years in prison alternated between having to keep moving on the treadmill, as it were, of the chain gang on the prison farm, where it made no difference whether the crops grew or not, and being shut up at night with the same gang. Mink even wished that he and Flem could wait to die together, forgetting about revenge. But he concluded: *"Cant neither of us help nothing now. Cant neither one of us take nothing back"* (p. 94).

Therefore, as soon as he was released from prison he began the same compulsive quest for revenge. The first part, his trip to Memphis to buy a gun, paralleled his trip to Jefferson, in *The Hamlet*, to buy shells. The money that Linda sent, on condition that he stay out of Mississippi, Mink renounced so completely that the thought of it was not even in his mind when he left the prison with $13.85. (Of course, Faulkner created suspense as to what happened to Linda's money.) Mink's odyssey is a miniature quest-romance, with the strangeness of the modern world intensifying the hazards and obstacles he had to covercome before reaching his goal: hitching rides on a paved highway in trucks; being cheated by a country storekeeper because of his own honesty; being robbed of ten dollars and paid back by the congregation of Goodyhay, Christ's Top Soldier; spending a night in a park and the depot in Memphis; finally spending $13.10 for an antiquated pistol and three bullets. Armed with this "treasure," this epic weapon, Mink ended his odyssey and approached the "castle," like Childe Harold coming to the Dark Tower: he had ridden in a cattle truck, picked cotton for a Negro and verified his information about Flem and Linda, and walked along the railroad track—"now a fading weed-grown branch line knowing no wheels any more save two local freight trains more or less every day" (p. 406). When he arrived at the unguarded mansion, Flem was visible through the window.

Unlike the account of Houston's murder, this narration contains no description of Mink's flight after killing Flem. Linda showed him the way out, and he merely went to earth where his old cabin had been. The purposeful journeys shift to those of Gavin, leaving the money with the warden at Parchman; of Ratliff to Parchman, discovering that Mink did not take the money; of Gavin and Ratliff, substituting the telephone for journeys in tracing Mink in Memphis; and finally of Gavin and Ratliff driving out to Mink's old place to give him his cash reward from Linda.

The story of Mink is ironically a combination of man in motion, compulsively traversing, chiefly on foot, the circles which define the limits of his necessity, and of man immobilized, in prison; both the motion and the immobility are fully in the Gothic tradition. What the southern scene and character add to the tradition is the fact that Mink's innocent freedom was almost as restricting and confining as his guilty imprisonment, and more lacking in creature comforts.

The emphasis on patterns of action before and after the chief acts of violence necessarily served to diminish somewhat the effect of those acts, in accordance with Faulkner's usual practice of distancing deeds of horror and minimizing the purely physical aspects of murder. In *Snopes,* however, Faulkner did not always do this or did so in ways that shift macabre and Gothic effects to other scenes than the murders or to other aspects than violence to the victim. Confrontations in which motion is frozen in tableaux dramatize the conflicts, with the usual contrast between motion and stasis. One such confrontation begins the conflict between Houston and Mink, when Mink went to Houston's pasture lot to get the cow he pretended he had sold. Faulkner said explicitly: "It was tableau: Mink with one leg over the top rail, Houston standing inside the fence, the pistol hanging in one hand against his leg, the Negro not moving either, not looking at anything, the whites of his eyes just showing a little. 'If you had sent me word, maybe I could a brought a pistol too'" (*The Mansion,* p. 15). Houston offered to put the pistol between them and race for possession of it, an echo of the contest between Lucas Beauchamp and Zack in "The Fire and the Hearth" but not here put into action.

In *The Mansion* the murder of Houston emphasizes the misfire and the sound of the shot; oblivious to Houston's body, Mink justified himself by his motive, the final insult of the one-dollar pound fee. *The Mansion* continues, in the next chapter, with the end of the trial and Mink's life sentence, with a shift forward to Mink at Parchman three years later. In *The Hamlet,* as has been indicated above, events between Mink's shooting of Houston and his capture are given at length. The shooting, however, is presented from Houston's point of view, from the moment he left the saddle, still alive. This subjective description of shock, pain, and ebbing consciousness is unusual in Faulkner. The dying victim confronted his murderer:

> . . . looking up out of the red roar, into the face which with his own was wedded and twinned forever now by the explosion of that ten-gauge shell—the dead who would carry the living into the ground with him; the living who must bear about the repudiating earth with him forever, the deathless slain—then, as the slanted barrels did not move: 'God damn it, couldn't you even borrow two shells, you fumbling ragged—' and put the world away. His eyes, still open to the lost sun, glazed over with a sudden well and run of moisture which flowed down the alien and un-remembering cheeks too, already drying, with a newness as of actual tears. [*The Hamlet,* p. 217]

The Gothic theme of the double, "wedded and twinned forever," re-appears, in the variation which had been used in *Light in August:* the faces of Joe Christmas and Percy Grimm blended in Hightower's vision of the "halo full of faces" of those whom he had known (p. 465).

The combination of poetic feeling and phrasing, naturalistic detail, and the last breath of arrogance distinguishes Houston's death from Faulkner's usual technique of avoiding the death agony, objectively or subjectively viewed, and lends a new dimension to Gothic horror. The entire passage is one of seven subjective treatments of "The Moment of Death in Modern Fiction" in which Robert Detweiler analyzed the experiences of each fictional "die-er." He discovered that "the basic elements of this final event" fall into three groups of characteristics. The first, "disjuncture," involves "astonishment, a curious sense of the invasion of the mundane at this time of heightened reality, a confusion of time and the senses," as in Houston's "shock of the ground while he knew he was still falling" (p. 217). Second is "interiorization," "an intense focus of the die-er on self—a hyper-selfconsciousness—and . . . a retreat into memory," as when Houston watched "his own 'shattered ends of sentience and will.'" The third, "fusion," the effort "to reunite seemingly disparate parts of oneself," followed when Houston tried "'to will the sentience to meet and fuse,'" and saw his face and Mink's "'wedded and twinned for-ever.'" Detweiler decided that "at the moment of death modern man . . . tries to find meaning in whatever fragments of life remain available to his consciousness," and that this "fusion of fragments of reality fills for an instant the empty center, identifies the empty subject, and creates meaning on the threshold of nothingness." The existential quality is manifest, confirmed by Detweiler's comparison with "the encounter with nothingness in Heidegger," and with "the reintegration of personality that accepts death as the supreme possibility." Robert Detweiler's analysis established both the characteristics of these "moments of death" and the achievement of the imagination which they represent, "to consider a new mode of thinking that can function in the proximity of death," but he was unable to appraise the episode in its larger context. In Faulkner's fiction the crucial significance of this "moment of death" lies in its contribution to Gothic horror as a *hapax legomenon.* Faulkner's achievement is the more remarkable in the technical virtuosity displayed in the shift, for Gothic horror, from omniscience to extreme "interiorization" in presenting a character who serves a double function in the themes of love and revenge.

So intent was Mink on his revenge that, ironically, the inseparability of slayer and slain never haunted *his* consciousness: Houston dead was merely a body to dispose of. The shift to Mink's point of view in the passage following Houston's death stresses the sound of the shot, as did the account in *The Mansion,* and the recoil of the gun; Mink's physical sensations are combined with the psychological tension which made the misfire a "vain click louder than thunderbolt," so deafening that he did not hear the crash which followed (p. 218).

More macabre even than the death of Houston is Mink's disposal of the body. Since Faulkner here shut away any ray of Gothic moonlight, darkness deepened the Gothic gloom when Mink returned to hide the corpse. The cry of the hound guided him through the "invisible corn" and the undergrowth to the brushpile where he had first concealed the body. The description of Mink's physical labors in dragging the body to the hollow tree, climbing the tree, and hauling up the body is merely the prelude to the most macabre details. The body became "wedged by one twisted arm," and Mink had to jump up and down on the shoulders until the body dropped, leaving him dangling by the rope tied to a tree stub above him. When the rope broke, Mink was interred in the tree with the corpse, and the rotten shell of the tree kept breaking as he tried to pull himself up:

... he climbed interminably, furiously perpetual and without gain, his mouth open for his panting breath and his eyes glaring at the remote September sky which had long since turned past midnight, until at last the wood stopped crumbling, leaving him dangling by his hands, panting, until he could pull himself up once more and straddle the rim. [p. 226].

The nightmare quality of this passage surpasses that of the familiar flight without progress.

The sound of the hound climaxed at night Mink's tormented days and drew him to the forest until one night he followed it: "Then the dog's voice stopped, again in mid-howl; again for an instant he saw the two yellow points of eyes before the gun-muzzle blotted them. In the glare of the explosion he saw the whole animal sharp in relief, leaping. He saw the charge strike and hurl it backward into the loud welter of following darkness" (p. 230). Like the stasis after motion, the alternation of darkness and light and of sound and silence in this passage exemplifies devices used throughout the story of Mink. The "tremendous silence" destroyed by the hound had "roared down about him" and stiffened like cement, "inside and without him too," until he ran blindly. The roaring silence through his sleepless nights was followed by a primrose sky at dawn, behind three buzzards. Later he saw their "black concentric spiraling as if they followed an invisible funnel, disappearing one by one below the trees" (p. 232). Having eliminated, he thought, the danger of the hound's leading to the body, Mink next had to cope with the problem of the buzzards.

The sequence with Lump Snopes adds to the suspense. The original confrontation between Mink and Lump, in which Lump learned that Mink had not even robbed Houston's body, is followed by the grotesque checker game, a nickel a game against Houston's supposed fifty dollars; Lump cheated at first, then tried to lose because if he won, Mink would never risk going to the body. Mink's agony of suspense heightens the Gothic quality. One is reminded of the poker game in "Was," where freedom from marriage and freedom for marriage were at stake. Checkers, however, is a board game like chess and therefore, according to Northrop Frye in *The Secular Scripture,* a game suitable in upward movement and in "romance and Eros contexts," contexts ironically unlike those of the contest between Snopeses.

Having decided that the game was a mistake, Mink knocked Lump out and tied him up before belatedly starting his last search for the body. He finally found his way to the tree, "the topless shell of the blasted oak rising against the leaf-frayed patch of rainless sky" (p. 252). Mink's struggles here reverse those in putting the body into the tree. The smell is a new horror, the hound a revived horror and impediment, returning even after Mink struck it with the axe. As Mink chopped into the rotten wood, horror increased:

. . . he knew now it was not imagination he had smelled and he dropped the axe and began to tear at the shell with his hands, his head averted, his teeth bared and clenched, his breath hissing through them, freeing one arm momentarily to fling the hound back though it surged against him again, whimpering, and then thrust its head into the growing orifice out of which the foul air seemed to burst with an audible sound. [P. 253]

And even this was not the worst. When he had finally got the body out and dragged it to a stream, as he "hurled it outward into the mist" he saw, "at the instant of its vanishing the sluggish sprawl of three limbs where there should have been four . . ." (p. 254). While he was groping for the missing arm, the hound disappeared. "A voice said: 'All right, Mink. We've got him. You can come out now'" (p. 255). In its startling effect, this moment resembles that in *Great Expectations* when the convict rises from behind the tombstone and addresses Pip. In jail that night Mink justified his failure by blaming the corpse: "'But the son of a bitch started coming to pieces on me'" (p. 258).

On the way to town in the surrey, Mink tried to jump out and almost broke his neck, a final bit of physical horror to contrast with the peaceful scene in Jefferson as the surrey entered town and passed children in bright dresses playing on lawns in the sunset and ladies in fresh dresses rocking and men coming home from work. The concentration on Mink after the murder eliminates the process of detection by which he was apprehended, but the information from Lump and the signs of search which Mink observed made clear that Mink never had a chance to escape and that only his single-minded concentration on his problems could have deceived him as to the outcome.

Although the murder of Houston and Mink's subsequent experiences constitute the most Gothic portion of *The Hamlet* and initiate the revenge theme which is completed in *The Mansion,* some incidents in *The Hamlet* which are related to the money theme are notably Gothic in effect. Mink's arrest is followed by "The Peasants," in which the spotted horses episode is one of the most comic and the most Gothic in *The Hamlet.* The wildness of the horses and the male lust for possession of them are dramatized in the violent action of the stampede, in which Henry Armstid suffered a broken leg and Tull's wagon was wrecked and Tull injured. Violence and comedy are grotesquely mingled in the scenes in Mrs. Littlejohn's hotel. Contrasting images of the blossoming pear tree and of Eula in the moonlight reintroduce the love-fertility theme and provide additional grotesque incongruities. Mrs. Armstid is the most pathetic of Faulkner's Suffering Wives; she is destitute and is abused by her husband, the victim of both his tyranny and Flem's injustice and greed.

The concluding episode in *The Hamlet* is the thoroughly Gothic tale of privation, greed, and madness of which the treasure hunt of Lucas Beauchamp is a transposition into a different key. The destitute Henry Armstid was driven mad by the false hopes aroused by Flem's salted treasure trove, by which he tricked Ratliff and Bookwright into buying the worthless Old Frenchman's place. The night scenes of the secret search are paralleled by those of Lucas seeking gold with the aid of a divining machine. The search for treasure at the Old Frenchman's place was truly a romance descent into a lower world, in which, as Myron Weybright observed, the vision of the treasure seekers was impaired by darkness and their perceptions were dulled by greed. Uncle Dick Bolivar, the human diviner with supernatural powers, adds another grotesque figure, with the same sound moral principles as Aunt Molly exhibited. Uncle Dick sensed evil: "'Hit's four sets of blood here lusting for trash'" (p. 346). The fourth, invisible, was Flem. The tableau at the end of *The Hamlet* shows the crippled and now insane Henry Armstid digging for treasure, to the amusement of the assembled onlookers. Among them is Flem, with Eula and the baby, impassively viewing the spectacle. The essence of Flem's Snopesism is concentrated in his parting words and gesture as he heads for Jefferson and greener fields to exploit. As Henry, "his gaunt unshaven face . . . now completely that of a madman," began to dig, "Snopes turned his head and spat over the wagon wheel. He jerked the reins slightly. 'Come up,' he said." In Jefferson Flem will meet success and doom.

The sequel to the spotted horses episode and to Mink's arrest is a series of court scenes, of respectable antiquity in Gothic fiction. There is a new twist to the unfair trial in romance, described by Frye in *The Secular Scripture,* in which the hero, as defendant, escapes by revealing his identity. In the first of the two actions, Armstid vs Snopes and Tull vs Eckrum Snopes, the "hero," Flem, escaped by denying his identity as owner of the horses and by Lump's committing perjury when he stated that he saw Flem give back Armstid's money to the Texan. In Tull vs Eckrum Snopes, Eck admitted to being the owner of the horse and was willing to pay Tull but was prevented from doing so by the judge's ruling that the horse did not belong to Eck because "ownership cant be conferred or invested by word-of-mouth" (p. 330). Instead of receiving damages, the Tulls became owners of the vanished horse. Justice was not done but the law was upheld. In the later trial Mink, the accused, was guilty and was convicted. The verdict of guilty called forth Mink's deadly but inarticulate threat to Flem: "'Tell that son of a bitch ———'" (p. 366).

The rest of Mink's life was lived in anticipation of gaining his freedom and killing Flem. After the extension of his sentence for his attempt to escape, one episode of violence in his life manifested his determination to live and gain his freedom in due time. By guile and courage he escaped murder by the rest of a gang in an attempted jail break. As soon as the one man who escaped and who swore vengeance on Mink was dead, Mink could be pardoned.

The climax which three volumes have been leading up to is a singularly quiet one. Finally at his destination after his epic journey, Mink prowled outside Flem's mansion, "unseen unheard and irrevocably alien like a coyote or a small wolf" (*The Mansion*, p. 411), until he ascertained that Flem was seated in his usual place and that Linda, to his surprise, was in the next room, not upstairs. Then Mink walked in and aimed his pistol, with the one remaining bullet, at Flem. As when he murdered Houston and when he tested the pistol, the gun misfired the first time. As Flem sat immobile, watching Mink, Mink rolled the cylinder back: "*Hit's all right* he thought *Hit'll go this time: Old Moster dont play jokes* and cocked and steadied the pistol again in both hands, his cousin not moving at all now though he was chewing faintly again, as though he too were watching the dull point of light on the cock of the hammer when it flicked away" (p. 416). To the reader this slow-motion murder scarcely seems serious until the chair "crashed to the floor" signals the success of Mink's shot.

Mink's wrath had a long-burning fuse, in contrast to the spontaneous explosion set off by Wash Jones's sudden recognition of Sutpen's contempt for him and his kind. But whereas Sutpen was still too "innocent" to know when he had committed unforgivable offenses against human dignity, Flem realized that Mink, as Charles Gregory said, had "the righteousness of the avenger of family dishonor on his side" and therefore expected nemesis to overtake him. Flem's acceptance of his fate, which allowed Mink a second try, justified Mink's belief that "Old Moster dont play jokes." Although the misfires in both of Mink's murders exemplify what Eric Bently calls "outrageous coincidence," that "notorious device of melodrama," the Falkner family history provided parallel examples which are cited by Blotner. At this point Mink's concept of Old Moster preserved him from the paranoiac reaction typical, Bentley said, of melodramatic vision. William R. Brown identified the paranoid process in Sutpen's delusion of grandeur and in Mink's delusion of persecution, manifest in Mink's concept of "them," testing his endurance. Brown regarded Mink as the most important of Faulkner's paranoid characters, his actions being inexplicable outside "a non-rational frame of reference." Brown distinguished between Old Moster, a concept of God which Mink came to believe in, and "they," the persecuting forces. All the hostile forces are agencies of a single hostile power concentrated in the earth. Both Mink's ethical code and his religious concepts are survivals of a kind of primitivism not represented in other Yoknapatawpha characters.

His mission accomplished, Mink's delusion of persecution seemed to subside. His flight after killing Flem is a kind of grotesque anticlimax, especially in comparison with *The Hamlet*. When Linda appeared, he threw the pistol at her and she returned it and showed him the way to the door.

Although this is the only murder in Yoknapatawpha staged in a "castle" and completely described, the effect is an ironic inversion of Gothic atmosphere. Mink reappears only at the end of his flight, in the cellar where his cabin had been; as Ratliff predicted, he wanted "jest to lay down in the dark and the quiet" (p. 418).

In *Snopes* the complicated counterpoint of Gothic revenge, courtly love, Alger success story, and comic or tragicomic battles of wits between Snopeses and non-Snopeses results in contrasts which reveal meaning and in ambiguities which conceal it. The only real triumph of the opponents of Snopesism, Ratliff's victory over Clarence Snopes in the election campaign in *The Mansion,* in July 1945, was one of the most comic and grotesque episodes in *Snopes* but scarcely a battle of wits, Clarence being endowed only with low animal cunning. But the contest involved the most serious local and national issues of that time and ours and only the picnic scene was comic. The codes of honor and motives of conduct of the five major characters who continue into the last two chapters of *The Mansion* reflect other themes which have merged into the revenge theme. In *Man in Motion* Warren Beck well defined the relationship: ". . . the Flem-Mink confrontation and the Linda-Gavin-Eula involvement are not plot and subplot but that plot-paralleling, with essential thematic reciprocation, which is found in most of Faulkner's work. . . ."

Mink becomes the central figure in the Snopes story, with Flem's role lapsing into inactivity in *The Mansion* and the subjective characterization of Mink eclipsing the two-dimensional Flem. Mink and Flem, more than Mink and Houston, are Gothic doubles, "wedded and twinned forever" by their birth and by the conflict in their codes which doomed Flem to death at Mink's hands. Mink's code of honor is a survival of the code of blood revenge which coexisted with Christianity during the Middle Ages: the insults to Mink's manhood inflicted by Houston's arrogance and Flem's indifference demanded ritual killing, as an insult by one gentleman to another once demanded a duel. Ab Snopes had demonstrated a similar code of honor in "Barn Burning" and in Ratliff's version of the same story in *The Hamlet.* Mink retained belief in the rightness of his code by his paranoid reasoning process, even to the extent of blaming the disintegrating corpse of Houston for his capture. Flem's code of materialistic opportunism could allow him to tolerate any humiliation so long as it was not made public and did not threaten his respectability: he could accept pay to father another man's child and would connive at his wife's adultery in the interests of economic advancement and social prestige. Money is a major symbol in relation to both Flem and Mink: the ten-dollar bill Mink's wife "earned" for him, the penniless Mink threw away; Flem used a roughly analogous kind of financing to advance his progress, and he kept the five-dollar bill which was the price of suffering for the Armstids. Mink was so honest that he would not take the money Linda sent when he did not intend to abide by her conditions, and that he made it easy for the storekeeper to cheat him. Flem's honesty was confined to accurate bookkeeping. When Mink thought intolerable provocation demanded a ritual killing, he killed as quickly as poor weapons and ammunition allowed. Both his gun and his pistol were ridiculous substitutes for the dueling pistol or the rapier that his courage and honesty, in another age and social class, would have warranted. So much were his killings affairs of honor that he did not rob Houston and sought no profit in killing Flem. Flem, on the other hand, drove Eula to suicide after tolerating her infidelity for eighteen years and gained from the flight of Manfred de Spain the position of president of the bank and ownership of the mansion. Flem's failure to protect or defend himself from Mink at the end may be a tacit admission that he had it coming to him, that, as Ratliff said, he had had "his lief fair and square" (p. 431), or may indicate utter boredom when Jefferson offered no more ready-made success patterns to imitate. Flem is the antithesis of Sutpen, who, like Faust, continued to strive, but neither Sutpen nor Flem could say to the passing moment, "Verweile doch! du bist so schön!"

But little Mink, in his den in the earth, had his moment of illumination which echoes successive apprehensions in *Snopes* of what Beck called "the ineffable within the bounds of human imagination." Mink took comfort in a concept like the Elizabethan "Death, the great leveler" theme and reflected that in death he would be

equal to any, good as any, brave as any, being inextricable from, anonymous with all of them: the beautiful, the splendid, the proud and the brave, right on up to the very top itself among the shining phantoms and dreams which are the milestones of the long human recording—Helen and the bishops, the kings and the unhomed angels, the scornful and graceless seraphim." [Pp. 435–36]

Unlike passages in *The Hamlet* in which some of the same allusions occur in relation to Ike and the cow, the rendition of Mink's intensity of feeling, when he may be at the point of death, greatly reduces the grotesque incongruity of the poetic concept and expression, an echo, as Richard Adams noted, of Synge's *The Playboy of the Western World:* Ike Snopes was unaware of the difference between man and beast; Mink was painfully aware of his own humanity and his humble status. Mink's sole reason for living being gone, the implication at the end is that, like Sam Fathers, he willed his own death, but the time and manner of his death are not revealed.

Linda Snopes Kohl is the most enigmatic figure in *The Mansion*. To have any sympathetic appeal in her role as accessory to Flem's murder, she should be a revenge heroine, but instead of having the courage of such heroines or of Mink, she duped her devoted knight Gavin, a lawyer, and made him an accessory before the fact in the murder of Flem, and she used as her tool the pathetic, stoic little Mink. Granted that Mink had lived thirty-eight years for the self-fulfillment of this murder, she was not justified in using him as she did nor, if she had sufficient reason for killing Flem, was she justified in accepting a home with Flem during the years while she waited for Mink to be freed and perform the deed. Comparison between Linda and Narcissa Benbow, a clearly unsympathetic character in *Sanctuary*, clarifies the implications. Narcissa betrayed the detective, her brother Horace, and thus aided the murderer, Popeye, for the sake of family respectability; Linda duped the detective, her devoted knight, and made him an accessory, and then paid the murderer. Perhaps the most ironic maiden in flight in Faulkner is Linda, in her coveralls, speeding away in her red Jaguar—a suggestive color—fleeing not from responsibility but from the unselfish devotion of Gavin which she had betrayed. At least she was honest enough to let him discover, through her possession of the Jaguar, both her reward to herself and the symbol of her crime, how she had used him. She left him the cold comfort of her lesser honesty after the greater deception.

If Linda's parting words are to be taken at their face value, as no doubt they should be, Gavin's code of honor may have doomed Linda: "I love you. . . . I have never loved anybody but you" (p. 425). Gavin as the courtly lover had refused Eula when she offered herself to him in *The Town* and had refused to marry the girl Linda, not only when she declared her love but her unreadiness to marry (*The Town*, p. 193) but forever after. In his idealism and his quixotic sense of honor, Gavin followed the "rule of courtly love" cited by Denis de Rougement in *Love in the Western World*, which "did not allow a passion of this kind [Tristan's] 'to turn into a reality,' to result in the 'full possession of his lady.'" It would seem, from what we know of Linda without ever getting into her mind, that Gavin could and should have married her, that that was what she returned to Jefferson for. She urged him to marry someone else only when it was painfully clear that he would not marry her. That his code of honor would not have allowed him to aid or connive at Linda's plan of revenge is clear: he warned Flem, his long-time opponent, he made every effort to locate and intercept Mink, and he posted a guard outside Flem's house—who happened not to be on duty when Mink arrived. Gavin tried to protect Linda from the knowledge that "her act of pity and compassion and simple generosity murdered the man who passes as her father . . ." (p. 391). The Jaguar revealed how mistaken he was in her motives.

After a mature lifetime of devotion to Eula and Linda, at the end of *The Mansion* Gavin is the Romantic hero defeated, not triumphant; the thought of Melisandre never enters his mind. Warren Beck's interpretation of Gavin in *Man in Motion* lacks adequate textual evidence and psychological validity: "Beyond his collusion, what he must the more lament is the cumulative cost to Linda, in the sacrifice of innocence, gentleness, and serenity, through her involvement with those of mankind who have warped her life." Melisandre, Gavin's wife, retained those qualities after being disillusioned in Gavin and married to a gangster. Moreover, if preservation of Linda's "innocence, gentleness, and serenity" had been Gavin's major concern, he would not have sent her, a nineteen-year-old southern provincial girl, to Greenwich Village in the late 1920s. If Kohl warped her life, Gavin was responsiible for sending her into Kohl's world. Flem could not have warped her life, for she had too little feeling for him to be influenced to accept his values. The only person with whom she was involved from girlhood on was Gavin. She said: "You're all I have, all I can trust. I love you!" (*The Town*, p. 193).

Gavin and Linda were like Pygmalion and Galatea, the classical version, Frye said in *The Secular Scirpture*, of the animation of statues in the romance themes of ascent. Gavin formed Linda's mind as, Margaret Mallison said, he had formed Melisandre's. Linda gave Gavin opportunity to take her down from her pedestal, when she invited him to the "housewarming" without benefit of clergy and then to her wedding to Barton Kohl: she might have been tempting him to be a young Lochinvar. When she returned to Jefferson a war widow, deaf and homeless except for Flem's mansion and without kith or kin, Gavin still resolutely saw in her his unchanging ideal, a woman who loved once, for life; that he, not Barton Kohl, could be the man, he refused to consider despite the evidence. As he had rejected Eula, he rejected Linda in Pascagoula, when she offered herself to him in unprintable terms. Only then did Linda urge Gavin to marry. When he did so, proving that he actually was matrimonial timber, Linda may well have sought a double revenge, against both Flem and Gavin, revenge against Gavin for her deafness and her wasted life, as it might well have seemed to her, and for rejecting her and then choosing another. Instead of granting Linda self-fulfillment as the woman he had formed according to his ideal image, Gavin doomed her to solitude in her silence. She became "the bride of quietness" when she rode off in her Jaguar, and Gavin lived with his queen in her castle. Her parting words were "I love you . . . I have never loved anybody but you" (p. 425).

Ratliff's role in the revenge tragedy is to aid Gavin and serve as commentator, a reliable witness, as he does throughout *The Town* and *The Mansion*. His comments represent the daylight view of the Gothic and romantic story: with instinctive wisdom and more knowledge of human nature than Gavin possessed, Ratliff is sympathetic but undeluded, imaginative but also rational. His views of Linda, Gavin, and Mink are relevant to the Gothic elements in *The Mansion*. Ratliff recognized that Linda was dangerous and that Gavin would act in accordance with her wishes. He warned Gavin that Mink might not be willing to take money as a substitute for revenge but said that if Gavin did not cooperate with Linda in dealing with Mink, she would simply get another lawyer, "'And then Flem Snopes wouldn't a had no chance a-tall'" (p. 370). It was Ratliff who so much doubted Mink's corruptibility by money that he went to Parchman and found that Mink did not take the money with him. When Gavin admitted his implication in Flem's murder, Ratliff calmly accepted what he had feared: "'What else is there beyond that for anybody to think up for you to do?'" (p. 427). It was Ratliff who saw the crowning irony of the end of Flem's ambitions and who passed a compassionate judgment on human beings: all of Flem's "gentle underhand" and "honest hard trompling" resulted in his cherished mansion becoming the possession of the last of the De Spains, a pitiable bedridden old lady and her old-maid schoolteacher daughter, included, with people in general, among "'The pore sons of bitches!'" (p. 429). Ratliff forced Gavin to recognize the truth, that Linda "'knowed all the time what was going to happen when he got out, that not only she knowed but Flem did too'" (p. 431). And Ratliff's final comment concludes the whole story of Gavin in *Snopes:* "'You done already been through two Eula Varners and I dont think you can stand another one'" (p. 434).

The Gothic atmosphere of *The Hamlet* and of Mink's part of *The Mansion* is fairly well dissipated at the end by the conditions of Flem's murder and such incongruous inversions and variations of the Gothic as the scarlet Jaguar, the defeat of the Romantic hero, and the reduction of the villain-hero to a small animal cowering in a den. But Mink's final union with the earth he had resisted and his meditation on death, in words not at his command, elevated the ending to the level of mystery and poetry and restored to Mink the dignity that attended his struggles in *The Hamlet*. Indomitable courage, unremitting passion, and unwavering integrity, however warped the values on which they are based, demand respect, if not emulation in the goals toward which they were directed. Faulkner used the devices of Gothic fiction of violence to raise Mink Snopes to semiheroic stature. In the story of Mink, Faulkner again exhibited the power of the imagination which distinguished the best of his earlier novels. The fact that in this part of *Snopes* he was continuing the Gothic mode confirms the significance of the Gothic tradition which he seemed to abandon in *The Town*. Gothicism was exceptionally congenial to Faulkner's creative imagination and his rich style, and it offered scope for original variations and inversions which could convey ironic comments on Yoknapatawpha society and characters.

CHAPTER TEN

FROM YOKNAPATAWPHA
TO THE WORLD

FAULKNER'S GOTHIC BEQUEST

A final panoramic view, as it were, of the unique Gothic realm which William Faulkner created in his Yoknapatawpha County shows what uses he made of the Gothic tradition and what nontraditional purposes he achieved by his distinctive varieties of Gothicism. The judgment of Faulkner's lifelong friend Phil Stone, reported by O. B. Emerson, provides a *mis*direction by which "to find directions out": Stone denied that Faulkner was a realist, "much less a photographic realist," and said that he was "obviously a romanticist, sometimes almost Gothic." Faulkner was *both* a realist and a romanticist and was positively Gothic: an artist can view life from various perspectives if his vision is sufficiently comprehensive and penetrating. Faulkner loved his land and his people too much to reject them in their everyday aspects, without romantic or Gothic makeup and lighting, and some of his characters share his love of the ordinary. He was enough of a romanticist to feel keenly the difference between the reality he observed and what his land and his people had been at their best, between the sometimes nightmarish present and the fine dreams they had cherished.

Faulkner achieved the fusion of dream and reality in his Yoknapatawpha novels. To Jacques Cabau, Faulkner's greatness lay in the fusion of two seemingly contradictory movements: "that of the left which carries the novel toward a realism of commitment, and that of the right which tends toward a romantic aesthetic." By assuming many points of view and imaginatively sharing the experiences of many diverse characters, by showing the outer world as it appeared to the mentally deficient, the psychologically disturbed, or the romantic idealist, Faulkner revealed the inner worlds of dream and nightmare and the razor's edge which

separated them. As the omniscient author or through a rational, humanistic central intelligence or narrator, he showed a world of everyday
experience, cherished in its multiplicity and uniqueness. The scope provided by this fictional world, despite its short history and limited boundaries, accommodated a variety of approaches, within a single novel or
within the Yoknapatawpha cycle. In this cycle, only *As I Lay Dying,
The Town,* and *The Reivers* are more in the romance vein than some
version of Gothic novel or romance. (Although *As I Lay Dying* has a
macabre quality and a partially Gothic effect, I deal with it in my article
as an ironic version of quest-romance.) For Faulkner, it is apparent,
Yoknapatawpha was essentially a Gothic realm. Of this mythic realm
in all its aspects, created from observed reality and inward vision,
Faulkner, as Richard Pindell said, was more than the "proprietor": "He
is the genius loci"; he is "finally the space that holds the inhabitants of
Yoknapatawpha County," and he "presides over the rites of passage of
his characters."

Consideration of individual novels in the preceding chapters was
chronological in time of action and logical in relationship between novels;
to avoid separating the two Compson novels and the two Sartoris novels
and to put them in order of present action, *Absalom, Absalom!* and *The
Sound and the Fury* were dealt with before *Sartoris.* Thus, Faulkner's
most extreme and traditional use of the Gothic came first. Now, however, a chronological survey of the Yoknapatawpha novels by dates
of composition and publication will show in what directions Faulkner
moved in his adaptations of Gothicism to his fictional county and how
his purposes modified his technical strategies and use of Gothic elements.

From *Flags in the Dust–Sartoris* (1929) through *Snopes* (1940, 1957,
1959), Faulkner varied the narrative method, from omniscient author
to limitation to a single point of view, but always with regard to both
the requisite dream-nightmare effects and the creation of suspense and
mystery. Mark Ratner well stated the effect Faulkner sought by his varied
narrative methods: like John Hawkes, Nathanael West, and William
Styron, his successors, Faulkner "gives us a comic-grotesque vision of
the horror of the American Nightmare, and symbolically offers the means
to the freedom of self-purgation."

In *Sartoris* the omniscient author virtually limits to young Bayard
his penetration into the depths of a consciousness, one beset by nightmares and plunged into nightmarish despair. In *Flags in the Dust* the
more extensive development of the Benbows, noted in chapter 4, provides
in Horace a second subjective-objective revelation of a young man whose
mind and motives are less mysterious than Bayard's. In *Flags in the Dust*
Byron Snopes is a full-scale psychological study; his mind and motives

when more completely revealed make him even more appalling as a study in sexual obsession than he is in *Sartoris*. The role of Bayard was left untouched when *Flags in the Dust* was shortened; therefore, mystery in *Sartoris* concerning the reasons for his suicidal despair at the death of his twin brother seems to be a defect in characterization: in all three characters as originally developed Faulkner used his omniscience to penetrate their minds and to reveal more than they understood. Young Bayard is haunted by memories of John; old Bayard and Simon are haunted by the ghost of Colonel John Sartoris. This first Yoknapatawpha novel in its Gothic aspects suggests the source of Gothicism in southern life and fiction. Lillian Smith said: "And everywhere there were the ghosts wandering restlessly through our everyday lives. Stories about haunted houses on the edge of town—what southerner does not remember!— merely took our minds off our own haunted lives and gave us reasons for our fears." Joseph Blotner told about the ghost of Rowan Oak; I have heard Mrs. Faulkner's daughter Cho-Cho and Cho-Cho's daughter Vicky tell those stories and affirm their belief that they had seen and heard supernatural manifestations.

The three central consciousnesses in *The Sound and the Fury* (1929), as noted in chapter 3, provide both structure and theme based on Freudian psychology. Dreamlike memory dominates 1 and 2, creating a mystery as to what actually occurred and what was distorted or imagined by Benjy and Quentin. Death is almost a presence in the Compson annals, preternaturally sensed by Benjy and the various dogs. Luster's fear of pappy's ghost is a more commonplace use of the supernatural than is characteristic of Faulkner's later works. In 4 the omniscient author does not resolve the mysteries in the first three parts; instead, the transcendent mysteries of Dilsey's Christian faith render negligible mere factual mysteries.

Written very soon after *The Sound and the Fury*, *Sanctuary* returns to the omniscient author of *Sartoris*, with a more sophisticated handling of central intelligences. By focusing chiefly on Horace Benbow and Temple Drake, Faulkner could present subjectively their nightmarish experiences and fantasies. By allowing himself freedom to shift to the omniscient author or to focus briefly on a few other characters, in a kind of sleight-of-hand dealing of his narrative cards, he could still achieve mystery and suspense by concealing some events or omitting some explanations. The almost intolerable nightmare effect of *Sanctuary* is due to the effective use of limited omniscience in presenting states of mind of characters under stress, climaxed by Horace's witnessing the lynching of Lee Goodwin.

After a single excursion into the complete fragmentation of narrative by presenting it solely through multiple points of view, in the semi-Gothic *As I Lay Dying,* Faulkner returned to the basic method of *Sanctuary* in *Light in August:* again focusing, not exclusively, on two chief characters, Joe Christmas and Hightower, for subjective presentation, the omniscient author could move freely from outside views of characters, as seen through the eyes of the author or of another character, to outside-inside author views which combine revelation of and comment on the consciousness of a major character, as with Joe, or to complete immersion in a consciousness, as in Hightower's final meditation. For Joe, the events so revealed were often nightmarish; Hightower lived in a romantic dream of the past; Byron Bunch, the comic hero, was divided between anxiety concerning Joe and a romantic dream concerning Lena. The central mysteries, of the identity of Joe and of the old man at the orphanage, are cleared up, except for the truth concerning Joe's father. Joe's motivations and the shaping of his character are complex but not mysterious, except for the motive for his final flight. The most notable use of preternatural powers in a Yoknapatawpha novel is that of the prescience and sense of divine guidance attributed to McEachern, Doc Hines, and Percy Grimm and echoed in Joe's "complete faith in an infallibility in events" derived from McEachern's influence and perhaps inherited from Doc Hines (p. 194).

Although *Light in August* is fully Gothic in all elements of the narrative except in the framing story of Lena, the voice of the omniscient author is in control. The ultimate in Gothic effect is achieved in *Absalom, Absalom!* from the points where the narrators take over (chapter 1, p. 9; chapter 2, p. 43); thereafter, although the omniscient author is not extinct, he speaks so seldom and so briefly that the reader scarcely notices him, even when seeing Quentin and Shreve through his eyes. By reducing the omniscient author passages and focusing on Quentin's consciousness in the revisions of the manuscript, Faulkner increased mystery and suspense. The narrators—Miss Rosa, Mr. Compson, and Shreve—and Quentin as narrator or central consciousness are caught up in a dream of the past, colored from the beginning by the romantic imagination of Miss Rosa and in the last chapters by the equally romantic but youthful creative imaginations of Quentin and Shreve, unlimited by direct knowledge such as Miss Rosa's of people and events. The dreams of Miss Rosa and Sutpen, and more remotely those of Henry, Charles Bon, and Judith, shaped and colored the events; human folly turned dreams to nightmares. In this novel the lack of factual knowledge leaves crucial events and motives mysterious, with only conjectural solutions. The narrators are haunted by the past, and, as Quentin thought, Sutpen's Hundred "would have to be haunted, could not but be haunted" (p. 213). In

Absalom, Absalom! Faulkner displayed his most thorough use of the Gothic tradition of the ninteenth century, even to the style in which the narrators expressed themselves.

Having gone as far as possible on that well-blazed trail, Faulkner struck out on a new track in the story-novels *The Unvanquished* and *Go Down, Moses.* In *The Unvanquished* the omniscient author retires: this is Faulkner's first novel told in the first person, by Bayard Sartoris, and the first dealing with the initiatory experiences of a boy and the coming-of-age of a young man. On the other hand, *Go Down, Moses* exemplifies the narrative methods used so far, except for multiple narrators as in *Absalom, Absalom!* Third-person narrator, somewhat like the long General Compson portion of chapter 7 in *Absalom, Absalom!* is used in "Was," with an omniscient-author prelude. The omniscient author is used with two central intelligences, Lucas and Roth, in "The Fire and the Hearth" and with one in "Pantaloon in Black" and "Go Down, Moses." In the Isaac McCaslin trilogy a new method was used which proved to have many advantages for Gothic narrative: a third-person central intelligence, without author mediation. The nostalgic reminiscence of Ike, his mind freely roaming in the past at some time in his old age, introduces a new sense of dreamlike mystery, in contrast with the waking nightmare of Rider, in "Pantaloon in Black," imprisoned in the flesh which separated him from the spirit of his dead wife. Ike's memories and the scenes remembered are so infused with a sacramental view of nature that his visions of the phantom buck and of the living bear are alike mysterious, and the dreamlike quality permeates his recollections of events he had anticipated in dreams and daydreams. The whole course of Ike's life, after he became twenty-one, hinged on his solution of one mystery, disclosed by the ledger entries: he chose to exercise his skills and wisdom, gained through initiation in the wilderness, in whatever wilderness remained accessible, rather than in the daily life of the land and the community which were his heritage.

In *Intruder in the Dust* the complete limitation to one central intelligence shows even more clearly than the McCaslin trilogy the advantages of this method for maintaining the mystery concerning facts until the process of discovering the truth has been completed. Unlike the usual novel of detection, *Intruder in the Dust* immerses the reader in a consciousness with many levels of awareness, exposed to present events and psychological stresses which produce a pervasive dreamlike effect, with nightmarish climaxes. So successful is the method that the un-Gothic nature of some of the elements, such as Chick Mallison's family and home, do not noticeably modify the Gothic effect.

When Faulkner used Chick Mallison in "Knight's Gambit," he adopted the same method, with similar results so far as Chick's more limited role made possible. But in *The Town* and *The Mansion* Chick is a narrator, in the first person, and thus operates entirely on the verbal level. The trilogy *Snopes* was planned by the time Faulkner wrote *Flags in the Dust*, before he began full use of the Gothic mode, but *The Hamlet* shows the effect of Faulkner's experience in using his author's omniscience to probe the consciousness of selected characters, most notably that of Ike Snopes, the cow lover, and of Mink Snopes, the man hater and murderer. The completely objective presentation of Flem Snopes throughout *Snopes* not only distinguishes him unfavorably from even the most humble of the other characters but, in a Gothic context, marks him as a coldly calculating rational man and therefore a villain. Eula also is seen objectively but is regarded with wonder and admiration that elevate her to the mythic status of a divinity. (Eula throughout *Snopes* is seen from masculine points of view.) Authorial comment and interpretation are supplemented by the use of V. K. Ratliff as a narrator of episodes. Although the suspense centers in the conflict between Flem Snopes and Frenchman's Bend, Flem is not an active character in the two nocturnal adventures which are the most Gothic narrative sequences, Mink's murder of Houston and his subsequent nightmarish experiences, and the treasure hunt by Ratliff, Armstid, and Bookwright, in which Flem's activities occur offstage. In the treasure hunt the preternatural skill of Uncle Bolivar as a treasure dowser adds a special Gothic touch.

The Town, the least Gothic Yoknapatawpha novel before *The Reivers*, is told entirely by three first-person narrators, V. K. Ratliff, Chick Mallison, and Gavin Stevens. The example nicely illustrates the limitations, for Gothic effect, of this narrator method unless the narrators are engaged in Gothic action or are deeply involved in relating a Gothic story, as were the narrators in *Absalom, Absalom!* In the Gothic tradition the first-person narrator was the victim or the observer of Gothic events; to this tradition the detective as narrator has been added. In *The Town* the vernacular effect of a first-person observer-commentator tends to diminish typically Gothic effects unless the event narrated lends itself naturally to exaggeration and grotesque imagery, as in the anecdote about Tom Tom and Turl. All three narrators have skill in language and lively imaginations, but their tone is too detached and reasonable for them to equal Miss Rosa or Quentin as Gothic narrators. Significantly, the most Gothic narrative sequence in *Snopes,* the revenge tragedy of Mink Snopes, is almost entirely absent in *The Town,* although Mink was imprisoned in Parchman during those years.

When Faulkner returned to Mink's story in *The Mansion,* he resumed the omniscient-author method, focusing on the consciousness of Mink for the chapters centered in his story: by so doing, Faulkner recaptured both the Gothic quality of Mink's part of *The Hamlet* and much of the imaginative power that seemed to be lacking in *The Town.* It seems that much of that power may have been derived from Faulkner's choice of the Gothic mode. The use of the three narrators from *The Town* for the non-Mink parts of *The Mansion,* either as first-person narrators or as third-person central intelligences, allows some mystery as to motives: Linda is seen only through their eyes, as she was also in *The Town,* and the mystery of her treatment of Gavin is never resolved. Although she is present in the action, she seems more enigmatic than the invisible Caddy did in *The Sound and the Fury.* As in *The Hamlet,* the dream-nightmare effects belong chiefly to the story of Mink, with some portions retold from *The Hamlet* with another turn of the Gothic screw.

Thus, Faulkner never abandoned the advantages of the omniscient author but tried various limitations of omniscience, always with the purpose of getting inside a character and involving the reader as fully as possible. With an inarticulate character or one of limited awareness and self-knowledge, such as Mink or Joe Christmas, the style must be the author's. The restriction or the relinquishment of authorial omniscience, however, had great advantages in securing reader cooperation and involvement in a Gothic tale. The most difficult and successful experiments with multiple points of view, with interior monologue or soliloquy, came early, in *The Sound and the Fury* and *As I Lay Dying.* Faulkner's predilection for the oral tradition, strong in *The Hamlet* and dominant in *The Town,* in much of *The Mansion,* and in all of *The Reivers,* is perhaps the most original feature of narrative method in his Gothic novels and the closely related romances. By never telling a Gothic tale in the first person from the point of view of the hero or heroine at the time of the action or in retrospect, Faulkner dissociated himself from the multitude of run-of-the-mill writers of Gothic romance.

In Yoknapatawpha the equivalents of the Gothic castles, symbols usually of past splendor and present decay, appear in most of the novels: the Sartoris plantation house in *Sartoris* and *Sanctuary;* the ruins of the Old Frenchman's place in *Sanctuary* and *The Hamlet;* the Compson house, in a state of dilapidation, in *Absalom, Absalom!* and *The Sound and the Fury;* Sutpen's Hundred in *Absalom, Absalom!* from creation to destruction; Miss Burden's house in *Light in August;* the McCaslin plantation, still a going concern, in *Go Down, Moses* and *Intruder in the Dust;* the Backus plantation in decline in *The Town* and as transformed by Mr. Harriss in "Knight's Gambit" and *The Mansion;* the old De Spain mansion as transformed by Flem in *The Town* and *The Mansion.* All these "castles" represent the plantation days of the past, and all of them had or have neighboring slave or servant quarters. Only one novel, *Intruder in the Dust,* lacks a "castle": the Mallison house is a comfortable middle-class residence in which the family live happily and usefully in the present. Although Will Varner's house, the only two-storey one in Frenchman's Bend, was scarcely a "castle," it housed a princess, Eula Varner, the Helen of Frenchman's Bend.

The scenes of enclosure, the "other rooms," in these "castles" or in other buildings, signify isolation, whether captivity or withdrawal or self-imprisonment: Bayard's room in *Sartoris* and the one where he spent the night at the MacCallums'; the bedrooms in the Compson house; in *Sanctuary* the bedrooms at the Old Frenchman place, at Sartoris, at Miss Reba's, at Ruby's, and in the jail. Finally in the courtroom, the last sanctuary, the occupants of these rooms are brought together. In *Light in August* all the rooms occupied by Joe Christmas were "other rooms," but in addition there were rooms at Miss Burden's and at Hightower's. Byron's room, however, was a refuge for Lena, an asylum in the same sense of the word as Hightower's house was an asylum for Joe Christmas, but unlike the asylum in which Joe had the first experiences he remembered. (We do not see Joe in jail.) In *Absalom, Absalom!* all the rooms in the Coldfield house were places of isolation and entrapment; the Coldfield attic and the rooms at Sutpen's Hundred of Ellen and Henry, in their last days, were places of living death. In *Go Down, Moses* the only rooms of warmth and love and family life were those where the fire burns on the hearth, in the cabins of Lucas Beauchamp and Rider. The hunters' bungalow and the tent in "Delta Autumn" represent more of the human fellowship in Ike McCaslin's life than did the various houses in which he lived, scarcely less dreary than Fonsiba's cabin. In *Intruder in the Dust* Lucas's cabin was again a refuge offering warmth and hospitality, but all the rooms in Chick's life, including his Uncle Gavin's law office, were places of communion and love. The only Gothic room in *Intruder in the Dust* is Lucas's jail cell, but for him that was an asylum, however precarious. In *Snopes* Mink's cabin was a place of isolation and retreat from which he was taken to jail and then to the penitentiary. Flem's mansion was a place of self-imprisonment. (In *The Mansion* Miss Reba's whorehouse is a place of entertainment, not of captivity.) The most Gothic scene in all these rooms is the one at Sutpen's Hundred where Quentin found Henry Sutpen, but the rooms most imbued with terror are Temple's bedroom and the corncrib at the Old Frenchman's place, in *Sanctuary.*

External nature ranges from the waste land despoiled by man, in *The Hamlet* and *Sanctuary* and *Absalom, Absalom!* and *Light in August,* to the pastoral and elegiac views of nature in *The Hamlet* and *The Mansion,* respectively. Productive plantations in *Sartoris* and *Go Down, Moses,* small farms in *Sartoris* and *The Hamlet,* and worn-out sharecroppers' or tenants' acres in the Frenchman's Bend area epitomize the agricultural economy and in context may be either Gothic or realistic. The most extended views of the natural scene in Yoknapatawpha are Gavin's panoramic survey from Seminary Hill in *The Town,* in which nature is least often a setting, and Chick's observations of his land and his vision of its place in the continent in *Intruder in the Dust.* Both Gavin and Chick show the romantic sensitivity to nature which is typical of Gothic fiction, but neither lives close to the land. Conversely, Ike McCaslin, despite his mystique of the land and the wilderness, shows little feeling for the areas which provide a living for man.

The forest of Gothic tradition is confined, in its most Gothic mystery, to the Isaac McCaslin trilogy in *Go Down, Moses:* it is no essential part of the environment of Faulkner's characters who contribute significantly to the welfare of the community. Recognizing that the wilderness theme is not a major one in Faulkner's chief works, William R. Brown considered the most normal and admirable characters in Faulkner to be Charles Mallison and Lucius Priest, town dwellers with no attachment to the soil or the wilderness. The wilderness represents a male ideal, not a social norm, and its devotees flee from both the town and women. To Brown's admirable characters should be added Gavin Stevens and V. K. Ratliff, who identify themselves with Jefferson but who maintain a relationship with the rural areas. Wooded areas in Yoknapatawpha County which impinge on farming land figure in action in *Sartoris, The Hamlet,* and *The Mansion,* and as background in *Intruder in the Dust.* In the last, two Gothic images are combined, the forest and the graveyard, in a clearing in the pines. The graveyard is the feature which appears in all the Yoknapatawpha novels discussed except *The Hamlet,* and it is the objective of the quest in *As I Lay Dying.* The graveyard in *Intruder in the Dust* is exceptional only in the fact that bodies are dug up as well as buried.

In these settings we not only find all the traditional Gothic character types, but we find them in every novel, played straight, ironically inverted, or parodied: the Romantic, Byronic, or Faustian heroes and, for good measure and medieval flavor, the courtly lovers; the tragic villain-heroes, the revenge villain-hero, the rational villains, the villain seducer, and the arch-villain of melodrama. The heroines, who may or may not be Persecuted Maidens, are less prominent than the heroes—in *The Sound and the Fury* Caddy appears only as a memory. What with adolescent heroes and heroes who can do without women, heroines would sometimes be as extraneous as in a horse opera. There is no traditional heroine in the action of *Intruder in the Dust* or *Go Down, Moses.* And *Snopes* makes do with two real heroines in three volumes, Eula Snopes and her daughter Linda, but they come closer to being romantic or romantic-Gothic heroines than do any other female characters. Evil Women or Temptresses are less numerous than villains and sometimes are disguised as heroines, like Narcissa, or beneath a bawdy exterior conceal a heart of gold, like Miss Reba. *Snopes* seems to lack a female villain until, at the end of *The Mansion,* Linda appears to qualify.

The parental figures who produced many of the heroes, heroines, and villains may be tyrannical or benevolent, but rarely were they successful as parents or grandparents: Sartorises, Compsons, Benbows, and Drakes failed to influence for good the children under their care, except for Granny Millard in *The Unvanquished.* All the parental figures in *Light in August* were disastrous if not positively malignant; so were Coldfields, Sutpens, and the conjectural Eulalia in *Absalom, Absalom!* In *Go Down, Moses* only Lucas and Molly and Rider's foster-parents were loving parents. In *The Hamlet* the Varners sold their daughter to Flem, much as the Compsons sold Caddy to Herbert Head in *The Sound and the Fury.* The Mallisons in "Knight's Gambit," *Intruder in the Dust, The Town,* and *The Mansion* were the most successful in bringing up a child, but, as Jean-Marie Magnan observed, Gavin was in a way the spiritual father of Chick. One might say, before *Snopes,* that the elder Mallisons were completely un-Gothic, but when Faulkner made Gavin and Margaret twins in *The Town,* he introduced a Gothic element, as Magnan recognized in including *The Town* in his study of incest in Faulkner. Faulkner exemplifies the truth of Irving Malin's statement that "the family is crucial in new American Gothic." In the record of ineffective or unloving parents, emotionally crippled children, and broken lives in Yoknapatawpha, Faulkner directly continued the Gothic tradition into the new American Gothic in which, Irving Malin said, "almost every work in the canon contains family terror."

The grotesques, which are the most easily recognizable of Gothic character types, appear in all the Yoknapatawpha novels, in part because Faulkner was both a Gothic and a comic novelist and combined the horror story with the comic tall tale, a combination, in the terms of Arthur Clayborough, of the regressive and the progressive in art. A lineup of Yoknapatawpha characters including Benjy Compson, Jim Bond, Ike Snopes, Tommy, Popeye, Miss Reba, Clarence Snopes, Doc Hines, Joanna Burden in her most Medusan aspect, Boon Hogganbeck, Labove, the child Eula, Flem and Mink Snopes, Old Het and Mrs. Hait, I. O. Snopes, and Old Meadowfill—to name only a few—would be horrible and ludicrous. The fact that Faulkner's grotesques, except those who are willfully or insanely evil, are presented with sympathy distinguishes them from those of some other Gothic writers and suggests the influence of Dickens in this as in other aspects of Gothicism.

Visible grotesqueness may or may not indicate psychological abnormality or sexual perversion, but characters who display such deviations from normality usually are indicative of themes typical of Gothic fiction, especially southern Gothic. William R. Brown considered that Faulkner's greatest contribution to understanding human nature lay in his ability to express the sensations and thoughts of abnormal states of consciousness of his characters and to draw implications from them. One such implication is that parental failures lie at the root of psychological deviations which are due to sexual immaturity. Lillian Smith explained the psychological and social effects of the women, like the Suffering Wives, who submitted to the southern concept of women and their subordinate role in society and who "dared not question what had injured them so much"; ". . . these women, forced by their culture and their heartbreak, did a thorough job of closing the path to mature genitality for many of their sons and daughters, and an equally good job of leaving little cleared detours that led downhill to homosexual and infantile green pastures, and on to alcoholism, neuroses, divorce, to race-hate and brutality, and to a tight inflexible mind that could not question itself." Mrs. Compson did about as well in achieving such results as she could with only four children, one of them an idiot. The fate of children in a motherless family—young Bayard Sartoris, the Benbows, the MacCallums, the McCaslins—by comparison seems less unfortunate. Narcissism, homosexuality, incest, and miscegenation are the specifically sexual themes in Yoknapatawpha which reflect the southern concept of upper class white women.

Narcissism is a characteristic of young Bayard Sartoris, all three Compsons, and Temple Drake and Narcissa Benbow. Old Bayard Sartoris was ineffectual in the paternal role, but the stern Judge Drake and his four sons wrought havoc by their strict policy with Temple. The narcissism of Lucas Burch in *Light in August* is not thematic except as it rounds out the catalogue of sexual perversions represented by the other characters. Young Bayard's narcissism is related to his obsessive love for his twin brother; this suggestion of incestuous homosexuality is reinforced by his visit to the all-male household of the MacCallums, which also includes twins. According to Lillian Smith, the trauma of the southern white male, occasioned by his having to break the infantile ties with his Negro foster-mother, sometimes caused him to turn away "from all women, shunning them white and black," and to spend "his real feelings on men and his hours in companionship with them." Both the MacCallums and the McCaslins, for whatever reasons, seemed to prefer male society when their shadowy wives died; there were no women in Ike McCaslin's Happy Hunting Grounds. Albert Devlin is the chief critic to recognize that the MacCallums represent pathological sexual adjustments. Faulkner emphasized this family not only by making the episode perhaps the finest passage about Bayard in *Sartoris* but also by returning to them in "The Tall Men" (1941). The homosexuality of Henry Sutpen and Charles Bon also has an incestuous quality, since it is based on the instinctive attraction between half-brothers. The theme of homosexuality is repeated in Quentin and Shreve in both *Absalom, Absalom!* and *The Sound and the Fury*. Mr. Compson having diagnosed Henry as both homosexual and incestuous, Quentin's subsequent identification with Henry suggests both perversions. In *Light in August* homosexuality is indicated in relation to Hightower and Byron and perhaps to Joe Christmas but is just one aspect of the overall theme of lack of normal healthy sexuality.

The strongest theme in this group is that of incest, involved in some characters, as noted above, with narcissism and homosexuality. John Irwin considered psychological incest and the consequent doublings to constitute a structure "that is central to Faulkner's work."

In this structure [he continued] the struggle between the father and the son in the incest complex is played out again and again in a series of spatial and temporal repetitions, a series of substitutive doublings and reversals in which generation in time becomes a self-perpetuating cycle of revenge on a substitute, the passing on from father to son of a fated repetition as a positive or a negative inheritance.

Incest was present from the beginning, even more obviously in *Flags in the Dust* than in *Sartoris*, in Horace and Narcissa Benbow. Similarly, incest was much further developed in the unpublished galleys of *Sanctuary* and was greatly reduced by Faulkner in the published version. (See chapter 5, pp. 95, 101.) In his first three Yoknapatawpha novels, *Flags in the Dust, The Sound and the Fury*, and *Sanctuary*, and again in *Absalom, Absalom!* the sixth, Faulkner was deeply concerned with the theme-cluster of narcissism, incest, and homosexuality. In *As I Lay Dying*, the fourth Yoknapatawpha novel Faulkner wrote, the theme of incest occurs again: the quest-romance hero is Jewel and the heroine is his mother, Addie. Faulkner's substitution of Gavin Stevens for Horace after *Sanctuary*, grafting onto Gavin some biographical details of Horace, may signify an intention to abandon these themes in twentieth-century Jefferson, but in making Gavin and Margaret twins in *The Town* he reintroduced Gothic doubles and thus reinforced the idea of incest.

Miscegenation, by southern standards a sexual perversion, appeared first as a major theme in the fifth novel, *Light in August,* and in the sixth, *Absalom, Absalom!* Here miscegenation is joined with the other three themes and is more abhorrent than incest. The next logical development would be to combine incest with miscegenation as an accomplished fact: this, of course, is what Faulkner did in *Go Down, Moses.* Isaac McCaslin's horror at discovering the secret of the ledgers, that his grandfather had a child by his own half-Negro daughter, equals Henry Sutpen's horror, as imagined by Quentin and Shreve, at discovering that Charles Bon had Negro blood and would thus, if he married Judith, be guilty not only of the venial sin of incest but also of the mortal sin of miscegenation, according to the southern code which Quentin attributed to Henry. (Ike was more horrified by the incest than by the miscegenation, but no white lady was involved and the miscegenation was a familiar fact of plantation life.) These southern themes are characteristic of the Yoknapatawpha novels through *Go Down, Moses* and thereafter disappear or cease to be an aspect of Gothic horror. In *The Reivers* Uncle Ned is called Uncle Ned McCaslin by the Priest family because he is the last descendant of Carothers McCaslin. Themes and action deal with racial etiquette but not directly with miscegenation.

The recurrence of these Gothic themes in Yoknapatawpha points to a basic weakness in the society, an inability of its members to enter into harmonious, vital relationships in family and social groups, which is confirmed in other Gothic themes. One group of themes deals with individual problems and the attempts to solve them. Isolation, alienation, and lack of love appear in *Flags in the Dust, The Sound and the Fury, Light in August,* and *Absalom, Absalom!* In *Go Down, Moses* Ike McCaslin appears to be alienated from his society except on hunting trips, and lack of love among the white McCaslins is a theme of the whole novel. The search for a remedy for such isolation has varied goals. It may be love or identity or a father or sublimation in an abstract ideal such as truth or justice. Glenn Sandstrom regarded the quest for identity as central in Faulkner's novels, from Temple Drake to Linda Snopes. Benjy, Caddy, and Miss Quentin sought love. Quentin sought death. Horace Benbow in *Sanctuary* sought justice and found reality. Joe Christmas sought his identity as a man and Byron Bunch sought love. In *Absalom, Absalom!* all the narrators, but especially Quentin, sought truth, and Quentin sought also understanding of himself and his heritage. He and Shreve conceived of Charles Bon as seeking a father and identity. In the wilderness Ike McCaslin sought communion with nature and values to live by. In *Intruder in the Dust* Chick Mallison sought truth and justice and with his success found his own mature identity and heritage. In *The Hamlet* Labove, Mink, and Houston sought physical love: in *The Town*

Gavin sought ideal love. In *The Hamlet* and *The Mansion* Mink sought human dignity. Only Gavin and Chick were not isolated and alienated before their quests.

The attempt to solve personal problems might take different directions: immature idealism might seek to reject reality and cling to a dream. André Bleikasten dealt at length with the theme of infantilism and immaturity in *Sanctuary:* "Novel of evil and tale of terror, *Sanctuary* is also the *roman noir* of childhood." Innocence itself "*is* the evil in so far as it is always already there as the center of corruption and of death." The dream might be one of innocence, like Quentin's, or Horace Benbow's before his belated initiation into reality, and like Ike McCaslin's when he refused to share the guilt of his ancestors. Gavin's idealism has some of this absence of involvement and its consequent guilt. Or it might be a dream of the past, with a similar lack of involvement in sinful humanity: Quentin had both dreams and died rather than relinquish them. Young Bayard had a dream of the past and a nightmare of guilt and died rather than live in desolation and despair. In *Light in August* Byron Bunch tried to live an uncommitted life of innocence until he began his quest for love, and Hightower tried to live outside of time in a vision of the past. What Robert Heilman called the dream that "embodies images of achievement that require action" is less prominent in Yoknapatawpha than "the dream that is out of line with reality" which "may be cherished with naive ignorance or with knowingness." The consequences of the two kinds of dream suggest other dreamers in Yoknapatawpha, as well as some cited above. The first kind of dream, if it "compels life instead of guiding it," may drive "the private dreamer" to madness (Sutpen); the second kind may make the dreamer quixotically eccentric (Gavin), innocuous (Ike McCaslin), "or even dangerous in the power to mislead" (Percy Grimm).

In contrast to the themes of individuals but not necessarily irrelevant to them are the extremely Gothic themes of family relationships and family heritage, often a heritage of doom. Only rarely does the positive and un-Gothic aspect, a heritage of love and fidelity, occur, as in the Negro Beauchamp family and the white Mallison-Stevens family. The note of doom is first sounded in *Flags in the Dust,* a fatality in the name "Sartoris" itself that haunts young Bayard. Quentin and Caddy Compson believed that there was a curse on the Compsons. Narcissa Benbow sacrificed her living brother and the Goodwins to the name of her dead parents. Joanna Burden bore, to her doom, the burden of her heritage and the black cross it laid upon her. Joe Christmas was equally doomed by his ignorance of his heritage and by the fact of his blood kinship to Doc Hines. Hightower chose one aspect of his heritage as the center of his dream and sacrificed to it his own personal and professional life. Isaac McCaslin repudiated his heritage and sacrificed the sons he might have had. Charles Mallison chose the best in his social heritage and by so doing preserved his integrity and achieved maturity. Even the Snopes heritage, miserable as it was, bound Mink and Flem fatally together as long as they lived. In the Yoknapatawpha novels the Gothic theme of family and social heritage signals the doom of those who look to the past and glorify the dead and implies Faulkner's abiding concern for the continuance of the family by those who have love, vitality, and courage to face the future.

Transcending individual concerns are themes based on the community, such as the theme of Negro-white relationships in *The Unvanquished, Go Down, Moses,* and *Intruder in the Dust.* The theme of truth recurs in various aspects: the themes of truth and justice *(Sanctuary),* of the truth of history *(Absalom, Absalom!)* of life-saving and spirit-saving truth *(Intruder in the Dust),* of essential human truth *(The Town* and *The Mansion).* When these themes involve a search, it is not primarily self-centered or self-seeking.

So far all of the themes dealt with are both Gothic and southern; other themes are derived from much older traditions and societies, from myth and world literature. The scapegoat is represented in the themes of Cain and Ishmael and Christ. The Christ imagery and allusions are obvious in *The Sound and the Fury.* In *Light in August* Joe Christmas was an Ishmael before becoming a scapegoat Christ figure. Henry Sutpen in *Absalom, Absalom!* became a wandering Cain but did his wandering offstage. Isaac McCaslin was a self-designated Christ figure but only as far as the carpenter stage. In *Intruder in the Dust* Chick saved Lucas from becoming a scapegoat and suffering crucifixion. Faulkner's use of this cluster of mythic themes was concentrated in the novels before 1940; in *Go Down, Moses* and *Intruder in the Dust* the use is strictly limited, no doubt because in the early forties he began work on *A Fable,* a full-scale use of the Christ story in a European setting.

Light in August marks the climax of the Christ theme in the Yoknapatawpha novels and combines that theme with the revenge theme that continued and reached its climax in *The Mansion.* Jason's persecution of Caddy and Miss Quentin in *The Sound and the Fury* was motivated by revenge for his disappointed hopes, his failure to get the job promised him by Herbert Head. In *Light in August* Lucas Burch, Judas to Joe as Christ, was motivated by revenge and greed; Doc Hines believed he was the instrument of divine vengeance; Percy Grimm was avenging White Womanhood. Forty years after she was outraged, Miss Rosa took her revenge against Sutpen by telling her story to Quentin Compson. Sutpen's whole design in *Absalom, Absalom!* was a means of revenge against plantation society but was not directed against any person. For a similar affront, Wash's revenge was personal and swift. Bayard's revenge against Grumby for killing Granny Millard is one of the fully Gothic tales in *The Unvanquished* and is contrasted with his refusal to take revenge against Redmond for killing John Sartoris. And finally, from *The Hamlet* to the end of *The Mansion*, Mink Snopes lived only to achieve his revenge against Flem, for the same denial of human dignity for which Wash had killed Sutpen and Mink had killed Houston. Mink was also a Cain, killer of blood kin. It is no mere coincidence that Hyatt Waggoner described Mink as "a fierce little Ahab, rebelling against the injustice of the gods": Ahab and Ishmael belong to *Moby-Dick*, which Fiedler considered as one of the three great American Gothic novels and which Waggoner compared in detail with Faulkner's novels.

The Faust theme occurs most impressively in the story of Sutpen, with his dreams of grandeur and his superhuman and ungodly aspiration. There is an allusion to Faust when Joe Christmas struck down McEachern. The comic Faust, who aspired only to money, status, and respectability appears near the beginning and near the end of the Yoknapatawpha cycle, in Jason Compson and Flem Snopes, who are pitted against each other in *The Mansion*. The image of Sutpen in the reader's mind points up the parody of Faust in Jason and Flem.

The themes of the land also have mythic parallels. Although Faulkner's early novels create an image of society that is reminiscent of and no doubt influenced by T. S. Eliot's "The Waste Land," especially *Sanctuary* and *Light in August,* in his later novels Faulkner developed the theme of man's exploitation of the land and contrasted this waste land with the Edenic wilderness that man had destroyed. Although both aspects of the land are presented in *Absalom, Absalom!* from the hewing of Sutpen's Hundred out of the wilderness to its final desolation, the accident of history was a factor in the destruction; it was fertile until cultivation was abandoned when the Civil War took men from the land. Miss Burden's sterile acres in *Light in August* present a parallel image. In *Go Down, Moses* the most complete and direct statement of the theme is Ike's lament and accusation in "Delta Autumn," and his prediction of the retribution in store. *The Hamlet,* the most fully rural novel in setting, contrasts fertility and the land, as symbolized in Eula, with sterility and exploitation, as symbolized in Flem. In both *The Hamlet* and "The Fire and the Hearth" the search for buried treasure is the objective correlative of the wrong use of the land.

The wilderness, the Eden, the paradise lost is a theme of *Go Down, Moses,* with echoes, in the story of Ike and his wife, of Adam and Eve and the Fall. The theme of the good earth, used with respect to maintain human life, is most vividly symbolized in Chick Mallison's image of "the beast the plow and the man," "the land's living symbol—a formal group of ritual almost mystic significance" (*Intruder in the Dust,* p. 147), but the theme is not developed. In *The Hamlet* the themes of love and fertility provide the pastoral tone and achieve a mythic transcendence, despite the comic subject, in the idyll of Ike Snopes and the cow. The relation of man to the land is most fully and mysteriously perceived by Mink Snopes in *The Mansion,* in his mystique of the pull of earth and man's bondage and his awareness of earth's beauty.

The last, the most frequently used, of these themes from the timeless past and the realm of myth and legend is the initiation theme, which is both personal and communal, initiation being successful only when the initiate experiences a rebirth which enables him to play a mature role in society. Faulkner's use of this theme exemplifies and corroborates Mircea Eliade's observation in *The Quest:* "The desire to decipher initiatory scenarios in literature, plastic arts, and cinema denotes not only a reevaluation of initiation as a process of spiritual regeneration and transformation, but also a certain nostalgia for an equivalent experience." In *Flags in the Dust* young Bayard refused initiation into an unglamorous peacetime society. By contrast, his grandfather Bayard, in *The Unvanquished,* had experienced initiation first in an ordeal of suffering and violence and then, by moral choice, an ordeal of forbearance. This choice of inaction which required moral courage was followed, as *Flags in the Dust* showed, by the elderly Bayard's life of inaction which was devoid of moral significance. Like young Bayard, Quentin in *The Sound and the Fury* refused initiation and chose death. Horace Benbow's whole experience in *Sanctuary* was an initiation into the social reality to which he had been blinded by his romantic ideals, but he rejected further commitment to an adult role, and Faulkner discarded him. In *Light in August* both Joe Christmas and Byron Bunch had initiatory experiences, but only Byron's succeeded. Sutpen's meditation in the cave in *Absalom, Absalom!* was a retreat to the womb, but his rebirth proved the need of mentors as guides to social responsibilities that accompany social privileges. His ignorance of what his chosen role entailed doomed him to failure. Henry Sutpen's experience in New Orleans was an abortive initiation.

The three last initiation themes are developed most fully, in a kind of logical sequence. Ike McCaslin's initiation into the cult of the hunters in *Go Down, Moses* was a failure because in spirit he never left the initiation retreat to return and play his part in the adult world. Chick Mallison's initiation in *Intruder in the Dust* was successful, both in his service to Lucas and the community and in his acceptance of himself and his people and his determination to work to overcome the evils in the land he loved. After *The Town* and *The Mansion* Faulkner returned to the initiation theme in *The Reivers,* in which the romantic, comic treatment does not conceal the underlying serious intent. By implication, this initiation is the most successful one in Yoknapatawpha, because Lucius Priest, the initiate, is the only character who lived a long life and produced a family continuing into the third generation when Lucius told his story. Faulkner's abiding concern with how a young person learns to take his part in carrying the world of the present into the future complements his concern for the continuation of the family.

The negative and the positive aspects of the personal themes, the flight-pursuit and the journey-quest, provide the Gothic patterns of action so consistently that both negative and positive aspects are present in all the novels discussed and are significant even in the least Gothic, *The Town,* where the quest of Gavin, the courtly lover, involves considerable pursuit and where there are episodes of frantic but comic flight and pursuit— Tom Tom and Turl, and Mrs. Hait and the mule. Flight from unrequited love kept Gavin in Europe from 1914 to 1919.

The extent to which Faulkner retained essential Gothic elements is impressive. He also transformed the Gothic mode in significant respects: by reducing it, by inverting it, and by parodying it. In *Sartoris* he undercut the Gothic effect by counterpointing the story of young Bayard with that of old Bayard and by using Aunt Jenny to deflate the Sartoris vainglory; both these effects are stronger in *Sartoris* than in *Flags in the Dust,* where the romantic-Gothic and grotesque-Gothic characterizations of Horace and of Byron Snopes divert attention from the Sartoris story. In *The Sound and the Fury* Faulkner provided a cheerful present scene in Benjy's and Quentin's sections and substituted psychological horror and pathos for mystery and suspense; the deaths take place offstage.

Omission of horror scenes is a favorite device with Faulkner. In *The Triumph of the Novel* Albert J. Guerard observed that "Dickens, Dostoevsky and Faulkner exhibit melodramatic imaginations in their most serious, most ambitious novels" and that "serious catastrophes," after prolonged anticipation, "are sometimes undertreated when their time at last comes." In *Sanctuary* after the omission of the rape and the understatement of the two murders, the lynching scene is a devastating shock. Similarly, the omission of the actual murder of Joanna Burden in *Light in August* leaves the reader unprepared for the retrospective account of Joe's death in horrible detail, especially after the shift from the terror of Joe's last flight to a focus on the triumphant pursuer, Percy Grimm. In *Absalom, Absalom!* also there is a break in the account of the murder of Sutpen like that in the murder of Joanna. The murders in *Intruder in the Dust* are distanced and understated, but the state of mind of Chick provides tension to lend Gothic suspense and mystery to setting and characters which in themselves are not Gothic. In *Snopes* the combination of Gothic and non-Gothic narrative sequences serves to modify the Gothic effects. Mink's two murders, of Houston and of Flem, admirably illustrate the two extremes of Faulkner's method, completely Gothic treatment and ironic understatement of violence.

In addition to diminishing some of the Gothic horror by such devices, Faulkner frequently, extensively, and significantly used ironic inversion, wherein characters and action are the reverse of what the Romantic or Romantic-Gothic tradition leads one to expect. This is done most completely in *Sanctuary*, to satirize the values and actions of respectable society: those who traditionally would be good guys are the villains, to whom those who are social outcasts are morally and humanely superior. Partial inversion in *Sartoris* had prepared for that in *Sanctuary*, especially in the characterization of Narcissa, who had demonstrated her exaggerated concern for outward appearances and her inner lack of the purity of the image she showed to the world. Because of the shifting points of view in *The Sound and the Fury*, inversion was less obvious and less consistent than in *Sanctuary* and the Gothic pattern less apparent; inversion is present in: the suicide-initiation, the Compson denial of Easter rituals and their meaning, the idiot-Christ, the unchaste Persecuted Maidens. Using the quest-romance pattern in *As I Lay Dying*, Faulkner achieved ironic inversion by having the hero and his allies serve age and death instead of youth and life. Inversion in *Light in August* is only occasional; it is the most consistent in Byron as the un-Byronic hero and most impressive in Joe Christmas as an ironic Christ or dying God. The combination in *Light in August* of Gothic and comic narratives and the inclusion of Northrop Frye's three types of heroes and of Ihab Hassan's major patterns in the ironic form, noted in chapter 5, uniquely exemplify Faulkner's use of ironic inversion in Gothic Yoknapatawpha novels. In *Go Down, Moses*, "Was" shows the most complete inversion of roles, of hunter and hunted, of animal and man, of man and woman, of victor and loser, all in the two patterns of the hunt and the courtly romance. Isaac McCaslin is an ironic Isaac, refusing to be sacrificed; an ironic Adam, losing Paradise but not entering the world; an ironic Gothic heir, relinquishing, not claiming, his inheritance; an ironic Christ, not serving humanity in a sinful world. The chief inversion in *Intruder in the Dust* is in the character of Chick and his initiation: he is a young and innocent detective, a mentor to his own uncle, an initiate with a woman mentor. In the southern tradition, Lucas is an ironic inversion, both as a character of stature and dignity and as the innocent victim instead of the uppity-nigger villain. *Snopes* uses ironic inversion most consistently in the "trickster-tricked" contests and in Flem, as an ironic Faust, seeking low goals and ceasing to strive when those goals were attained. In *The Mansion,* Gavin and Linda become ironic, Gavin as the defeated romantic hero and even, in Pascagoula, a Joseph to Linda as Potiphar's wife, and Linda as the triumphant but morally guilty heroine of the revenge tragedy and the defeated heroine of the courtly love romance. In the revenge tragedy, Mink is an unheroic hero, endowed for the part only with an indomitable will. His murder of Flem goes beyond mere underplaying of violence and in the actual death scene becomes ironic in characters, circumstances, and action.

Closely allied to ironic inversion is parody, which is inherent in Gothic romance. Parody is more comic in effect than irony, which may be bitterly satiric. In *Sartoris* Caspey and Simon are parodic stereotypes of comic Negro characters, and Byron Snopes is a parody of the Byronic hero, not, like Byron Bunch, an ironic inversion with worth and dignity of his own. With Flem in mind, a similar contrast can be perceived between Jason as a parody of Faust and Flem as an ironic inversion who won success in his own limited terms, with Sutpen as the genuine Faust figure providing the pattern in Yoknapatawpha to be inverted. Parody and burlesque accompany the basic sober irony in *Sanctuary* in the characters and actions of Gowan as a romantic hero, Fonzo and Virgil as rustic innocents, Miss Reba and her friends as respectable ladies, and Clarence Snopes as a state Solon. The whole story of Joe Christmas in *Light in August* is a kind of uncomic parody of the archetypal mythic hero; Bobbie is a parody of Barbara Allen, Byron and Lucas are parodies of rival knights, and Lena is a parody of the Persecuted Maiden. The final parody is Lena, Byron, and the baby as the Holy Family. Parody in *Light in August,* however, is superimposed on irony and coexists with multiple levels of meaning and with literary and mythic parallels. In *Go Down, Moses* the pursuit of Turl in "Was" is a parody of a foxhunt, and Sophonsiba is a parody of a Scott-type romantic heroine, in an inversion of a courtship. In "The Bear" Ike's prudish wife is a parody of the Temptress, toned down as seen through Ike's eyes. The most frequent subject of parody in *Snopes* is that of courtly love: in *The Hamlet* Eula with her suitors, Houston and Mink and their loves, and above all, Ike Snopes and the cow; in *The Town* Gavin and Manfred de Spain as rivals for Eula followed by Gavin and Matt Levitt as rivals for Linda; in *The Mansion* (and "Knight's Gambit") Gavin and Melisandre as the knight and the princess in her castle. The most vivid parodic image is that of Mink as the maiden in flight. But the most original and spectacular single passage in the parodic vein is that of Ike and the cow which parodies, as Richard Pindell said, "more than the archetypal journey theme so beloved by the Romantics. In its quixotic excesses, its gracefulness and grotesqueness, it is a demonic parody of an art like Faulkner's that is the natural expression of a love for the earth, which marries imagination and will in an achievement that encourages man to realize his potential."

In addition to the ways in which Faulkner transformed or modified the Gothic elements he used are the ways in which he added new elements. First of all, he based the setting and characters on actual places and contemporary times or the relatively recent past, in an interrelated series of novels. He added individual characters which are not derived from traditional Gothic types: Dilsey, Molly Beauchamp, Aunt Jenny Du Pre, Granny Millard, and Miss Habersham; Lena Grove; Lucas Beauchamp; V. K. Ratliff. In his experiments with point of view Faulkner covered all levels of intelligence, from speechless idiots to highly intelligent, sensitive, and articulate characters; he even entered Hightower's and Mink's minds near death and Houston's at the moment of death. These are additions to the basic ingredients, as it were. Other additions are related to new purposes to which Faulkner adapted the Gothic.

These new purposes were rarely achieved in a single novel; the limited area and society made realistically possible the recurrence of characters, the repetition of incidents, the allusions to local legend, and the continued development of accounts of families and related themes, as in the novels dealing with the Sartorises, the Benbows, the Compsons, the Stevens-Mallisons, and the whole trilogy *Snopes*. The Yoknapatawpha chronicles covered enough time to reflect the historical process of change in Mississippi and, by extension and suggestion, in the South and the New World. This process, epitomized in the colloquy between Cass Edmonds and Ike McCaslin in "The Bear" and in the historical prologues in *Requiem for a Nun,* represents the conversion of the dream of Europe and of the early settlers of America into the nightmare of the present. Thus, Faulkner used the Gothic mode for the purposes of "America's serious literature" as stated by David Madden: for "depicting the *nightmare* results of public and individual guilt." *Absalom, Absalom!* epitomizes, in one novel and four generations, the rise, flourishing, decline, and destruction of the plantation society, but the whole process is reinforced by the parallels with other leading families, Sartorises, Compsons, and McCaslins in particular, in which social change is mirrored in individual consciousness. The Gothic novel which deals with the more or less remote past or with a very limited scene and society in the present and with characters who are oriented to the past cannot attempt such a broad view as Faulkner's of social change and its impact on successive generations.

Only the Indian short stories, *The Unvanquished*, and *Absalom, Absalom!* deal directly with events in the period before Reconstruction. The rest of the Gothic narratives about Yoknapatawpha deal with the twentieth century, chiefly with a time of action approximately that of the writing; Ike's memories in *Go Down, Moses* are recalled in his old age, and he is still living at the time of narration in *The Reivers*, 1961. The bulk of the material which Faulkner adapted to his new purpose deals with the society of Yoknapatawpha from about 1900 to the end of *The Mansion*, in 1946, most of it within the span of Faulkner's own memory. The whole social structure is covered, the caste and class system, the legal system, the churches. In *Yoknapatawpha: Faulkner's "Little Postage Stamp of Native Soil"* I cover the mythic society and indicate factual parallels.

The breakdown of the family in training the young, the disruption of families by miscegenation and caste distinctions, the physical and mental degeneracy in "normal" white families are dramatized in the stories of the Sartorises, Compsons, Sutpens, and McCaslins. The corruption of the legal system by respectable white society is demonstrated in *Sanctuary*, in the trial of a white man; the inability of law forces to protect Negro prisoners is a factor in "Pantaloon in Black," *Light in August*, *Intruder in the Dust*, and "Dry September." *Light in August* covers the whole range of indictments of white society: the lack of Christian brotherhood and the failure of the Church; the failure of the legal system, when the supposed race of a man is taken as proof of guilt; the failure of organized charity in caring for orphans and the failure of families of all white classes in bringing up children; the stranglehold of the past on minds and lives in the present. The cumulative effect of these failures of society is well illustrated by Joanna Burden's retelling of the story of Colonel Sartoris's white-supremacy killing of the Burden men during Reconstruction, with an implicit analogy, it develops, between Colonel Sartoris and Percy Grimm, both of whom acted as they were conditioned to act by their society and its codes.

Of all the failures and weaknesses with which he dealt, Faulkner seemed most concerned with the failure of the family and society to preserve and observe meaningful rituals by which to initiate the young into mature life. In the various initiation experiences of young men in Yoknapatawpha, only Ike McCaslin's was conducted by a responsible group of older men according to a well-established pattern which the boy was familiar with and eagerly anticipated mastering. The failure was due to Ike's own shortcomings. The other initiations were improvised and irregular, and the successful ones, including that in *The Reivers*, involved women who were not typical of southern wives and mothers. Chick Mallison, seeking a guide to the proper moral imperative, found it in neither society nor his beloved Uncle Gavin but only in Miss Habersham. One of the great strengths of Faulkner's characterizations in his Gothic novels is his intense sympathy with and understanding of young people; his indictment of families and society is that they have failed to give their children love and emotional security or to instill in them by precept and example sound moral and ethical principles, truths to live by.

By great good fortune Faulkner had at his disposal what the original Gothic novelists, and even those of the generation before his, had lacked: the insight into the unconscious provided by Freud. Thus, in dealing with the irrational and instinctual aspects of the psyche, Faulkner was able to combine the subjective techniques of modern fiction with knowledge of depth psychology. His structural use of the id, the ego, and the superego in *The Sound and the Fury* and the Freudian interpretation of *Sanctuary,* as explained by Carvel Collins and Dr. Lawrence Kubie, have been noted. William Brown regarded Faulkner's preoccupation with horror and perversion as evidence that he was a good writer: he "creates, reproduces, delves into, and draws implications from the very consciousness of the psychotic," using full technical symptomatology based on psychiatric theory and practice. Faulkner also possessed innate perception which allowed him to anticipate the work of later psychologists; according to Glenn Sandstrom, Faulkner had a "profound perception into the darkest and deepest wells of the human personality" and "a brilliant, raw psychological intuition which could cut like a laser to the center of human thought and emotion." Nowhere is this intuition more fully exercised than in the exhaustive probing into sociopathological causes of murder in *Light in August,* beginning with the dawn of self-awareness in Joe. As if the study of alienation and obsession in Joe were not enough, Faulkner matched it with that of Hightower, rooted in quite different causes and manifest in stasis rather than in violence. To pour into a whole row of old bottles of Gothicism a new wine fermented by a powerful creative imagination, stimulated by technical knowledge, and irradiated by intuition, this was Faulkner's distinctive achievement in Gothic characterization.

The Gothic revival of interest in the irrational side of man's consciousness tended to undervalue the rational side which had been too exclusively the concern of the age of reason. This lack of balance Faulkner could avoid because the scope of the Yoknapatawpha cycle allowed him to include characters who combined imagination and sympathy with reason and whose lives were more satisfactory and useful than those of either the irrational or the too rational characters. V. K. Ratliff, Gavin Stevens, and Chick Mallison are normal in the terms of William Brown's definition: they have ideals, humanistic moral values, and fundamental decency, and they manage to maintain the equilibrium which is a defense against chaos: "The maintenance of this tenuous equilibrium is so important as sometimes to require even that evil be condoned." Such characters are naturally rare in Gothic novels but can be accommodated in the Yoknapatawpha cycle because, first, the ample scope permits non-Gothic elements, and, second, the point of view of normal characters under stress involves multiple levels of consciousness and irrational phenomena which serve to illuminate the dark and secret areas in man's psyche. The apparent paradox of light out of darkness was neatly expressed by Alfred Kazin, referring to Faulkner's novels: "The essential thing in all these books was a sense of havoc and conflict, of human storm, blood madness and the irrational, of the unconscious possessing the human spirit but using it . . . to make history. History always implies meaning."

As the omniscient author, Faulkner could express his moral and ethical convictions, or he could use normal characters as spokesmen or reflectors, such as those mentioned above. He could always convey his meaning through the narrative events and thematic ideas. Instead of the good-evil polarity that Gothic romance often took over from medieval romance and that even Gavin echoed in his theory about the conflict in Joe Christmas between good white blood and bad black blood, Faulkner represented evil as white: in *Sanctuary, Light in August, Absalom, Absalom! Go Down, Moses,* and *Intruder in the Dust,* and finally in Clarence Snopes in *The Mansion* and Butch Lovemaiden in *The Reivers.* Only in *Sanctuary* are black and white relationships and black characters not involved. The white man's burden, the black cross, the white man himself had raised by his own guilty deeds. Joe Christmas, the one apparently Negro criminal in action in Yoknapatawpha, was not certainly a Negro and in any case was a victim from birth of white society and white heredity, with Doc Hines as his grandfather. In the later novels, in which there are enough normal characters to convey moral and ethical meaning directly, Faulkner finally enunciated his basic principles: the ideal character is one who, like Chick, acts as a responsible member of society to change what is wrong. As Gavin said, Chick must refuse to bear "injustice and outrage and dishonor and shame" (*Intruder in the Dust,* p. 206). The same principles, Faulkner showed, apply to all men, black or white, and human dignity must be respected, regardless of caste or class. *Intruder in the Dust* dramatizes both the American Dream and the American Nightmare by revealing the unconscious reasons for and the conscious reactions to race hatred which violates these principles. No more serious new purpose could be conceived for revitalizing the Gothic tradition.

The originality of Faulkner's adaptations of the Gothic tradition and the imaginative power of his creations provide the basis for his influence on other writers, particularly the southern Gothic novelists. John Irwin's interpretation of the implications of the doubling and incest images extends to the whole of the Yoknapatawpha cycle:

For Faulkner, doubling and incest are both images of the self-enclosed—the inability of the ego to break out of the circle of the self and of the individual to break out of the ring of the family—and as such, both appear in his novels as symbols of the state of the South after the Civil War, symbols of a region turned in upon itself. Thus, the temporal aspects of doubling and incest evoke the way in which the circle of the self-enclosed repeats itself through time as a cycle, the way that the inability to break out of the ring of the self and the family becomes the inability of successive generations to break out of the cyclic repetition of self-enclosure.

The comprehensive but irregular scheme which connects the Yoknapatawpha novels demands much of the reader; he must work out his own synthesis of the many characters and events and determine what the unifying elements are beneath the multiplicity; the Gothic strand is only one of many. A total setting is created, seen at night and by day, in all seasons, through more than a hundred years. The country and the people are observed by a multitude of characters of all degrees of intelligence and sensitivity, of varied temperaments and moral proclivities. By using the Gothic strand so extensively, Faulkner was implicitly allying himself with "the tradition of the new," which, Leslie Fiedler said, finds parody "a kind of *necessary* final act of destroying the past." Believing, as he said to Jean Stein, that "life is motion, and motion is concerned with what makes man move—which is ambition, power, pleasure," Faulkner belonged naturally to the tradition that accepts change and will not be held in bondage to the past. By choosing the Gothic mode, he was recognizing that man's "moral conscience is the curse he had to accept from the gods in order to gain from them the right to dream." He recreated the motivating dreams of the past in a specific region and showed how its society was destroyed by what was wrong with its dreams or by its failure to attain and maintain what was right. He was answering, in terms of that society, the questions posed by David Madden in the introduction to *American Dreams, American Nightmares:* "What is the psychological basis for the development of dreams and nightmares? What in human nature explains the flowering and withering of American Dreams? What in man wilfully perverts the Dream into nightmare? What, even in the most fervent dreamer, prevents realization of the Dream, or even wishes it to fail and celebrates its decline or death?"

To his gallery of Gothic characters Faulkner added some untypical new characters which have won a permament place in American literature as representing individual worth regardless of distinctions of class or caste: Dilsey, Molly Beauchamp, Lucas, Sam Fathers, Joe Christmas, and finally, Uncle Parsham and Uncle Ned McCaslin. These characters in Yoknapatawpha serve to illustrate David Madden's statement: "From the beginning, the Indian and the Negro have been the most visible contradictions of the [American] Dream." The supposed Negro blood of Joe Christmas made him a visible man, as the obvious Negro blood of Ralph Ellison's hero made him an invisible man. The change in Faulkner's interest and concern from the pseudoaristocrats to the common man, both black and white, was also clearly revealed in Mink Snopes, whose murderous intent and action are somehow purged of baseness by his unfaltering will to prove himself a man, and in V. K. Ratliff, born as V. K. Suratt in *Flags in the Dust,* who would be the ideal man of good will if he had sired others of his kind. Ratliff is the one major character who played an active role in all three volumes of *Snopes* and whose point of view and ideas bear considerable resemblance to Faulkner's. Necessarily, such normal characters as Ratliff and Gavin Stevens and Chick Mallison and Granny Millard and Aunt Jenny Du Pre and Miss Habersham do not appear frequently in the most Gothic contexts, but they serve as a standard by which to estimate the Gothic characters: these normal characters, according to William Brown's criteria, are generally free from excessive guilt feelings and repressions and other crippling psychic conflict; they can perceive reality as it appears in the light of day and can make commonsense distinctions between beliefs and delusions. They wake from their dreams, but they do not forget them.

The absurdity of Faulkner's fictional world has been remarked on by various critics. William Brown considered that superabsurdity is at the center of this world and saw a parallel with Camus and the myth of Sisyphus. In *The Absurd* Arnold Hinchliffe cited R. W. B. Lewis, *The Picaresque Saint* (1960), as including Camus, Faulkner, and Graham Greene among novelists whose ambiguous heroes respond to absurdity. Hinchliffe noted that in *Radical Innocence,* limited to American writers since World War II, Ihab Hassan took absurdity for granted. Richard Hauck devoted the last two chapters of *A Cheerful Nihilism* to Faulkner and John Barth. In the absurd world there is no value or meaning. But on the margins of Faulkner's absurd world are always those who provide value and meaning, as Ratliff and Gavin do for the absurd world of the Snopeses. The allusion to Camus suggests existential qualities combined with the Gothic. The existentialist approach, in fact, has value for most of the Yoknapatawpha novels and has been dealt with in three articles by William J. Sowder on Thomas Sutpen, Joe Christmas, and Lucas Beauchamp (in *Intruder in the Dust*), and by Robert Slabey in an article on *As I Lay Dying*.

William Faulkner belongs to the literary tradition of the Western world, before and after the Enlightenment, and has carried that tradition forward in the twentieth century to reflect the concerns of artists of his own and younger generations. William Brown said that "Faulkner feels the reality of a metaphysical power as inimical as the Furies of Aeschylus or Conrad's Powers of Darkness." I cannot resist adding, with amazement and amusement, the view of Faulkner advanced by Yashar Kemal, a Turkish novelist whom Paul Theroux met on the Orient Express: ". . . the greatest Marxist writer was William Faulkner." Theroux envisioned Yashar's dream of a socialist paradise, "a Soviet pastoral where the workers own the means of production and complete sets of Faulkner." Although I do not endorse the Marxist interpretation of Faulkner, examination of his work in the light of the absurd or of existentialism or of any other significant literary or philosophical frame of reference related to aspects of his work is likely to be valid and rewarding. Gothicism, however, encompasses more elements of content and technique than does any other traditional or current literary trend and, as an amalgam, can and does coexist with various other patterns. Preeminent among the predecessors from whom Faulkner received his Gothic heritage were Charles Dickens and Joseph Conrad and the great nineteenth-century Americans Melville, Hawthorne, and Mark Twain. In "Faulkner: The European Roots" Richard P. Adams stated that "the author whose name or whose work or characters Faulkner mentioned most often . . . was Dickens." In his comparison of *Absalom, Absalom!* with works of Dickens, Louis Berrone concluded that Faulkner's characters correspond to characters in Dickens and "often become vicious, impious, and grotesque because of inordinate future-boundness or past-boundness, and because of self-bound attitudes toward change that blind them to communal obligations."

Albert J. Guerard's comparative study of Dickens, Dostoevsky, and Faulkner, *The Triumph of the Novel*, was not available soon enough to receive the consideration it merits. Guerard stresses the melodramatic imagination of the three novelists and hence deals with narrative qualities, patterns, and techniques which are also characteristic of Gothic fiction. Although he rarely uses "Gothic," his critical analysis abounds in "fantastic," "grotesque," "dream-like," "macabre" and other terms indispensable in discussion of Gothicism. He ends his discussion of Faulkner with "*Absalom, Absalom!*: The Novel as Impressionistic Art" and concludes that this novel "is, perhaps, the greatest American novel." The triumph is, perhaps, that of the American *Gothic* novel.

Faulkner, in turn, added to the richness of the Gothic heritage and has bequeathed it to the world. The achievement which set an example for the next generation of southern writers was formidable. Alfred Kazin called Faulkner's novels "the most intensely imagined and comprehensive record of separateness, powerlessness, poverty, mania, defeat, of a pride and secret renewal unknown to anyone but an isolated Southerner." Leslie Fiedler, in *Waiting for the End,* regarded Faulkner as "the last of the old Southern writers," who "helped create the legend of the South" by "his notion of a baffled aspiration to the tragic, nurtured by dreams and memories, falling away always, in fact, into melodrama or farce." In *An End to Innocence* Fiedler said that for us, the readers, "the truth of Faulkner's world is a symbolic truth; and across his gothic landscape is fought not the historical war between North and South, but the eternal war between the dream of nobility and order and the fact of disorder and failure and sorrow." "Faulkner and Melville and James," Fiedler said, "these are the American novelists who function as living influences today."

Flannery O'Connor's picturesque statement of the problem of the southern writer is deservedly familiar: "The presence alone of Faulkner in our midst makes a great difference in what the writer can and cannot permit himself to do. Nobody wants his mule and wagon stalled on the same track the Dixie Limited is roaring down." But unlike the Dixie Limited, the Gothic track can run in any territory. References in the preceding chapters to Flannery O'Connor and others of her generation of southern writers have indicated that the Gothic journey may successfully follow other southern tracks.

By pure serendipity, aided by my natural procrastination, evidence hot off the press was provided to show Faulkner's continued domination of the southern literary scene. In the *Saturday Review* for September 4, 1976, Bruce Cook began "New Faces in the Faulkner Country": "Looking back, it may seem that William Faulkner was always there, looming gigantically, a presence, a writer who so dominated the tradition that it appeared to have originated with him." Much of that tradition which he seemed to have originated, Faulkner had inherited and transformed. Cook continues, confirming what has been said in this book concerning the post-Faulkner generation of southern novelists: ". . . there can be no doubt that the work of William Faulkner has had a direct, deep, and widespread influence on some of them. . . ." The problem that confronts the southern heirs to the literary heritage Faulkner left them was stated by Louis Rubin, quoted by Cook: "'The Faulknerian ordering of the Southern experience must be adapted, changed, revised, so that what is still valid can be used, while what is outmoded will not get in the way." Cook quite rightly points out that the South is changing, but wrongly seems to think that those changes, especially urbanization, will necessarily mark an end to such Faulknerian elements as a sense of place. But the pervasive elements of Gothicism found in Faulkner can be adapted to other settings with which the characters do not identify themselves, to Hollywood in Nathanael West's *The Day of the Locust,* to New York in Ralph Ellison's *Invisible Man,* to Italy in William Styron's *Set This House on Fire.* The influence of Faulkner is not necessarily the chief source of Gothicism in later writers; but his work, like that of Dickens, contributes significantly to the Gothic tradition and to its capacity to accommodate the dreams and nightmares of modern civilization, rural or urban, American or European, Asian or Antipodean. One of the fringe benefits of my own involvement in Faulkner criticism has been the friendship of a chance-met Australian woman writer, Patsy Adam-Smith, who became a Faulkner fan because Yoknapatawpha reminded her so much of Tasmania, where she grew up. The extent to which Faulkner is recognized as one of the great writers of the world can be appreciated only in light of evidence: Faulkner criticism and translations, the records of visitors to the Faulkner Collection at the University of Mississippi, and academic interest in Faulkner which produces whole issues of scholarly journals devoted to Faulkner in the United States and France, as well as a stream of doctoral dissertations, 137 in the United States in the five-year period from 1970 through 1974.

William Faulkner inherited the Gothic tradition from his European and American predecessors and so absorbed it, consciously or unconsciously, into his own creative imagination that he enriched the tradition for the pleasure of readers and the profit of writers. But let writers beware of the folly of seeking the Gothic treasure only in the soil of the Deep South. For Gothic writers who would emulate the Brontës or Dickens or Hawthorne or Faulkner, the world is all before them. The Dixie Limited itself, Percy Adams assures us, "is not resting on a siding in Yoknapatawpha County; it has no local transitory load but an enormous schedule to meet as it goes throughout the world and passes other 'Specials,' each carrying its great band of international passangers." Yoknapatawpha has won a place on the timeless map of the Gothic world, and William Faulkner remains its "Sole Owner and Proprietor."

NOTES/BIBLIOGRAPHY/INDEX

FOREWORD: A Reader's Guide

In this book a bibliography-index provides the essential information about critical sources which is usually given by a system of obtrusive or elusive superscript numbers in the text, often called footnote numbers. But the notes are rarely footnotes, conveniently located by a downward glance from the number, but are usually found at the back of the book, grouped by chapters. In lieu of this system each author cited is named in the text, with the title if more than one work by that author has been used, and in the bibliography-index at the back of the book a complete entry for each author and each work cited is given in a single alphabetical listing. Each bibliographical entry is followed, in square brackets, by the index number, in boldface type, of the page in the text and by the page number(s) in the source for the passage(s) cited on that page in the text, as in the following example:

Beck, Warren, *Faulkner: Essays by Warren Beck.* Madison: University of Wisconsin Press, 1976. [**91**: 242, 263; **99**: 243; **202**: 632]

Please note the punctuation: a colon between index number and source number(s) and a semicolon between index and source page-number *groups*. An index number without a source page number indicates a citation of that work without reference to a specific passage. Repetition of an index number in a second cluster of numbers indicates a break on that page in the sequence of the references to that source, either a break in thought or a shift to another source before another reference to the previous source. (See the first column of numbers under "Fiedler, *Love and Death in the American Novel*": **14, 14** and **17, 17** are examples of the two kinds of repetition of index numbers.)

Entries under an editor's name have no index or source numbers unless the editor is quoted. (See the two entries under "Bloom, Harold" and the one after "Corrigan, Robert W.")

The same index and source page-number system used for nonfiction works cited in the text applies to the nonfiction works of Faulkner and to Joseph Blotner's *Faulkner: A Biography,* listed in the first section of the bibliography/index. Quotations from Faulkner's novels in the text are followed in parentheses by page numbers in the edition specified in the list of novels.

With no superscript numbers to nudge him, the reader can cheerfully ignore the bibliography or can more easily refer to the author's name in the bibliography than to an entry in an end note. For a few authors of several works cited, like Leslie Fiedler and Northrop Frye, a title has to be given in the text, but short titles or key words are usually adequate, such as *Love and Death* for the chief book by Fiedler and "Calvinistic" or "Apocalyptic" to distinguish between Ilse Dusoir Lind's articles on *Light in August.*

A few authors and even fewer single works have been cited often enough to require listing of numbers in columns instead of horizontally. Frequent citation of an author serves as an implicit critical annotation as to the usefulness of that author for my purpose.

The Ph.D. dissertations listed, with most of the other dissertations on Faulkner, are available for use in the Faulkner collection in the University of Mississippi Library. Most of them are in book form, enlarged and reproduced from microfilm. A print-out in October 1975 by the Comprehensive Dissertation Query Service listed more than 270 dissertations on William Faulkner's works. I have referred to only those dissertations which proved germane to my subject; none of these dealt with Gothicism as such.

Those readers who make use of footnotes will find the requisite information in the bibliography, in a single listing without duplication of data. Those who find notes an interruption or irritation can ignore the bibliography. By authors' names in the text and the data in the bibliography I have identified and given due credit to all writers who have contributed to my understanding of the fictional tradition represented in Gothicism and to my interpretation of Gothicism in Faulkner's Yoknapatawpha novels.

BIBLIOGRAPHY

The following works of fiction and nonfiction by William Faulkner and the biography by Joseph Blotner are published in New York by Random House.

Yoknapatawpha novels and stories:
Flags in the Dust, ed. Douglas Day. 1973.
Sartoris. © 1929, 1956.
The Sound and the Fury. Modern Library College ed., photographic reproduction of 1st printing, 7 October 1929.
Sanctuary. © 1931, 1958.
Light in August. Vintage ed., photographic reproduction of 1st printing, 6 October 1932.
Absalom, Absalom! Modern Library ed., facsimile of 1st ed., 1936.
The Unvanquished. Photographic reproduction of 1st printing, 15 February 1938.
Go Down, Moses. Modern Library ed., © 1942.
Intruder in the Dust. 12th printing, © 1948.
Knight's Gambit. 4th printing, © 1949.
Collected Stories of William Faulkner. N.d.
Requiem for a Nun. N.d.; © 1950, 1951.
Snopes: A Trilogy. 3 vols. 1964.
    1 *The Hamlet.* 3rd ed. rev., 1964.
    2 *The Town.* 4th printing, © 1957.
    3 *The Mansion.* 3rd printing, © 1959.

Collections of nonfiction:
William Faulkner: Essays, Speeches, and Public Letters. ed. James B. Meriwether, 1965. "On Privacy" [**182**: 62]
Lion in the Garden: Interviews with William Faulkner, 1926–1962. Eds. James B. Meriwether, Michael Millgate. 1968.

Published version of recorded conferences and speeches:
Faulkner at Nagano. Ed. Robert A. Jelliffe. Tokyo: Kenkyusha, 1956. (Identified in the text by "Faulkner" and the title or "Nagano.")

56: 104	**88**: 143	**159**: 78
63: 103	**145**: 51, 78, 92	**182**: 97

Faulkner in the University: Class Conferences at the University of Virginia, 1957–1958. Eds. Frederick L. Gwynn, Joseph L. Blotner. Charlottesville: Univeristy of Virginia Press, 1959. (Identified in the text usually by "Faulkner" without the title.)

38: 97, 98	**69**: 2	**157**: 236, 246
39: 94	**109**: 199	**160**: 60
54: 268	**115**: 199	**162**: 142
55: 61	**121**: 97, 118	**167**: 142
55: 87	**129**: 119	**183**: 246
56: 17	**139**: 39	**186**: 50, 150
60: 85	**145**: 51, 78, 92	**190**: 141
63: 263	**153**: 275	

KEY: Bold-faced numbers indicate pages of *this* book on which reference to cited work appears. Numbers following colon indicate the specific page reference in the *cited* work.

Biography:
Blotner, Joseph L. *Faulkner: A Biography.* 2 vols.: 1:1–909; 2:913–1846. 1975.
(Identified in the text by "Blotner.")

46: 1:698, 829	**110:** 1:701–02	**184:** 2:1097
78: 1:209	**139:** 2:1077	**188:** 2:962
83: 1:531–32	**155:** 1:177	**213:** 1:116, 54
86: 1:583–84	**164:** 1:657	**222:** 1:138–39, 660, 669–70
90: 1:492		

Bibliographies and catalogues:
Bassett, John. *William Faulkner: An Annotated Checklist of Criticism.* New York: David Lewis, 1972.
McHaney, Thomas L. *William Faulkner: A Reference Guide.* Boston: Hall, 1975.
Massey, Linton R., comp. *William Faulkner: "Man Working," 1919–1962: A Catalogue of the William Faulkner Collections at the University of Virginia.* Charlottesville: Bibliographical Society, University of Virginia, 1968.
Petersen, Carl. *Each in Its Ordered Place: A Faulkner Collector's Notebook.* Ann Arbor: Ardis, 1975.

Adamowski, Thomas H. "The Dickens World and Yoknapatawpha County: A Study of Character and Society in Dickens and Faulkner." Ph.D. dissertation, Indiana University, 1969. [**33:** 261, 263; **44:** 277; **47:** 264; **67:** 89; **110:** 139, 132, 146; **167:** 227; **173:** 233; **174:** 251, 233; **191:** 51, 52]
–––. "Joe Christmas: The Tyranny of Childhood." *Novel: A Forum on Fiction* 4 (Spring 1971), 240–51. [**130:** 250]
Adams, Percy G. "Faulkner, French Literature, and Eternal Verities." *William Faulkner: Prevailing Verities and World Literature.* Eds. Wolodymyr T. Zyla, Wendell M. Aycock. *Proceedings of the Comparative Literature Symposium,* vol. 6. Lubbock: Interdept. Comm. on Comp. Lit., Texas Tech. University Press, 1973, pp. 7–24. [**248:** 21]
Adams, Richard P. "Faulkner: The European Roots." *Faulkner: Fifty Years after "The Marble Faun."* Ed. George H. Wolfe. University: University of Alabama Press, 1976, pp. 21–41. [**246:** 25]
–––. *Faulkner: Myth and Motion.* Princeton: Princeton University Press, 1968. [**215:** 29]
Appel, Alfred. "The Grotesque and the Gothic." *A Season of Dreams: The Fiction of Eudora Welty.* Baton Rouge: Louisiana State University Press, 1969, pp. 73–103. [**21:** 74]
Axton, William F. *Circle of Fire: Dickens' Vision and Style and the Popular Victorian Theater.* Lexington: University of Kentucky Press, 1966. [**91:** 223; **104:** 111]
Barrett, William. "Backward toward the Earth." *Time of Need: Forms of Imagination in the Twentieth Century.* New York: Harper, 1972, pp. 96–129. [**30:** 125; **61:** 106; **67:** 104, 114; **73:** 107]
Baumbach, Jonathan. *The Landscape of Nightmare: Studies in the Contemporary American Novel.* New York: New York University Press, 1965. [**22:** 15]
Beach, Joseph Warren. "William Faulkner: The Haunted South"; "William Faulkner: Virtuoso." *American Fiction, 1920–1940.* New York: Macmillan, 1941, pp. 123–69. [**52:** 143]

KEY: Bold-faced numbers indicate pages of *this* book on which reference to cited work appears. Numbers following colon indicate the specific page reference in the *cited* work.

Beck, Warren. *Faulkner: Essays by Warren Beck.* Madison: University of Wisconsin Press, 1976. [**91:** 242, 262; **99:** 243; **202:** 643]

———. *Man in Motion: Faulkner's Trilogy.* Madison: University of Wisconsin Press, 1961. [**185:** 105; **192:** 139; **193:** 149, 165; **193:** 200; **202:** 171; **214:** 29; **215:** 180; **217:** 183]

Bentley, Eric. "Melodrama." *Tragedy: Vision and Form.* Ed. Robert W. Corrigan. San Francisco: Chandler, 1965, pp. 217-31. [**17:** 223, 222; **18:** 221; **26:** 221; **46:** 224; **213:** 221]

Bergonzi, Bernard. *The Situation of the Novel.* Harmondsworth, Middlesex: Penguin, 1972. [**9:** 79; **13:** 98, 99-100]

Berrone, Louis. "Faulkner's *Absalom, Absalom!* and Dickens: A Study of Time and Change Correspondences." Ph.D. dissertation, Fordham University, 1973. [**246:** 244]

Bleikasten, André. *"The Most Splendid Failure": Faulkner's "The Sound and the Fury."* Bloomington: Indiana University Press, 1976. [**54:** 119-20, 148, 114; **65:** 173]

———. "La Terreur et la nausée, ou le langage des corps dans *Sanctuaire."* *Sud—Revue trimestrielle,* no. 14/15: *Faulkner* (1975), 81-116. [**233:** 88, 89]

Bloom, Harold. "The Internalization of Quest-Romance." *Romanticism and Consciousness.* Ed. Harold Bloom. New York: Norton, 1970, pp. 3-24. [**15:** 12]

Bloom, Harold, ed. *Romanticism and Consciousness: Essays in Criticism.* New York: Norton, 1970.

Bowling, Lawrence E. "Faulkner and the Theme of Innocence." *Kenyon Review* 20 (Summer 1958): 466-87. [**63:** 477, 481, 467]

Breyer, Bernard R. "A Diagnosis of Violence in Recent Southern Fiction." *Mississippi Quarterly* 14 (Spring 1961): 59-67. [**48:** 67]

Brooks, Cleanth. "Faulkner's *Sanctuary:* The Discovery of Evil." *Sewanee Review* 71 (Winter 1963): 1-24. [**100:** 13]

———. "The Narrative Structure of *Absalom, Absalom!"* *Georgia Review* 29 (Summer 1975): 366-94. [**43:** 366, 367, 368; **47:** 384]

———. *William Faulkner: The Yoknapatawpha Country.* New Haven: Yale University Press, 1963. [**29:** 295, 296, 311; **40:** 319, 318; **43:** 438]

Bross, Addison C. *"Soldiers' Pay* and the Art of Aubrey Beardsley." *American Quarterly* 19 (Spring 1967): 3-23. [**19:** 23, 6]

Brown, Calvin. "Faulkner's Manhunts: Fact into Fiction." *Georgia Review* 20 (Winter 1966): 388-95. [**122:**]

Brown, William R. "Faulkner's Paradox in Pathology and Salvation: *Sanctuary, Light in August, Requiem for a Nun."* *Texas Studies in Literature and Language* 9 (Autumn 1967): 429-49. [**96:** 431; **101:** 431, 432]

———. "William Faulkner's Use of the Material of Abnormal Psychology in Characterization." Ph.D. dissertation, University of Arkansas, 1965.

34: 127, 116, 138, 143
62: 149
62: 159, 158
65: 166
96: 56
116: 86
121: 55

123: 76, 79, 80
125: 64, 65, 68, 72
130: 443
167: 27-37
186: 33-34
192: 35, 41, 42
213: 164, 183, 171, 193

228: 16, 27
230: 59
242: 10, 9, 4
243: 34-35, 37
245: 30-31, 33
245: 275
246: 163

Brylowski, Walter. *Faulkner's Olympian Laugh: Myth in the Novels.* Detroit: Wayne State University Press, 1968. [**169:** 68; **176:** 173; **186:** 201; **188:** 144; **189:** 147; **191:** 139]

KEY: Bold-faced numbers indicate pages of *this* book on which reference to cited work appears. Numbers following colon indicate the specific page reference in the *cited* work.

Cabau, Jacques. *La Prairie perdue: histoire du roman américain.* Paris: Editions du Seuil, 1966. [**24:** 228; **25:** 57; **114:** 230; **118:** 229; **121:** 232; **134:** 236; **220:** 35]

Cawelti, John G. "The Concept of Formula in the Study of Popular Literature." *Criticism and Culture.* Papers of the Midwest Modern Language Association, no. 2. Iowa City: *MMLA,* 1972, pp. 115-23. [**5:** 123, 122]

Chase, Richard. "The Stone and the Crucifixion: Faulkner's *Light in August."* *Kenyon Review* 10 (Autumn 1948): 539-51. [**112:** 544; **115**]

Clayborough, Arthur. *The Grotesque in English Literature.* Oxford: Clarendon Press, 1965. [**12:** 182; **229:** 99]

Coindreau, Maurice-Edwar. *Mémoires d'un traducteur: Entretiens avec Christian Guidicelli.* Paris: Gallimard, 1974.

Collins, Carvel. "A Conscious Literary Use of Freud?" *Literature and Psychology* 3 (June 1953): 2-4. [**53; 309**]

–––. "Nathanael West's *The Day of the Locust* and *Sanctuary."* *Faulkner Studies* 2 (Summer 1953): 23-24. [**13; 115:** 23-24]

–––. "William Faulkner's *The Sound and the Fury."* *Explicator* 17 (December 1958), item 19. [**55**]

Conley, Timothy K. "Beardsley and Faulkner." *Journal of Modern Literature* 5 (September 1976): 339-56. [**19:** 348]

Cook, Bruce. "New Faces in the Faulkner Country." *Saturday Review* (4 September 1976): 39-41. [**248:** 39, 41]

Cook, Richard M. "Popeye, Flem, and Sutpen: The Faulknerian Villain as Grotesque." *Studies in American Fiction* 3 (Spring 1975): 3-14. [**46:** 12, 9, 10, 11]

Coolidge, Archibald C., Jr. *Charles Dickens as a Serial Novelist.* Ames: Iowa State University Press, 1967. [**6:** 105]

Corridori, Edward L. "The Quest for Sacred Space: Setting in the Novels of William Faulkner." Ph.D. dissertation, Kent State University, 1971. [**41:** 124; **58:** 101; **67:** 101; **76:** 132; **91:** 73; **149:** 53; **165:** 59; **199:** 157]

Corrigan, Robert W., ed. *Tragedy: Vision and Form.* San Francisco: Chandler, 1965.

Cowan, James C. "Dream-Work in the Quentin Section of *The Sound and the Fury."* *Literature and Psychology* 24, no. 3 (1974): 91-98. [**53**]

Cowley, Malcolm. *The Faulkner-Cowley File: Letters and Memories, 1944-1962.* New York: Viking, 1966. [**35:** 13; **138:** 113; **143:** 113]

Creighton, Joanne V. "Self-Destructive Evil in *Sanctuary."* *Twentieth Century Literature* 18 (October 1972): 259-70. [**102:** 269]

Cullen, John, in collaboration with Floyd C. Watkins. *Old Times in the Faulkner Country.* Chapel Hill: University of North Carolina Press, 1961. [**122:** ch. 13]

Dauner, Louise. "Quentin and the Walking Shadow: The Dilemma of Nature and Culture." *Arizona Quarterly* 21 (Summer 1965): 159-71. [**70:** 163, 159; **71:** 164-65]

Davis, Roger L. "William Faulkner, V. K. Ratliff, and the Snopes Saga (1925-1940)." Ph.D. dissertation, University of California, Los Angeles, 1971. [**76:** 44, 47]

Detweiler, Robert. "The Moment of Death in Modern Fiction." *Contemporary Literature* 13 (Summer 1972): 269-94. [**208:** 275, 276, 279, 292, 294]

Devlin, Albert J. "Parent-Child Relationships in the Works of William Faulkner." Ph.D. dissertation, University of Kansas, 1970. [**78:** 144]

–––. "*Sartoris:* Rereading the MacCallum Episode." *Twentieth Century Literature* 17 (April 1971): 83-90. [**231:** 83]

KEY: Bold-faced numbers indicate pages of *this* book on which reference to cited work appears. Numbers following colon indicate the specific page reference in the *cited* work.

Dussinger, Gloria R. "Faulkner's Isaac McCaslin as a Romantic Hero Manqué." *South Atlantic Quarterly* 68 (Summer 1969): 377–85. [**146**: 380; **148**: 378; **154**: 379; **155**: 381–82; **157**: 381; **159**: 383; **181**: 282; **181**]

Early, James. *The Making of "Go Down, Moses."* Dallas: Southern Methodist University Press, 1972. [**137**: 32–34, 15]

Eberly, Ralph D. "Immediacy, Suspense, and Meaning in William Faulkner's *The Sound and the Fury:* An Experiment in Critical Analysis." Ph.D. dissertation, University of Michigan, 1953. [**68**: 1–2]

Ehrstine, John. "Byron and the Metaphysic of Self-Destruction." *The Gothic Imagination.* Ed. G. R. Thompson. Pullman: Washington State University Press, 1974, pp. 94–108. [**18**: 94, 95; **35**: 102]

Eliade, Mircea. *The Quest: History and Meaning in Religion.* Chicago: University of Chicago Press, 1969. [**23**: 121, 66; **154**: 124, 126; **155**: 93, 95, 97; **156**: 113, 114; **158**: 113, 115; **236**: 69; **236**: 125–26]

–––. *Rites and Symbols of Initiation: The Mysteries of Birth and Rebirth.* 1958; rpt., New York: Harper Torchbooks, 1965. [**147**: 70; **167**: 53–54, 55; **172**: 116; **174**: 61, 64; **174**: 15; **179**: 114]

Emerson, O. B. "Bill's Friend Phil." *Journal of Mississippi History* 32 (May 1970): 135–45. [**220**: 145]

Esslinger, Pat M., et al. "No Spinach in *Sanctuary.*" *Modern Fiction Studies* 18 (Winter 1972–1973): 555–58. [**90**: 558, 557]

Fadiman, Regina K. *Faulkner's "Light in August": A Description and Interpretation of the Revisions.* Charlottesville: University Press of Virginia, 1975. [**135**: 203, 209]

Ferguson, Robert C. "The Grotesque in the Fiction of William Faulkner." Ph.D. dissertation, Case Western Reserve University, 1971. [**20**]

Fiedler, Leslie A. "The Dream of the New." *American Dreams, American Nightmares.* Ed. David Madden. Carbondale: Southern Illinois University Press, 1970, pp. 19–28. [**16**: 24, 26, 27; **244**: 27]

–––. *An End to Innocence: Essays in Culture and Politics.* Boston: Beacon, 1955. [**169**: 150; **247**: 198]

–––. *Love and Death in the American Novel.* Rev. ed., New York: Dell, Delta Books, 1967.

7: 26, 27, 134	**25**: 172, 194	**99**: 322
14: 47, 53, 54, 25	**26**: 259, 312	**103**: 324, 323
14: 68, 79	**31**: 414, 154, 470	**134**: 470
15: 56	**32**: 475	**139**
16	**34**: 134	**148**: 210
16: 205, 369, 421	**64**: 345	**149**: 212
17: 179, 181	**64**: 111, 112	**154**
17: 134, 34	**71**: 415	**169**: 365–66, 367
18: 38	**81**: 322–24	**185**: 53
19: 296	**93**: 321	**187**: 334
23: 128, 26	**96**: 346	

–––. *No! in Thunder: Essays on Myth and Literature.* Boston: Beacon, 1960. [**15**: 279; **56**: 18]

–––. *The Return of the Vanishing American.* New York: Stein and Day, 1969. [**24**: 134; **28**: 18; **139**: 50–51; **150**: 116–17]

–––. *Waiting for the End.* New York: Stein and Day, 1964. [**247**: 11]

Fletcher, Mary D. "William Faulkner: The Calvinistic Sensibility." Ph.D. dissertation, Louisiana State University and Agricultural and Mechanical College, 1974. [**71**: 52, 53; **93**: 145; **115**: 146, 147, 159]

KEY: Bold-Faced numbers indicate pages of *this* book on which reference to cited work appears. Numbers following colon indicate the specific page reference in the *cited* work.

Foster, Ruel E. "Dream as Symbolic Act in Faulkner." *Perspective* 2 (Summer 1949): 179-94. [53]

Frazer, Sir James G. *The Golden Bough: A Study in Magic and Religion.* 1 vol. abridged ed. 1922; rpt., New York: Macmillan, 1944. [162: 1]

Frazier, David L. "Gothicism in *Sanctuary:* The Black Pall and the Crap Table." *Modern Fiction Studies* 2 (Autumn 1956): 114-24. [103]

Frederickson, Michael A. "A Note on 'The Idiot Boy' as a Probable Source for *The Sound and the Fury.*" *Minnesota Review* 6, no. 4 (1966): 368-70. [55]

Freud, Sigmund. *The Standard Edition of the Complete Psychological Works of Sigmund Freud.* Trans. and ed. James Strachey et al. 24 vols. London: Hogarth Press, 1953-1974. "Narcissism," vol. 14; "The Uncanny," vol. 17. [34: vol. 14: 76, 98; 77: vol. 17: 238, 234; 105: 235]

Frye, Northrop. *Anatomy of Criticism: Four Essays.* Princeton: Princeton University Press, 1957. [4: 195; 6: 185; 34: 40; 37: 223, 221; 48: 273; 130: 42; 132: 203, 206; 133: 148; 133: 147-50, 147; 135: 157]

–––. *The Secular Scripture: A Study of the Structure of Romance.* Cambridge: Harvard University Press, 1976.

3: 38	92: 139	153: 123
5: 23, 28, 4	93: 142	174: 113, 114
9: 53	95: 139	185: 155, 156
15: 110	120: 129	189: 117, 118
23: 15	140: 146	210: 156
26: 5	141: 124	212: 123
51: 36, 37	142: 121	217: 155
89: 138	143: 121	

–––. *A Study of English Romanticism.* Studies in Language and Literature. New York: Random House, 1968. [6: 15, 16, 28; 9: 80; 97: 60]

Garber, Frederick. "Meaning and Mode in Gothic Fiction." *Racism in the Eighteenth Century.* Ed. Harold E. Pagliaro. Studies in Eighteenth Century Literature, 3. Cleveland: Case Western Reserve University Press, 1973, pp. 155-69. [89: 156; 100: 162]

Garzilli, Enrico. *Circles without Center: Paths to the Discovery and Creation of Self in Modern Literature.* Cambridge: Harvard University Press, 1972. [15: 10; 23: 117; 41: 57; 46: 54]

Geismar, Maxwell. "William Faulkner: Before and after the Nobel Prize." *American Moderns: From Rebellion to Conformity.* New York: Hill and Wang, 1958, pp. 91-106. [163]

Gelfant, Blanche H. "Faulkner and Keats: The Ideality of Art in 'The Bear.'" *Southern Literary Journal* 2 (Fall 1969): 42-65. [8: 46; 145: 49, 50; 157: 64]

Gershman, Herbert. *The Surrealist Revolution in France.* Ann Arbor: University of Michigan Press, 1969. [12: 170-71]

–––. "Toward Defining the Surrealist Aesthetic." *Papers on Language and Literature* 2 (Winter 1966): 47-56. [12: 48]

Gibian, George, ed. "The Grotesque in Russian and Western Literature." *Yearbook of Comparative and General Literature* 13 (1964): 56-59. [91: 58]

Gold, Joseph. "Dickens and Faulkner: The Uses of Influence." *Dalhousie Review* 49 (Spring 1969): 69-79. [6: 74-78; 11: 71]

Greer, Scott. "Joe Christmas and the 'Social Self.'" *Mississippi Quarterly* 11 (Fall 1958): 160-66. [121: 164]

KEY: Bold-faced numbers indicate pages of *this* book on which reference to cited work appears. Numbers following colon indicate the specific page reference in the *cited* work.

Gregory, Charles T. "Darkness to Appall: Destructive Designs and Patterns in Some Characters of William Faulkner." Ph.D. dissertation, Columbia University, 1968. [**30**; **55**: 160, 162; **75**: 82; **82**: 161; **83**: 80; **113**: 183–84; **191**: 42, 67, 54, 64; **218**: 61]

Guerard, Albert J. *Thomas Hardy: The Novels and Stories.* Cambridge: Harvard University Press, 1949. [**31**: 4]

———. *The Triumph of the Novel: Dickens, Dostoevsky, Faulkner.* New York: Oxford University Press, 1976. [**237**: 39; **246**: 339]

Hagopian, John. "*Absalom, Absalom!* and the Negro Question." *Modern Fiction Studies* 19 (Summer 1973): 207–11. [**40**: 210]

Hart, Francis R. "The Experience of Character in the English Gothic Novel." *Experience in the Novel: Selected Papers from the English Institute.* Ed. Roy Harvey Pearce. New York: Columbia University Press, 1968, pp. 83–105. [**4**: 85–86]

Hartman, Geoffrey H. "Romanticism and 'Anti-Self-Consciousness,'" *Romanticism and Consciousness.* Ed. Harold Bloom. New York: Norton, 1970, pp. 46–56. [**4**: 56; **24**: 51]

Hassan, Ihab. "The Daydream and Nightmare of Narcissus." *Wisconsin Studies in Contemporary Literature* (Spring-Summer 1960): 5–21. [**10**: 6; **12**: 5; **193**: 5, 8]

———. *The Dismemberment of Orpheus: Toward a Postmodern Literature.* New York: Oxford University Press, 1971. [**12**: 71, 74; **16**: 24, 27]

———. "The Novel of Outrage: A Minority Voice in Postwar American Fiction." *American Scholar* 34 (Spring 1965): 239–53. [**16**: 252]

———. *Radical Innocence: Studies in the Contemporary American Novel.* Princeton: Princeton University Press, 1961. [**21**: 78; **23**: 118; **37**: 236; **65**: 34–35; **74**: 9; **84**: 57; **107**: 331; **108**: 100, 206, 104; **131**: 60]

———. "The Victim: Images of Evil in Recent American Fiction." *College English* 21 (December 1959): 140–46. [**20**: 145]

Hathaway, Baxter. "The Meanings of Faulkner's Structures." *English Record* 15 (December 1964): 22–27. [**56**: 25]

Hauck, Richard B. "The Prime Maniacal Risibility: William Faulkner." *A Cheerful Nihilism: Confidence and "The Absurd" in American Humorous Fiction,* chap. 6. [**245**]

Haury, Beth B. "The Influence of Robinson Jeffers' 'Tamar' on *Absalom, Absalom!*" *Mississippi Quarterly* 25 (Summer 1972): 356–58. [**41**]

Heilman, Robert B. "The Dream Metaphor." *American Dreams, American Nightmares.* Ed. David Madden, Carbondale: Southern Illinois University Press, 1970, pp. 1–18. [**7**: 7; **10**: 1; **233**: 4, 17]

———. "Tragedy and Melodrama." *Tragedy: Vision and Form.* Ed. Robert W. Corrigan. San Francisco: Chandler, 1965, pp. 245–57. [**38**: 248, 254; **66**: 257; **198**: 255–56]

Hinchliffe, Arnold P. *The Absurd,* rev. ed. *The Critical Idiom,* no. 5. London: Methuen, 1974. [**245**: 93–94, 97]

Hoffman, Frederick J. and Olga W. Vickery, eds. *William Faulkner: Three Decades of Criticism.* East Lansing: Michigan State University Press, 1960.

Howard, Alan B. "Huck Finn in the House of Usher: The Comic and Grotesque Worlds of *The Hamlet.*" *Southern Review: An Australian Journal of Literary Studies* 5 (June 1972): 125–46. [**193**: 126, 133, 125]

Hume, Robert D. "Exuberant Gloom, Existential Agony, and Heroic Despair: Three Varieties of Negative Romanticism." *The Gothic Imagination.* Ed. G. R. Thompson. Pullman: Washington State University Press, 1974, pp. 109–27. [**17**: 112]

KEY: Bold-faced numbers indicate pages of *this* book on which reference to cited work appears. Numbers following colon indicate the specific page reference in the *cited* work.

Humphrey, Robert. "Form and Function of Stream of Consciousness in William Faulkner's *The Sound and the Fury.*" *University of Kansas City Review* 19 (Autumn 1952): 34-40. (Revised for *Stream of Consciousness in the Modern Novel* [1954].) [56: 40]

Hurt, Lester E. "Mysticism in 'Go Down, Moses.'" *English Record* 15 (December 1964): 17-22. [144: 18; 146: 22; 149: 22]

Irwin, John T. *Doubling and Incest/Repetition and Revenge: A Speculative Reading of Faulkner.* Baltimore: Johns Hopkins University Press, 1975.

31: 6, 10, 74	45: 43	65: 91
32: 11-19, 20	49: 107	66: 28-29
34: 83-84	50: 78	69: 213, 124
37: 25-26	51: 157	70: 42
39: 116, 117	54: 5	71: 37
39: 77	54: 1	71: 37, 46, 47
41: 148, 149	59: 38, 39	78: 55, 56, 59
41: 17-20	60: 69	231: 157
44: 49	62: 42, 43	244: 59
	64: 35, 43	

Kayser, Wolfgang. *The Grotesque in Art and Literature.* Trans. Ulrich Weisstein. Bloomington: Indiana University Press, 1963. [20: 188]

Kazin, Alfred. *Bright Book of Life: American Novelists and Storytellers from Hemingway to Mailer.* Boston: Little, Brown, 1973. [8: 29, 26; 243: 26; 247: 25]

Kerr, Elizabeth M. "*As I Lay Dying* as Ironic Quest." *Wisconsin Studies in Contemporary Literature* 3 (Winter 1962): 5-19. Rpt. in *William Faulkner: Four Decades of Criticism.* Ed. Linda W. Wagner. East Lansing: Michigan State University Press, 1973, pp. 234-43. [186; 221]

———. "*The Reivers:* The Golden Book of Yoknapatawpha County." *Modern Fiction Studies* 13 (Spring 1967): 95-113. [182; 186; 221]

———. *Yoknapatawpha: Faulkner's "Little Postage Stamp of Native Soil.* New York: Fordham University Press, 1969. 2d ed., rev., Fordham Rose Hill Books, 1976. [241]

Kornfeld, Milton H. "A Darker Freedom: The Villain in the Novels of Hawthorne, James, and Faulkner." Ph.D. dissertation, Brandeis University, 1970. [10: 2; 60: 116, 114, 120; 191: 134, 125, 133; 192: 125]

Kubie, Lawrence S., M.D. "William Faulkner's *Sanctuary.*" *Saturday Review of Literature* (20 October 1934). Rpt. in *Faulkner: A Collection of Critical Essays.* Ed. Robert Penn Warren. Englewood Cliffs, N.J.: Prentice-Hall, 1966, pp. 137-46. [10: 139, 138; 10: 140; 28: 139; 88: 145; 93: 141; 98: 142; 99: 141; 101: 144-45; 103: 145; 104: 142-43]

Lang, Eleanor M. "Hawthorne and Faulkner: The Continuity of a Dark American Tradition." Ph.D. dissertation, Lehigh University, 1970. [57: 90; 63: 118]

Langford, Gerald. *Faulkner's Revision of "Absalom, Absalom!": A Collation of the Manuscript and the Published Book.* Austin: University of Texas Press, 1971. [51: 9, 41, 41-42, 41]

———. *Faulkner's Revision of "Sanctuary": A Collation of the Unrevised Galleys and the Published Book.* Austin: University of Texas Press, 1972. [105; 105: 23]

Langston, Beach. "The Meaning of Lena Grove and Gail Hightower in *Light in August.*" *Boston University Studies in English* 5 (Spring 1961): 46-63. [128]

Larkin, David, ed. *Fantastic Art.* New York: Ballantine, 1973. [194]

Lawson, Lewis A. "The Grotesque-Comic in the Snopes Trilogy." *Literature and Psychology* 15 (Spring 1965): 107-19. [**191:** 114; **192:** 110, 111; **192:** 112, 113; **194:** 115; **200:** 113; **201:** 119]

Lawson, Richard A. "Patterns of Initiation in William Faulkner's *Go Down, Moses.*" Ph.D. dissertation, Tulane University, 1966. [**149:** 8, 27; **150:** 47, 53; **155:** 75; **160:** 31]

Lensing, George S. "The Metaphor of Family in *Absalom, Absalom!*" *Southern Review* 11 (January 1975): 99-117. [**36:** 106, 105; **41:** 103, 104; **45:** 114, 116]

Levin, Harry. *The Gates of Horn: A Study of Five French Realists.* New York: Oxford University Press, Galaxy Books, 1966. [**3:** 23; **10:** 55; **13:** 458-59]

Levins, Lynn G. *Faulkner's Heroic Design: The Yoknapatawpha Novels.* Athens: University of Georgia Press, 1976.

———. "The Four Narrative Perspectives in *Absalom, Absalom!*" *PMLA* 85 (January 1970): 35-47. [**35:** 36, 37, 39; **38:** 37; **47:** 36] (This essay is the basis of chap. 2 above.)

Lévy, Maurice. *Le Roman "Gothique" anglais, 1764-1824.* Toulouse: Association des publications de la faculté des lettres et sciences humaines de Toulouse, 1968. [**4:** 53; **5:** vi, viii; **8:** 640; **12:** 606; **19:** 71, 53; **26:** 612]

Lind, Ilse Dusoir. "Apocalyptic Vision as Key to *Light in August.*" *Studies in American Fiction* 3 (Autumn, 1975): 133-41. [**123:** 137; **131:** 133, 135; **132:** 134; **132:** 135; **133:** 133]

———. "The Calvinist Burden of *Light in August.*" *New England Quarterly* 30 (September 1957): 307-29. [**113:** 307; **116:** 325; **126:** 310-11]

———. "The Design and Meaning of *Absalom, Absalom!*" *PMLA* 70 (December 1955): 887-912. [**30:** 898] Rpt. in *William Faulkner: Three Decades of Criticism.* Eds. Frederick J. Hoffman and Olga W. Vickery. East Lansing: Michigan State University Press, 1960. *William Faulkner: Four Decades of Criticism.* Ed. Linda W. Wagner. East Lansing: Michigan State University Press, 1973.

———. "The Realization of Expressionism in *Light in August.*" Paper read at MLA convention, San Francisco, December, 1975. Xeroxed. [**7:** 4; **129:** 28]

Lovecraft, Howard Phillips. *Supernatural Horror in Literature,* with a new introduction by E. F. Bleiler. Republication of 1945 ed., New York: Dover, 1973. [**18:** 13; **18:** 37; **20:** 19]

Lytle, Andrew. "The Working Novelist and the Mythmaking Process." *Daedalus* (Spring 1959), pp. 326-38. [**26:** 331]

MacAndrew, Elizabeth. "The Gothic and Popular Literature." Paper read at the National Convention of the Popular Culture Assoc., Milwaukee, Wis., May 1974. Xeroxed. [**5:** 4, 3; **32:** 12]

Madden, David, ed. *American Dreams, American Nightmares.* Crosscurrents: Modern Critiques. Carbondale: Southern Illinois University Press, 1970. [**9:** xvii; **10:** xxxvi; **150:** xxxix, xlii; **249:** xxxix; **244:** xxxviii, xxxi-xxxii]

Magnan, Jean-Marie. "Incest et mélange des sangs dans l'oeuvre de William Faulkner." *Sud*—Revue trimestrielle, no. 14/15: *Faulkner* (1975), 150-84. [**227:** 151]

Malin, Irvng. "Flannery O'Connor and the Grotesque." *The Added Dimension: The Art and Mind of Flannery O'Connor.* Eds. Melvin J. Friedman and Lewis A. Lawson. New York: Fordham University Press, 1966, pp. 108-22. [**20:** 108]

———. *New American Gothic.* Crosscurrents: Modern Critiques. Carbondale: Southern Illinois University Press, 1962. [**20:** 4, 9; **22:** 11, 80; **23:** 106; **62:** 6; **70:** 127, 79; **229:** 8]

KEY: Bold-faced numbers indicate pages of *this* book on which reference to cited work appears. Numbers following colon indicate the specific page reference in the *cited* work.

Martin, Carter W. *The True Country: Themes in the Fiction of Flannery O'Connor.* Nashville: Vanderbilt University Press, 1969. [**24:** 160]

Masters, R. E. L. *Patterns of Incest.* New York: Ace Books, 1970. [**15:** 55]

Materassi, Mario. *I romanzi di Faulkner.* Rome: Edizioni di Storia e Letteratura, 1968. [**30:** 211-15; **54:** 95, 96; **89:** 142-43]

Matthews, J. H. *Surrealism and the Novel.* Ann Arbor: University of Michigan Press, 1969 (© 1966). [**13:** 27]

Mayoux, Jean. *Vivants Piliers: Le Roman anglo-saxon et les symboles.* Paris: Julliard, 1960. [**91:** 242; **96:** 256, 253]

McHaney, Thomas L. "*Sanctuary* and Frazer's Slain Kings." *Mississippi Quarterly* 24 (Summer 1971): 223-45. [**90:** 237, n. 25]

Meats, Stephen. "Who Killed Joanna Burden?" *Mississippi Quarterly* 24 (Summer 1971): 271-77. [**127**]

Mellard, James M. "Caliban as Prospero: Benjy and *The Sound and the Fury.*" *Novel: A Forum on Fiction* 3 (Spring 1970): 233-48. [**61:** 241]

Meriwether, James B. *The Literary Career of William Faulkner: A Bibliographical Study.* Princeton: Princeton University Library, 1961. [**138:** 30] Rpt. Columbia: University of South Carolina Press, 1971.

Miller, Arthur. "Tragedy and the Common Man." *Tragedy: Vision and Form.* Ed. Robert W. Corrigan. San Francisco: Chandler, 1965, pp. 148-51. [**199:** 150-51]

Miller, James E., Jr. "William Faulkner: Descent into the Vortex." *Quests Surd and Absurd: Essays in American Literature.* Chicago: University of Chicago Press, 1967, pp. 41-65. [**73:** 53, 56]

Millgate, Michael. *The Achievement of William Faulkner.* New York: Random House, 1966. [**47:** 164; **52:** 162; **88:** 120, 317]

———. "'A Fair Job': A Study of Faulkner's *Sanctuary.*" *Review of English Literature* 4 (October 1963): 47-62. Rpt. in *The Achievement of William Faulkner,* pp. 113-23. [**106:** 123]

Monk, Samuel. "The Sublime: Burke's Inquiry." *Romanticism and Consciousness.* Ed. Harold Bloom. New York: Norton, 1970, pp. 24-41. [**19:** 27, 39]

Morell, Giliane. "'Pourquoi ris-tu,' Darl?—le temps d'un regard." *Sud*—Revue trimestrielle, no. 14/15: **Faulkner** (1975), 128-49. [**89:** 145]

Moseley, Edwin M. *Pseudonyms of Christ in the Modern Novel: Motifs and Methods.* Pittsburgh: University of Pittsburgh Press, 1962. [**129:** 142]

Muhlenfeld, Elisabeth S. "Shadows with Substance and Ghosts Exhumed: The Women in *Absalom, Absalom!*" *Mississippi Quarterly* 25 (Summer 1972): 289-304. [**36:** 293, 290]

Murphy, Denis M. "*The Sound and the Fury* and Dante's *Inferno:* Fire and Ice." *Markham Review* 4 (October 1974): 71-78. [**69**]

Muste, John. "The Failure of Love in *Go Down, Moses.*" *Modern Fiction Studies* 10 (Winter 1964-1965): 366-73 [**143; 158:** 367]

Newton, Eric. *The Romantic Rebellion.* New York: Schocken, 1964. [**13:** 148, 153; **17:** 130]

Micoll, Allardyce. *The World of Harlequin: A Critical Study of the Commedia dell'Arte.* Cambridge: Cambridge University Press, 1963. [**144:** 48, 49-50, 202]

Noble, Donald R. "Faulkner's 'Pantaloon in Black': An Aristotelian Reading." *Ball State Teachers College Forum* 14 (Summer 1973): 16-19. [**143**]

O'Connor, Flannery. "Some Aspects of the Grotesque in Southern Fiction." *Flannery O'Connor: Mystery and Manners: Occasional Prose.* Eds. Sally and Robert Fitzgerald. New York: Farrar, Straus & Giroux, Noonday Press, pp. 36-50. [**247:** 45]

O'Connor, William Van. *The Grotesque: An American Genre and Other Essays.* Crosscurrents: Modern Critiques. Carbondale: Southern Illinois University Press, 1962. [**23**: 19]

O'Donnell, George Marion. "Faulkner's Mythology." *Kenyon Review* 1 (Summer 1939). Rpt. in *Faulkner: A Collection of Critical Essays.* Ed. Robert Penn Warren. Englewood Cliffs, N. J.: Prentice-Hall, 1966, pp. 22–33. [**104**: 28] Rpt. also in *William Faulkner: Three Decades of Criticism.* Eds. Frederick J. Hoffman and Olga W. Vickery. East Lansing: Michigan State University Press, 1960. *William Faulkner: Four Decades of Criticism.* Ed. Linda W. Wagner. East Lansing: Michigan State University Press, 1973.

Parker, Herschel. "What Quentin Saw 'Out There.'" *Mississippi Quarterly* 27 (Summer 1974): 323–26. [**43**: 368, 370, 373]

Pearce, Richard. "Faulkner's One-Ring Circus." *Wisconsin Studies in Contemporary Literature* 7 (Autumn 1966): 270–83. [**117**: 280, 271]

Percy, Walker. "The Delta Factor." *Southern Review* 11 (January 1975): 29–64. [**8**: 47]

Perry, J. Douglas. "Gothic as Vortex: The Form of Horror in Capote, Faulkner, and Styron." *Modern Fiction Studies* 19 (Summer 1973): 153–67. [**80**: 153, 154, 156; **98**: 154; **102**: 161; **103**: 161]

Phillips, Robert S. "The Gothic Architecture of *The Member of the Wedding.*" *Renascence* 16 (Winter 1964): 59–72. [**15**: 61, 65; **23**: 60; **24**: 63; **64**: 60]

Pindell, Richard P. "The Ritual of Survival: Landscape in Conrad and Faulkner." Ph.D. dissertation, Yale University, 1971. [**166**: 174; **221**: 191, 193; **240**: 236]

Pitavy, François L. *Faulkner's "Light in August."* Trans. Gillian E. Cook. Bloomington: Indiana University Press, 1973. [**108**: 153–54; **109**: 85; **117**: 83]

———. "The Landscape of *Light in August.*" *Mississippi Quarterly* 23 (Summer 1970): 265–72. [**27**: 266, 270, 272]

Pommer, Henry F. "*Light in August:* A Letter by Faulkner." *English Language Notes* 4 (September 1966): 47–48. [**129**]

Porte, Joel. "In the Hands of an Angry God: Religious Terror in Gothic Fiction." *The Gothic Imagination.* Ed. G. R. Thompson. Pullman: Washington State University Press, 1974, pp. 42–64. [**6**: 43; **14**: 43, 45; **129**: 47; **133**: 63, 61]

Poteet, Lewis J. "Dorian Gray and the Gothic Novel." *Modern Fiction Studies* 17 (Summer 1971): 239–48. [**7**]

Praz, Mario. *The Romantic Agony.* Trans. Angus Davidson. 1933; rpt. New York: Meridian, 1951. [**7**; **17**; **116**]

Putzel, Max. "What Is Gothic about *Absalom, Absalom!?*" *Southern Literary Journal* 4 (Fall 1971): 3–19. [**30**; **30**: 18]

Railo, Eino. *The Haunted Castle: A Study of the Elements of English Romanticism.* 1927; rpt. New York: Humanities Press, 1964. [**18**; **19**: 49; **35**: 51; **78**: 186]

Ramsey, William C. "Coordinate Structures in Four Faulkner Novels." Ph.D. dissertation, University of North Carolina, 1971. [**53**: 53, 70; **82**: 123, 165, 164; **188**: 100]

Rank, Otto. *The Double: A Psychoanalytic Study.* Trans. and ed. Harry Tucker, Jr. Chapel Hill: University of North Carolina Press, 1971. [**37**: 75, 76–77, 79, 83; **71**: 51, 54, 77, 57; **78**: 75]

Raper, J. R. "Meaning Called to Life: Alogical Structure in *Absalom, Absalom!*" *Southern Humanities Review* 5 (Winter 1971): 9–23. [**33**: 16]

Ratner, Marc L. "Rebellion of Wrath and Laughter: Styron's *Set This House on Fire.*" *Southern Review*, n.s. 7 (Autumn 1971): 10007–20. [**221**: 1020]

KEY: Bold-faced numbers indicate pages of *this* book on which reference to cited work appears. Numbers following colon indicate the specific page reference in the *cited work.*

Ray, Paul C. "What Was Surrealism?" *Journal of Modern Literature* 1 (1970): 133–37. [**12**: 134]

Rogers, Robert. *A Psychoanalytic Study of the Double in Literature*. Detroit: Wayne State University Press, 1970. [**7**: viii, 22–23; **36**: 5; **37**: 28–29]

Rossky, William. "The Pattern of Nightmare in *Sanctuary;* or, Miss Reba's Dogs." *Modern Fiction Studies* 15 (Winter 1969–1970): 503–15. [**89**: 504, 505, 507; **92**: 505; **97**: 511–12, 514; **103**: 512]

Rougemont, Denis de. *Love Declared: Essays on the Myths of Love*. Trans. Richard Howard. New York: Pantheon, 1963. [**9**: 23, 11, 43; **14**: 11; **64**: 209]

———. *Love in the Western World*. Rev. ed., trans. Montgomery Belgion. New York: Pantheon, 1956. [**216**: 35]

Sandstrom, Glenn. "Identity Diffusion: Joe Christmas and Quentin Compson." *American Quarterly* 19 (Summer 1967): 207–23. [**64**: 207, 216; **121**: 217; **122**: 214; **130**: 222; **232**: 207; **242**: 223]

Scott, Arthur. "The Myriad Perspectives of *Absalom, Absalom!*" *American Quarterly* 6 (Fall 1954): 210–20. [**46**: 220, 215]

Seyppel, Joachim. *William Faulkner*. Rev. and trans. by the author. New York: Ungar, 1971. [**36**; **93**: 76, 52]

Simpson, Lewis P. "Faulkner and the Southern Symbolism of Pastoral." *Mississippi Quarterly* 28 (Fall 1975): 401–15. [**145**: 412; **155**: 414]

Singleton, Marvin K. "Personae at Law and in Equity: The Unity of Faulkner's *Absalom, Absalom!*" *Papers on Language and Literature* 3 (Fall 1967): 354–70. [**40**: 367]

Slabey, Robert M. "The 'Romanticism' of 'The Sound and the Fury.'" *Mississippi Quarterly* 16 (Summer 1963): 146–59. [**55**: 151, 153]

Smith, James L. *Melodrama. The Critical Idiom*, no. 28. London: Methuen, 1973. [**17**: 17, 26–27, 34, 39]

Smith, Lillian. *Killers of the Dream*. Rev. ed. 1949; rpt. Garden City, N. Y.: Doubleday Anchor Books, 1963. [**162**: 197; **222**: 95; **230**: 132, 133–34; **230**: 116]

Smith, Margarita G., ed. *The Mortgaged Heart*. 1971: rpt. New York: Bantam, 1972. [**21**: 319]

Stein, Jean. "William Faulkner." *Writers at Work*. Ed. Malcolm Cowley. New York: Viking Compass Books, 1959, pp. 119–41. [**244**: 138–39] Rpt. in *Lion in the Garden: Interviews with William Faulkner, 1926–1962*. Rpt. also in *William Faulkner: Three Decades of Criticism*. Eds. Frederick J. Hoffman and Olga W. Vickery. East Lansing: Michigan State University Press, 1960.

Stein, William Bysshe. "Faulkner's Devil." *Modern Language Notes* 76 (December 1961): 731–32. [**191**]

———. "The Wake in Faulkner's *Sanctuary*." *Modern Language Notes* 75 (January 1960): 28–29. [**103**: 28–29]

Steinberg, Aaron. "'Intruder in the Dust': Faulkner as Psychologist of the Southern Psyche." *Literature and Psychology* 15 (Spring 1965): 120–24. [**168**: 121; **181**: 123; **181**: 123; **183**: 124]

Stephens, Rosemary. "Mythical Elements in 'Pantaloon in Black.'" *University of Mississippi Studies in English* 11 (1970): 45–51. [**143**]

Stoehr, Taylor. *Dickens: The Dreamer's Stance*. Ithaca: Cornell University Press, [**73**: 111; **92**: 101]

Stone, Emily Whitehurst. "How a Writer Finds His Material." *Harper's Magazine* (November 1965), pp. 157–61. [**156**: 161]

Stoneback, H. R. "Faulkner's Blues: 'Pantaloon in Black.'" *Modern Fiction Studies* 21 (Summer 1975): 241–45. [**144**: 243, 242]

Straumann, Heinrich. *William Faulkner.* Frankfurt am Main: Athenäum, 1968. [**100**: 137–39]

Summers, Montague. *The Gothic Quest: A History of the Gothic Novel.* 1938; rpt. New York: Russell, 1964. [**8**: 198, 398; **15**: 220; **17**: 397; **97**: 141; **27**: 407]

Swiggart, Peter. *The Art of William Faulkner's Novels.* Austin: University of Texas Press, 1962. [**30**: 151; **64**: 94]

Sypher, Wylie. "Aesthetic of Revolution: The Marxist Melodrama." *Tragedy: Vision and Form.* Ed. Robert W. Corrigan. San Francisco: Chandler, 1965, pp. 258–67. [**47**: 260]

Tanner, Tony. *City of Words: American Fiction, 1950–1970.* New York: Harper, 1971. [**6**: 16; **11**: 51]

Taylor, Walter. "Horror and Nostalgia: The Double Perspective of Faulkner's 'Was.'" *Southern Humanities Review* 8 (Winter 1974): 74–84. [**140**: 80, 82; **141**: 75]

Theroux, Paul. *The Great Railway Bazaar: By Train through Asia.* New York: Ballantine, 1976. [**246**: 40, 41]

Thomas, Frank Howard, III. "The Search for Identity of Faulkner's Black Characters." Ph.D. dissertation, University of Pittsburgh, 1972.

66: 63, 70–71	**119**: 155	**151**: 224, 235, 236
66: 99, 96	**121**: 157, 168	**152**: 250, 251
75: 21	**122**: 206	**168**: 280
79: 20	**130**: 207	**181**: 273, 280
81: 41, 16, 18, 23	**143**: 262	**181**: 273, 280

Thompson, G. R., ed. *The Gothic Imagination: Essays in Dark Romanticism.* Pullman: Washington State University Press, 1975. [**5**: 3; **6**: 1; **22**: 6]

Thompson, Lawrence. "Mirror Analogues in *The Sound and the Fury.*" *English Institute Essays,* 1952. New York: Columbia University Press, 1953, pp. 83–106. [**70**] Rpt. in *Faulkner: A Collection of Critical Essays.* Ed. Robert Penn Warren, Englewood Cliffs, N. J.: Prentice-Hall, 1966. *William Faulkner: Three Decades of Criticism.* Eds. Frederick J. Hoffman and Olga W. Vickery. East Lansing: Michigan State University Press, 1960. *William Faulkner: Four Decades of Criticism.* Ed. Linda W. Wagner. East Lansing: Michigan State University Press, 1973.

Thomson, Philip. *The Grotesque. The Critical Idiom,* no. 24. London: Methuen, 1972. [**20**: 27]

Tompkins, J. M. S. *The Popular Novel in England, 1770–1800.* 1932; rpt. Lincoln: University of Nebraska Press, 1961. [**26**: 62]

Tritschler, Donald H. "Whorls of Form in Faulkner's Fiction." Ph.D. dissertation, Northwestern University, 1957. [**90**]

Tuck, Dorothy. "Faulkner, *Light in August:* The Inwardness of the Understanding." *Approaches to the Twentieth Century Novel.* Ed. John Unterecker, New York: Crowell, 1965, pp. 79–107. [**109**: 81; **112**: 85; **115**: 85; **130**: 88; **134**: 106]

Varma, Devendra. *The Gothic Flame, Being a History of the Gothic Novel in England: Its Origins, Efflorescence, Disintegration, and Residuary Influences.* 1957; rpt. New York: Russell, 1966. [**7**; **72**: 92]

Varnado, S. L. "The Idea of the Numinous in Gothic Literature." *The Gothic Imagination.* Ed. G. R. Thompson. Pullman: Washington State University Press, 1974, pp. 11–21. [**7**: 12; **146**: 18]

KEY: Bold-faced numbers indicate pages of *this* book on which reference to cited work appears. Numbers following colon indicate the specific page reference in the *cited* work.

Vickery, Olga W. *The Novels of William Faulkner: A Critical Interpretation.* Rev. ed., Baton Rouge, Louisiana State University Press, 1964.

30: 84, 87, 88, 89	**116:** 76, 68	**169:** 135
83: 20	**121:** 78–79	**176:** 137
92: 109	**121:** 68	**177:** 139
95: 110	**126:** 71	**181:** 143
96: 110	**133:** 79	**187:** 198
99: 107, 108	**134:** 82, 83	**198:** 200
101: 105	**149:** 133	**199:** 167, 168, 172
107: 82	**152:** 128	
109: 66, 67	**157:** 133	

Waggoner, Hyatt H. *William Faulkner: From Jefferson to the World.* Lexington: University of Kentucky Press, 1959. [**156:** 214; **198:** 188; **235:** 188]

Wagner, Linda W., ed. *William Faulkner: Four Decades of Criticism.* East Lansing: Michigan State University Press, 1973.

Waldberg, Patrick. *Surrealism.* London: Thames and Hudson, 1968. [**12:** 11; **13:** 16]

Walpole, Horace. *The Castle of Otranto.* New York: Collier Books, 1963. [**22:** 20]

Warren, Robert Penn, ed. *Faulkner: A Collection of Critical Essays. Twentieth Century Views.* Englewood Cliffs, N. J.: Prentice-Hall, 1966.

Weinstein, Arnold L. *Vision and Response in Modern Fiction.* Ithaca: Cornell University Press, 1975. [**33:** 150–51; **36:** 139, 143; **47; 68:** 137]

Wellek, René. "Romanticism Re-examined." *Romanticism Reconsidered: Selected Papers from the English Institute.* Ed. Northrop Frye. New York: Columbia University Press, 1963. [**5:** 132]

Weybright, Myron D. "A Study of Tensiveness in Selected Novels of William Faulkner." Ph.D. dissertation, Northwestern University, 1971. [**187:** 229, 254–55; **189:** 196; **212:** 216]

Wolf, Leonard. *A Dream of Dracula: In Search of the Living Dead.* New York: Popular Library, 1973. [**11:** 139, 141]

Wolfe, George H., ed. *Faulkner: Fifty Years after "The Marble Faun."* University: University of Alabama Press, 1976.

Zyla, Wolodymyr T., and Wendell M. Aycock, eds. *William Faulkner: Prevailing Verities and World Literature.* Proceedings of the Comparative Literature Symposium, vol. 6. Lubbock: Interdept. Comm. on Comp. Lit., Texas Tech. University Press, 1973.

KEY: Bold-faced numbers indicate pages of *this* book on which reference to cited work appears. Numbers following colon indicate the specific page reference in the *cited* work.